"This is a remarkable collection of papers. Each one is worth spending time with individually, while the collection as a whole is an invaluable survey of the Contemporary Freudian tradition. Ken Robinson and Joan Schächter, prominent members of that tradition, have put together almost 20 papers, spanning some 40 years, which address themes such as the unconscious mind; psychic development; the body and psychosexuality; and aggression and destructiveness. Some are acknowledged classics; others may take the reader into new territory. Together they show the evolution over time of Contemporary Freudian thinking and reveal the richness and diversity of what is a central current in today's psychoanalysis."

**Dr Michael Parsons** is a Fellow and Training Analyst of the British Psychoanalytical Society

"This collection of papers of the wide family of Contemporary Freudian Analysts will help all of us, including those in the UK, to keep Freudian thinking in a lively and creative way. The collection exemplifies the enormous wealth of Contemporary Freudian thinking. Thanks to the efforts of the editors Ken Robinson and Joan Schächter, this book should become obligatory reading for all analysts."

**Dr Elisabeth Brainin**, member and Training Analyst of the Viennese Psychoanalytic Society

# The Contemporary Freudian Tradition

This is the first book dedicated to the Contemporary Freudian Tradition. In its introduction, and through its selection of papers, it describes the development and rich diversity of this tradition over recent decades, showing how theory and practice are inseparable in the psychoanalytic treatment of children, adolescents and adults.

The book is organized around four major concerns in the Contemporary Freudian Tradition: the nature of the Unconscious and the ways that it manifests itself; the extension of Freud's theories of development through the work of Anna Freud and later theorists; the body and psychosexuality, including the centrality of bodily experience as it is elaborated over time in the life of the individual; and aggression. It also illustrates how within the Tradition different exponents have been influenced by psychoanalytic thinking outside it, whether from the Kleinian and Independent Groups, or from French Freudian thinking. Throughout the book there is strong emphasis on the clinical setting, in, for example, the value of the Tradition's approach to the complex interrelationship of body and mind in promoting a deeper understanding of somatic symptoms and illnesses and working with them. There are four papers on the subject of dreams within the Contemporary Freudian Tradition, illustrating the continuing importance accorded to dreams and dreaming in psychoanalytic treatment.

This is the only book that describes in detail the family resemblances shared by those working psychoanalytically within the richly diverse Contemporary Freudian Tradition. It should appeal to anyone, from student onwards, who is interested in the living tradition of Freud's work as understood by one of the three major groups within British psychoanalysis.

**Ken Robinson** works as a psychoanalyst in private practice in Newcastle upon Tyne. He is a member of the British Psychoanalytical Society, Honorary Member of the Polish Society for Psychoanalytical Psychotherapy and Visiting Professor of Psychoanalysis at Northumbria University.

**Joan Schächter** trained as a psychiatrist before training as a psychoanalyst in the British Psychoanalytic Institute. She worked a consultant psychotherapist in the NHS for many years. Since retiring from the NHS she works in private psychoanalytic practice.

THE NEW LIBRARY OF PSYCHOANALYSIS
General Editor: Alessandra Lemma

The New Library of Psychoanalysis was launched in 1987 in association with the Institute of Psychoanalysis, London. It took over from the International Psychoanalytical Library which published many of the early translations of the works of Freud and the writings of most of the leading British and Continental psychoanalysts.

The purpose of the New Library of Psychoanalysis is to facilitate a greater and more widespread appreciation of psychoanalysis and to provide a forum for increasing mutual understanding between psychoanalysts and those working in other disciplines such as the social sciences, medicine, philosophy, history, linguistics, literature and the arts. It aims to represent different trends both in British psychoanalysis and in psychoanalysis generally. The New Library of Psychoanalysis is well placed to make available to the English-speaking world psychoanalytic writings from other European countries and to increase the interchange of ideas between British and American psychoanalysts. Through the *Teaching Series*, the New Library of Psychoanalysis now also publishes books that provide comprehensive, yet accessible, overviews of selected subject areas aimed at those studying psychoanalysis and related fields such as the social sciences, philosophy, literature and the arts.

The Institute, together with the British Psychoanalytical Society, runs a low-fee psychoanalytic clinic, organizes lectures and scientific events concerned with psychoanalysis and publishes the *International Journal of Psychoanalysis*. It runs a training course in psychoanalysis which leads to membership of the International Psychoanalytical Association—the body which preserves internationally agreed standards of training, of professional entry, and of professional ethics and practice for psychoanalysis as initiated and developed by Sigmund Freud. Distinguished members of the Institute have included Michael Balint, Wilfred Bion, Ronald Fairbairn, Anna Freud, Ernest Jones, Melanie Klein, John Rickman and Donald Winnicott.

Previous general editors have included David Tuckett, who played a very active role in the establishment of the New Library. He was followed as general editor by Elizabeth Bott Spillius, who was in turn followed by Susan Budd and then by Dana Birksted-Breen. Current members of the Advisory Board include Giovanna Di Ceglie, Liz Allison, Anne Patterson, Josh Cohen and Daniel Pick.

Previous members of the Advisory Board include Christopher Bollas, Ronald Britton, Catalina Bronstein, Donald Campbell, Rosemary Davies, Sara Flanders, Stephen Grosz, John Keene, Eglé Laufer, Alessandra Lemma, Juliet Mitchell, Michael Parsons, Rosine Jozef Perelberg, Richard Rusbridger, Mary Target and David Taylor.

For a full list of all the titles in the New Library of Psychoanalysis main series as well as both the New Library of Psychoanalysis 'Teaching' and 'Beyond the Couch' subseries, please visit the Routledge website.

# The Contemporary Freudian Tradition

Past and Present

Edited by Ken Robinson and Joan Schächter

LONDON AND NEW YORK

First published 2021
by Routledge
2 Park Square, Milton Park, Abingdon, Oxon OX14 4RN

and by Routledge
52 Vanderbilt Avenue, New York, NY 10017

*Routledge is an imprint of the Taylor & Francis Group, an informa business*

© 2021 selection and editorial matter, Ken Robinson and Joan Schächter; individual chapters, the contributors

The right of Ken Robinson and Joan Schächter to be identified as the authors of the editorial material, and of the authors for their individual chapters, has been asserted in accordance with sections 77 and 78 of the Copyright, Designs and Patents Act 1988.

All rights reserved. No part of this book may be reprinted or reproduced or utilised in any form or by any electronic, mechanical, or other means, now known or hereafter invented, including photocopying and recording, or in any information storage or retrieval system, without permission in writing from the publishers.

*Trademark notice*: Product or corporate names may be trademarks or registered trademarks, and are used only for identification and explanation without intent to infringe.

*British Library Cataloguing-in-Publication Data*
A catalogue record for this book is available from the British Library

*Library of Congress Cataloging-in-Publication Data*
Names: | Robinson, Ken, editor. Schächter, Joan, editor.
Title: The contemporary Freudian tradition: past and present / edited by Ken Robinson and Joan Schächter.
Description: Milton Park, Abingdon, Oxon; New York, NY: Routledge, 2021.| Series: The new library of psychoanalysis | Includes bibliographical references and index. |
Identifiers: LCCN 2020019387 (print) | LCCN 2020019388 (ebook) | ISBN 9780367483555 (hardback) | ISBN 9780367483562 (paperback) | ISBN 9781003039495 (ebook)
Subjects: LCSH: Freud, Sigmund, 1856-1939. | Psychoanalysis.
Classification: LCC BF173.C5675 2021 (print) | LCC BF173 (ebook) | DDC 150.19/5209—dc23
LC record available at https://lccn.loc.gov/2020019387
LC ebook record available at https://lccn.loc.gov/2020019388

ISBN: 978-0-367-48355-5 (hbk)
ISBN: 978-0-367-48356-2 (pbk)
ISBN: 978-1-003-03949-5 (ebk)

Typeset in Bembo
by codeMantra

# Contents

|   | About the editors and contributors | xii |
|---|---|---|
|   | Previously published material | xvii |
| 1 | Introduction<br>KEN ROBINSON AND JOAN SCHÄCHTER | 1 |
| 2 | Phantasy and its transformations: a Contemporary Freudian view<br>JOSEPH SANDLER AND ANNE-MARIE SANDLER | 35 |
| 3 | Unconscious phantasy and après-coup: the Controversial Discussions<br>ROSINE JOZEF PERELBERG | 47 |
| 4 | The vicissitudes of preparing and sustaining a young child in psychoanalysis<br>ANGELA JOYCE | 70 |
| 5 | The oedipal experience: effects on development of an absent father<br>MARION BURGNER | 89 |
| 6 | Oedipus at play<br>KEN ROBINSON | 107 |

## Contents

7  Female masturbation in adolescence and the development of the relationship to the body    126
M. EGLÉ LAUFER

8  Modes of communication—the differentiation of somatic and verbal expression    138
ROSE M. EDGCUMBE

9  The soma and the body: navigating through the countertransference    155
MARINA PERRIS-MYTTAS

10  Pregnancy, miscarriage and abortion. A psychoanalytic perspective    176
DINORA PINES

11  Masculinity, femininity and internalization in male homosexuals    188
MERVIN GLASSER

12  Doubt in the psychoanalysis of a paedophile    205
DONALD CAMPBELL

13  "I'm like a shattered windscreen": struggles with sadism and the self    234
MARIANNE PARSONS

14  The patient's discovery of the psychoanalyst as a new object    251
RONALD BAKER

15  The dream space, the analytic situation and the eating disorder: clinging to the concrete    269
SARA FLANDERS

16  The fate of the dream in contemporary psychoanalysis    287
SUSAN LODEN

17  How come your house does not fall down?    309
LUIS RODRÍGUEZ DE LA SIERRA

18 Measure for measure: unconscious communication
   in dreams                                                    328
   JOAN SCHÄCHTER

19 Regression, curiosity and the discovery of the object        343
   ROSEMARY DAVIES

   Name index                                                   363
   Subject index                                                366

# About the editors and contributors

## Editors

**Ken Robinson** works as a psychoanalyst in private practice in Newcastle upon Tyne. He is a member of the British Psychoanalytical Society, Honorary Member of the Polish Society for Psychoanalytical Psychotherapy and Visiting Professor of Psychoanalysis at Northumbria University. He has published on the history of psychoanalysis, the nature of therapeutic action, and other topics; and he contributes to conferences and lectures and facilitates seminars in the UK and abroad. He provides training analysis for trainings in adult and child and adolescent psychoanalytic psychotherapy in the North East of England.

**Joan Schächter** is a training and supervising analyst of the British Psychoanalytical Society. She trained as a psychiatrist and worked at the Cassel Hospital and the Brent Centre for Adolescents. She was for many years a consultant psychotherapist in the NHS. She now works in private practice. She co-wrote *The Late Teenage Years* with Luis Rodriguez de la Sierra (2013). She teaches in the UK and abroad.

## Contributors

**Ronald Baker** was a training and supervising analyst of the British Psychoanalytical Society. He published articles on various aspects of the psychoanalytic process—on assessment (1980), humour

(1993), "the neutral position" (2000)—as well the paper on the concept of the "new object" in this collection. He also had a deep interest in films, publishing a paper on "Deconstructing Dirty Harry" (1999).

**Marion Burgner** was a training and supervising analyst of the British Psychoanalytical Society. Prior to becoming an adult analyst, she trained in child and adolescent psychoanalysis at the Hampstead Clinic, where she worked for many years. She was also a staff member at the Brent Adolescent Centre. She worked in a Tavistock Clinic Project offering psychotherapy to patients who were HIV positive. She was also part of a research project at the Anna Freud Centre offering analysis to young adults who had suffered a breakdown. She published and taught widely both in the UK and abroad.

**Donald Campbell** is a training and supervising analyst, Distinguished Fellow and past President of the British Psychoanalytical Society, and former Secretary General of the International Psychoanalytic Association. He also served as Chair of the Portman Clinic in London, where he worked for thirty years as a child, adolescent and adult analyst, with violent and delinquent individuals and patients suffering from a perversion. He has published papers and chapters on such subjects as adolescence, doubt, shame, metaphor, violence, perversion, child sexual abuse, self-analysis and horror film monsters. Most recently he co-authored a book with Rob Hale, *Working in the Dark: Understanding the Pre-suicide State of Mind* (2017).

**Rosemary Davies** is a training and supervising analyst of the British Psychoanalytical Society and works in private practice. She is an Honorary Senior Lecturer at University College London where she has taught Freud reading seminars and a seminar series on Contemporary Clinical Theory. She has delivered papers in the UK and abroad including a paper on The Setting, Whose Frame is it Anyway? at the European Psychoanalytic Federation in 2015. Her publications include editing and contributing to various psychoanalytic books, and papers on "Anxiety, The Importunate Companion" (2012) and "Rivalry, Benign or Belligerent Sibling of Envy?" (2018).

**Rose M. Edgcumbe** trained as a child and adolescent analyst at the Hampstead Clinic. She worked there for many years, writing and contributing to many publications. She also trained in adult analysis at the British Psycho-Analytical Society. She taught child analysis and child development in the UK and abroad. Her *Anna Freud. A View of Development, Disturbance and Therapeutic Technique* (2000) is already acknowledged as a classic text.

**Sara Flanders** obtained her PhD in English Literature in the United States before coming to the UK to train as a psychoanalyst. She is a training and supervising analyst of the British Psychoanalytical Society. She is a staff member at the Brent Adolescent Centre and works in private practice. She edited *The Dream Discourse Today* (1993), and *Reading French Psychoanalysis* (2010) with Dana Birksted-Breen.

**Mervin Glasser** was a training and supervising analyst of the British Psychoanalytical Society. He helped to establish the Brent Adolescent Centre and Centre for Research into Adolescent Breakdown with Moses and Eglé Laufer. Later he moved to the Portman Clinic where he became Chairman until his retirement. He is best known for his work on perverse and violent patients, especially for his creation of the concept of the "core complex", described in this collection, which remains influential in Contemporary Freudian thinking.

**Angela Joyce** is a training and supervising analyst of the British Psychoanalytical Society and a Child Psychoanalyst trained at the Anna Freud Centre London, where she worked for many years. She works in private practice in London. She is currently Chair of the Winnicott Trust and a Trustee of the Squiggle Foundation. She edited with Lesley Caldwell *Reading Winnicott* (2011), contributed the Introduction to volume 6 of *The Collected Works of D. W. Winnicott* (2016) and edited the papers from the London 2015 Conference *Donald Winnicott and the History of the Present* (2017).

**M. Eglé Laufer** is a training and supervising analyst of the British Psychoanalytical Society. She and **Moses Laufer** (also a training and supervising analyst) set up the Centre for Research into Adolescent Breakdown and the Brent Centre for Adolescents in 1967. The centre offers a consultation and treatment service which initially included analytic treatment. Eglé and Moses Laufer published and edited several books on the work of the centre, most notably *Adolescence and Developmental Breakdown* (1984). Eglé

Laufer has published and taught widely in the UK and abroad. She has retired from clinical practice.

**Susan Loden** is a training and supervising analyst of the British Psychoanalytical Society. After a first career in book publishing, she trained in psychotherapy at the British Association of Psychotherapists, took an academic degree in Developmental Psychoanalytic Psychology at the Anna Freud Centre/University College London, and then trained as a psychoanalyst at the Institute of Psychoanalysis in London. She is especially interested in psychoanalytic theory and technique as it was developed by Freud's followers following the introduction of the structural model of the mind and has lectured and taught the subject in the UK and abroad. She works as psychoanalyst in private practice.

**Marianne Parsons,** a child and adult psychoanalyst, a member of the British Psychoanalytical Society, has contributed papers to books and journals. Formerly Head of Clinical Training at the Anna Freud Centre and Editor of the *Journal of Child Psychotherapy*, she worked for many years at the Portman Clinic. She was a member of the Violence Research Group led by Mervin Glasser and ran the Portman Clinic Diploma in Forensic Psychotherapeutic Studies. Currently, she chairs the Training Analysis Committee for the Independent Psychoanalytic Child and Adolescent Psychotherapy Association and teaches and supervises widely on many psychoanalytic trainings.

**Rosine Jozef Perelberg** is a training and supervising analyst and President of the British Psychoanalytical Society. She is visiting professor in the Psychoanalysis Unit at University College London and Corresponding member of the Paris Psychoanalytical Society. Previously she completed a PhD in Social Anthropology at the London School of Economics. She has written and edited twelve books, amongst most recent *Murdered Father, Dead Father: Revisiting the Oedipus Complex* (2015); *The Greening of Psychoanalysis,* edited with Gregorio Kohon (2017), and *Sexuality, Excess and Representation* (2019). She works in London in private practice.

**Marina Perris-Myttas** is a clinical psychologist; a training and supervising analyst of the British Psychoanalytical Society, a member of Institut de Psychosomatique, Paris and a corresponding member of the Hellenic Society. She works in private practice in

London. Previously she worked in the National Health Service where she led a psychoanalytically informed service for personality disorders and headed a multidisciplinary training programme in psychotherapy for Mental Health Professionals. She has published and presented papers in the UK and abroad.

**Dinora Pines** was a training and supervising analyst of the British Psychoanalytical Society. Prior to training she worked as a consultant dermatologist. She was a staff member at the Brent Adolescent Centre for many years and taught widely in the UK and abroad. Her collected papers entitled *A Woman's Unconscious Use of Her Body*, were published in 1993 and republished in 2010.

**Luis Rodríguez de la Sierra** is a training and supervising analyst of the British Psychoanalytical Society for adult and child and adolescent psychoanalysis. He did his medical training in Barcelona, and he qualified as a psychiatrist in Barcelona and London, where he also trained as a group psychotherapist. He worked for many years in the NHS and at the Anne Freud Centre; he now works for the London Clinic of Psychoanalysis and in private practice. He lectures and teaches here and abroad. He has published papers on child analysis and drug addiction. He has edited *Child Analysis Today* (2004) and has written *The Late Teenage Years* with Joan Schächter (2013).

**Joseph Sandler** and **Anne-Marie Sandler** were training and supervising analysts of the British Psychoanalytical Society. Joseph Sandler was the first Freud Memorial Professor of Psychoanalysis in the University of London. Anne-Marie trained first at the Hampstead Clinic, where she worked for many years, also serving as Director. Joseph was a key figure in the Hampstead Clinic Index, working with colleagues to define and refine definitions of psychoanalytic concepts. Some of this work is collected in *From Safety to Superego* (1987). They published many papers and books, together and separately; *Internal Objects Revisited* (1998) represents their creative integration of a theory of internal objects and ego psychology. They taught extensively in the UK and abroad.

# Previously published material

Baker, R. (1993). The patient's discovery of the psychoanalyst as a new object. *Int. J. Psycho-Anal.*, 74: 1223–1233. Reprinted with permission from *International Journal of Psychoanalysis*.

Burgner, M. (1985). The oedipal experience: effects on development of an absent father. *Int. J. Psycho-Anal.*, 66: 311–320. Reprinted with permission from *International Journal of Psychoanalysis*.

Campbell, D. (2014). Doubt in the psychoanalysis of a paedophile. *Int. J. Psycho-Anal.*, 95(3): 441–463. Reprinted by permission of the publisher (Taylor & Francis Ltd, http://www.tandfonline.com).

Edgcumbe, R. M. (1984). Modes of communication—the differentiation of somatic and verbal expression. *Psychoanal. St. Child*, 39: 137–154. Reprinted by permission of the publisher (Taylor & Francis Ltd, http://www.tandfonline.com).

Glasser, M. (1996). Masculinity, femininity and internalization in male homosexuals. *Bull. Brit. Psychoanal. Soc.*, 32(11). Reprinted with permission from the Glasser family.

Laufer, M. E. (1982). Female masturbation in adolescence and the development of the relationship to the body. *Int. J. Psycho-Anal.*, 63: 295–302. Reprinted with permission from *International Journal of Psychoanalysis*.

Loden, S. (2003). The fate of the dream in contemporary psychoanalysis. *J. Amer. Psychoanal. Assn.*, 51(1): 43–70. Reprinted with permission from *Journal of the American Psychoanalytic Association*.

Perelberg, R. J. (2006). The controversial discussions and après-coup. *Int. J. Psycho-Anal.*, 87(5): 1199–1220. Reprinted by permission of the publisher (Taylor & Francis Ltd, http://www.tandfonline.com).

*Previously published material*

Pines, D. (1990). Pregnancy, miscarriage and abortion. A psychoanalytic perspective. *Int. J. Psycho-Anal.*, 71: 301–307. Reprinted with permission from *International Journal of Psychoanalysis*.

Davies, R. *Regression, Curiosity and the Discovery of the Object Time and Memory*, ed. R. R. Perelberg. London: Routledge, 2007. Reprinted by permission of the publisher (Taylor & Francis Ltd).

Sandler, J. and Sandler, A. (1994). Phantasy and its transformations: a contemporary Freudian view. *Int. J. Psycho-Anal.*, 75: 387–394. Reprinted with permission from *International Journal of Psychoanalysis*.

Flanders: S. The dream space; the analytic situation and the eating disorder: clinging to the concrete. In *Dreaming and Thinking*, ed. R. J. Perelberg, London: Routledge. Reprinted by permission of the publisher (Taylor & Francis Ltd).

# 1

# INTRODUCTION

Ken Robinson and Joan Schächter

**The rich diversity of the Contemporary Freudian group**

Far from being uniform, the Contemporary Freudian group is notable for its rich diversity. The group has its roots in Freud, Anna Freud and the Hampstead Clinic, which after the Freuds' emigration from Vienna became a centre for Freudian thinking; it has built on that foundation and continues to develop, both in relation to it and independently of it. Some current Contemporary Freudian analysts (particularly but not only child analysts) see themselves as more aligned with Anna Freud's extension of Freud's thinking. Others give more emphasis to cross-fertilization with the work of psychoanalysts (Klein or Winnicott, for example) from other groups within the British Society. One example is Joseph and Anne-Marie Sandler's review of various aspects of the concept of "internal objects" in *Internal Objects Revisited* (1998). Based on papers from 1976 onwards, it offers "a theoretical basis for integrating a theory of internal object relations into an ego-psychological—or, more properly, a post-ego-psychological—frame of reference" (Sandler 1998, p. xii). And still others regard themselves as working independently of Anna Freud's filter, exploring, for example, a return to Freud partly inspired by French psychoanalysis—Green, Laplanche, Pontalis and the work of the Paris Psychosomatic School (particularly Aisenstein, Marty, and Smadja). Contemporary Freudian analysts have also been working with Italian colleagues over the past ten years, focusing on a common interest in the body, its presence in the session and the associated relevance of the counter-transference. As a result, no simple definition of the Contemporary Freudian tradition can do justice to it. Instead, its nature is best approached through the idea of "family resemblances" which offers an analogy for connecting particular uses of the same word or phrase through "a complicated network of similarities overlapping and criss-crossing" (Wittgenstein 1968, PI 66). The concept of "family resemblances" makes it possible to distinguish both the family of psychoanalysts in general, and particular families of psychoanalysts. To be a psychoanalyst, the individual must, in this sense, share a sufficient number of resemblances but will not share all. Psychoanalysts, in general, share at least some "resemblances", an interest in the unconscious and in psychic determinism, for example; and in the work of particular families some resemblances are more prominent and differently nuanced, both theoretically and in clinical practice. In British psychoanalysis, the Contemporary Freudian, Kleinian and Independent "families" came into existence out of the disagreements about what resemblances psychoanalysts should share, which led to the Controversial Discussions (1942–1944). Following these Discussions, it was agreed that, primarily for the purposes of training, the Klein group would be known as the "A" group and the Anna Freud group would become the "B" group. The non-aligned British Freudians became the Middle group. In 1987, the "B" group was renamed the Contemporary Freudian group by its members (see Robinson 2011). The concept of family resemblances shifts the focus away from historical roots and allegiances (although they are significant and we shall note them) and onto the theoretical and clinical characteristics that shape the tradition.

From a Contemporary Freudian perspective, it is useful in mapping these resemblances to bear in mind the metapsychological points of view which have their origin in Freud's work: the topographical and the structural models, the dynamic, the economic and the developmental perspectives. These points of view are not the sole province of Contemporary Freudian analysts, nor would they all now think in economic terms, but the Contemporary Freudian approach does characteristically rest on them, with differences of emphasis between individual analysts. We shall refer in passing to these points of view (even though in practice they run together and separating them is a convenience) as we identify the resemblances that inform the Contemporary Freudian approach. We shall concentrate on the following areas of interest which constitute resemblances: the unconscious, the developmental approach, the body and psychosexuality and aggression. Finally, we shall comment on resemblances within Contemporary Freudian technique and practice.

## The unconscious

For Freud the unconscious is both a topographical and dynamic concept. It has its place in his depth model of the mind alongside the preconscious and the conscious, but it cannot be understood without the notion of repression. Freud's understanding that the unconscious can only be known via its derivatives, by way of the traces that it leaves in consciousness, is central in the Contemporary Freudian approach to clinical work. Several Contemporary Freudian analysts have contributed to elucidating Freud's theory. Anne-Marie and Joseph Sandler have tried to clarify the implications of Freud's discussion of censorship in relation to his account of two censorships in "The Unconscious": "the first ... is exercised against the *Ucs.* itself, and the second against its *Pcs.* Derivatives.... In psychoanalytic treatment the existence of the second censorship, located between the systems *Pcs.* and *Cs.* is proved beyond question" (Freud 1915, p. 193). In their papers on the past and the present unconscious, the Sandlers (1983, 1994a) point out the confusions that have developed surrounding the meaning and use of term "the unconscious" and consequently the meaning of "unconscious phantasy". They distinguish theoretically and clinically between preconscious phantasies predominantly related to the transference which are operating in the present of the analysis and unconscious phantasies which have arisen in early childhood and have been repressed; the preconscious phantasies are of course in part derivatives of the early phantasies. "Whereas the past unconscious acts and reacts according to the past, the present unconscious is concerned with maintaining equilibrium in the present" (Sandler and Sandler 1984, p. 372). This view also places emphasis on the stabilizing function of unconscious phantasy with important implications for technique. Taking a different approach, partly in response to the Sandlers' work, Clifford Yorke (1996, 2001) surveyed the concepts of the preconscious and the unconscious as they appear in Freud's work and in more recent usage. He emphasizes the importance of maintaining clear metapsychological differentiations in the face of a tendency to collapse the two terms, especially in the failure to distinguish the descriptive and dynamic usages of the term unconscious clinically. Whereas, in their revision of Freud, the Sandlers took what they deemed to be appropriate from their "own clinical experience and from object relational and Kleinian theory while trying to avoid simplistic formulations" (Sandler 1998, p. xii). Yorke was sceptical about the possibility of a compromise between Freud and Klein seeing them instead as in conflict (Yorke 1994). Yorke preferred an earlier paper by Sandler and Nagera (1963) on aspects of the metapsychology of fantasy which had sought to

> bring out something of the confusion which attends the use of the terms 'fantasy' and 'unconscious fantasy,' and to offer a number of thoughts, based on Freud's work, which may lead to a clarification of the scientific and semantic problems involved.
>
> (p. 192)

The Sandlers and Yorke, then, disagree, but their differences are witness to the on-going vitality of debate within the Contemporary Freudian tradition as its analysts visit and revisit Freud's metapsychology and strive for greater conceptual clarity.

Freud first outlined the topographical model in his *Interpretation of Dreams* (1900), setting out a method by which to elucidate the meaning of the unconscious elements in dreams. Dreams and dream interpretation remain one of the royal roads, a privileged medium of access to the patient's unconscious (Flanders 1993, Perelberg 2000, Loden, Rodriguez de la Sierra and Schächter this volume). Since dreams reveal aspects of the past that have had to be turned away from consciousness, they bring to the surface something hitherto not known, albeit represented in disguised form. They may, for example, reveal important memories and traumatic experiences that can be constructed through the work of interpretation, which further the analytic process (Loden this volume). And once the transference is in full flow, dreams can be understood as communicating aspects of the past alive in the current transference relationship. Dreams in analysis are considered not only for their potential encoded meaning but also for the meaning of their function within the analytic process. On another level, they may also be seen as reflecting elements of the patient's ego capacity to tolerate unconscious affects and conflicts, and the ego's capacity to symbolize (Flanders and Schächter

*Introduction*

this volume). Some Contemporary Freudian analysts make use of Winnicott's ideas concerning the relation between transitional space, play and the dream, and of the developments in psychoanalytic thinking about the structure of dreams and dreaming (Flanders 1993, Perelberg 2000).

More generally within this theoretical perspective, early experiences held in the unconscious can never be recalled as they really were, for two reasons: first because they may never have been mentally represented, second, even when earlier experiences seem to be remembered they are filtered through later experiences. The existence of the repression barrier which creates the infantile amnesia means that individuals remember little (if anything) in the way of explicit memories of their first years of life. What are recalled in adult analysis are experiences which have been revised in the process of later remembering, as well as having been acquired second-hand. Early experiences then do not remain as they actually were but can only be constructed within the analytic process. This is especially true where there has been trauma. Freud's concept of "Nachträglichkeit" is essential in understanding the complexity of the unconscious and unconscious mental functioning (Perelberg 2007, 2015). This is one of the points at which Contemporary Freudian analysts have found the French understanding of Freud helpful, in, for example, grasping the complex process of après-coup ("Nachträglichkeit") in relation to mnemic traces, inscription and unrepresented and proto-mental states.

Whilst all the papers in this volume inevitably involve discussion of the unconscious, we have chosen two papers to include in this section, both of which have important implications for clinical technique and practice, Joseph and Anne-Marie Sandler's "Phantasy and Its Transformations: A Contemporary Freudian View" and Rosine Perelberg's "Unconscious Phantasy and Après Coup: the Controversial Discussions". Both engage with topics that were part of the Controversial Discussions.

The Controversial Discussions are not only essential to understanding the development of psychoanalysis in Britain, but they helped to focus Contemporary Freudian ideas and still do, as these papers (and Davies's this volume) show. The Controversial Discussions addressed central questions in psychoanalytic theory, central then and central now: for example, does the infant have a functioning ego from birth; what is the role of the environment and object relationships in relation to the internal world and internal object relations; is destructive aggression primary or a product of excessive frustration or trauma; how do we understand unconscious phantasy; when does the oedipal development occur? One of the problems highlighted by the Discussions was that central psychoanalytic concepts had become ambiguous or diffuse in their meaning. In the papers by the Sandlers and Perelberg, we see examples of the important contributions that Contemporary Freudian analysts have made to clarifying key concepts in relation to psychoanalytic practice.

Taking their lead from Freud, Joseph and Anne-Marie Sandler distinguish two levels of censorship, one between the systems unconscious and the preconscious, the other between the preconscious and conscious. Behind the first, the repression barrier, lies the "past unconscious"; its phantasies are subject to infantile amnesia and can only be reconstructed through interpretation. Behind the second lies the "present unconscious". The Sandlers focus on this second censorship, redefining the preconscious as the realm of the "present unconscious", "the realm of *current* unconscious subjective experience". As such it exists in the here and now and is more readily accessible, even though its phantasies are also repressed should they disturb psychic equilibrium. It is here that transference phantasies exist and can be interpreted.

Rosine Perelberg, who brings a rich knowledge of French psychoanalysis to Contemporary Freudian thinking and practice, argues that the concept of après-coup collapses the distinction between past and present: they are intertwined in a "mutual process of reinterpretation". Against the background of the Controversial Discussions, and drawing on Paula Heimann's contribution on regression as well as Isaacs (together with the ensuing discussions of them), she too makes a central metapsychological distinction: between two types of "après-coup", the descriptive and the dynamic, parallel to the distinction between the descriptive and the dynamic unconscious. The one is concerned with retrospective attribution of meaning in the unfolding progression of a session, the other is at the heart of Freudian metapsychology and Freud's understanding of temporality. Perelberg argues that the dynamic "après-coup" is rooted in Freud's recognition of the essential discontinuity between infantile sexuality and adult sexuality. The resolution of the Oedipus complex institutes re-structuring of earlier development with sexuality at its core. The seeds of later sexuality are present in infantile sexuality but are both re-organized and given fresh meaning: as Freud put it succinctly "There are thus good reasons why a child sucking at his mother's breast has become the prototype of every relation of love. The finding of an object is in fact a refinding of it" (1905, p. 222). Freud's remark catches the regressive and progressive aspects of "après-coup", but, as Perelberg's paper demonstrates, the temporality embodied in the concept is multi-dimensional.

## The developmental approach

Interpretations of the individual's past are rooted in our theories of child development and mental functioning and are based on reconstructions from the patient's verbal and non-verbal material. Freud's theory emphasizes the formative power of infancy and childhood in the development of the adult personality: the personality is built from identifications as a response to loss. We pass through libidinal phases, from oral, through anal and phallic, to puberty and the adolescent genital organization; and in the process of ego development the infant and child's relation to the environment is formative as the ego faces challenges in managing the demands of the drives, the dynamic unconscious and the superego. Freud's theory depends on the vicissitudes of object-relating and attachment in relation to the drives in infantile life. Behind adult disturbance, there is an "infantile neurosis", with fixation points left behind by impairments and arrests in development. Under stress the adult might regress to these points, a regression expressed through various symptom formations—conversion hysteria, obsessive compulsive or psychotic (a break with reality).

Against this background, the Contemporary Freudian developmental perspective embraces a complex notion of temporality within which the gradual process of psychic structuring takes place. A broad and complex account of psychic development which occurs in time and over time is central to this psychoanalytic model (Perelberg 2007, this volume). Development does not take place in a linear, cumulative fashion (Davies this volume). Freud's concepts of phases of development and the timelessness of the unconscious, together with his dynamic concepts of regression, fixation, repetition compulsion, the return of the repressed, play an important role in Contemporary Freudian thinking.

Freud wrote in "On Narcissism": "... a unity comparable to the ego cannot exist in the individual from the start; the ego has to be developed" (1914, p. 77). Contemporary Freudian analysts tend to assume that initially the infant has no continuous sense of self; rather, sporadic experiences of self and other alternate with experiences of non-differentiation. These early experiences are essentially bodily: "the ego is first and foremost a bodily ego" (Freud 1923, p. 26), derived from multiple physical contacts with the mother/caretaker and in response to the bodily pressures of the drives (hunger, thirst, cold, pain, etc.). From these early un-differentiated experiences, there is a gradual development of differentiation between inside/outside, self/other, phantasy/reality, which gives rise to the development of psychic structures. These maturational processes occur within the context of differentiating and then separating from the matrix of the early relationship with the mother, gradually enabling the capacity to tolerate absence and dependence to develop. This view of early development can be seen as a theory of psychic "coming to be" where the maturational task is that of building a stable, separate self with capacities for self-maintenance, self-regulation and ultimately self-reflection. Here some Contemporary Freudian analysts find the economic point of view useful in distinguishing the relative degrees of libidinal investment in the self and others required for self-esteem and object-relationships.

Freud had theorized development through infancy and childhood to puberty and adolescence largely by extrapolation from the data of his analyses of adults with only limited observation "in children at first hand". Anna Freud and her colleagues at The Hampstead Clinic (renamed the Anna Freud Centre after her death in 1981) drew on direct clinical experience of psychoanalytic work with children and adolescents, and extensive observational experience of infants and children through to adolescence. As she put it:

> The facts of infantile sexuality, the Oedipus and castration complexes, the problem of ego and superego development, and role of aggression having been established, psychoanalytic study then turned to the child's first year of life, i.e. to the beginning of mental functioning and the first emotional contact of the infant with his environment.
>
> (1955 [1954], p. 589)

The Hampstead Clinic became an important centre for research into development from birth to early adulthood. Much of its research was carried out predominantly in study groups in which analytic and psychotherapeutic work with children and adolescents was discussed from the perspective of the impact of specific illnesses on the development and psychic functioning of the individual patients. Dorothy Burlingham and colleagues worked with blind children, George Moran and colleagues worked with children and adolescents who had developed brittle diabetes. These studies shed light on the complex relationship between external and internal traumas. Willi Hoffer investigated early development, notably the mouth-ego as a stage of body-ego development (1950) and the emergence of "the primal sensation of self" (1949, p. 55). Joseph Sandler and colleagues carried forward the Hampstead Index established by Burlingham, which aimed to examine and define psychoanalytic concepts on the basis of extensive clinical data across development. It was a co-operative project that led to a great number of influential publications (many in *The Psychoanalytic Study of the Child*), some of them collected together in Sandler's *From Safety to Superego* (1987), including papers on, for example, the superego and the representational world and his concepts of "safety" and the "safety principle". Sandler's clarification of the way in which the ego "makes every effort to maintain a minimum level of safety feeling … through the development and control of integrative processes" (pp. 7–8), with its emphasis on perception as mastery, has important implications for clinical practice. It means, for example, that as well as paying attention to patients' defensive manoeuvres to reduce anxiety, we must also be aware of their attempts to offset anxiety by heightening the feeling of safety. In 1996, Peter Fonagy and Mary Target published the results of using the rich resource of the Index to investigate "Predictors of Outcome in Child Psychoanalysis" in "a Retrospective Study Of 763 Cases at The Anna Freud Centre".

The Index led to the development of the Diagnostic Profile as a method of organizing material into an overview of the functioning of a patient at a particular point of life against the background of his/her development from birth in relation to the environment and in relation to a spectrum of "variations of normality", on the one hand, and the pathological, on the other (A. Freud 1965, p. 147). Its developmental perspective is characteristic of Contemporary Freudian thinking, and it is still in use today, revised in 2016 by Jennifer Davids, Viviane Green, Angela Joyce and Duncan McLean (2017). Alongside this synchronic profile, some Contemporary Freudian analysts in the Anna Freudian mould also draw on her diachronic concept of developmental lines (Parsons this volume), which allows the clinician to understand diagnostically how the patient has progressed along various lines in relation to each other and the effect of disharmony between them (1963, 1981).

Much more is now understood about the importance of pre-oedipal development, particularly the very early mother-infant interactions, and the toddler's anality, sadism and experiences of separation, but Freud's concept of the Oedipus complex in its full complexity remains central in Contemporary Freudian thinking and practice. It is understood as a pivotal element of psychic structuring, which lays the foundations for the development of personal and sexual identity in adolescence. The role of the father is seen as fundamentally important from early development onwards, both by his presence and by his absence (Burgner this volume). More recently, Contemporary Freudian analysts have studied the impact of the absent father (and "the third" paternal function he represents) in violent, suicidal and perverse patients (Campbell 1995; Perelberg 1995, 1999, 2011, 2015a). From another angle, Peter Fonagy and Mary Target have made early attachment the centre of their researches, especially in relation to developmental psychopathology and borderline states. They offer to complement and extend psychoanalytic developmental theory about the "child's perception of psychic reality", writing, for example, about "the integration of the 'psychic equivalent' and 'pretend' modes into a reflective mode at around the oedipal stage" (1996).

Mervin Glasser's concept of the "core complex", which grew out of his work with perverse and violent patients at the Portman Clinic, draws on the developmental vicissitudes of the symbiosis and separation-individuation stages of early development with their struggles with dependence and independence, closeness and separation and the associated fears of being engulfed or isolated. Glasser's patients had encountered an environment, notably a mother experienced as both "avaricious" or intrusive and "indifferent" or rejecting, that fed into these terrors rather than enabling them to become tolerable, leaving the patients fixated, with profound consequences for their sexuality, aggression and personality development (Glasser 1979, this volume; Campbell and Schächter this volume). Many Contemporary Freudian analysts make use of Glasser's concept in understanding patients' difficulties with experiencing dependence and separateness, manifested in oscillations between contact and avoidance in the transference and counter-transference.

The processes of separation and individuation and oedipal development are revisited in adolescence. Adolescence is normally a tumultuous phase of life, when the sexually mature body, with its potential for procreation and aggression, has to be integrated, leading to a re-working of earlier infantile and childhood conflicts and the development of an adult sense of gendered identity. As Freud pointed out in his concept of "Nachträglichkeit", earlier traumatic experiences are transformed and re-signified in the light of oedipal and adolescent development. In adolescence, we see how the body may be used to carry the burden of un-metabolized affective experiences related to infantile conflicts. Contemporary Freudian analysts have made particularly significant contributions over many years, and continue to do so, to studying and treating adolescents, notably in research into adolescent breakdown at the Brent Adolescent Centre (E. and M. Laufer 1984, 1997, and Eglé Laufer this volume).

Moses and Eglé Laufer have drawn attention to the importance of offering adequate psychoanalytic treatment to adolescents who are struggling with developmental tasks, especially with integrating the newly developed sexual body into the self-representation, in order to avert breakdown and developmental foreclosure (1984, 1997). Most recently, Joan Schächter and Luis Rodriguez de la Sierra, working in this tradition, have delineated later adolescent development in *The Late Teenage Years: from Seventeen to Adulthood* (2013). Parsons (this volume) discusses disturbances in the relation between sensuality and sexuality in the analysis of a 19-year-old girl with a fragmented sense of self, drawing on Anna Freud's conceptualizations of developmental lines and Winnicott's concept of transitional space.

Later phases of sexual life (pregnancy, motherhood, fatherhood, menopause, ageing) are also important events in the psychic life of the individual allowing for further development and re-working of earlier conflicts or leading to the acute re-emergence of unresolved conflicts (Pines 1993).

The papers chosen for this section represent the Contemporary Freudian tradition of developmental thinking from Marion Burgner and Eglé Laufer to analysts writing today, represented by Angela Joyce and Ken Robinson.

In her paper "The Vicissitudes of Preparing and Sustaining a Young Child in Analysis" Angela Joyce describes the ways in which the Anna Freud Centre engaged with a young mother who had suffered severe traumas in her country of origin: she sought help with her toddler daughter who screamed relentlessly. Whilst focussing on the repetition of unelaborated traumas through the generations, Joyce describes the different phases of treatment, all of which were suddenly interrupted by the mother. A period of parent–infant psychotherapy ameliorated the mutually unsatisfying relationship between mother and daughter, lessening the hostility and allowing them to play together. At the same time, the daughter was attending the Centre nursery. A good enough engagement with the Centre enabled the mother to accept a recommendation for analysis for her daughter. The need for analysis was based on the assessment that the child's development was being compromised by her on-going difficulties with affect regulation, and an unconscious fantasy shared with her mother that separateness is catastrophic. The analysis continued for one year. It was ended precipitately by her mother. Joyce discusses the complex issues involved in taking a child into analysis, which include taking account of the counter-transference evoked by the parent-child pair.

Joyce describes vividly and movingly the painful cycle of engagement and rupture which this mother felt unconsciously compelled to repeat in her relationship with her daughter and with the therapists at the Centre. Whilst not under-estimating the impact on the child of the sudden interruption of her analysis, Joyce speculates that the experience of being heard and thought about by her analyst within a consistent setting would have been internalized to some degree, modifying the child's developing internal world (see Baker this volume). To an extent, the nursery staff and the child's analyst could be thought of as providing the necessary developmental help to facilitate the child's capacity to better regulate her own affective states.

Several other analysts included in this volume also make use of the concept of developmental help. In her paper "The Oedipal Experience: Effects on Development of an Absent Father" Marion Burgner makes use of an allied concept, the analyst as a new developmental object. Burgner's paper grew out of a Hampstead Clinic study group. In this case, the group examined the effects on the child, in analysis, of the loss of the father through separation or divorce in the first five years of life. Burgner first describes the findings of the group together with case material and then presents two adult analytic cases to explore the feasibility of analysis where a marked structural deficit from the oedipal phase has been carried over into later life. The study group found that a major theme for the

*Introduction*

children was the taboo on incest which was fragile for boys left alone with mothers. They were confronted symbolically with parricide and incest, with an absent father and having a mother all to themselves. Their damaged oedipal development left them prone to being driven by pre-oedipal needs and exclusively tied to their pre-oedipal mother, fearful of losing her and driven by anxiety to seek closeness, even if on the surface they seemed to function at a pseudo-oedipal level. Because the task of relinquishing pre-oedipal ties and facing incest and parricide was too much for these children, they carried their pre-oedipal attachments forward through later developmental stages. There were problems also in the formation of the superego, which tended to be over-strict with aggression turned towards the self, and with sexual identity. Burgner comments on the girls experiencing the loss of their father as confirming that they were not attractive enough. Clinically, it was found that the children needed a therapeutic approach that helped them with reality testing, and the availability of the analyst as a new object, as a safe, predictable figure, unlike the parents.

Against this background Burgner turns to her work with adults. Both the cases that she describes were able to gain something from analysis, but both stopped their treatment prematurely when they could not tolerate working on the incestuous oedipal material that was finding its way into transference and that brought with it considerable narcissistic vulnerability.

Ken Robinson writes of what can go wrong in the oedipal phase, first giving an account through a vignette of normal development. Robinson brings together Freud and Winnicott, arguing that they share a conviction that a capacity to entertain illusion and reality simultaneously, without one cancelling out the other, makes engagement in illusion and play possible, and he extends this to describe transitional play as a fundamental aspect of the parental function in the oedipal stage. He emphasizes that the development of sexuality at this time is inseparable from the development of mind and the sense of a self as personally engaged in the world. The parents hold the reality of generational difference and the incest taboo so that the child is free to play at being the lover of the chosen parent, to explore emerging sexual fantasies, wishes and feelings. The parents are responsible too for gradually meting out the dis-illusionment that it is they who occupy their bed and they who make babies. In his clinical example, Debra, Robinson describes a case where such play was not possible. Debra's tender, potentially playful overtures to her father were treated as if they were adult sexual advances, leading to sexual abuse. In the course of the analysis, Debra had to develop a capacity to play rather than re-enact her abuse in the transference as she moved towards treating her analyst as a new developmental object in relation to whom she could explore some of her hitherto distorted oedipal feelings. Robinson stresses that in providing a framework in which such play may happen, the analyst must be neither afraid nor narcissistically excited. He concludes that what is needed is firm holding of the situation on the model of the parents' holding.

Moses and Eglé Laufer have published extensively on the subject of adolescent development and adolescent breakdown, illustrated with many clinical examples (1984, 1995, 1997). They have elaborated the particularities of the adolescent developmental tasks, especially the need to integrate the mature sexual body into the overall sense of identity. In her paper "Female Masturbation in Adolescence and the Development of the Relationship to the Body", Eglé Laufer explores the functional role of masturbation in the female adolescent, differentiating this from its role in male adolescents. She focuses on the reported cessation of masturbation in adolescent girls, specifically the suppression of the use of the hand. Whereas Freud had linked the cessation of masturbation to the girl's experience of disappointment in her own body—the lack of a penis—Eglé Laufer proposes that it is rather related to the fear of bringing into consciousness passive homosexual wishes in relation to the mother, and to the anxiety aroused as a result of experiencing the post-pubertal body as now having the potential of living out the destructive retaliatory wishes against the mother's body. In the pre-oedipal period, masturbation carries the meaning for the child of feeling that her own body is capable of providing satisfaction independently of her mother. Masturbation, she points out, always has an active and a passive component and is thus likely to be affected if the individual is struggling with intense conflict in this area. The need to struggle against the desire to masturbate in adolescent girls may lead to the compelling need to attack their own bodies actively with their hand. From her clinical experience she understood that the impulse for self-cutting occurred at times when the patient experienced a fear of giving in to the regressive wish to be passively cared for. The self-damage was preceded by an outburst of uncontrolled hostility against the mother, the sexual partner or the analyst.

We would like to refer here to a paper by Clifford Yorke, "The Development and Functioning of the Sense of Shame" (1990) which for reasons of length, we had to omit from this collection. In exploring the development of the sense of shame, particularly through child observations in the nursery and in analytic treatment, Yorke distinguishes shame from guilt and explores its function as a regulator of self-esteem and a motivator of behaviour. As many clinicians have observed, guilt brings material into the analysis and shame keeps it out: the Sandlers' second censorship (this volume) has "as its fundamental motivation the avoidance of conscious feelings of shame, embarrassment and humiliation". Yorke's paper links with Campbell's elaboration of the importance of the fear of shame in his proposal of a developmental concept of a shame barrier (this volume). Yorke points out that whilst unconscious guilt can mobilize defences against its full conscious experience, there is no defence against shame once the affect has been elicited. For most if not all Contemporary Freudian analysts, the recognition and interpretation of the role of shame is an important element of clinical technique.

## The body and psychosexuality

The physical reality of the body and the vicissitudes of the development of psychosexuality through the libidinal phases remain important for Contemporary Freudian analysts in understanding infantile sexuality and the individual's internal world. Burgner and Edgcumbe (1975) extended Freud's classification of the phases, adding the phallic-narcissistic stage, in which the difference between the sexes has to be accepted in order to develop a stable gender identity. It is because of this emphasis on the body and its relation to the unfolding of the libidinal phases that many Contemporary Freudian analysts retain Freud's dating of the onset and development of the biphasic Oedipus complex. The place of the Oedipus complex in the development of identifications and sexual object choice are fundamental in the psychic structuring of the individual (Burgner, Glasser, and Robinson this volume).

The role of the body and its representation within the mind are fundamental in understanding the earliest affective experiences. The body is the site of the earliest affective experiences, which over time become represented at a psychic level, as the ego and its functions develop within the matrix of the relationship with the mother. Traces of early bodily experiences that have never reached representation are often expressed through the body in the form of behaviours or physical symptoms later in life. In her collection of papers, *A Woman's Unconscious Use of her Body* (1993) Dinora Pines discussed the ways in which unbearable feelings and conflicts arising in early infantile life in women patients are expressed through the body, particularly in relation to skin disorders and disturbances in their psychosexuality.

In this volume, the Contemporary Freudian emphasis on the body is represented by three papers that deal in turn with delineating a developmental path from somatic to verbal expression, the relation of the soma and the body, and a specific aspect of female sexuality in the form of miscarriage and abortion.

Rose Edgcumbe's paper "Modes of Communication—the Differentiation of Somatic and Verbal Expression" grew out of her own earlier papers and discussions in two study groups in the Anna Freud Centre. The study groups had been concerned with characteristic tendencies to "react to specific stimuli with individually specific patterns of cognitive, emotional, behavioural and physiological responses" and with the interaction of constitutional, developmental and environmental factors in early development in the formation of these patterns. Edgcumbe's paper delineates normal development, emphasizing the importance of the mother's capacity to tune into her infant so as to gather together the infant's somatic expressions into the service of communication, first in action and then verbally. Such interaction is the foundation on which the infant develops a capacity for mental representation which informs communication with others and oneself. Where this interaction does not happen, or is impaired, owning and being able to symbolize affect may be stunted. More specifically, where the environment responds physically at the expense of the verbal, the infant may be inhibited in talking and prioritize body language; or where feelings are "talked away" it might be difficult for the child to be able to use appropriate somatic discharge—crying, for example. In keeping with her emphasis on unique patterns of response, Edgcumbe offers a rich array of cases, both child and adult. It is impossible to do justice to them in a synopsis, but suffice it to say that they both vividly portray individual cases and raise important theoretical and clinical questions: for example, when is a somatic phenomenon a communication, even unconsciously, from the point of view of the patient?

*Introduction*

Edgcumbe's classic paper has its roots in Freud's and Anna Freud's work on the somatic and communication, and she shares with them a keen awareness of the complexity of psychosomatic phenomena across specific cases. Marina Perris-Myttas's paper "The Soma and the Body" is an instance of the Contemporary Freudian tradition's enduring concern with the mind-body relationship, and the psychic representations of the body. She too draws on Freud's metapsychology regarding the constitution of the drive, integrating it with the work of Winnicott on somato-psychic development, and the conceptualizations of the French School of Psychosomatics, to investigate the notion of the soma as a psychoanalytic concept. Against this background, she describes the use of the counter-transference to explore the inter-relationship between the libidinal body and the soma in the analytic process, illustrating her view of the impact of differing kinds of early trauma on the development of the body-mind relationship.

Perris-Myttas describes the process of working through her intense and at times overpowering counter-transference experiences with two female patients. The first patient, Zoe, used her over-libidinized body to communicate and distract her analyst from the psychic domain where she would have to confront painful feelings of loss and traumatic separation. The second patient, Liona, who suffered from physical illnesses throughout her life, appeared detached from her libidinal body, only to sweep her analyst into a wished-for idealized transference in which there was to be no separation. When the end of the analysis appeared on the scene, Liona became somatically ill, transmitting her inner fragmentation in a concrete way to her analyst's body. The analyst, at first overwhelmed by this experience, came to understand that a process of somatic regression had taken place in the face of a traumatic loss of the idealized primary object. This early trauma interrupted the development of what Winnicott termed "the psyche's in-dwelling in the soma".

Perris-Myttas concludes that recognizing and working through the different "textures" of counter-transference, where there is a regressive process of drive defusion in relation to early trauma, can help the analyst arrive at a place where "we can speak to the soma through the voice of the body" to recover the developmental processes of drive representation and elaboration. She suggests that understanding the distinction between the body and somatic processes may open the way for further explorations in the field of psychosomatics.

In the third paper, "Pregnancy, Miscarriage and Abortion. A Psychoanalytic Perspective", Dinora Pines also takes account of the vicissitudes of the transference-counter-transference relationship as she focuses on the revival of early separation-individuation conflicts in pregnancy, and the uses a woman unconsciously makes of her body in an effort to avoid or to resolve these conflicts, especially where ambivalence towards the mother remains intense and unresolved. Pines posits that if the little girl has not felt satisfied by her mother at the pre-oedipal stage, nor felt that she herself has satisfied her, she can never make up for this basic loss of a primary sense of well-being in her body. She suggests that adolescent girls who precociously embark on sexual relationships are attempting to re-experience the most primitive contact with their mothers. The pubertal development of a sexual body enables the girl to split off and deny painful emotional states by substituting bodily sensations, in itself a regressive process that may stir up anxieties around separation and individuation. Like Burgner (this volume), Pines is aware of the impact in these cases of fathers who have in some sense or other been absent and therefore unavailable to influence the difficult mother and daughter relationship.

A woman with such a developmental trajectory may encounter problems in pregnancy. She may not have the capacity to regress to re-experiencing "a feeling of primary unity" with her mother through her own experience of "the unseen foetus, concretely within her body", and she may be unable to identify narcissistically with it, "as if it were herself in her mother's body". Instead of being able to identify with the mother as a generous, life-giving force, she may identify with her as a murderous figure resulting in negative feelings and fantasies being projected onto the foetus, threatening the pregnancy. Pines gives three brief but detailed clinical examples in which the patients' lack of an internalized satisfying relationship with their mothers, alongside a deeply ambivalent tie to them, led to difficulties with conception, miscarriage, and repeated abortions. In the final case, careful analysis of the patient's defensive need to re-enact a sado-masochistic relationship within the transference together with analysis of her dreams enabled an exploration of the incestuous fantasies and sadism which had resulted in her abortions. Whereas this patient welcomed the menopause as a release from becoming pregnant and could not experience her analyst as a life-giving force so as to create an analytic baby, the other patients were able to use their analysis to create their own families. Pines's paper typifies the Contemporary Freudian concern with both normality and pathology within a developmental perspective. She points out that pregnancy faces a woman with a further stage of emotional identification with the pre-oedipal mother which may lead to a new adaptive position within both her inner and outer object world, or an intensification of unresolved conflicts.

## Aggression

The role of aggression and destructive impulses is an area about which there has been, and remains, considerable controversy, deriving partly from Freud's changing thinking about aggression and the destructive instincts. Freud never arrived at a final, coherent conceptualization of aggression, wrestling with where to place aggression in his instinct theory which was always dualistic. Briefly, in his early work Freud thought of aggression as a component of the sexual instinct, later he considered it as connected with the self-preservative instinct, even as deriving from it. It was not until 1920 that he conceptualized a separate aggressive instinct, the death instinct. It is this later theory, in which the destructive instinct is in opposition to the life instinct, and the conflict between these instincts is seen as a fundamental conflict in psychic life, that has been the source of controversy. Laplanche and Pontalis (1973) comment that although a textual examination of Freud's writings cannot establish an absolutely unequivocal sense of the term "aggressive instinct", or precise lines of demarcation between the death instinct, the destructive instinct and the aggressive instinct, it does confirm that Freud rarely writes of an aggressive instinct except in a restricted sense; for the most part it designates the death instincts turned outwards.

Freud's speculation about the "death instinct" as a hypothetical concept emerged from his recognition in his clinical work of a "compulsion to repeat" and an unconscious need for punishment that leads to destructive tendencies being turned back upon the ego. Both necessitated a revision of his view that the pleasure-unpleasure principle was the governing principle in the economy of psychic life. The repetition compulsion he argued has an instinctual character and he defined instinct as "an urge inherent in organic life to restore to an earlier state of things" (1920, p. 36). Initially he was particularly interested in the operations of the death instinct within the organism as part of the fresh metapsychological insight it gave into the vicissitudes of aggressive or destructive tendencies, but he soon became more concerned with the ways in which it is turned outwards when the fusion of life and death instincts gives way to defusion. Destructiveness, then, arises in Freud's theory when the death instinct becomes unbound from the life instinct. The death instinct then operates in the opposite direction to the binding function of the life instinct, leading to a destruction of the ego's capacity to symbolize and to melancholic depression and suicide, in which the "pure culture of the death instinct" is turned on the ego (1923, p. 53). The French School of Psychosomatics utilizes this conceptualization to understand severe psychosomatic illnesses. No matter how speculative, Freud's theory allowed him new clinical understanding not only of melancholia but also of, for example, the negative therapeutic reaction, obsessional neurosis, and sadism and masochism. These different elements of Freud's thinking are to some extent reflected in the range of views existing amongst Contemporary Freudian analysts concerning the development and clinical understanding of destructiveness.

Some Contemporary Freudian analysts use the concept of the death instinct clinically to refer to a destructive drive. More specifically, some conceptualize the death instinct as operating separately from the life instinct, essentially as a primary destructive instinct directed against internal objects from the beginning, or early on in the infant's life. From this perspective, there may be less emphasis on developmental factors (including environmental factors) leading to a predominance of destructivity in the individual's psychic economy. Others prefer the first instinct theory's emphasis on self-preservative aggression, some seeing self-preservative aggression as being employed defensively against overwhelming experiences of helplessness (hilflösichkeit), which Freud saw as a basic problem of early infantile life that is never completely overcome in later development. Some think that the concept of an aggressive instinct brings into focus a loving part of a superego complex which provides an internal source of guidance, aims and self-esteem—an ego ideal seen as a compliment to the punitive superego (Yorke 1995).

Many Contemporary Freudian analysts today emphasize destructiveness as the result of the failure to achieve sufficient integration of the aggressive and libidinal drives, as a result of: "adverse external or internal conditions, such as absence of love objects, lack of emotional response from the adult environment, breaking of emotional ties as soon as they are formed, [and] deficiency of emotional development for innate reasons" (A. Freud 1949, p. 41). Hoffer (1950) described the absence of self-directed aggression in healthy infants as reflecting the existence of sufficient libidinal cathexis of the infant's own body, such that aggression was deflected outwards, in contrast to deprived children who frequently attack their own bodies. Such destructiveness is closely associated with deficits in secondary narcissism and a vulnerability to fears of fragmentation and annihilation. Marianne Parsons's (2006) account of the normative development of aggression concentrates on the power of love to bind hatred, following Anna Freud's idea that what is pathological in destructiveness is not the aggressive tendency *per se* but the defusion of libidinal and aggressive urges.

Anna Freud developed the concept of "identification with the aggressor" (1937) to explain how aggression may be split off and projected, sometimes as a defence against anxiety. Later, Mervin Glasser explored the relation of self-preservative and sado-masochistic aggression to further our understanding of the function and nature of violence (Glasser 1998). The work of Glasser and colleagues at the Portman Clinic with perverse and violent patients has led to new formulations, in particular, the "Core Complex", which have led to a wider understanding of the uses of sexuality to modify aggression, as will be seen from Donald Campbell's paper in this volume. For Glasser, sadism is a way of relating to another through torture, keeping the object alive but at a distance and under control in fantasy. Drawing on Glasser, some of the work from the Young Adults Research Group at the Anna Freud Centre which investigated the analyses of patients who had been physically violent towards others or themselves was gathered together into a book, *Psychoanalytic Understanding of Violence and Suicide* (1998), edited by Rosine Perelberg. These conceptualizations of the complexity of aggressive and destructive impulses inevitably prompt us to consider further the vicissitudes of narcissism, and the expression of narcissistic rage (Perelberg 1998 and 2015). They also bring into fresh focus the role of the "absent" father in the life of violent patients.

All three papers chosen to represent Contemporary Freudian work in the area of aggression are concerned with sadism. Although Mervin Glasser's paper "Masculinity, Femininity and Internalization in Male Homosexuals" (which has hitherto been only privately available in print) focuses on one very particular group of patients, it contains an especially useful account of aggression, sadism and the core complex. With the caveat that homosexuals are a heterogeneous group and that he is writing only about those who present themselves as patients, Mervin Glasser asks what psychoanalysis can offer to the explanation of the phenomenon of homosexuality. He stresses that the answer must be multifactorial and narrows his focus to one aspect: the type of homosexual who conducts himself in a way which caricatures women. Using correspondence between Benjamin Britten and Peter Pears as well as clinical material, Glasser describes the interacting elements that make up the "core complex" and its effects. He describes being caught between conflicting impulses towards the object who is experienced as both avaricious and indifferent. Because an individual caught in the throes of the core complex wishes to engage intimately with his object to the point of merger, that object is experienced as threatening annihilation. This provokes a defensive urge to destroy the object or at least to get to a safe distance from it. Glasser sees this as a conflict which every infant experiences, and he argues that the solution or attempted solution to it contributes significantly to the aetiology of different psychopathologies, as well as to 'normality'. In the particular homosexual group that he chooses to focus on, the solution is to sexualize destructive aggression towards the mother, converting it into sadism, thus protecting her and controlling her, at the expense of intimacy. The pseudo-femininity of this group is two-edged: it allows a relationship to be sustained with the mother but at the same time it is a cruel caricature of her. Glasser draws out the profound implications of this solution to core complex anxieties for identification. The core complex brings with it such a fear of intrusion, that threatens a take-over or annihilation of the personality, that identification is problematic, leading to simulation rather than identification resulting in an insubstantial sense of identity.

Understanding sadism is essential in working with paedophilic patients as the second paper in this section shows, Donald Campbell's "Doubt in the Psychoanalysis of a Paedophile". Few psychoanalysts have written about the analysis of paedophilic patients or about paedophilia. Perhaps this is because if such patients access psychotherapy, it is likely to be once a week in an NHS setting, like the Portman Clinic where both Mervin Glasser and Don Campbell worked; perhaps it is because of problems of confidentiality which Campbell helpfully discusses at the end of his paper. Campbell presents a single-case study to set out three types of doubt that mark working with someone who has been subject to incestuous sexual abuse. Abused by his father, mother and uncle (and perhaps others), the patient brought all three into the consulting room. Campbell describes "honest" doubt in the analyst about where fantasy ended and reality began, "inherent" doubt stemming from the trauma of abuse that left the patient's mind fragmented and confused, and the sadistic imposition of doubt that is first experienced by the victim at the hands of his abuser and then turned by the victim upon others, notable those he abuses and the analyst. Campbell sees sadistic doubt as an essential part of paedophilia: the patient took sadistic gratification from projecting doubt into the boys whom he abused as part of failed attempts to master his own experience as a victim. Campbell portrays the unfolding of the analysis so as to capture the complex movement of doubt between patient and analyst as Campbell finds a way through his own affective responses to understand the process, even though finally the emphasis is on doubt, both "honest" doubt in the analyst and doubt used in the service of self-deception in the patient as a defence against a fierce superego knowing what he had done.

The third example of Contemporary Freudian thinking about aggression, "'I'm like a shattered windscreen': Struggles with Sadism and the Self" comes from another analyst who has worked at the Portman Clinic, Marianne Parsons. Her paper discusses aspects of the analysis of a late adolescent girl whose intense core complex anxieties propelled her into self-destructive sado-masochistic relationships with others and with her own body. This pattern of relating precluded the intimacy she longed for and transformed sensuality into sadism. Parsons is concerned to explore the role of sensuality in relation to drive integration and the development of the capacity for satisfying adult sexual relationships. She suggests that the capacity for intimacy and concern for the other is based on the internalization of satisfying emotional and sensual experiences in infancy. Parsons outlines her understanding of the developmental distortions in her patient's capacity for instinctual binding and affect regulation as related to inconsistent parental care. She describes a confusing mix of neglect and overstimulation that not only undermined the child's potentiality to internalize pleasurable and safe sensory experiences (the basis of a coherent body ego) but also intensified dependency conflicts such that it was not possible to achieve genuine autonomy and separateness during adolescence. Parsons understands her patient's sado-masochistic mode of relating as being primarily defensive, to shore up a confusing and at times fragmented sense of self. She makes use of Glasser's concept of the core complex to understand her patient's oscillation between a wish for fusion and fear of abandonment and annihilation.

Parsons describes some of the transference and counter-transference vicissitudes within a six-year analysis, in which both participants struggled to withstand the patient's need to control and distance her object through the compulsive use of sado-masochistic behaviour. The patient experienced herself as detached, worthless and empty, needing to provoke a fight in order to feel alive. Her regressive wishes to be passively cared for by her female analyst had to be ferociously defended against in the initial years of analysis. Parsons describes how her patient could slowly acknowledge her wishes to be cared for and held, in response to the analyst's careful attention to her affective states. The patient's intelligence and capacity to express herself verbally, partially based on a previous period of analysis in latency, clearly expressed and sustained a libidinal attachment to a potentially helpful analyst.

## Technique and practice

Many of the papers in this volume describe clinical work that demonstrates some of the main resemblances, with inevitable similarities and differences, of a Contemporary Freudian analytic approach. However, the perspective on temporality and the complexity of early development, including the view that a coherent ego capable of fantasy formation is not present at birth, underpins all the work described here. As does the analyst positioning himself as equidistant from the id, ego and superego, and working practically in a way that draws on both the topographical and structural points of view.

The patient is regarded as a collaborator in the analytic process, developing a therapeutic alliance with the analyst which involves both conscious and unconscious attitudes. The patient's positive investment in the analysis and the positive transference to the analyst underpin the forward movement in the process. This movement builds on free association, and the analysis of the obstacles that beset it, as well as analysis of the patient's transferences. The method of free association which Freud recognized as a route into the dynamic unconscious even before he focused on the royal route in dreams, is a *sine qua non* of the analytic process, as too is the collaborative interpretation of dreams, through tracing associations, recognizing how dreams are being used within sessions, and through being alert to their possible significance within the transference neurosis (Flanders, Loden, Rodriguez de la Sierra, and Schächter this volume). In parallel with the patient's free associations and reports of dreams, the analyst listens with free floating attention (Robinson 2015), in an attitude of abstinence and neutrality (Baker 2000) and on the basis of empathy and the possibility of communication directly between unconscious and unconscious. Freud thought of empathy as an embodied activity (Pigman 1995). In keeping with their emphasis on the body, Contemporary Freudian analysts listen with their soma as well as their psyche (Perris-Myttas this volume).

Interpretations remain at the centre of the therapeutic process with its aim of enabling psychic change. The act of interpreting embodies the analyst's separateness, which may be one reason for the borderline patient to reject interpretations. The analyst aims to identify the predominant affects in the session, the conflicts which are being activated, and the underlying anxiety and the defences used to maintain some psychic equilibrium. Interpretations tend to move from the surface to depth, facilitating the patient's engagement in the process, and avoiding over-whelming the patient or pushing him into a pseudo-intellectual analysis. By identifying the defences and underlying anxiety in the session, the analyst aims to decrease rather than increase the resistances. Interpretations may initially be aimed at furthering the process, enabling the patient to experience trust in the person of the analyst and the process. Timing of interpretation is paramount; this entails waiting and listening to the network of the patient's associations as they gradually reveal the current unconscious transference phantasies and conflicts. Extra-transference interpretations and other interventions are regarded as necessary tools in furthering the process towards interpretation of the particular transference phantasy activated in the session (Couch 2002). Dennis Duncan in a series of papers (1989, 1990, 1993) explored in detail, the process of formulating interpretations. He described the "flow of the session" in which various interpretations are thought but not made, "the collateral interpretation", that illustrate the shifts occurring in the session as a result of the analyst's internal dialogue between inherent and acquired theories, in response to the patient's communications.

The transference neurosis is a central aspect of the analytic process: it helps to organize the way in which the treatment unfolds. Psychic activity and affective investment gather around it as the presence of the analyst offers her/him as an object of transference. The Contemporary Freudian perspective rests on Freud's formulation of the transference both as a resistance to the flow of free associations and as a playground in which what cannot yet be remembered can be enacted through repetition. If all goes well enough the analyst can "succeed in giving all the symptoms of the illness a new transference meaning and in replacing his ordinary neurosis by a 'transference-neurosis'" (Freud 1914, p. 134). Counter-transference is defined as the analyst's unconscious responses to the patient's transferences; it needs to be differentiated from the analyst's transference to the patient, from the analyst's affective response to the patient and from empathy. The mutual influence of patient and analyst in the analytic relationship is complex. In the playground of the transference the patient, as it were, casts the analyst in a particular role and, as Joseph Sandler has described in his concept of "role responsiveness" (1976), "evokes or provokes an unconscious role response in the analyst that actualizes an aspect of the transference" (Campbell this volume). Sandler made a central contribution to understanding enactment within the analytic process, a frequently discussed theme within analytic discourse generally.

Some Contemporary Freudian analysts distinguish, as Anna Freud did, between the patient's relation to the analyst as a transference object and as a new developmental object in relation to whom the patient might seek developmental help to overcome developmental impairments or deficiencies in his/her ego-development (Baker and Robinson this volume). This is especially the case with patients suffering from borderline, psychotic and narcissistic disorders. Such developmental help—offering an auxiliary ego or naming affects, for example—kick-starts development that has been arrested (Parsons this volume). It is part of the Contemporary Freudian extension of analytic technique beyond neurotic disorders.

Contemporary Freudian analysts pay attention to the development of the analytic process and how this can best be facilitated with each patient in relation to our understanding of their psychic structure and defensive organization. The overall therapeutic aim is to enable the patients to become aware of the ways in which their defences distort their experience and limit their capacities, both inside and

## Introduction

outside the analysis. This process leads to the uncovering of the affects and associated phantasies against which the patient is defending her/himself. It involves both interpretation of unconscious conflict and phantasies and the construction of new meanings.

Whether named explicitly or not, the concept of the analyst as a new object is present throughout this volume. Ronald Baker's paper "The Patient's Discovery of the Psychoanalyst as a New Object" (1993) is included in our selection of papers to represent this aspect of Contemporary Freudian thinking, alongside four papers that emphasize the continuing importance of dreams in Contemporary Freudian technique and practice, and Rosemary Davies's paper on "Regression, Curiosity and the Discovery of the Object". Baker is concerned with particular aspects of the nature of therapeutic action, focusing in general on the relationship between interpretive and non-interpretive factors in therapeutic change and in particular on the relationship between two different views that the patient might have of the analyst, as a transference object or as a new object. Non-interpretive factors are broad ranging, from the setting itself, through benevolent neutrality and empathy, to non-retaliatory survival. Baker surveys the literature to conceptualize the two types of object. Although he covers many contributions, he shows a special affinity with the work of Hans Loewald who also developed a concept of a "new developmental object" and who has been an influential figure for others too in the Contemporary Freudian tradition. Baker's clinical example is a woman who attacked and derided him for a considerable period, casting him in transference as a moaning, critical mother. He in turn felt exasperated, able to identify with a mother who couldn't get rid of her moaning child, but used the feelings generated in him as a communication of her own feelings as a child. These were interpreted but to Baker's mind what was fundamentally important was not to enact being the transference object but instead to tolerate and survive the attacks. This neutrality in the face of an invitation to retaliate is important (along with non-interpretive factors) with patients who suffer from structural deficit or developmental arrest. Baker regards such neutrality as an implicit transference interpretation, helping the patient to free herself from re-enacting a transference relationship to experience him as a new object, as indeed his patient did. In these ways his work is related to Chused's idea of the "*informative experience*" which Davies draws on.

The authors of the four papers concerned with dreams (Sara Flanders, Susan Loden, Luis Rodriguez de la Sierra and Joan Schächter) restate the importance of dreams in analysis as offering a unique access to the patient's internal world and providing a space in the patient's mind and in the analysis, within which previously unacknowledged affects and conflicts may be thought about and understood. Loden and Schächter both record that the debate about the place of dreams in psychoanalytic practice has a long history, beginning with Freud noting the disappearance of the section on dreams in the International Journal in 1932. They point out that there is a marked tendency for the understanding of dreams to be confined to interpretation of their place in the transference and counter-transference relationship, replacing dream interpretation as "the royal road to understanding the unconscious".

Susan Loden's paper "The Fate of the Dream in Contemporary Psychoanalysis" (2003) argues that the trend to give exclusive importance to the patient-analyst relationship and the transference comes at a cost: in-depth interpretation of dreams may be lost and along with it the opportunity through dream analysis to strengthen the patient's capacity for self-inquiry. She believes that this is particularly the case with borderline patients who are often deemed not to possess the capacity to take in analysis of the unconscious content of their dreams. Against the background of a comprehensive review of thinking about dreams and dreaming as well as the technique of dream interpretation from Freud to the present day, Loden describes the importance of the dream in relation to the development of ego capacities and the implications of this potential development for technique. She demonstrates that dreams provide not simply an opportunity for the interpretation of unconscious content, though that remains fundamental, but a basis for a collaborative process of associative understanding which furthers both the patient's capacity to experience a benign "dissociation" within his ego and the development of self-reflection.

To consolidate her argument, Loden presents a detailed account of the analysis of 50-year-old female borderline patient. Loden argues that her patient, like similar patients, was helped by "the fact that affect can be reported at one remove in the dream" whilst the dream can be experienced as "authentic". Collaborative work allowed the patient to bridge thought and feeling as memories from childhood found their way into the analysis through dreams.

Joan Schächter notes in her paper "Measure for Measure: Unconscious Communication in Dreams" that "the dream can function as a place in which split-off elements can be kept alive until conditions are prestigious for their integration". She is drawing on Cecily De Monchaux (1978) whom she uses as a starting point for her exploration, agreeing with her that dreams and their reporting in the session can offer a privileged space for unconscious communication. She uses a sequence of dreams from an adult patient after his first analytic break which illustrated and expressed the patient's central oedipal and sexual conflicts, in which his bisexual conflicts and castration anxiety featured strongly. But her emphasis is not so much on what could be gleaned from the dream's content but what was conveyed in the process of the patient's telling of his dreams and the analyst's reception of them. Verbal interpretation, Schächter records, was "limited" so that the analyst had to draw on "the experience of the unconscious affective content of the dreams within the analytic relationship", content rooted in "bodily states and memories". At different times Schächter felt, for example, overwhelmed, or imprisoned as a passive listener. Her paper shows how dreams, early in an analysis, which evoked unconscious communication, opened up resonances within the analyst, which preconciously and unconsciously understood, allowed the patient's conflicts to emerge within the transference relationship, so furthering the analysis.

In their different ways, both Loden and Schächter consider dreaming as not just providing access to the unconscious but as furthering the process of analysis and helping to structure the patient's inner world and psychic capacities. Sara Flanders' paper "The Dream Space, the Analytic Situation and the Eating Disorder: Clinging to the Concrete" contributes further to this theme. It describes aspects of the analysis of a young woman with a bulimic eating disorder, focussing on the ways in which the profound anxieties stirred up by the demands of the analytic situation, its boundaries and limits and intimacy, are manifested in her dreams and in the transference and counter-transference relationship. Initially the emphasis was on the analyst's separateness and then in a more paranoid way, on intrusion, and later, on a developing capacity to take things in that had to countered by the erection of a "no entry" sign. For this patient, the dream offered a privileged space for the expression not only of rage and other intense affects but also of the to and fro of the unfolding analysis, signalling a capacity to be interested in her inner world and thus to begin to tolerate the analyst's interest and interpretation with the inevitable intrusion these bring into the patient's inner world. Flanders emphasizes her patient's difficulties in symbolizing complex and conflictual emotional states and the fluctuations in this capacity which became linked to the patient's experience of the analytic setting and the presence and absences of her analyst. She brings out the tension between psychic development and the demands that it made on her patient to further integrate her feelings, demands that could lead to a retreat into concrete defensive functioning.

In his paper, "How Come Your House Never Falls Down?", Luis Rodriguez de la Sierra explores the understanding and use of dreams in child analysis. Briefly reviewing Freud's thinking about the dreams of children, he notes the relative absence of writing on this subject. Rodriguez de la Sierra gives a detailed clinical illustration of psychoanalytic work with a nine-year-old boy who presented with predominantly oedipal problems. Whilst the boy's play and verbal material provided clear indications of his conflicts, his dreams enabled the analyst to get a clearer picture of the current conflicts with which his patient was struggling in the transference. Whilst he did not necessarily interpret the meaning of the dreams directly, Rodriguez de la Sierra shows how he used this understanding to inform his interventions. The dreams, which could be dismissed by the patient as "only a silly dream", allowed the boy to begin to confront his aggression and feared retaliation; and when this process was underway, more direct dream interpretation was possible and useful. The work that is described shows in action the notion of developmental help, developed by Anna Freud, as an essential therapeutic tool in psychoanalytic work with some children.

Rosemary Davies's paper "Regression, Curiosity and the Discovery of the Object" is also concerned with the analyst's tact in knowing when to stay in the background and when to intervene. She depicts her work with Stephen, a patient who regressed in the early stages of his analysis, conceptualizing the regression itself, the process of Stephen's emergence from it, and the analytic attitude that she held. In his second year of treatment, he experienced a sudden thought on leaving his session that he might follow his analyst through into her house. It constitutes a turning point but is frightening for him. Davies skilfully draws out its significance: it represents Stephen's emergence from regression, his burgeoning curiosity and his fears of destructiveness and retaliation. Reviewing the literature on regression Davies bases her approach in Freud's concepts of formal regression and primary narcissism, using the latter as a helpful description of a clinical phenomenon, and in Winnicott's extension of them, drawing too on French psychoanalysis in the form of Green, the Botellas, Laplanche and Roussillon. Both Freud and Winnicott stress the destructive hatred unleashed by emergence from primary narcissism into reality, the world of others and other minds. Rather than Stephen's regression being the result of hatred, Davies shows his need to destroy his object as a developmental step towards acceptance of reality. Throughout the analysis, Davies maintains a stance in which receptivity to regression (including inherent hatred of the analyst's otherness) is paramount, with the emphasis on resilience and receptivity rather than activity.

Davies concludes her paper with two important caveats. First, that in a case like Stephen's curiosity is developmental and creative rather than intrusive, and second that the analyst's ability to sustain and reflect on her own feelings and thoughts, whilst essential, may nevertheless be difficult for a patient who is struggling to experience and to verbalize intense affects. The analyst, she suggests, must know "when to hold off and when to hold forth".

## Concluding remarks

This collection of papers has been selected to represent both past and current thinking within the Contemporary Freudian tradition and to demonstrate the evolution of differing strands of important theoretical and clinical developments over time. The earlier papers (and some later ones) come from analysts who were associated with the Anna Freudian strain of the Contemporary Freudian tradition. There is always a danger with such strains that orthodoxy will smother creativity, but we believe that these papers show the individuality of their authors and retain their freshness. Alongside them are more recent papers that represent a different and vibrant strain of engagement with central questions and concepts from fresh perspectives. Contemporary Freudian analysts are a broad family. We believe that the papers collected here, considered together, offer a clear perspective on the contribution of Contemporary Freudian analysts to British Psychoanalysis.

## References

Baker, R. (1993). The patient's discovery of the psychoanalyst as a new object. *Int. J. Psycho-Anal.*, 74: 1223–1233.

Baker, R. (2000). Finding the neutral position. *J. Am. Psychoanal. Assoc.*, 48: 129–153.

Burgner, M. and Edgcumbe, R. M. (1975). The phallic-narcissistic phase: a differentiation between pre-oedipal and oedipal aspects of phallic development. *Psychoanal. St. Child*, 30: 161–180.

Campbell, D. (1995). The role of the farther in a pre-suicide state. *Int. J. Psycho-Anal.*, 76: 315–323.

Couch, A. (2002). Extra transference interpretations: a defence of classical technique. *Psychoanal. St. Child*, 57: 53–92.

Davids, J., Green, V., Joyce, A. and McLean, D. (2017). Revised provisional diagnostic profile: 2016. *J. Infant Child Adolesc. Psychother.*, 16: 149–157.

De Monchaux, C. (1978). Dreaming and the organizing function of the ego. *Int. J. Psycho-Anal.*, 59: 443–453.

Duncan, D. (1989). The flow of interpretation-the collateral interpretation, force and flow. *Int. J. Psycho-Anal.*, 70: 693–700.

Duncan, D. (1990). The feel of the session. *Psychoanal. Contemporary Thought*, 13: 3–22.

Duncan, D. (1993). Theory in vivo. *Int. J. Psycho-Anal.*, 74: 25–32.

Flanders, S. (ed.) (1993). *The Dream Discourse Today*. London: Routledge.

Fonagy, P. and Target, M. (1996). Predictors of outcome in child psychoanalysis. A retrospective study of 763 cases at the Anna Freud Centre. *J. Am. Psychoanal. Assoc.*, 44: 27–77.

Freud, A. (1937). *The Ego and the Mechanisms of Defence*. London: Hogarth Press.

Freud, A. (1949). Aggression in relation to emotional development; Normal and pathological. *Psychoanal. St. Child*, 3: 37–42.

Freud, A. (1955 [1954]). *The Writings of Anna Freud*, Vol. 4. New York: International UP, 1968.

Freud, A. (1963). The concept of developmental lines. *Psychoanal. St. Child*, 18: 245–265

Freud, A. (1965). *Normality and Pathology in Childhood*. New York: International Universities Press.

Freud, A. (1981). The concept of developmental lines—their diagnostic significance. *Psychoanal. St. Child*, 36: 129–136.

Freud, A., Nagera, H. and Freud, W. E. (1965). Metapsychological assessment of the adult personality. *Psychoanal. St. Child*, 20: 9–41.

Freud, S. (1900). The interpretation of dreams. *S.E.*, 4 and 5: 1–627.

Freud, S. (1905). Three essays on the theory of sexuality. *S.E.*, 7: 124–246.

Freud, S. (1914). On narcissism. *S.E.*, 14: 67–102
Freud, S. (1915). The unconscious. *S.E.*, 14: 159–215.
Freud, S. (1920). Beyond the pleasure principle. *S.E.*, 18: 1–64.
Freud, S. (1923). The ego and the id. *S.E.*, 19: 1–66.
Glasser, M. (1979). Some aspects of the role of aggression in the perversions. In *Sexual Deviations*, ed. I. Rosen. Oxford: OUP, pp. 278–305.
Glasser, M. (1998). On violence: a preliminary communication. *Int. J. Psycho-Anal.*, 79: 887–902.
Hoffer, W. (1949). Mouth, hand and ego-integration. *Psychoanal. St. Child*, 3: 49–56.
Hoffer, W. (1950). Development of the body ego. *Psychoanal. St. Child*, 5: 18–23.
Laplanche, J. and Pontalis, J. B. (1973). *The Language of Psycho-Analysis*. London: The Hogarth Press.
Laufer, M. and Laufer, M. E. (1984). *Adolescence and Developmental Breakdown – A Psychoanalytic View*. New Haven, CT and London: Yale University Press.
Laufer, M. (ed.) (1995). *The Suicidal Adolescent*. London: Karnac Books.
Laufer, M. (ed.) (1997). *Adolescent Breakdown and Beyond*. London: Karnac Books.
Loden, S. (2003). The fate of the dream in contemporary psychoanalysis. *J. Am. Psychoanal. Assoc.*, 51: 43–70.
Parsons, M. (2006). From biting teeth to biting wit: the normative development of aggression. In *Aggression and Destructiveness: Psychoanalytic Perspectives* ed. C. Harding. London: Routledge, pp. 41–48.
Perelberg, R. J. (1995). A core phantasy in violence. *Int. J. Psycho-Anal.*, 76: 1215–1231.
Perelberg, R. ed. (1998). *Psychoanalytic Understanding of Violence and Suicide* London: Routledge.
Perelberg, R.J. (1999). The interplay between identifications and identity in the analysis of a violent young man. *Int. J. Psycho-Anal.*, 80: 31–45.
Perelberg, R. J. (ed.) (2000). *Dreaming and Thinking*. London: Karnac Books.
Perelberg, R. J. (2007). Space and time in psychoanalytic listening. *Int. J. Psycho-Anal.*, 88: 1473–1490.
Perelberg, R. J. (2011). A father is being beaten: constructions in the analysis of some male patients. *Int. J. Psycho-Anal.*, 92: 97–116.
Perelberg, R. J. (2015). *Murdered Father, Dead Father. Revisiting the Oedipus Complex*. London: Routledge.
Pigman, G. W. (1995). Freud and the history of empathy. *Int. J. Psycho-Anal.*, 76: 237–256.
Pines, D. (1993). *A Woman's Unconscious Use of Her Body. A Psychoanalytical Perspective*. London: Virago.

Robinson, K. (2011). A brief history of the British Psychoanalytical Society. In *100 Years of the IPA. The Centenary History of the International Psychoanalytical Association 1910–2010*, eds. P. Loewenberg and N. L. Thompson. London: Karnac Books.

Robinson, K. (2015). The ins and outs of listening as a psychoanalyst. *Empedocles Eur. J. Philos. Commun.*, 6: 169–184.

Rodriguez de la Sierra, L. and Schächter, J. (2013). *The Late Teenage Years: From Seventeen to Adulthood.* London: Karnac Books.

Sandler, J. (1976). Counter-transference and role responsiveness. *Int. R. Psycho-Anal.*, 3: 43–47.

Sandler, A.-M. and Sandler, J. (1983). The second censorship, the three box model and some technical implications. *Int. J. Psycho-Anal.*, 64: 413–425.

Sandler, A.-M. and Sandler, J. (1984). The past unconscious, the present unconscious: interpretation of the transference. *Psychoanal. Inq.*, 4: 367–399.

Sandler, A.-M. and Sandler, J. (1994a). The past unconscious and the present unconscious: a contribution to a technical frame of reference. *Psychoanal. St. Child*, 49: 278–292.

Sandler, A.-M. and Sandler, J. (1994b). Phantasy and its transformations: a contemporary Freudian view. *Int. J. Psycho-Anal.*, 75: 387–394.

Sandler, J. (1987). *From Safety to Superego: Selected Papers of Joseph Sandler.* London: Guilford Press.

Sandler, J. and Nagera, H. (1963). Aspects of the metapsychology of fantasy. *Psychoanal. St. Child*, 18: 159–194.

Sandler, J. and Sandler, A.-M. (1998). *Internal Objects Revisited.* London: Karnac Books.

Wittgenstein, L. (1968). *Philosophical Investigations.* Trans. by G. E. M. Anscombe. Oxford: Basil Blackwell.

Yorke, C. (1990). The development and functioning of the sense of shame. *Psychoanal. St. Child*, 45: 377–409.

Yorke, C. (1994). Freud or Klein: Conflict or compromise. *Int. J. Psycho-Anal.*, 75: 375-385.

Yorke, C. (1995). Freud's psychology. Can it survive? *Psychoanal. St. Child*, 50: 3-31.

Yorke, C. (1996). Childhood and the unconscious. *Am. Imago*, 53: 227–256.

Yorke, C. (2001). The unconscious: past, present and future. In *Within Time and Beyond Time. A Festschrift for Pearl King*, eds. J. Johns and R. Steiner. London: Karnac Books, pp. 230–251.

# 2

# PHANTASY AND ITS TRANSFORMATIONS
## A Contemporary Freudian view[1]

### Joseph Sandler and Anne-Marie Sandler

Now that half a century has passed since the Freud-Klein Controversies (reported by King and Steiner 1991), we are in a position to look back and see that the controversies within the British Society are significantly different now from what they were then, although in a certain sense they are, of course, derivatives of the conflicts of the past. Inevitably, over the past 50 years the different groups in the Society have influenced one another, and there can be little doubt that much of the impetus for this cross-fertilisation has come from the systematic discussion of clinical material, with the fine details of psychoanalytic theory taking second place. So, for many members of the Contemporary Freudian group, much greater emphasis has been put, over the years, on the importance of the earliest internal influences on the child's development, on the existence of transference phantasies, anxieties and resistances from the outset of the analysis and on the need for these to be interpreted from the beginning. In this context, the understanding of processes of projection and externalisation in the transference has been significantly appreciated. Similarly, in the Klein group, we have seen a decreased emphasis on the early interpretation of deep anxieties and, as Elizabeth Spillius (1988) has pointed out, less stress is being laid on destructiveness, and there is less use of concrete part-object language, and a variety of other changes. To Spillius's list of changes, we would add our impression that the concepts of defence *mechanisms* (as opposed to defensive phantasies), and of resistance, are beginning to be discerned in Kleinian presentations, just as the notion of projective identification can be seen in the writings of some members of the Independent and Contemporary Freudian groups.

The views of the object-relations theorists in the Group of Independent Analysts have certainly affected the thinking of many in the Contemporary Freudian group. It is now widely accepted that the psychoanalytic view of motivation cannot be simply reduced to sexual and aggressive drives or their derivatives, and the link between motivation—both conscious and unconscious—and the tie to the object has been given increasing importance. The work of Donald Winnicott has also had a profound effect on Freudian thinking about infant development and infant-mother relationships. We cannot comment on the changes which have occurred in the Group of Independent Analysts under the influence of the Contemporary Freudian and the Klein groups, although we have no doubt that they are significant. Our reason for saying this is that the Independent Group consists of analysts, each of whom wishes to be independent of the two other groups, and as a consequence the views of its members are very diverse.

However, in spite of all these changes, some fundamental differences between the groups remain. While we shall put what follows in mainly theoretical terms, the differences between us still reflect, as we see them, important differences in approach both to psychoanalytic theory and technique.

At a meeting of the British Society on 13 January 1943, as part of the Controversial Discussions, Susan Isaacs presented her paper on "The nature and function of phantasy" (in King and Steiner 1991). As we have heard, she pointed out in that paper that the meaning of the word 'phantasy' had been extended over the preceding years. She concluded that "the psychoanalytical term 'phantasy' essentially connotes *unconscious* mental content, which may seldom or never become conscious", and went on to extend the concept of unconscious phantasy even further than before, to include practically every variety of unconscious mental content, both knowable and unknowable—an extension which was a central point of disagreement in the Controversial Discussions, as Anne Hayman has shown us in her excellent and comprehensive presentation at this Conference (Hayman 1994).

## Phantasy and its transformations

The extension of psychoanalytic concepts beyond their original meaning has been a frequent occurrence in the history of psychoanalysis, and this can serve a useful function in the advancement of psychoanalytic thinking. Such concepts can be referred to as "elastic",[2] but elastic concepts can only be stretched up to a certain point before they snap. In our view, this has occurred in relation to unconscious phantasy, resulting in a number of conceptual and clinical problems, some of which we shall try to address today.

We may all be clear about the role and function of conscious phantasies or daydreams in our mental life, but the concept of unconscious phantasy has suffered from a major ambiguity in regard to the meaning of the term "unconscious". You will recall that in Freud's topographical theory of the mind a firm distinction was made between the systems Preconscious (*Pcs*) and Unconscious (*Ucs*). While the system unconscious contained childhood libidinal wishes that had been repressed, and which were subject to primary process functioning, the Preconscious was seen as following quite different principles. Further, although the Preconscious was regarded as being the repository of thoughts, wishes and ideas which were able to be called into consciousness relatively freely, Freud also postulated a *censorship* between the Preconscious and Conscious systems, as well as attributing the capacity for reality-testing to the Preconscious (1915).

The existence of a censorship between the preconscious and consciousness, in addition to the censorship between the system Unconscious and the Preconscious, was referred to by Freud on a number of occasions. In 1915 he spoke of "a new frontier of censorship", going on to say that

> the first of these censorships is exercised against the *Ucs* itself, and the second against its *Pcs* derivatives. One might suppose that in the course of individual development the censorship had taken a step forward ... in psychoanalytic treatment the existence of the second censorship, located between the systems *Pcs* and *Cs*, is proved beyond question.
> (1915, p. 193)

Descriptively speaking, the Preconscious can be considered to be unconscious, although the two systems were regarded as being governed by completely different rules, and this has made things rather complicated. They were complicated still further by the introduction of the structural theory in 1923, when it became (and still is) common usage to refer to the *id* and the unconscious parts of the *ego* and *superego* as "the unconscious". All of this has contributed to the confusion surrounding the meaning of unconscious phantasy. In one sense, unconscious phantasy can be taken to refer to early phantasies of the child which had subsequently been repressed into the system unconscious of the topographical theory, a system contrasted with the systems preconscious and conscious, distinguished from them by its functioning according to the primary process, and characterised by timelessness, by the equality of opposites and so forth. On the other hand, unconscious phantasy can be *preconscious* phantasy, showing a degree of secondary-process thinking and awareness of reality. It is perhaps because of the widening gap between our clinical observations and current psychoanalytic theories that we still make use of the concept of *the unconscious* alongside our other concepts, and it is important to know that the meaning of this term changes according to the context in which it is used. What has happened is that the adjective 'unconscious' has been transformed into a noun.[3] As a consequence, the conceptual distinction between the system Unconscious and the system Preconscious has tended to be lost, the two systems becoming confused; and this confusion is still to be found in the writings of some of our most distinguished psychoanalytic writers.[4]

Because it is inevitable that the term "unconscious" will continue to refer to "all that is unconscious", we need to find a way to distinguish between the two sorts of unconscious phantasy we have been discussing. What we want to put forward is a frame of reference that will allow us to make such a distinction, and to take into account the clinical observation that the products of preconscious functioning *are themselves often subject to repression or are otherwise defended against and prevented from reaching consciousness*. The best examples of such preconscious content being defended against are unconscious transference thoughts and phantasies, in which unconscious secondary-process thinking is certainly involved.

We hope that we have been able to make the point that there are two broad classes of unconscious phantasies, and we shall try to show that the distinction between the two is not only theoretically but also clinically relevant. As it is clear that the term "the unconscious" is here to stay, it seems convenient to make use of a distinction which we have elaborated in a number of previous papers

(Sandler and Sandler 1983, 1984 and 1986). This is the distinction between the *past unconscious* and the *present unconscious*, and consequently a distinction between phantasies in the past unconscious and phantasies in the present unconscious.

Phantasies in the *past unconscious* are those which are believed to occur in the first years of life, and which can be thought of as existing behind the so-called repression barrier (i.e. behind Freud's "first censorship"). The repression barrier is responsible for the infantile amnesia, and we are all aware of how little can be remembered from the first four or five years of life. What we do remember or recall in analysis tends to be in the form of isolated fragments which have been revised in the process of later remembering—if they have coherence, this has usually been added later. In addition, much that is recalled from the first few years has been acquired second-hand. The phantasies of the past unconscious are *constructs* which are extremely important for our psychoanalytic work, but our conception of the past unconscious comes from *reconstruction*, and the phantasies we assume to exist in the past unconscious are our reconstructions based upon the patient's analytic material, on our *interpretation* of the past, interpretations which are rooted in our psychoanalytic theory of mental functioning and our theory of child development.[5]

That part of the unconscious which we can refer to as the *present unconscious* can be thought of as having a very different type of functional organisation and is in many ways similar to the system Preconscious of Freud's topographical model. It is the realm of *current* unconscious subjective experience. Phantasies in the present unconscious—especially here-and-now unconscious transference phantasies—are much more accessible to our analytic work. As wishful impulses and phantasies arise in the present unconscious—phantasies which can be considered to be in part *derivatives* of the past unconscious—they have to be dealt with by *the person of the present*, by the adult part of the person. One can put it thus: "Whereas the past unconscious acts and reacts according to the past, the present unconscious is concerned with maintaining equilibrium in the present ..." (Sandler and Sandler 1984, p. 372). These phantasy derivatives of the past can be regarded as being different in structure from the phantasies of early childhood, from the phantasies which date from before the construction of the repression barrier and the resulting infantile amnesia. The phantasies in the present unconscious are more closely linked with representations of present-day persons and are subject to a higher level of unconscious secondary-process functioning. *Thus it follows that unconscious transference phantasies exist in the present unconscious, not in the past unconscious.*

The phantasies or impulses arising in the present unconscious, *to the extent that they arouse conflict*, disturb the equilibrium of the present unconscious and, accordingly, have to be dealt with outside consciousness, have to be modified, disguised or repressed. It is here that the whole range of the mechanisms of defence, and indeed all sorts of other compensatory mechanisms, come in. These mechanisms serve to disguise the unconscious wishful phantasy by means of manipulations of the self and object representations involved in the phantasy. Parts of the self-representation involved will be split off and displaced to the object-representation (projection and projective identification), and parts of the object representation absorbed into the representation of the self (a process analogous to identification). All this is a reflection of what has been called *the stabilising function of unconscious phantasy*. This function involves a response in the present unconscious to all sorts of affective disturbances of inner equilibrium, whatever the sources of these disturbances may be (Sandler 1986; Sandler and Sandler 1986).

Although an unconscious phantasy may have been substantially modified within the present unconscious in order to render it less disruptive, its path to the surface, to conscious awareness, may be impeded by a resistance due to what has been referred to earlier in this paper as the "second censorship", that is, the censorship spoken of by Freud as existing between the systems Preconscious and Conscious. In the present frame of reference, this has been located between the present unconscious and consciousness. This censorship has been described as having as its fundamental motivation the avoidance of conscious feelings of shame, embarrassment and humiliation. Developmentally, it can be linked first with the step of substituting conscious phantasising for play, and the need to keep such phantasies secret. What happens then has been described as follows:

> As the child develops the increasing capacity to anticipate the shaming and humiliating reactions of others (with all the additions he has made to his expectations arising from his own projections), so he will become *his own* disapproving audience and will continually internalise the social situation in the form of the

second censorship. Only content that is acceptable will be permitted through to consciousness. It must be *plausible* and not ridiculous or 'silly'. In a way the second censorship is much more of a *narcissistic* censorship than the first, but the narcissism involved often tends to centre around fears of being laughed at, as being thought to be silly, crazy, ridiculous or childish—essentially fears of being humiliated.

(Sandler and Sandler 1983, pp. 421–422)

A very simple—and much simplified—example of a patient in analysis with one of us (J. S.) may be useful to illustrate the points made in the paper in a very general way. A male patient came a few minutes late to his session and complained about the fact that his girlfriend had not permitted him to use his alarm clock to wake in time for his analysis because it woke her as well, so he had woken late. He thought that she had been very selfish. He had taken a minicab to come to the analysis, but the car was very uncomfortable—the springs were bad, and the driver had driven over every pothole in the road. He then went on to tell the analyst how badly he had been treated by his employer. He had been given so much to do that he had to work late the previous evening, and his employer didn't seem to care about his well-being at all. The employer had work which he had to do himself but had at the last moment left it to the patient to do. He would complain at work but didn't want to lose his job. (These associations were, of course, those which the patient had permitted to enter his consciousness and could report in the analysis.) The analyst then commented that perhaps the patient was also angry with him for having mentioned on the previous day the dates when he would be taking his holiday. The analyst reminded him of how surprised the patient had been that analysis was stopping earlier than expected and suggested that he was in conflict about his anger with the analyst because he thought that the analyst would get angry and replace him with another patient. On the other hand, he resented his not being allowed to fix the dates just as he resented his girlfriend not allowing him to use an alarm clock. He must have been feeling that the analyst was giving him a rough ride, just as the minicab driver did, but perhaps in fact he wanted to make things rough for the analyst in order to get even. (This interpretation was directed towards the underlying current unconscious transference phantasy that the analyst was treating him badly and to the wish to retaliate.) The patient fell silent for a minute and then exploded with anger. "You're damn right", he said, "you boss me about, telling me when I can come and when I can't". He proceeded to elaborate on this theme, saying how times should be arranged to suit his own needs, but ending with the comment that the analyst would probably throw him out because he had been so rude. Days later, it was possible to reconstruct what had gone on in the transference in terms of the patient's interaction with his father during the oedipal period, and after some months we could trace this pattern to a significantly earlier aspect of his relationship with his mother.

We want to emphasise the need to interpret what is most dominant and affectively laden in the present unconscious rather than to talk about the past. The patient was in resistance due to his transference conflict in the here-and-now, and it was this conflict which had to be interpreted. Reconstruction of the past, i.e. of the past unconscious, is more appropriate once the resistances in the here-and-now have been analysed. In the present instance, the patient had not been able to allow into his consciousness the transference phantasy which was active in his present unconscious (that the analyst was giving him a rough time), but had defensively displaced it in his associations on to his employer and the cab driver. This defensive displacement was much more consciousness-syntonic than the unconscious transference thoughts. Later it was also possible to see, through the transference-countertransference interaction, how he had almost certainly had a hand in provoking both his employer and his girlfriend into acting as they did.[6]

Our purpose in presenting this rather ordinary fragment of analysis was simply to illustrate the conceptual difference between the past and present unconsciouses, and the clinical value of making this particular theoretical differentiation. However, we also wanted to lay the ground for concluding this paper by referring briefly to a concept mentioned earlier, that is, the stabilising function of unconscious phantasy.[7]

The products of the stabilising function of unconscious phantasy may, of course, find their way into consciousness, modified to a greater or lesser extent by the second censorship, and can show themselves as any type of derivative. (The derivative of the censored phantasy in the present unconscious need not necessarily be in the form of a conscious daydream or free associations in analysis.) But, in any case, in order to pass the second censorship, the products of the stabilising function have to be modified further—must have to undergo a sort of secondary revision—in order to be made plausible, non-silly, non-stupid (except in specially licensed forms such as dreams and humour).

In the very active work that occurs continuously in the present unconscious, a great deal of phantasy dialogue is involved. This dialogue can be said to be with one's introjects (Sandler and Sandler 1978), but more precisely, *they are dialogues in phantasy with the representatives of one's introjects in one's unconscious phantasy life.*[8]

The central point in the "stabilizing" or "gyroscopic" regulation of unconscious phantasy is the maintenance of safety and well-being in the face of disruptive urges of various kinds (Sandler 1986; Sandler and Sandler 1986). What is organised into the form of unconscious phantasy we are describing serves the function of creating and maintaining a feeling of self-preservation. In doing this, defences are used in relation to the self and object representations involved in the phantasy. These defences may be all sorts of projections, identifications and projective identifications, displacements, externalisations, as well as reversals of one kind or another.

It would appear that the extent to which this occurs only began to be realised in the mid-1930s with the analysis of those resistances in which defensive displacement between self and object representations occurred in the general context of transference. Anna Freud had written of combined projection and identification in so-called altruistic surrender—living through another— and of identification with the aggressor as a defence, in *The Ego and the Mechanisms of Defence* in 1936. Then, in 1946, Melanie Klein put forward her concept of projective identification. Although the latter concept has been used in an extremely broad way, we have all become more aware of the defences that make use of displacements between self and object representations. It is these displacements that will occur in the process of creating unconscious stabilising phantasies that restore the person's feeling of cohesion and of integrity of the self.

Finally, it should be said that one thing is certain about the concept of unconscious phantasy, whether we use it as introduced by Freud or in some modified form: psychoanalysis cannot do without it.

## Notes

1 This paper first appeared *Int. J. Psycho-Anal.*, 75 (1994): 387–394.
2 In writing on the value of the elasticity of certain psychoanalytic concepts, I (J.S.) suggested that

> Elastic concepts play a very important part in holding psychoanalytic theory together. As psychoanalysis is made up of formulations at various levels of abstraction, and of part-theories which do not integrate well with one another, the existence of pliable, context-dependent concepts allows an overall framework of psychoanalytic theory to be spelled out, but can only articulate with similar part-theories if they are not tightly connected, if the concepts which form the joints are flexible ... The elastic and flexible concepts take up the strain of theoretical change, absorbing it while more organised newer theories can develop
>
> (Sandler 1983, p. 36)

3 In Freud's last work, *An Outline of Psycho-Analysis*, published just three years before the Controversial Discussions, he remarked, "The theory of the three qualities of what is psychical [he refers here to the qualities unconscious, preconscious and conscious] ... seems likely to be a source of limitless confusion rather than a help towards clarification" (1940, p. 161).
4 One of the factors fostering the tendency to absorb the notion of the unconscious ego and superego of the structural theory into the notion of "the unconscious" is the fact that Freud's structural theory did not succeed in completely and successfully replacing the topographical model (in spite of the claims of the "ego psychologists").
5 In this conception the past unconscious represents more than the person's *id* or the system *Unconscious* of the topographical model. Inasmuch as it represents "the child within" (Sandler 1984) it can be regarded as far more developmentally complex, involving age-appropriate (but at best preoperational) secondary processes as well as primary process functioning.
6 This provocation could be called a form of projective identification, but my own view is that the term should be used specifically for the provocative externalisation of a split-off aspect of the self-representation (rather than an aspect of the object-representation) for purposes of defence.
7 In an earlier publication (Sandler and Sandler 1986) this was referred to as the "gyroscopic" function of unconscious phantasy. This section draws on material published there and in a further paper (Sandler 1986).
8 There is always a pressure to anchor the phantasies in the present unconscious in reality. In some way we try to *actualise* our unconscious wishful phantasies (Sandler 1976a; 1976b), but we need to do this in a

way which is plausible to us. We make extensive use of what is perhaps the most overworked function of the mental apparatus, i.e. rationalisation, in order to make our implausible actions plausible to ourselves and to others. We have to anchor, to externalise, to fit our unconscious phantasies into reality in one way or another. In this context "psychotic" phantasies do not represent the direct emergence of the past unconscious, but rather the fact that the psychotic (or borderline) patient's style of rationalisation and vision of reality, as well as his understanding of the way other people's minds function, are different from and alien to our own as a consequence of impaired or deviant reality-testing.

## References

Freud, A. (1936). *The Ego and the Mechanisms of Defence*. London: Hogarth Press.
Freud, S. (1915). The unconscious. *S.E.*, 14: 159–204.
Freud, S. (1923). The ego and the id. *S.E.*, 19: 3–66
Freud, S. (1940). An outline of psycho-analysis. *S.E.*, 23: 139–208.
Hayman, A. (1994). Some remarks about the controversial discussions. *Int. J. Psychoanal.* 75: 345–361.
Isaacs, S. (1943). The nature and function of phantasy. In *The Freud-Klein Controversies: 1941–45*, ed. P. King and R. Steiner. London: Routledge, 1991, pp. 264–321.
King, P. and Steiner, R. (eds.) (1991). *The Freud-Klein Controversies: 1941–45*. London: Routledge.
Klein, M. (1946). Notes on some schizoid mechanisms. *Int. J. Psychoanal.*, 27: 99–110.
Sandler, J. (1976a). Dreams, unconscious fantasies and 'identity of perception'. *Int. J. Psychoanal.*, 3: 33–42.
Sandler, J. (1976b). Countertransference and role-responsiveness. *Int. R. Psychoanal.*, 3: 43–47.
Sandler, J. (1983). Reflections on some relations between psychoanalytic concepts and psychoanalytic practice. *Int. J. Psychoanal.*, 64: 35–45.
Sandler, J. (1984). The id or the child within. In *Dimensions of Psychoanalysis*, ed. J. Sandler. London: Karnac Books, pp. 219–239.
Sandler, J. (1986). Reality and the stabilizing function of unconscious fantasy. *Bull. Anna Freud Centre*, 9: 177–194.
Sandler, J. and Sandler, A.-M. (1978). On the development of object relationships and affects. *Int. J. Psychoanal.*, 59: 285–296.
Sandler, J. and Sandler, A.-M. (1983). The 'second censorship', the 'three box model' and some technical implications. *Int. J. Psychoanal.*, 64: 413–425.

Sandler, J. and Sandler, A.-M. (1984). The past unconscious, the present unconscious, and interpretation of the transference. *Psychoanal. Inq.*, 4: 367–399.

Sandler, J. and Sandler, A.-M. (1986). The gyroscopic function of unconscious fantasy. In *Towards a Comprehensive Model for Schizophrenic Disorders*, ed. D. B. Feinsilver. Hillsadale, NJ: The Analytic Press.

Spillius, E. B. (ed.) (1988). *Melanie Klein Today: Vol. 2, Mainly Practice*. London: Routledge.

# 3

# UNCONSCIOUS PHANTASY AND APRÈS-COUP
## The Controversial Discussions[1]

### Rosine Jozef Perelberg

**Introduction**

In this paper, I would like to suggest a distinction between the descriptive après-coup and the *dynamic après-coup*. This parallels Freud's distinction between the descriptive unconscious and the dynamic unconscious in the topographical model of the mind. The descriptive après-coup refers to the way in which the concept has found a use, especially but not only in the French literature, to refer to retrospective signification in the moment to moment progress of a session.[2] In this paper, I will outline *dynamic après-coup* which, I suggest, is at the core of Freudian metapsychology. Dynamic après-coup establishes a link between trauma, castration, repetition compulsion, sexuality, and temporality in the context of the transference.

In recent years, a series of debates centred on this concept can be found in the literature. One took place in the Paris Psychoanalytical Society, between Ignês Sodré and Michel Neyraut, whose texts, together with Jean Cournut's, were published in the *Revue Francaise de Psychanalyse* (1997). Another took place in 2005, between Haydee Faimberg and Ignês Sodré, published in the *International Journal of Psychoanalysis* (2005). In reading through these papers, one gains access to the atmosphere of the two psychoanalytic cultures, in terms of the presence or absence of the links between the concept of après-coup and the Freudian metapsychology, an idea which I will develop in this paper. Dana Breen has indicated that not mentioning the concept does not mean that it is not being used (2003). The thesis I will develop in this article is the intrinsic link that après-coup has with other concepts in Freudian metapsychology.

Four papers were discussed in the Controversial Discussions, over a series of ten meetings between January 1943 and July 1944. In this paper, I will concentrate on two of the papers discussed during six of the meetings. The first was written by Susan Isaacs on "unconscious phantasies" and was discussed over five meetings. The other was written by Susan Isaacs and Paula Heimann on "regression". Pearl King has suggested that the discussion of this latter paper took place at only one meeting because there was so much consensus about the issues (King and Steiner 1991, p. 686). My impression is different. I think that regression was an issue that permeated most of the discussions and some of the crucial points of difference had already been established, as I will outline below.

These two papers and the discussions that followed them to my mind contain core issues central to psychoanalysis not only at the time, but also later on. In fact, I suggest that they have been central to the discussions in the British Society on the nature of unconscious phantasies in their connection with the issues of temporality and sexuality and the Oedipus complex. It is worth revisiting these discussions because in so many ways the issues were then more clearly discussed than they have been since in the British Society. Green has suggested, in the French translation of the Controversial Discussions, that "these controversies are the most important document of the history of psychoanalysis" (King and Steiner 1996, p. xi, my translation). Furthermore, I wish to discuss these issues in the light of the concept of après-coup.

This paper will be divided into three main parts. In the first, I will briefly outline my understanding of concept of après-coup in Freud's work, and its connections with the concept of unconscious phantasies, sexuality and Freud's different notions of time. In the second, I will use the concept of après-coup to illuminate the issues raised in the 1942 Controversial Discussions in the British Society and indicate how it might have shed light on differences between ideas. In the third part, I will give a clinical example that illustrates the way in which the dynamic concept of après-coup has illuminated a moment of my clinical practice.

My suggestion is that the concept of après-coup is central to an understanding of Freud's formulations, and works as a "general illumination" in his conceptual framework, as discussed by Marx in his Introduction to *A Critique of Political Economy*:

> In all forms of society, it is a determined production and its relations which assign every other production and its relations their rank and influence. It is a general illumination (Beleuchtung) in which all the colours are plunged and which modifies their special tonalities. It is a special ether which defines the specific weight of every existence arising in it.
>
> (Marx 1964, p. 27).

This quotation points out the presence of the structure in its effects, i.e. the notion of structural causality. Althusser argues that this is contained in the notion of *Darstellung*, a key element of the Marxist theory of value (Althusser 1970). It also suggests, however, that although the structure is present in its effects, it cannot be seen, so that the concept points to the efficacy of an absence. I tend to think of après-coup in this way. As a central idea in Freud, it illuminates everything else. What is central to the notion of après-coup in Freud is the fundamental discontinuity between two different times, discontinuity brought about by the centrality of the Oedipus complex that is structurally inserted between these two notions of time. Bernard Chervet (2006) has suggested that the concept of après-coup is inherent to the conception of thinking itself in Freud's work, which works in multiple directions, includes affects and representations and requires time for elaboration.

## Freud and après-coup

Freud's conceptualisation of the psychic apparatus postulates that distinct timings must be at work. Experiences are registered in the psychic apparatus, which is a system that exists in space and time, and these are re-experienced and externalised through the analytic process. Repetition, irreversibility and oscillation are all present in the functioning of the mind. Freud was always considering different notions of time at any given moment of his work, as evidenced by the complexity of both his theoretical writings and his analyses of clinical cases.

The first concept of time in Freud's formulations is that of the *evolution and development* of the individual, in terms of both the biological development of the baby and the emergence of functions and behaviour patterns which result from exchanges between the organism and its environment. This is the genetic perspective, based on the notion of developmental continuity.

A second concept of time refers to the *structuring of the individual* and the distinction between the ego, the id and the super-ego. Freud (1923) suggested that at birth no ego exists. It is primary repression which institutes the separation between the id and the ego, between primary and secondary processes which are, hereafter, regulated by different conceptions of time. Time in the unconscious is atemporal and can only be accessible in terms of its derivatives in the system Pcpt-Cs.

Freud suggested that the different timings in the id and the ego are thus inaugurated by repression. But when does repression occur? Here a third notion of time must be introduced. In 1926, Freud suggested that most of the repression which we deal with in our therapeutic work represents cases of repression by deferred action (*après-coup*). By this he meant that experiences, impressions and memory traces may be revised at a later date, when the individual reaches a new stage of maturation (Laplanche and Pontalis 1985, p. 111).

Although the full exposition of his theory appears in 'The Wolf Man', which can be viewed as providing a mythological perspective of Freud's theories on time, one can only grasp the full extent of the complexity of Freud's models of temporalities by reading many of his papers, each of which indicates a new dimension that cannot be comprehended without taking the others into account. It is not until the metapsychological papers of 1915 that the notion of après-coup acquires full significance. I will return to this point in a moment.

## Inscription of après-coup in the metapsychology

Après-coup is inscribed in Freud's metapsychology, the set of papers that can be seen as having no connection with a theory of practice, but are rather an expression of an intellectual tradition, a path taken by Freud in his work that is crucial to the understanding of his formulations. In Britain and America, with rare exceptions, the metapsychological papers are regarded as a relic of the past.

It is in France that these papers come alive and are part of an intellectual debate. As Jean Claude Rolland has emphasised, the metapsychological papers cannot be read in the same way as so many of the more clinical papers. They are pervaded by a sense of strangeness in which it is almost as if it is Freud's unconscious that speaks to the reader's unconscious, opening doors which illuminate the enigma of the unconscious. Rolland points out how these writings had to be in place before Freud could take the leap towards the even stranger text of 'Beyond the Pleasure Principle' and the structural model of the mind (Rolland 2005).

Repression establishes the rupture between conscious and unconscious, which is now only accessible through its derivatives. It is thus only retrospectively that one can access unconscious phantasies. From that perspective, phantasy, like time, is multi-determined, and to my mind one cannot select any one of the layers in Freud's work as 'central'. What gives depth to the Freudian theory of the mind is indeed its fluidity, the dynamics between the various concepts. One only has to read the clinical papers such as 'The Rat Man', 'The Wolf Man' and 'Little Hans' or the paper on Leonardo to comprehend the way in which unconscious phantasies are only accessed through their derivatives, retrospectively in terms of *après-coup*. Primal phantasies—*Urphantasien*—as discussed above, are there from the beginning, although they have to be "reactivated" in the individual history. In *all* these unconscious phantasies, Freud seems to be concerned with the question of how sexuality comes about for human beings.

Thomä and Cheshire (1991) have pointed out the two directions implied in the concept of Nachträglichkeit. Reactivation of predispositions, or of these schemata and clichés as defined by Freud (1912, 1918), might stimulate associations to, and memories of, similar situations in the past. Freud in fact described a disposition with regard to Nachträglichkeit which suggests that the concept operates in two different directions:

> On different occasions and for different purposes (for example, explanatory as opposed to therapeutic), Freud approaches his concept from two different standpoints in time: sometimes he looks backwards from the point of view of the therapist reconstructing a phenomenal-developmental sequence of events and experiences, and sometimes he is looking forward as if through the eyes of the

original traumatic event which is setting off a series of potentially pathogenic developments, some of whose effects are going to be 'carried over' into the future.

(p. 420)

Nachträglichkeit was usually translated by Strachey as 'deferred action'. This translation has been considered unsatisfactory by many authors because the idea of the delayed effect of an early trauma is often combined in Freud's usage with that of the retrospective reconstruction of the psychological significance of that trauma. Consequently, (1) translators have the problem of whether or how to signal this aspect of the concept—which the German does not suggest; and (2) it has been thought that the concept implies a kind of 'backward causality' which challenges conventional notions of temporality.[3]

Thomä and Cheshire add the following note:

The essential difference between the verbs nachtragen and 'to defer' consists in the fact that they express exactly opposite relations to time: the former is backward-looking (nach = 'after', so after what?), whereas the latter is forward-looking (defer ... until when?). Both words have linguistic roots in verbs of motion, though different ones: in the case of 'defer', it is obviously the Latin ferre, which means 'to carry' (or tragen); while tragen seems to come from the Germanic root meaning 'to drag' or 'to draw along' (in spite of the temptation to derive it intuitively from the Latin trahere!)

(p. 422)

However, the term does also carry a relevant metaphorical meaning, namely 'to bear a grudge'.

Whereas Strachey's preferred rendering calls attention to forward-looking elements of the micro-theory, Lacan by contrast focuses on its backward-looking aspects by adopting the usage 'retro-action' and cognates in his French (e.g. Lacan 1966, p. 839 and 1977, p. 48).

This double movement, regressive and progressive, however, has to be articulated with Freud's other notions of time, as time for Freud's is multidimensional. *My image is that of a heptagon*, rather than a linear perspective, even a bi-directional one. This is the diachronic heterogeneity of the psychic apparatus (Green 2000). The concept of après-coup in Freud is intrinsically linked to the notions of trauma, memory, sexuality and unconscious phantasy. It is related to a theory of the mind that includes multiple temporalities—progressive and regressive movements take place together and condition each other reciprocally. These include development, regression, repression, fixation, repetition compulsion, the return of the repressed and the timelessness of the unconscious. These different dimensions of time constitute a dominant structure (Althusser 1970), and this dominance resides in the après-coup.

## The Controversial Discussions

Questions of time, life and death, as well as beginnings were certainly present at the time of the Controversial Discussions. Freud had died in England, away from his country of origin, as a Jewish refugee from Nazi persecution, saved by the generosity and concern of his friends. The presence of the Second World War surrounded the discussions, and at times the participants had to take refuge in the basement of the Institute in the middle of a debate. A decision had even to be made allowing those with families to leave, as if it was not obvious that personal survival might at times take priority over the survival of ideas.

London and the bombings were the backcloth of these controversies. It is not surprising that temporality was indeed at the core of these discussions, and that it seemed one was attempting to separate the present from both the past and the future, when the present had such enormous and tragic dimensions.

Previous examinations of the Controversial Discussions have concentrated on the debates surrounding disagreements over timing and the nature of phantasy, as well as disputes over whether the earliest months display vivid, complex oral-cannibalistic phantasies involving internal objects and massive introjection and projection, or whether they are mainly narcissistic and auto-erotic (see Hayman 1994; King and Steiner 1991). In examining the debates in the Controversial Discussions in this paper, I would like to concentrate on key differences expressed in the discussions in relation to temporality. In the process, I will focus on the concepts of regression, the Oedipus complex and unconscious phantasy in its connection with sexuality. Although the concept of après-coup was not once mentioned during the controversies, I will suggest that it helps to illuminate the depth of differences between the ideas expressed at the time in important ways. Furthermore, I think that some of these key differences still exist today.

There is an "official" version of the debates in the British Society, which works almost like a "founding myth" that goes more or less like this: this was a time when two factions were in conflict with each other, each trying to prove the other one wrong (Freudians and Kleinians). In the middle there were the natives of the island, who had a balanced view, in that they agreed with most of the new ideas, but not with all. They were the moderates, who became known as the middle group.

My perspective is that a closer examination of the discussions, and the concentration on the issues of temporality and metapsychology, indicates that some of the most crucial criticisms came in fact from this "middle group", and from the perspectives expressed by Glover, Ella Sharpe, M. Brierley and Sylvia Payne, as well as Hoffer and Friedlander.

## The papers in the Controversial Discussions

The first paper was presented by Susan Isaacs, on the nature of unconscious phantasy. It put forward the idea that unconscious phantasies are "the primary content of unconscious mental processes", and "the mental corollary, the psychic representative of instinct" (King and Steiner 1991, p. 275). These ideas are consistent with Freud's ideas about primal phantasies, although the two formulations are different in terms of both content and structure. For Freud, these primal phantasies are castration, seduction and primal scene. For Klein, unconscious phantasies are particularly derived from the death instinct.

In reading through the five discussions that followed this paper, I noticed that regression became a key concept, around which questions concerned with temporality were debated. Although only one evening was dedicated to specifically discussing Isaacs' paper on "regression", the concept was discussed nearly every evening of the Controversies.

## Regression

Freud had distinguished three levels of regression: topographical, temporal and formal. He gave a fuller definition in a note added to *The Interpretation of Dreams* in 1914:

Three kinds of regression are thus to be distinguished: a. topographical regression, in the sense of the schematic picture [of the psychical apparatus]; b. temporal regression, in so far as what is in question is harking back to older psychical structures; and c. formal regression, where primitive methods of expression and representation take the place of the usual ones.

(p. 548)

## Backward and forward movements

In the commentary below, delivered in the first of the ten discussions, which was dedicated to the paper on unconscious phantasy, Jones equated phantasy with hallucinatory wish fulfilment. Two central ideas relate to his understanding of regression.

First, he believes that one reaches early expressions of fantasies through regression. Here "early" means "early on in time". Green has pointed out that

> the term is untranslatable in French, as neither 'précoces' or 'primitives' encompasses what should each time be designated as happening early in life. Melanie Klein argues that that what is linked to the most ancient past is necessarily what is most determining and more fundamental to the psyche.
> (Green 1996, xii, my translation)

Second, according to Jones there is continuity between later manifestations and earlier ones. This is related to the notion of *genetic continuity*, an idea much emphasised at the time of the Controversial Discussions by the supporters of Melanie Klein. These two points were at the centre of many of the ten discussions, although challenged by several participants, such as Brierley, Payne, Hoffer and Friedlander.

There is, however, another idea, namely that later manifestations may reactivate earlier ones, in other words, the notion of a double movement, forwards and backwards. Is this idea of a bidirectional temporal movement equivalent to après-coup?

Can one identify these ideas—back and forth movement, polysemia of meaning, non-previous determination of meaning, retrospective re-structuring of earlier representations—in terms of their link with sexuality in Jones's comments in his first intervention in the Controversial Discussions?

> If, for example, we compare a phantasy or reaction after puberty with a corresponding one between the ages of, say, three and five, then we may surely say that either may reinforce the other. *The continued unconscious operation of the earlier one may strengthen the later one, while contrariwise an emotional event at the later age may through regression reanimate and reinvest an earlier attitude*
> (King and Steiner 1991, pp. 323–324)

Jones emphasises the double movement, progressive and regressive. Later phantasies may reactivate through the process of regression earlier ones. Conversely, earlier phantasies may "reinforce" later ones. One is not clear yet about what he means by the term "reinforce".

Jones made several points. First, he emphasised the relevance of the early impulses and suggests that they have a "greater intensity" than later ones. Second, he suggests that there is "something" that attracts the regression. Third, he assumes that what is found in adults can retrospectively also be found earlier on. This will be related to the concept of *genetic continuity*, an idea consistently emphasised throughout the Controversial Discussions by authors such as Isaacs and Jones. The dimension which is missed out altogether in this comment is re-signification, a re-structuring of earlier events in the light of later events and, most importantly, the Oedipus complex. The notion that something is waiting to find meaning in the future, which illuminates an event in the past, a crucial aspect of après–coup in the way it has been discussed before in this paper, is missing. This is clear in the following statement, as Jones continued:

> The presence of such phantasies in older subjects had long ago led me to deduce the actual existence of them in young infants, and this inference has in my opinion been amply confirmed by the analysis of them carried out by Mrs. Klein and others as well as by the observational data to which Mrs. Isaacs has often drawn our attention.
> (Ibid., p. 324)

A different emphasis is present in the comments made by Friedlander, who suggests that through the mechanism of regression, *later phantasies acquire aspects of earlier ones, so that what one has access to is a retrospective modification of early phantasies.* Thus, oral phantasies expressed in later years may not be derived from the oral phase itself but may have acquired their oral aspect through regression. One could suggest that this is a component of après-coup.

In continuing his comments, Friedlander emphasises the notions of stages of development, fixations and developmental arrest. Friedlander also indicates the backwards and forwards movement of the libido. She adds that in Klein's thinking the process of development is seen in a more static form, and that the concept of regression has no place in this theory. The whole of the libido remains fixated on these early phantasies throughout life, without undergoing the biological developmental phases described by Freud.

M. Brierley, in her intervention, coins the very interesting term *retrospective sophistication*, which I think comes close to the concept of après-coup:

> I think, personally, that some of the precocity attributed to Mrs. Klein's infant is due to this simple fact, that an adult cannot make any content of infantile experience intelligible to other adults without subjecting the experience itself to some degree of falsification or *retrospective sophistication*.
> (Ibid., p. 471, my italics)

Glover thought that the regression in oral hallucinatory gratification activates the memory traces of the actual experiences at the sensory end of the apparatus. He also thought that many Freudian concepts had been left out—these include the biological progression of an instinct series, the early formation of object images, fixation points, regression, the possibility of permanent withdrawal of cathexes from pre-oedipal fixation systems and, last but not least, the theoretical and clinical significance of the Oedipus complex.

Anna Freud, also focusing on the theory of regression under discussion, early on in the discussions seemed not to identify the profound differences implied in the discussions for the metapsychology, as she pointed out that the differences concerned the first year of life only. However, she later indicated that the discussions indicated differences for the whole theory of the unconscious.

She highlighted the following points, in connection with our present theme of temporality:

> As concerns the new *theory of regression* Mrs. Isaacs herself speaks of divergence of opinion. But I think that *she underestimates the far-reaching consequences of her point of view, when followed to its logical end, for the theory of the neuroses. It shifts all emphasis from the later stages of development to the earliest ones*, gives secondary importance only to the level on which the breakdown of the personality occurs, puts the concept of fixation-points out of action and, incidentally, gives rise to nearly all the existing differences of the technique of psychoanalytic treatment.
>
> (Ibid., p. 329, my italics)

Throughout most of the discussions, there was an attempt to clarify the issue of temporality in psychoanalysis. At times the debates seemed to be locked in terms of whether one should emphasise earlier events or later ones. Was the manifestation of an unconscious phantasy a product of an earlier event (as the Kleinians were emphasising) or a later one, that acquired earlier aspects through regression (as the Freudians and the "middle group" were **both** emphasising)? My sense is that the concept of après-coup solves the dichotomy of whether earlier ones or later ones are more important as it indicates the way in which in Freudian metapsychology the later events resignify earlier ones which then emerge with a new meaning. For Freud this is centrally indicated in relation to the Oedipus complex, and I will now look at the way this concept was thought about in the discussions of the two papers.

## The Oedipus complex

A crucial aspect of the discussions centred on ideas related to the Oedipus complex. The differentiation between the positions expressed in the debates is not simply a dichotomy between the positions of the Kleinians vs. the Freudians, with a third group in the middle. Once again, some of the crucial issues that relate to the Oedipus complex, its structural function and temporality are raised by those who were later to belong to the middle group as well as some (Anna) Freudians, who objected to the positions expressed by the Kleinians.

If, on the one hand, I am covering old ground, at the same time I do not cease to be surprised about the way in which differences between, say, the Kleinian Oedipus complex and the Freudian view tend to be blurred even today in the British Society.

As Kohon suggests:

> Not only was the Oedipus complex then made to appear earlier in life (e.g. by Melanie Klein and her followers), but it was transformed into something radically different: it ceased to be the model of sexuality and meaning for the subject.
>
> (1999, p. 8)

In the Freudian model there is a reorganisation that takes place with the oedipal situation, and sexuality is its motto. In the first of the Controversial Discussions, Sylvia Payne questioned the concept of unconscious phantasies as proposed by Susan Isaacs both in terms of the content and time of phantasies:

> In the first place I should like to say that I cannot see any reason for denying the presence of some form of primitive phantasy from the beginning of extra-uterine mental life.... [However] I do not think that phantasy, using the word in the usual sense, occurs until there has been a psychic experience which involves the reception of a stimulus and a psycho-physical response.
>
> (King and Steiner 1991, pp. 333–334)

Although Ella Sharpe agreed that there was a continuity between the early phantasies and later ones (thus agreeing with the notion of genetic continuity), she criticised the new definition of unconscious phantasy proposed by Isaacs for not allowing for a clear differentiation that she thought important; that is, between early 'phantasies' and the sophisticated, classical oedipal ones. She listed a number of differences: the classical Oedipus complex required ego development and reality recognition of frustration, repression, the use of symbolic substitutes, and the superego, which was inseparable from 'Freud's Oedipus complex', which she distinguished from what she called the 'super-id' of the primitive state.

Isaacs thought Sharpe made too great a distinction between the earlier and the later Oedipus complex. She wished to stress the genetic continuity by using the same term. Payne thought that although she herself believed in genetic continuity, there should be a different word for the earlier and the later states. 'We don't call a foetus a man', she said.

Ella Sharpe pointed out very importantly that:

> ...the Freudian Oedipus complex is of a different nature altogether, involving ego organization and repression which is inseparable from reality adaptation. The Oedipus complex is bypassed when the wish psychosis is retained to any strength. ...
>
> The term 'super-ego' is only correctly used when it designates what it says: a superego. This superego is inseparable from the Oedipus complex of Freud. Some other term should be found such as 'id-ideal' in contrast to ego-ideals for those derivatives of the incorporation of the actual object when ego differentiation has hardly begun. The superego in the Freudian sense is accessible to influence and amelioration, that which derives from the belief in actual incorporation is inaccessible and adamant, the belief in righteousness as adamant as implacable evil.
>
> (Ibid., p. 339)

Barbara Low also stressed the reorganisation that takes place with the Oedipus complex, and I think that the following statement was one of the clearest on this issue, throughout the whole of the controversies:

> Does Mrs. Isaacs interpret Freud's theory of phantasy as a developing situation, dependent upon new psychic situations as they arise? *For example, the phantasy of the introjected mother (good or bad) must surely be modified (and perhaps completely changed) with the onset of the Oedipus conflict.*
>
> (Ibid., p. 392, my italics)

In her paper and statements, Paula Heimann emphasised the "early" and "pre-genital", which take the place of the oedipal. Willi Hoffer to my mind made the most clarifying comments on the issue of the Oedipus complex as retrospectively reorganising the psychic apparatus. Moreover, he pointed out the different emphases in the Freudian and the Kleinian perspectives. He said that "according to Freud, neuroses are the specific diseases of the sexual function; according to Klein's theory, the neuroses might be called the specific diseases of the destructive function" (Ibid., p. 723).

Hoffer pointed to three main characteristics of the Freudian Oedipus complex. First, the attainment of the phallic phase implies an important distinction between the penis as an organ and the penis as an erotogenic zone. The second characteristic is the ability to choose an object; the third is the castration complex. He emphasises that it is only retrospectively that one can decide if an earlier event may be pathogenic or not. It is the later event that transforms and gives meaning to the earlier one. Is this not the concept of après-coup? The following emphases on the role of sexuality seem to me to complete the essential component in the concept. Hoffer thinks that Klein has proposed a new theory of neurosis:

> According to Freud's view it is the happenings of this stage which decide about the onset of infantile neurosis. Under the strain of the Oedipus conflict the phallic organization may break down; due to anxiety caused by the intervention of the ego and superego the phallic aims are renounced and regression takes place to fixation points on former pre-genital levels. *Thus it is impossible to decide whether a given pre-genital phase will prove pathogenetic or not before the phallic phase has given evidence of either its stability or instability.*
> 
> (Ibid., p. 722, my italics)

He points out the dominant element in each model: anxiety in the Kleinian model, sexuality in the Freudian.

In the case of Emma (1895, pp. 353–356), Freud had already wished to underline the centrality of sexuality in the process of signification. For him it is not possible to separate the question of time from infantile sexuality, its origins and transformations.

These last points indicate the radical difference between the notion of genetic continuity (central to the Kleinians in the discussion), which emphasise the continuity between infantile sexuality and adult sexuality, on the one hand, and the notion of après-coup, on the other. This latter notion implied the radical discontinuity between infantile sexuality and adult sexuality with the re-structuring that takes place with the Oedipus complex, the incest taboo and the institution of the differentiation between genders and generations.

## A clinical example

In this section, I would like to indicate how the dynamic concept of après-coup underpins my understanding of a moment in my clinical practice.

### Francis

A woman in her twenties, tall with long, black hair, a sculptress, Francis came into my consulting room asking to start an analysis because of her wish to improve her relationships. She had had an analysis in her country of origin, in her mother tongue, which she had found helpful. Francis is married, in a loving relationship, and has two daughters.

At the time I am describing. Francis had been having dreams which involved celebrities which indicated, I believe, her idealisation of me and her narcissistic identification with me. She thought that I had a clear style, she once said to me that I spoke in a way that she found "organic", she felt that it was part of me.

During the session I intend to describe, Francis had been telling me about her admiration for me. She also talked about other artists, whom she also admired greatly. It is a source of suffering for her when she feels that there is nothing she can offer. Then she went on to tell me about a weekend trip to Salzburg, where she had seen many statues dedicated to Mozart. The whole town revered him as a 'total celebrity'.

I said: "Looking at other artists and me as celebrities leaves you feeling depleted, with nothing".

There was a silence for a while. Then Francis talked about a painting that she had seen in an exhibition that morning. It portrayed a little girl of about eight years of age, and its eroticism was shocking. A woman was inclined towards the girl, kissing her on her lips. The little girl's head was tilted backwards, in a position of total surrender, and yet at the same time giving an impression of actively participating in the kiss. She wore lipstick and mascara; this make up seemed to be the marker of the woman's kiss on her. It is as if she had become this woman, Francis exclaimed.

Francis paused and there was a vibrant silence in the session.

She then said that it made her think of her relationship with her mother in a new way. She recollected how passionate she felt about her mother. Yet, in a fight they once had, she had thought about saying to her mother "You are going to fuck me to death".

(I thought that there was a transformation from the idealisation of me, which left her feeling depleted, to this other layer of erotic surrender, the repetition in each session of this experience of being fucked to death, surrendering to the kiss which is her phantasy of what takes place between the analyst and the patient in the session.)

I said: "When you surrender to me in your sessions, you not only feel depleted, but fucked to death".

Although I had thought about what I was going to say, there was an element of surprise in my saying it, and we were both silent for quite some time.

In the movement of the session, there was a flow between different moments in time. From the present of the session, to the image of the picture, to a recollection of an experience as a young girl in her relationship with her mother (the kiss), a moment in adolescence that illuminated her experience as a little girl and both moments in the past illuminating and giving a further meaning to the present of the session. Conversely, in the present of the session these various moments of her past story acquired new meaning, in a process of re-signification. A possibility was expressed of linking that which takes place in the session to the past, and back to the present.

Four dimensions of time were present in the session:

1. The surrender to her analyst in the present
2. The erotic image of the picture of a woman and a little girl seen earlier that day
3. A souvenir of her experience of passion for her mother when she was a little girl
4. The memory of her adolescent fight with her mother when she had wanted to tell her "You'll fuck me to death".

In the here and now of the session, both the past and the present are interpreted and understood après-coup, in the experience of a "temps éclaté" [shattered time] (Green 2000).

## Discussion

Over the years, the concept of après-coup has come to mean many different things in the psychoanalytic literature. The concept has been extended so that more narrowly and descriptively it has been equated with the process of thinking retrospectively about one's own thoughts and work (see, for instance, Pontalis 1977), or the retrospective and progressive dimensions of time in given sessions. Sandler (1983) has suggested that psychoanalytic concepts may be elastic and become stretched. He saw this type of flexibility as playing an important part in the development of psychoanalytic theory; but it remains a puzzle as to how it is possible for such disparate meanings to be so widely accepted as if the disparity did not actually exist.

The theoretical concern with the connections between the past and the present and the implication for a theory of technique has been relevant in the history of thinking in the British Society. Joseph and Anne-Marie Sandler, for instance, have in several papers (1984, 1994a, 1994b) distinguished between the past unconscious and the present unconscious. In their view, the past unconscious can be regarded as acting like a dynamic "template", a structuring organisation that gives form to current wishes or wishful fantasies, which are then further modified in the present unconscious before gaining access to consciousness; it is "the child within" which gives form to all the intrapsychic content that arises in the depths—in particular unconscious wishes and wishful fantasies.

Gill (1982) has suggested the centrality of the transference in the psychoanalytic process and suggests that the transference is an amalgam of past and present. Ruth Riesenberg Malcom has suggested that the 'here-and-now' of the analytic situation is indeed the expression of the patient's past in its multiple transformations. In any transference interpretation, the analyst is interpreting both the past and the present as is present in the here and now of the analytic situation (1999). Green (2000) has suggested the term "shattered time" to indicate the "collapse" between past and present in the analytic process, and especially in the analyses of dreams.

Dana Breen has cogently indicated how the "here and now" type of interpretation in the British School of psychoanalysis is never a "pure present". She indicates that progressive and retrospective time go inherently together, "one being a requisite for the other" (Breen 2003). Ignês Sodré has indicated the many similarities between the concept of après-coup and that of "mutative interpretation" (1997). I think that both these authors use the concept in the descriptive sense and not in the dynamic sense as I am proposing here.

My perspective is that the concept of après-coup cuts across a discussion of whether one is addressing the past or the present, as it indicates clearly that one is addressing both at the same time, with a mutual process of reinterpretation: the present reinterprets the past, as the past leaves the seeds which will find their fulfilment in the present, albeit with no sense of predetermination, as discussed in this paper. Moreover, I have also indicated the way in which the dynamic concept of après-coup is profoundly embedded in Freudian metapsychology.[4] One of the shortcomings of the process of extending the concept of après-coup is that some of key aspects of Freud's metapsychology have been lost in some of the papers cited above: the links between trauma, repetition and infantile sexuality. One feels echoes of some of the key issues discussed during the Controversial Discussions. At the time, concepts like the Oedipus complex and unconscious phantasies, which had a specific meaning in Freudian terminology, were expanded to mean something quite different. My suggestion is that there is a similar process taking place now with the concept of après-coup which, if it is expanded to mean many different things, loses some of the crucial meanings that connect it to Freudian metapsychology.

In this paper, I have suggested the distinction between descriptive and dynamic après-coup. Descriptive après-coup refers to the way in which the concept has found a use especially but not only in the French literature, where it means retrospective signification in the moment to moment progress of a session. I have proposed in this paper the concept of *dynamic* après-coup, which I think is at the core of Freudian metapsychology.

The paper was then divided into three main parts. In the first part, I delineated my understanding of the dynamic concept of après-coup in Freud. I suggested that it is one of the crucial dimensions of time, amongst at least seven others (timelessness of the unconscious, repetition compulsion, the return of the repressed, fixation, development, structuring and regression) and that, moreover, it has the role of a dominant concept, in the way suggested by Althusser in relation to the role of the economic in Marx's work. In other words, it gives meaning to everything else. Moreover, I pointed out the crucial connection it has in Freud's work with the notions of trauma and infantile sexuality.

I then used the concept to illuminate crucial differences in the 1942 Controversial Discussions in the British Society. In summarising the complexity of views expressed on the issue of temporality, there was overall support for the idea of genetic continuity. Some important differences were also expressed, however.

I have suggested that that the concept of après-coup might have helped to solve the dichotomy between early and later phantasies, as it indicates the way in which in Freudian metapsychology later events resignify earlier ones which then emerge with a new meaning. For Freud this is central to the Oedipus complex, structurally inserted between two different notions of time.

In presenting my clinical example, I indicated the double movement present in the notion of après-coup (prospective and retrospective), like Proust's madeleine, which encompasses at least two spaces, and two periods of time, which can only be discovered retrospectively.

There is a scene of childhood trauma that is retrospectively understood in terms of what takes place in the here and now of the transference situation. It is indeed in relation to the transference and the transference interpretation that the après-coup can be depicted and constructed. The whole process takes place in the "analytic site", which brings together transfer, process, interpretation, and counter-transference, and within which the après-coup takes place (Donnet 2005). Furthermore, and very importantly for the understanding of the dynamic concept of après-coup, in both examples the après-coup is defined by the primacy of sexuality, the erotic passivation in the transference that evokes the traumatic childhood sexual scene. In the Freudian model, as in the way the examples were understood in this chapter, sexuality and sexual phantasies are at the centre of the re-elaboration of meaning.

## Notes

1 This paper first appeared *Int. J. Psycho-Anal.*, 87: 1199–1220.
2 I have chosen to use the concept in its French version, instead of the German *Nachträglich* (adjective), *Nachträglichkeit* (noun) because "après-coup" evokes an intellectual field of debate in France, where the concept has not only been first recovered by Lacan but been more centrally discussed than in any other language. One has only to attend any of the scientific meetings of the Paris Psychoanalytical Society, or any congress in France to hear how the concept is part of the current vocabulary of French psychoanalysts in a way that I have not encountered in any other country. This can also be attested by reading the main

psychoanalytic journals in France. Haydee Faimberg has suggested that the fact that these are common words in the German language perhaps may be one explanation of why the concept has not acquired the same importance in the German psychoanalytical culture as it has in France. The very process of translation has demanded reflection (see Faimberg 2005, p. 1). Laplanche has also suggested: "It is therefore in France, and in close relation to the problems of translation, that the importance of Nachträglichkeit has made itself felt" (1999, p. 26). The suggestion is that one is already dealing with an *interpretation* of a concept, which implies a particular understanding of it (Ibid., p. 263).

3 Faced with this issue, the translators of the new French 'standard edition' have decided nevertheless to adopt a single term which has two-way connotations. Explaining that they propose to render nachträglich as 'après-coup' and Nachträglichkeit as 'effet d'après coup', Bourgogne et al. (1989) write that:

> Lacan is responsible for having restored this concept its full importance, which Freud forged from the time of the seduction theory and maintained throughout the whole extent of his writings. Our only innovation, for this translation, is to have rendered the noun … by the term effet d'après-coup (and not effet après-coup which, like the English 'deferred action', conveys the impression of a simple delay in the action effected by the past on the present, whereas l'effet d'après-coup is effective along the reverse vector also: from the present toward the past. The distinction being signalled here, piquantly by a single letter (or maybe two) in French, is something like that between a delayed or belated effect and an 'after effect', where the latter implies the continuing consequence of some previous event.
>
> (pp. 82–83)

4 Amongst the authors in Britain who have used the concept in the dynamic way I am defining it in this paper I would draw particular attention to Kohon (1986, 1999).

## References

Althusser, L. (1970). Marx's immense theoretical revolution. In *Reading Capital*, eds. L. Althusser and E. Balibar. London: Verso, pp. 182–193.

Birksted-Breen, D. (2003). Time and the après-coup. *Int. J. Psycho-Anal.*, 84: 1501–1515.

Bourgogne, A., Cotet, P., Laplanche, J. and François, R. (1989). *Traduire Freud*. Paris: Presses Universitaires de France.

Chervet, B. (2006). L'après-coup, prolégomènes. *Rev. Franç. Psychanal.*, 70: 671–700.

Cournut, J. (1997). Le sens de l'après-coup. *Rev. Franç. Psychanal.*, 61: 1239–1246.

Donnet, J.-L. (2005). *La Situation Analysante*. Paris: Presses Universitaires de France.
Faimberg, H. (2005). Après-coup. *Int. J. Psycho-Anal.*, 86: 1–6.
Freud, S. (1895 [1950]). Project for a scientific psychology. *S.E.*, 1: 281–391.
Freud, S. (1900). The interpretation of dreams. *S.E.*, 4 and 5.
Freud, S. (1909a). Analysis of a phobia in a five-year-old boy. *S.E.*, 10: 1–150.
Freud, S. (1909b). A case of obsessional neurosis. *S.E.*, 10: 151–250.
Freud, S. (1910). Leonardo da Vinci and a memory of his childhood. *S.E.*, 11: 59–137.
Freud, S. (1912). The dynamics of transference. *S.E.*, 12: 97–108.
Freud, S. (1915a). Instincts and their vicissitudes. *S.E.*, 14: 111–140.
Freud, S. (1915b). Repression. *S.E.*, 14: 141–158.
Freud, S. (1915c). The unconscious. *S.E.*, 14: 159–204.
Freud, S. (1918). From the history of an infantile neurosis. *S.E.*, 17: 3–122.
Freud, S. (1923). The ego and the id. *S.E.*, 19: 3–66.
Freud, S. (1926). Inhibitions, symptoms and anxiety. *S.E.*, 20: 75–172.
Gill, M. M. (1982). *Analysis of Transference Vol. I*. New York: International University Press.
Green, A. (1996). Introduction. In: King P and Steiner R, eds. *Les Controverses Anna-Freud Melanie Klein 1941-45*. Paris: PUF.
Green, A. (2000). *Le Temps Eclaté*. Paris: Les Editions de Minuit.
Hayman, A. (1994). Some remarks about the 'Controversial Discussions'. *Int. J. Psycho-Anal.* 75: 343–358.
King, P. and Steiner, R. (eds.) (1991). *The Freud-Klein Controversies 1941—1945*, London: Routledge.
King, P. and Steiner, R. (eds.) (1996). *Les Controverses Anna Freud Melanie Klein 1941–1945*. Paris: Presses Universitaires de France.
Kohon, G. (1986). *The British School of Psychoanalysis: The Independent Tradition*. London: Free Association Books.
Kohon, G. (1999). *No Uncertainties to be Recovered*. London: Karnac Books.
Lacan, J. (1966). *Ecrits*, Paris: Éditions du Seuil.
Lacan, J. (1977). *Écrits: A Selection*, transl. Alan Sheridan, New York: W.W. Norton & Co. Revised 2002, transl. Bruce Fink.
Laplanche, J. (1999). *The Unconscious and the Id*. London: Rebus Press
Laplanche, J. and Pontalis, J.-B. (1985). *Fantasme Originaire, Fantasme des origines, Origines du fantasme*. Paris: Hachette.
Marx, K. (1964). *A Contribution to a Critique of Political Economy [1867]*. London: Lawrence & Wishart.
Neyraut, M. (1997). Considérations rétrospectives sur l'après-coup. *Rev. Franç. Psychanal.* 61: 1247–1254.
Pontalis, J.-B. (1977). *Entre le Rêve et le Douleur*. Paris: Gallimard.

Riesenberg Malcom, R. (1999). *On Bearing Unbearable States of Mind*. London: Routledge.

Rolland, J. C. (2005). The metapsychological papers. In *Freud: A Modern Reader*, ed. R. J. Perelberg. London: Whurr, pp. 93–108.

Sandler, J. (1983). Reflections on some relations between psychoanalytic concepts and psychoanalytic practice. *Int. J. Psychoanal.*, 64: 33–45.

Sandler, J. and Sandler, A.-M. (1984). The past unconscious, the present unconscious and interpretation of the transference. *Psychoanal. Inq.*, 4: 367–399.

Sandler, J. and Sandler, A.-M. (1994a). Phantasy and its transformations: a contemporary freudian view. *Int. J. Psycho-Anal.*, 75: 387–394.

Sandler, J. and Sandler, A.-M. (1994b). The past unconscious and the present unconscious: a contribution to a technical frame of reference. *Psychoanal. St. Child*, 49: 278–292.

Sodré, I. (1997). Insight et après-coup. *Rev. Franç. Psychanal.*, 61: 1255–1262.

Sodré, I. (2005). 'As I was walking down the stairs, I saw a concept that wasn't there…'. Or, après-coup: a missing concept? *Int. J. Psycho-Anal.*, 86: 7–10.

Thomä, H. and Cheshire, N. (1991). Freud's concept of Nachträglichkeit and Strachey's 'deferred action': Trauma, constructions and the direction of causality. *Int. Rev. Psycho-Anal.* 3: 401–445.

# 4

# THE VICISSITUDES OF PREPARING AND SUSTAINING A YOUNG CHILD IN PSYCHOANALYSIS

Angela Joyce

The formative setting of the family, whatever its cultural variations, is suffused with residues of its unique history, which plays a central part in the psychological development of the new generation. In her seminal work "Ghosts in the Nursery" which explores the repetition of trauma down the generations, Selma Fraiberg (Fraiberg et al. 1975) points to the process of repression of painful feelings in the recollection of memories of a traumatic past, accompanied by identification with the aggressor by the victim of that trauma. These mechanisms facilitate the parent to not recognise the emotional pain that they are inflicting on their child, in identification with the person from their own past, a repetition of the pain they themselves experienced in childhood. Freud (1920) originally alerted us to the presence of the repetition compulsion as an aspect of the seeking after mastery when the ego feels overwhelmed. More recently, Christopher Bollas (Bollas 1999), following André Green (Green 1983), has written about the consequences for the child's development of a psychically dead mother. He avers that a traumatised mother may become psychically dead and in turn deadens her child. Psychoanalytic thinking can help us understand how the best intentions go awry, when the ordinary wishes of a mother—to make things right for her child and for her to be happy—have not been fulfilled and indeed seem to have been over-ridden by quite contrary forces.

In this paper, I will explore the repetition into the next generation of trauma suffered by a mother, its impact on the mother-child relationship and consequently upon the child's development. The trauma was embedded in the presenting symptom of screaming by a nearly three-year-old girl Sylvia. Aspects of it became built into the way her mother Mary managed the family's relationship with the Anna Freud Centre, ultimately leading to the breakdown of treatment in a way reminiscent of the original trauma. The family were involved with the Centre for approximately 20 months. From this story, I will draw out some ideas about the issues involved in taking a child into analytic treatment, a process that is multi-layered, and always inclusive of countertransference responses.

A parent who is not be able to console a screaming infant because of something inconsolable in their own past may react to the child's distress with rage and cruelty rather than with compassion. The screaming child in the mother, and the cruelty towards her own child self, may then be translated into minute emotional interactions between the mother and infant, within which the child is formulating the earliest knowledge of self and other. As I got to know Sylvia and her mother, it became evident that neither had experienced the sort of developmental process that Winnicott would have recognised as being "good enough" (Winnicott 1960a, p. 145). Despite the mother Mary's best efforts to "make everything right for Sylvia", she was far from happy and both were very distressed.

## The referral

Sylvia and her mother Mary were referred to the Parent-Infant Project at the Anna Freud Centre. Mary had confided to the Health Visitor at the GP's surgery that she was at the end of her tether with Sylvia who would do nothing she was told, they just ended up screaming and shouting at each other. They were refugees from a part of the world where there was war, and Mary was now seeking a new life in England.

## The family and the first session

In the first meeting, I was told a story of trauma and loss that had been overwhelming for Mary. The details of this story are specific to this family but in many families, all over the world, stories of traumas suffered are passed down the generations, either consciously as family history, or unconsciously as bewildering intimations of horrors that cannot be countenanced.

Mary had been pregnant with Sylvia and due to marry the father of her child when the civil war broke out and her husband-to-be was killed. Her father, a brother and a sister were also killed. With a surviving sister she fled and eventually reached safety in a bordering country where another brother lived, and Sylvia was born. They lived there until Sylvia was 18 months old and then came to London, a long journey in more ways than one. Sylvia became the symbol both of her mother's survival and the reminder of the death of the father and killing of her family.

There were several striking features of this first meeting and the story as it unfolded. Mary and Sylvia sat far apart from each other, Sylvia near to David (mother's new partner) and Mary sat slightly with her back to them. Sylvia seemed paralysed she was so still, until I simply acknowledged the pain of Mary's story, which threatened to overwhelm me as I listened to it. Sylvia began to play with the toys set out around us. Mary described Sylvia screaming at her so much and in such a way that, she said, *"it sounded as though I was killing her"*. This unconscious and repeated reference to the trauma in the family history, represented now in relation to the child, was the first indication of the impact of the un-integrated and therefore un-mourned loss of the father (Sylvia's and Mary's) on Mary's mothering of Sylvia.

However, I was soon to learn that these were not the only losses of significance in Mary's life. As Mary watched David enjoying playing with Sylvia, she observed how difficult it was for her to play like that: she could not. She explained that when she was aged three years her parents had separated, and in the custom of their culture, she and her brother had gone to live with their father and his new wife. The new wife had been kind, but Mary had not had any further contact with her mother until she was grown-up, even though she was living in the same town. She had coped with this by becoming a little grown-up-girl, looking after her younger siblings, longing for their freedom to play, but unable to do so.

As Mary told me of her early life Sylvia stood beside her and put her hand on her shoulder, their first physical contact during the session. I said to Sylvia that she understood that her mummy got upset and she wanted to make her better. She withdrew her hand, but Mary turned towards her and after a hesitation drew her daughter to her and cuddled her in her lap. Sylvia put her thumb in her mouth and stared at me, listening to her mother's story about her lost childhood. This was a very powerful moment and I felt very moved by it.

## Discussion

After this first session, I conjectured that the traumatic circumstances within which Mary's baby was born, containing war, death and forced migration, gave new meaning to the loss of her own mother in childhood. In the way Mary related to Sylvia, unconsciously, against all her conscious wishes, she created a space that was suffused with danger and risk, reflected in the fantasy of killing her. As a consequence, her daughter was unable to use her as a safe base for exploration and play. This was graphically displayed in Sylvia's distance from her mother, and in how frozen she was for much of the session. This detail of the material conveys the repetition of the trauma with the next generation. The fantasy of killing her daughter evoked by the screaming, reflected the trauma of the war. I also speculated that Sylvia became the unconscious target for her mother's projection of her own abandoned little girl self; that, in the après coup, the first loss was reorganised and given new and violent meaning in the light of the later traumatic losses in the war.

Both Sylvia's and Mary's early development was marked by "impingements"—intrusions from the environment (Winnicott 1952). These impingements demanded reaction, rather than the child being held in such a way that the maturational process could proceed well enough, giving rise to a sense of going-on-being in Winnicott's terms, gathering authorship of one's own urges and wishes, and ultimately taking responsibility for them. For Sylvia the presenting symptom, her not doing what she was told, screaming and shouting, suggested that her mother's request for co-operation might evoke in her a sense of having to capitulate or collapse; perhaps she was not able to cooperate without a sense of her self being compromised, equivalent to the killing and murder in her mother's fantasy. For Mary, the loss of her mother had led to the loss of her sense of being a child, able to play. She identified with her lost mother but could not mourn her, she became the child-mother who had now to "mother" others in the absence of her own lost mother. I was later to learn that her mothering of her siblings had a bullying quality, perhaps to externalise an internal sense of the mother-child relationship, suffused with loss and consequent hatred and cruelty. When Mary became a mother herself in such tragic circumstances, she was faced with the return of this internal scenario, now made real, with her own real baby.

## Varieties of intervention

I will now describe the different ways in which we responded to this family, to try to meet their needs and to help Sylvia find a better path for her development. There were three overlapping phases of the work: parent-child joint sessions for four and a half months; nursery for eighteen months; psychoanalysis for a year, and ongoing but frequently interrupted parent work for approximately sixteen months.

## First phase

In the first phase, Sylvia and her mother were offered weekly parent-child joint sessions to address those aspects of their relationship that were in difficulty. Mary did not want David involved at this point as she was very unsure of the relationship. Coincidentally there was a place available in the nursery, and Sylvia started there a couple of months after Mary had first made contact with the Centre. At this point, Mary had been working three days a week, she was a very competent and resourceful woman and already had a university degree. Sylvia had been looked after by a child-minder during work time, but was now able to be taken to and from nursery by her mother.

## Parent-child work

Parent-infant psychotherapy is rooted in the view that the child's development takes place within the affect and fantasy-laden matrix of the relationship with the parents. Its focus is on the exploration of those relationships as they impinge on the unfolding maturational process of the child. Work with a parent and toddler together is very similar to this, with the essential difference that the child's language is sufficiently developed for the content of the clinician's interventions to have specific meaning. The work takes place in an attractive room, sitting on cushions on the floor, with suitable play materials provided. The clinician becomes a participant observer of their interactions, which are the focus of therapeutic interventions.

In contrast to more usual psychoanalytic work, the transference to the therapist is not often addressed directly; rather it is noted, and especially the countertransference that we find is aroused most strongly by the presence of such young children with their parents. Interventions are more often focused on the parents' transferences to the child. It is here that the internal representations, the family scripts in the parents' minds are being recreated anew with this next generation. If the transference to the therapist comes to constitute an interference in the work, classically a resistance, then it is addressed; as it was from time to time with Mary.

Mary and Sylvia settled into their weekly sessions with me but from the outset Mary expressed ambivalence through frequent lateness. She was initially very keen to focus on and play with Sylvia, but I felt that I was already being invited to take part in something depriving; Mary was depriving herself and Sylvia of the full time we could have together. I wondered also if the lateness expressed anxiety about getting too attached to me, and this was corroborated after the first break in our sessions. The first day they were due to return they arrived at the end of the session. Mary had thought that the time of the end of the session was the beginning of it. This afforded some opportunity to reflect on her feelings of being left over the break and how, in this context, she set up a situation where she *so* desperately wanted the session with me that she ended up not getting it at all.

In these meetings, I learned more about the link of the symptom of screaming with the terror of separation in this mother and in her child. Sylvia's birth was followed by her mother becoming very depressed as she felt faced with the reality of the death of Sylvia's father. Perhaps as a defence against this, during Sylvia's early months it seemed that the mother and baby pair were enveloped in a cocoon, un-separated and focused around more or less constant breastfeeding. Later Mary was to describe Sylvia as "just wanting to get right inside me" in her liking for close proximity. At ten months Sylvia began to crawl, and with this ability to be physically separate, she began to scream. The experience of physical separation activated an immense amount of terror and panic in this child, which then became structured into their relationship and echoed terrors in her mother's own past. Sylvia refused to be weaned from the breast or eat other food, and only allowed this to happen after they arrived in the UK.

Over several sessions we were able to broach the subject of Sylvia's father's death. He was referred to as "Daddy B". Mary expressed her unhappiness that Sylvia referred to her boyfriend David as Daddy; to her he was just a friend. She was reminded of the loss of her own mother and had never called her stepmother Mum, just father's "wife". She wanted to protect Sylvia from echoes of her own experience; she spoke of not thinking about the loss of her fiancé B until Sylvia's birth when she just cried and cried. She and Sylvia were so close they always slept together and even now they did whilst David slept in the single bed. In another session Mary said that Sylvia had her own daddy (not David) and she had told her that he lived with the angels. I asked Sylvia where she thought her Daddy lived and she pointed to a house across the street. I said that she might be puzzled why he didn't come to visit; she came over to me and whispered that he had got ill and died. This verbalisation of her fantasy of the death of her father shocked her mother who thought she had no idea about his death. Despite this I think Sylvia's capacity to represent the death of her father must have reflected her mother's ability at some level to convey it as representable. Later in her analysis Sylvia indicated her interest in "Daddy" in her play, confused and conflicted though it was with her relationship with David.

Gradually a sense of safety with me allowed them to begin to show in subtle ways what was wrong between them. It could be summed up in this way: that both mother and child had enormous child-like needs and only one of them could be a child. This meant that there was tremendous competitiveness between them. I became aware of this as Mary related to me as a child towards the maternal adult in the room, whilst Sylvia wanted Mary to be the mother. Mary was not able to be; such was the enormity of her own need. Sometimes it was difficult to include Sylvia in the discourse of the sessions as she responded to her mother's need by taking herself off to a corner of the room leaving her mother to me to sort out.

With great effort they became more able to play together, although Mary struggled with a sense that it was a waste of time and found it hard to enjoy. In this somewhat safer environment Sylvia developed her imaginative capacity to pretend, which was sometimes based age appropriately on her identifications with her mother. Even so she often had to contend with her mother refusing a pretend cup of tea as Mary's more cruel, rejecting self was asserted. Mary's internal bully was turned inwards as she condemned her own incapacities but also she found it hard not to give in to the pull to treat her daughter in this depriving way. However, they were able to begin to negotiate aspects of their relationship that previously had been the centre of much difficulty and Sylvia became calmer and less distressed.

In the face of an increasing attachment to me, Mary's ambivalence became more evident, and she began to talk about a dilemma she had been presented with—the chance to work full time. The Easter break was approaching, and in the UK the last Sunday of March is Mother's day. As they were leaving at the end of the Friday session just before Mother's day, Sylvia picked up the paper daffodil she had made in the nursery for her mother. Mary gasped, and said to me that she was terribly sorry but she had forgotten to bring the Mother's day card for me that she had intended to. As this was the end of the session and they were going out of the door, we could not explore the meaning of this. She cancelled the next session and then it was Easter. She failed to return for the session after the Easter holidays and sent me a note that she was working full time and could not come to see me. I was now the one helplessly to experience loss; Mary had recreated and reversed her own history in her relationship with me. I was the "mother" to whom she was so attached, but I was to be left in this unpredictable capricious way as she had been as a young child.

## Sylvia in the nursery

Anna Freud (1979) described the task of nursery school as guiding the small child's first steps outside the familiar home surroundings; offering the first substitutes for parental care and authority; facilitating entry into a community of peers and furthering speech development and physical mastery, manual skills and intellectual curiosity. The Anna Freud Centre nursery also always regarded as essential the filling of gaps left for whatever reason in the parental care, irrespective of whether these omissions are in the area of physical nurture, affectionate support or mental stimulation (Wilson 1988; Zaphiriou 2000).

As Sylvia and Mary settled into parent-child work with me, Sylvia appeared to settle into the nursery very quickly and surprisingly stayed for the full day within a week of starting. She was apparently confident with staff and children and readily approached any adults but in a rather inappropriate manner. She arrived smiling and eager each morning, taking part in a wide variety of activities and building positive relationships. Although she could be excitable and occasionally argumentative, there was nothing in her behaviour at first that caused undue concern. However little things began to be noticed:

> It was observed that she sucked her index finger of her right hand while stroking the hair of one of the assistants. This happened repeatedly and also with the mother of another child who was in the nursery at story time.

Snuggling up to adults and fiddling with their hair as a means of comfort happened on a regular basis and soon the staff began to note that Sylvia seemed distressed over very minor incidents and needed a great deal of attention and comforting:

> She became frightened of a dead wasp, and when watching some worms in the garden, she panicked and later talked of worms in her mouth.

At this time Sylvia mentioned on two occasions that her mother "beat" her for screaming at home. There was a steady improvement for several weeks however, and Sylvia seemed to be learning to cope with frustrations without always dissolving into tears. Her mother told the teacher at this time that she had noticed "a big change" for the better in Sylvia since she started nursery.

There was a breakdown of the parent-child work when mother began full time work, and Sylvia was brought and collected by a child minder. We realised that it wasn't only that the Centre staff had been left in the lurch by the new regime, but this meant that Sylvia had to endure the virtual loss of her mother. Sylvia's behaviour changed dramatically. She again became tearful over minor incidents throughout the day. After two or three days her distress seemed to change to rage and it became very difficult to comfort or console her. The staff encouraged her to talk about whatever seemed the matter, to which she was sometimes able to respond, but at other times not. She would create situations where she would be rejected by another child, e.g. *deliberately playing with a favourite toy of another child and goading him about it.* This would provoke an outburst in the other child and Sylvia could then feel attacked and aggrieved. Her earlier capacity to negotiate situations with other children disappeared. The Centre began to witness the screaming that Mary had originally described. The tempers, rages and anguish were expressed through the most dreadfully loud and piercing screams. Everyone could hear them. They sounded as though Sylvia was being killed. These incidents would be interspersed with calmer happier moods when Sylvia was able to be consoled by an adult, or to work it through herself.

Mary made herself contactable only by phone and the teacher conveyed the concerns of the staff. We had the problem: of how to help this child in the face of the actual loss of her mother as an available parent. Although we were witnessing a reaction to events in the present, Sylvia was showing us the fragility of her internal world. It seemed she was unable to maintain a sense of the availability of her mother as a source of comfort and solace in her absence, a failure to establish object constancy (Anna Freud 1965). Sylvia's rage destroyed her internal sense of Mary as a potentially available object—whatever sense of object constancy she might have acquired seemed to have left her. The original separation following the start of crawling when she began the screaming had remained a traumatic marker in her internal equilibrium and was once again activated in the face of current experience.

We began to consider intensive individual treatment for Sylvia. We were concerned whether this was the right time for her to start an analysis, although it was felt that she was "crying out" for it. Should she be offered such intensive treatment in the face of the actual loss of the mother and could we re-engage the mother in joint parent-child work? We would at least need to raise the mother's concern about Sylvia's state of mind and help her think through her choices in relation to her child's needs. We decided to refer Sylvia for a full assessment for individual treatment because it seemed that there was good evidence that her internalisation of the difficulties in her relationship with her mother might best be worked with in that form, in addition to the work of the nursery.

Perhaps we were also motivated by a wish to make up for the gap in Sylvia's life, made manifest again by her mother's unavailability through work but indicative of a much deeper gap connected to the traumatic meanings of the loss. Psychoanalysis could provide Sylvia with the experience of a new developmental object (Hurry 1998) who could bear the onslaught of the scream, and would not be overwhelmed, dysregulate and abandon her in the face of her distress.

The developmental task of the regulation of affective states was already severely compromised and required the kind of developmental assistance that analytic work could make available.

I re-engaged Mary and reinforced the teacher's message that Sylvia was in severe distress following her return to work. This was met with surprise as at home Sylvia had become amenable, unprovocative, and altogether a different child. Mary was concerned about what was reported from the nursery but felt that she could not go back on her decision to work full time, as she would have to live off state benefits and Sylvia would also suffer as a consequence. The reality issues had to be recognised, but we felt that Mary's conflicts over her mothering, as well as her own needy self was a significant part of her decision. It seemed that if Sylvia's newfound good relationship with her mother was to be believed, it was being preserved at a cost: it felt too precarious for her to risk spoiling it. However, it seemed that she also felt safer in the nursery to show her distress perhaps in the hope of it being attended to.

Mary agreed to a diagnostic assessment for Sylvia and supported our decision to recommend intensive psychoanalytic treatment four times per week. She also agreed to support this process actively by coming to see me once a week to work with her parenting of Sylvia. Now with hindsight perhaps I can see some naiveté on my part; maybe I was taken in despite the evidence that Mary could not sustain close and intense contact and had already given me a taste of the repetition of her history in cutting off regular contact with me before.

## Second phase: nursery and analysis and parent work

Sylvia's analyst began meeting with her non-intensively a few weeks before the summer holidays. As the term drew to a close Sylvia was very pre-occupied with its ending and her analyst verbalised her fear about missing important people who disappeared. In the nursery the significance of the summer holidays was talked about and the teacher reassured Sylvia that she would be coming back, and that Sylvia would also return. I worked with Mary on our re-engagement and on the fact that she was planning to take Sylvia back to her home country over that summer break for the first time. This was clearly of enormous significance to her.

Sylvia did not return after the holidays, and Mary failed her appointment with me. On the phone she told the teacher that she had decided to move Sylvia to the nursery of the school she would attend when she was five years old. She gave no reason for this but agreed that she would bring Sylvia in to say goodbye. We were stunned; once again the staff at the Centre were put into a situation where we were to suffer unpredicted and unprepared-for loss, carrying the emotions which Mary had long ago experienced and repressed. Sylvia also was the victim of this, re-traumatised as her mother repeated her own history.

When Mary brought Sylvia in to say goodbye, I met with her and we talked about what was happening: the repetition of unprepared for loss. Mary was very confused between the part of herself that had felt abandoned by me over the break, and the part that wished to wipe me out so that she would not know her neediness. Initially, she was quite unable to see Sylvia's needs as separate from her own. She declared that the world was a dangerous jungle and the nursery was too soft and indulgent; another school would toughen her up. I took up her feelings towards me for leaving her during the weeks of the summer, that far from being soft she felt I had cruelly abandoned her to the too tough, dangerous jungle of the world. She conceded that she had felt bad and wanted to get rid of the feelings. The best way seemed not to return. She began to talk about Sylvia missing her analyst and the nursery staff and acknowledged that these attachments were also important to her. Perhaps she felt threatened by them, afraid she would lose Sylvia to this too-soft place. She agreed that Sylvia could return, but she had enrolled for a college course at the time she was due to see me and claimed she was unable to change it.

We were left in a difficult position of having Sylvia back in nursery and analysis, but without Mary's commitment to regular sessions to support the work. In fact, the failure of the home environment to hold and sustain Sylvia was repeatedly enacted. The arrangements Mary made for Sylvia's care outside nursery hours were capricious and unpredictable. There were frequent and unannounced changes of childminders and every time there was a change, Sylvia's distress was palpable. Mary's meetings with me were equally unpredictable, and I came to realise that I had to wait for her approaches to me, as my pursuit of her only made her run the other way. The distress and anger felt by the staff on Sylvia's behalf was strong, as we observed and experienced the re-traumatising of this little girl time and again.

Sylvia played out her predicament in her analytic sessions. For example, she changed places alternately with the baby doll, as baby or mother. The baby was put in the locker because she screamed and "Mummy"

Sylvia in a strict voice said "She's got to listen to me—Daddy (David) has gone to another country—you won't see him" The analyst wondered aloud if Daddy had gone because the baby was screaming, to which Sylvia said yes. The screaming-baby-Sylvia felt responsible for sending Daddy away, and perhaps not just this Daddy David but her birth daddy who had been killed before her birth.

At other times Sylvia would be literally screaming, bringing this part of her directly into the sessions. Her analyst wrote:

> In the room I mentioned her upset and angry feelings when we had to finish the session yesterday "before she was ready". Sylvia clung on to her anger for a long time, in a demonstrative way: talking to me angrily, saying I was not to touch her things when she made a "fire" to bake her dough. I said the fire was like her hot burning feelings. She responded by throwing the toys from her locker in the bin. I said she was worrying that I would not like her fire feelings and would throw her out. Sylvia replied, "You are not a nice mummy".

The analyst commented some weeks later that although Sylvia's distress was very obvious, her anger and provocation could be quite relentless. She speculated that this also drove her mother away and that there was some sort of mutual cruelty between a very guilty mum and a vengeful child.

## Mary's marriage

We learned of Mary's plans to marry David later in the autumn term, and they were married in November. Simultaneously one of the several changes of childminder occurred in the usual unplanned way. Sylvia's life was a roller-coaster of change that burdened her with the requirement to react to outside impingements with little space to experience a sense of self. There was very little sense of a holding environment (Winnicott 1960b), in her life outside the Centre, and the staff were constantly called upon to provide this for her. Her sense of guilt and responsibility for the bad things is evident in the following extract from the nursery file:

> I (the nursery assistant) called Sylvia to show her the bulbs we planted which had been dug up by the squirrels and asked her

if she knew who was digging them up. She said in a little guilty voice "Me". I said "No, it's the squirrels who think it's food and dig them up every night". After that she shouted "Naughty squirrels" her face deforming in a rage. Her anger seemed to be defused that way and unusually there were no arguments or rages during playtime. I said to her that the squirrels were hungry not naughty, and she started a game with playmates about "three little girls crying for food"

Here we can see how Sylvia was very troubled by a generalised sense of being the author of the bad things that happen, but when this was contradicted she switched to the enraged other who condemned the naughty squirrel/Sylvia. The "hunger" was not just for physical food but for emotional nurturance too. Her inner world was being formed by persecutory and guilt laden relationships. There was little room for concern, and even though the nursery staff were extremely attentive to her sensitivities, there was slow progress in enabling her to modify her internal representation of herself in relation to others.

Sylvia was challenged to deal with her mother's marriage to David. She wanted her mummy to herself; she wanted to be with the parental couple, she wanted David to herself. Babies took on a new meaning in her play as she was faced with the possibility at least in her fantasy that there would be new babies on the way. She was full of conflict and despair as she was both involved in the plans for the wedding and also faced being excluded as her parents were to go away on their honeymoon without her. In her analytic sessions her analyst was able to talk about these things, allowing Sylvia to use her as a containing, holding presence who could understand her pain. Sylvia fell asleep on her lap, a sure sign of confidence in her analyst, but also of her regressive baby needs in the face of the developmental demands which were beyond her emotional capacity.

In Mary's occasional sessions she struggled with the notions of soft and tough, conveying a fundamental feeling that the quest to understand was foreign, especially to understand her child and the child part of herself. Giving Sylvia the status of a child to be understood was tremendously conflictual because it challenged her own experience as a child who was not accorded such treatment. She told me that she had said to Sylvia that she did not want a Sylvia who cries but another one and would send her to her room until she stopped. Perhaps it was just too difficult for this mother who had survived such cumulative trauma (Khan 1963) to begin to abandon her tough, resilient exterior which presumably had protected her to some degree from complete despair; and yet it did become a conflict for her, as the forgotten mother's day card had indicated. Indeed, despite the indicators that Mary had dealt with the trauma of the war with dissociative defences, she struggled with the possibility of her own developing reflective process which would put her in touch with the psychic pain of traumatic loss.

Approaching the Christmas break we were concerned that there would be a repeat of the reaction to the separation over the summer, but this did not transpire. However, in the new term Mary threatened to remove Sylvia again, this time with some warning and concern for her. Sylvia's volatility and extremely controlling behaviour in the nursery did not endear her to the other children and although this was worked with, inevitably there were consequences. Sylvia was unhappy as none of the children would play with her. This led to a more productive communication with Mary as we were able to share our joint experience of the manifestations of Sylvia's disturbance—her low frustration tolerance, her bullying, her screaming tempers and the possibility of Mary acting out was prevented.

After a very difficult winter, Mary decided that she would leave work and spend more time with Sylvia. She was able to do this from a practical point of view because she could now rely upon her husband's financial care. Mary also re-engaged with me, and for a short time was able, with her husband David, to explore their difficulties in parenting this very troubled child in regular weekly sessions. I felt that I was seen as presenting a too soft approach in my search to help them understand Sylvia's predicament, and that this played into a struggle they were having as a couple, in which Mary took the "too soft part" and David the "tough" one. The propensity to split and exploit the un-integrated fragmented aspects of the self in this complicated family was very difficult to work with, and ultimately the work broke down although in a way which was not so completely unforeseen as before.

David was offered a placement of several months' duration abroad with his firm. The question then was that if he were to take it, would Mary and Sylvia accompany him. Sylvia was due to move from the nursery to the local school as she was now approaching five years old, but plans had been put in place for her analysis to continue. In the event the family did go abroad, and on their return did not respond to any of our attempts to re-engage them. Once again an ending was made final, like a killing cut that could not be healed.

## Discussion

The central theme in this case was the catastrophic impact of separation and loss in the context of violent trauma. The original loss in Mary's history of her mother at aged three had its own impact, evidenced in her memories of looking after her siblings in identification with her lost mother. We do not know what becoming a mother might have evoked in Mary if there had not been the intervening trauma of the losses of her soon-to-be husband, her father, brother and sister in the war. However, by the time Sylvia was born in exile, this mother was in an overwhelmed state where separation, even the normal developmental separation of her baby's crawling, was felt to be catastrophic. Sylvia's ordinary maturational achievements were coloured by the powerful significance of separation and loss. Sylvia's screaming reflected the unprocessed trauma felt by her mother and now disowned and projected into her baby. The unconscious meaning of the scream was shaped by the killing and contributed to the sense of cruelty and danger that so suffused the feelings generated in everyone who heard it.

We can also think of the symptom of screaming developmentally in terms of Sylvia's unprocessed and unregulated affects. At that critical time in her infancy, unmodified negative affects would have had a profound and permanent effect upon her developing brain (Perry et al. 1995). Neuronal pathways, thus privileged, left her vulnerable to the repetition of saturating negative affect when events re-evoked the same panic. Separation felt to be catastrophic necessitated her screaming.

In his paper "Dead Mother Dead Child" (1999), Christopher Bollas writes about the traumatising event that arrives from the outside and impacts on the members of a family so that they mutate: the changes wrought are of such a quality that the self of the traumatised person can feel itself to be a mutant; no longer human.

> The traumatised person has experienced a process of continuous radical shifting from his idiom to something else and his self is derived from an event and its structure.
>
> (pp. 100–101)

One of the striking features of Mary's engagement with the Anna Freud Centre and me was the way in which she manufactured events around each re-presentation of loss especially the termly breaks. She thus replayed her evocation of her original trauma, the loss of her mother at three years, given new meaning by the traumatic losses of her family members in the war. The essential ingredients of these events were that they were unexpected and were to be final, a cutting off that felt like and were, a killing, and they were to be the way in which she was to be known. Indeed, this family is remembered at the Centre for two things in particular: Sylvia's screaming so that one thought she was being killed, and Mary's peremptory cutting off treatment virtually without a trace. They are known by the events created to re-conjure the past. In Bollas's terms perhaps the self of the mother (traumatised and then re-traumatised) became defined for her in this way: the creator of events that carried the impact and the meaning of the original trauma. She became the author of her own re-traumatisation and because she was now a mother, involved her child, as representative of her child self in the continuous re-enactments.

### Implications for treatment

With the benefit of hindsight what can we glean and learn about the decision to take this little girl into intensive treatment? There is no doubt in my mind that we were motivated by the extremely powerful feelings Sylvia aroused in the staff. The extent and expression of her psychic pain in the context of her mother's repeated abandonments, seemingly often on a weekly if not daily basis as one new childminder replaced another without warning, required a response to intervene. This felt compelling. Perhaps the sense of compulsion was a warning to heed, but the decision was not taken lightly. It was thoroughly discussed before being referred to the diagnostic service for an assessment for treatment.

In addition, despite the enactments, Mary made good contact with me; she engaged me not just with the tragedy of her story but also with her genuine if inconsistent struggles to understand the predicament in which she found herself.

Ultimately what carried the decision was that at three years old, this child's internal self-structure was already marked by the meaning that separation was a disaster: a threat or experience of psychic death that manifested in the scream. It seemed that only intensive treatment could begin to tackle this. At three a child's self-structure is still in the process of formation, and intensive intervention stands a good chance of making an impact. We cannot say that it did not. Certainly Sylvia used her analyst to process her volatile affects. However, in this treatment not only did the external events of Sylvia's home life impinge on the analytic endeavour, but her psychoanalyst also felt that the continuous events in the nursery around Sylvia's disruptive behaviour interfered with her focus on this child's internal world and her co-construction of meaning out of her experiences. It seems that perhaps in identification with the maternal object, Sylvia already had a well-developed propensity to create catastrophic events through which she filtered her relation to the world.

To take any child into analytic treatment is a huge commitment for all concerned. Nothing can be guaranteed at the outset and it is very difficult to predict what a particular child will do internally with the opportunity. The most pessimistic view of this analysis was that we colluded with Mary in the evocation of her past traumas repeated with her daughter by being unable to hold the frame and prevent the repetition. Sylvia was left without any preparation for the ending of her analysis and so her analyst could be added to the list of people whom she had lost. A more optimistic view would be that the year of psychoanalytic treatment with a new developmental object contributed to the building up of an internal world where softness could be integrated with toughness as psychic reality could be broached and not avoided, and where there could be some attempt to withstand the constant draw to enactment through the repetitive creation of catastrophic events.

## References

Bollas, C. (1999). Dead mother, dead child. In *The Dead Mother: The Work of André Green*, ed. G. Kohon. London: Routledge, pp. 87–108.

Fraiberg, S., Adelson, E. and Shapiro, V. (1975). Ghosts in the nursery: a psychoanalytic approach to the problem of impaired infant-mother relationships. *Journal of the American Academy of Child Psychiatry*, 14: 387–422.

Freud, A. (1965). *Normality and Pathology in Childhood*. London: Hogarth Press.

Freud, A. (1979). The nursery school from the psychoanalytic point of view. In *Psychoanalytic Psychology of Normal Development*. London: Hogarth Press, 1982.

Freud, S. (1920). Beyond the pleasure principle. *S.E.*, 18: 1–64.
Green, A. (1983). The dead mother. In *On Private Madness*. London: Hogarth Press, 1986, pp. 142–173.
Hurry, A. (1998). *Psychoanalysis and Developmental Therapy*. London; Karnac Books.
Khan, M. R. (1963). The concept of cumulative trauma. *Psychoanal. St. Child*, 18: 286–306.
Perry, B. D. Pollard, R., Blakely, R., Baher, W. and Vigilante, D. (1995). Childhood trauma, the neurobiology of adaptation, and user-dependent development of the brain, how 'states' become 'traits'. *Infant Ment. Health J.*, 16: 271–291.
Wilson, P. (1988). Therapeutic intervention through the nursery school. *Bull. Anna Freud Centre*, 11: 307–316.
Winnicott, D. W. (1952). Psychosis and childcare. In *Collected Papers: Through Paediatrics to Psychoanalysis*. London: Hogarth and the Institute of Psychoanalysis, 1958, pp. 219–228.
Winnicott, D. W. (1960a). Ego distortion in terms of the true and false self. In *Maturational Processes and the Facilitating Environment*. London: Hogarth Press, 1965, pp. 140–152.
Winnicott, D. W. (1960b). The theory of the parent infant relationship. In *Maturational Processes and the Facilitating Environment*. London: Hogarth Press, 1965, pp. 37–55.
Zaphiriou, M. (2000). Preventive work in a toddler group and nursery. *J. Child Psychother.*, 26: 209–233.

# 5

# THE OEDIPAL EXPERIENCE
## Effects on development of an absent father[1]

## Marion Burgner

Freud's unequivocal stand on the importance of the Oedipus complex in the genesis of the transference neuroses is well known to all of us, though it is perhaps of interest that he did not actually use the term 'Oedipus complex' until 1910; before that, he had, of course, written widely about the topic, sometimes referring to it as the 'nuclear complex', and as early as 1897, in a letter to Fliess, he wrote:

> One single thought of general value has been revealed to me. I have found, in my own case too, falling in love with the mother and jealousy of the father, and I now regard it as a universal event of early childhood....
>
> (Freud 1897, p. 265)

Deepening analytic knowledge of development in the first three years of life as well as a difference in emphasis, perhaps even a change, in the content of our patients' disturbances have made us increasingly aware of the contribution of pre-oedipal experiences to child and adult psychopathology. Many analysts have in recent years questioned a number of issues classically connected with the Oedipus complex, and sometimes the centrality of the complex itself. I too found myself faced with a number of important questions while working in a study group[2] at the Hampstead Clinic. This group was set up to examine the effects of the loss of the father through parental separation or divorce in the first five years of life;

none of the children studied came from families where the father was the remaining parent and the mother was absent. We were not studying children from one-parent families, rather those children whose fathers had left, or been largely absent from, the home in the children's early years. The children studied (13 in all) were either in psychoanalytic treatment, assessed diagnostically or attending the Nursery School, which is run on psychoanalytically informed lines. The data in this paper, except when otherwise stated, were obtained from analytic treatment. In the first part of this paper, before proceeding to a discussion of adult disturbance, I should like to present some of the findings of this study group. Essentially, therefore, I am discussing analytic patients and what happened in their analyses; I am not considering the increasing number of individuals who grow up in the community with, for whatever reason, only one parent.

It is important to note that initially I felt we were perhaps faced with the ubiquitousness of the Oedipus complex, and I wondered whether there was anything new to say. Lebovici (1982) has written how:

> today's psychoanalysts have to diagnose and treat concrete cases of the oedipal situation in their everyday practice, and also of the theory they thereby evolve concerning a too frequently erroneous extension of a reference which, while inherent in the mental life of man and his culture, at the same time generates a resistance to psycho-analysis through the very monotony of its generalizations.
>
> (p. 202)

# Childhood

### *The pattern of oedipal development*

In defining what the constituents were of a so-called normal Oedipus complex, we found that our group of children continually drew our attention to the prohibition against incest, a taboo which becomes alarmingly tenuous for boys whose fathers are absent and who are left alone, or largely alone, with their mothers. We also found relevant a formulation by Laplanche and Pontalis (1973), with its emphasis on what happens at an unconscious level within and between the parents and is then internalized by the child, a series of psychic events which is at best blurred for the child living with one parent. They write:

> It should be pointed out that in concentrating on the triangular relationship itself, we are led to assign an essential role in the constitution of a given Oedipus complex to the other poles of this relationship—the unconscious desires of both parents, seduction, and the relations between the parents—as well as to the subject and his instincts. It is the different types of relation between the three points of the triangle which—at least as much as any particular parental image—are destined to be internalized and to survive in the structure of the personality.
>
> (p. 286)

Loewald (1979) too, in his discussion of parricide, stresses the lack of distinction between reality and fantasy in the individual's psychic life:

> Responsibility to oneself in the sense of being responsive to one's urgings... involves facing and bearing the guilt for those acts we consider criminal. Prototypical, in oedipal context, are parricide and incest. From the standpoint of psychic reality it matters little if these acts are in objective reality merely fantasies or symbolic acts.
>
> (p. 761)

Thus, these children were faced in their lives with the symbolic effects of parricide and incest: an absent father and an available mother.

In the children studied, we found a persistence of modes of behaviour from earlier phases, with a corresponding lack of dominance at the phallic oedipal phase and beyond. Analytic material or observed behaviour which appeared to carry the stamp of oedipal, triangular conflicts in fact contained major elements from pre-oedipal developmental phases: such elements were characterized by primitive fears of object loss and an anxiety-driven wish for closeness. It seemed that it was the maturational drive pressures as well as initially perhaps our own analytic set that lent to the child a mere appearance of dominance at the oedipal level. In these children, their tie to the original object remained relatively unchanged, and it was this adhesiveness that, in part, contributed both to the lack of dominance at each phase and to the distorted oedipal phase.

Stress within the family does not begin at the point of parental separation, and the relationship between the parents is inevitably affected long before this happens. It is ongoing and cumulative and can result in the child's increased pre-oedipal needs and the mother's decreased capacity to meet them. Such capacity may be affected by the mother responding to the separation as a narcissistic injury with accompanying depressive affect. This interaction sets the scene for a persistence of pre-oedipal needs and for a persistence of an internal object relationship based primarily on these needs, which colour later developmental phases.

John[3] was three and a half years old when his father left, and nine and a half when he began analysis. John's pre-oedipal longings to have exclusive possession of mother were exacerbated when he was nearly two years old and his sister (who became mother's favourite child) was born. Following the sister's birth, the marriage deteriorated and mother became less available to John to whom she related impatiently, rejecting him as she herself felt rejected by her husband. A year later father left the family home and mother took refuge in a new relationship, the first of many. It emerged in the analysis that John blamed himself for his pre-oedipal wish to have mother to himself and that he viewed father's departure as punishment for his greedy longing and as confirmation of the omnipotence of his wishes to be alone with mother. His need to please and impress mother, as an insurance against losing her later, coloured his subsequent development.

We were initially led to assume that interactions between the child, the mother and the interchangeably present or absent father were oedipal in content, whereas in fact they were pre-oedipal in terms of the dyadic emphasis between child and mother. We thus have to emphasize the importance and inevitability of triadic interaction long before such interaction carries an actual oedipal stamp. 'Triangulation', to use Lebovici's (1982) word, should not be confused with the Oedipus complex proper. It appeared from our material that only when the mother could make a reasonably lasting relationship with a man other than the father was the child able to experience a triangular oedipal relationship.

Just as we were struck by the incidence of pseudo-oedipal behaviour, we became similarly aware of the pseudo-latency in the children studied. For instance, when John started analysis in his tenth year, it was noted that he still had to negotiate a distorted oedipal situation and that the outcome would probably also show a similar

## The oedipal experience

distortion; his attempts to escape into latency would therefore lack the hallmark of developmental progress and would represent an attempt at defensive, non-integrated adaptation which would inevitably prove maladaptive.

It could well be that the inconsistencies and dangers in negotiating the oedipal phase with its inherent anxieties over incest and parricide, and in relinquishing the exclusiveness of the dyadic, pre-oedipal relationship with a mother who is also the one remaining constant object, proves too much for these children; thus, they seem to carry with them the exaggerated ambivalent investment of the primary object into latency, adolescence and even into adulthood.

After the separation from the father, these children live in constant dread of the loss of the remaining object, the mother. Such feelings were well expressed by a four-year-old girl, Mary. At the diagnostic assessment she was withdrawn and inhibited but she was more able to talk about her real concerns in a follow-up interview a year later. Mary viewed her real worries as connected with mother getting upset when she and her younger brother were naughty and then threatening to abandon them; according to the child, her mother would often threaten to leave them alone in the house or to place them in a children's home.

The degree of persistence we have noted in these children—in their problems over giving up earlier patterns of drive expression and over the continuing immaturity of the level of relating to their primary object, the mother—is also reflected in other areas of their personality. Prior to treatment, we found that cognitive ego functioning was sometimes interfered with. It was as if they could not allow themselves to use their normal curiosity to gather information about their bodies, their parents, the physical world and—eventually—to participate in formal learning at school, but rather that they felt compelled to restrict their curiosity overall; by circumscribing their understanding and knowledge, they felt they made themselves less vulnerable to knowing about their real and dangerous predicament; they had kept it a secret from themselves. In fact, in the children treated, cognitive ego functions showed improvement well before other areas of the personality.

### Superego structuralization

In company with many psychoanalysts, we did not accept the classical concept that superego structuralization and introjection only occur after the resolution of the oedipal conflict. In normal development, after all, we see an organization of pre-oedipal and oedipal elements into a superego structure around the oedipal phase, while final structuralization has to wait on adolescence and its outcome. While the children investigated showed—at best—a distorted oedipal phase, the internalization of parental introjects seemed to proceed both at pre-oedipal and oedipal levels without a coherent oedipal organization and often resulted in an early, over-strict superego formation and damaged narcissistic and sexual identifications.

Omnipotent thinking was prevalent, and these children saw themselves as responsible for the parental separation, and therefore as capable of magically reuniting them. Similarly, they expected their analysts to work such magic for them and responded with enraged disappointment at the inevitable failures. If the father leaves at a time when the child normally resorts to omnipotent thinking, anxiety about the power of his wishes may mobilize fears of retaliation. In turn, this may result in premature superego structuralization and in a harsh response to any type of hostile or negative feeling; the benign quality of the superego remains undeveloped. Often, overt aggression is turned against the self.

Sometimes the child makes use of fantasied objects (idealized or punitive) to ward off the pain of the reality situation and to preserve the integrity of the self. John, for example, dealt with his pain and disillusionment in his real parents by introjecting idealized parents, thereby sustaining himself with a strong moral code. His rigid concept of right and wrong also helped him to harness his greedy longings for exclusiveness, which he feared would be punished by further loss. It was only after analytic work was accomplished on the de-idealization of father that John was able to experience the more benign aspects of his superego and enjoy work and play with less destructive self-criticism.

## Identification and sexual identification

These children had problems over establishing a masculine or feminine identity. Fears of incest in the boys and lack of an oedipal father for the girls also hindered sexual identifications. Inevitably, the boys lacked a constant male model as an object for identification, with some concomitant confusion over the phallic, castrating qualities of the mother. Just as inevitably, the girls' doubts and conflicts over the mother's femininity (as distinct from the fantasies they had about her underlying sadism to the father) made her a conflictual identificatory model and enhanced their bisexual problems. It was significant that in all the girls the loss of the father was experienced as confirmation of their inadequate bodies. Their pervasively low self-esteem and dissatisfaction were important factors in their longing for a complete body, a complete family.

Since none of the children studied had yet reached adolescence, we could not with certainty predict the outcome of their sexual identifications. However, a study made some years ago by the Centre for the Study of Adolescence of 90 adolescents who approached the Brent Consultation Centre[4] for help during a three-year period showed that the extent and quality of disturbance was greater the earlier the age when the loss of the father occurred. Compared with their counterparts from two-parent families, those adolescents showed a greater tendency towards depression, certain fundamental difficulties in forming stable and durable relationships, a tendency to leave school earlier and a tendency to take jobs below their capacity.[5]

## Aims and techniques of treatment

One of the most interesting facets of our study was the discussion on relevant therapeutic techniques with these children. We eventually understood that these children had lived through a cumulative experience which their internal world was not yet structured enough to deal with and which, when internalized, produced a consequent disharmony in their inner self-object relationships as well as an imbalance between the mental structures. These children, it emerged, needed a different emphasis in our clinical approach from that used for children with internalized neurotic conflicts. We considered that the initial therapeutic emphasis should be directed towards the fostering of reality testing, to differentiate carefully with the child between fantasy and reality and between the result of projections as opposed to unalterable reality situations.

For most of these vulnerable children danger was lodged in their ongoing and painful experience of being trapped in a situation which they could not alter and which they often felt they compounded—whether they were caught in the crossfire of parental quarrels and violence or in mother's angry, depressive response to the father's departure and to his intermittent appearances and disappearances. For John, it became clear early on that his daily life, in and out of the analysis, was dominated by his confusion over external unpredictabilities. He saw himself as helpless, a victim of external disasters, and he blamed his parents, his analyst, his teachers and anyone else to hand for his inability to take responsibility for himself. Since these children often do not enter treatment because of internalized neurotic conflict but because of their continuing maladaptive responses to disharmonies between the internal and external world, analysis first has to demonstrate to the child his growing, adaptive capacity to deal with these external difficulties, an inner capacity which was not available to him at the time of the original, cumulative trauma.

It also seems that with these children the importance of the analyst as a real person should not be minimized. In part, the analyst's importance lies in his or her role as a safe, predictable object who does not act in the same crazy fashion as the parents. As Anna Freud (1965) has written:

> all individuals, as they develop and mature, have a hunger for new experience which is as strong as the urge to repeat... The child who enters analysis sees in the analyst a new object and treats him as such, so far as he has a healthy part to his personality. He uses the analyst for repetition, i.e. transference, as far as his neurosis or other disturbance comes into question.
>
> (p. 38)

## Adulthood

Alerted then to the complexities and snares of quasi-oedipal and post-oedipal problems in children who lacked a consistent, triangular oedipal experience and who had to rely upon fantasy configurations, I turned to a consideration of adult patients who had had similar experiences in their childhood. Did they inevitably carry into their adult lives the distortions we had become aware of in our child patients? I also had in mind the passage in 'King Oedipus' where the horror of the incestuous union is visited upon the children of Oedipus and Jocasta. After Jocasta's suicide by hanging and Oedipus blinding of himself with her golden brooches, the unseeing King addresses his sobbing daughters:

> I think of your sorrowful life in the days to come, when you must face the world: the holy days, High days and days of state, joyless

# The oedipal experience

for you, returning sadly home while others play. And when you look for marriage, will there be men, Will there be one man brave enough to outface the scandal that will cling to all my children and children's children?.

(Sophocles 1947, pp. 71–72)

The ethic of the Old Testament, the relentlessness of Greek tragedy and the repetition compulsion and determinism of Freud are all contained in this one extract from 'King Oedipus', and I wondered to what extent the uneasy balance between early fantasy and reality manifested itself in the adult lives of analytic patients with such childhood experiences of separated parents.

In our work as child analysts, we are aware of the developmental importance of the oedipal process as the organizing phase of pre-oedipal experiences and relationships into the triangular oedipal constellation. We assume that without, at best, a partial negotiation and experience of this phase, the constant necessary reorganization of relationships in later childhood, adolescence and adulthood may be distorted. As adult analysts we frequently work with patients where the negotiation of the Oedipus complex has plainly gone awry and we will reconstruct and interpret both the pre-oedipal and oedipal elements in the transference. But what of those patients whose oedipal development has been severely affected—that is if the triangular relationship has happened at all—due to the loss or absence of a father and the simultaneous psychic experience of a potentially dangerous mother in the early years of childhood? Is it possible for such patients to experience analysis as a facilitating and adequate working-over of the original painful and perhaps totally depriving situation or does a narcissistic deficit persist which is reflected in their adult object relationships? With these questions in mind, I should like to present two brief case studies.

## First case illustration

Mrs. A started analysis in her late thirties, protesting that she had no memories of her father who had died when she was seven, on their return to this country; prior to his death, he had been away on military service for much of her early childhood; however, she was still miserably mourning her mother who had died 12 years earlier, shortly after the birth of Mrs. A's first child. Mrs. A's mother was the daughter of an undertaker and, as a child, would—she recounted to Mrs. A—climb into the coffins in the workshop and pretend she was dead. Mrs. A entered analysis with a history of severe incapacitating depression, suicide attempts and a marriage that had been replete for the past 16 years with a sado-masochistic interaction of violent physical and verbal fights; there had been no sexual relationship with her husband for the past three years and she had been frigid throughout the marriage.

Mrs. A's analysis was characterized from the first week by a paradoxical transference—she longed for me to be the caring, holding mother and she was also terrified that I would criticize her, condemn her for her internal badness, discard her, 'put her away', just as mother had when she was sent to boarding school at the age of four. Her pervasive anxieties about abandonment found early expression in a suicide gesture which mirrored her feelings about my abandoning her over the weekend, her dispatch to boarding school, and mother's continuous depressive withdrawal from her, as seemed likely from babyhood onwards; father's absences and eventual death were not relevant in this part of the analysis. Her despairing search for a caring mother prompted Mrs. A into countless, exciting, apparently seductive approaches to myself, male professional contacts, her male doctor and so on, and yet none of these was essentially oedipal and she was relentlessly compelled to seek a caring, maternal closeness and ultimately to destroy it: the cycle seemed to consist of idealization of the object, realization of fallibility, disappointment, pain, rage, attempted destruction of the self or the object, an attack which came together in the suicidal attacks on the internal self/object. In the transference, I was not only the dangerous 'addictive' mother who would keep her forever (just like Woody Allen's analyst and Mrs. A's weeping mother who had kept her daughter sleeping in the parental bedroom from the time the father died until she was 19) but also the longed-for mother, 'the first person' she had ever trusted. Holiday breaks were a torment for Mrs. A, but so were sequences of analytic time since they inevitably led to the next break.

The view Mrs. A had of herself fluctuated enormously, though there were times in her analysis when heightened self-esteem was reflected in her improved appearance and acknowledged good feelings about the self. Some years before her analysis began, she had a gynaecological operation which she experienced as an 'assault'; menstruation was felt in the beginning phase of treatment as a crab crawling within and eating the inside of her body and her children were often viewed as inevitably damaged issue emerging from her damaged body. In her first analytic session she talked of her constant fears during her older daughter's first year that she would die; furthermore, her younger child's referral for analysis highlighted her feeling of transmitted damage. The engulfing menstrual pain was understood in the course of her analysis as linked with the murderous rage which frequently threatened and engulfed her. Our work also uncovered a repressed memory at the base of her menstrual pain, a pain which disappeared during the analysis. Mrs. A claimed that she had lived without sex for so long and was so terrified of what it implied that she now could not contemplate a sexual relationship. As on previous occasions, her associative comments were to her operation, the pain, the gaping wound, the horror of the hospital situation. She was, I suggested, equating sexual experience, a potentially pleasurable experience between herself and another person, as a rape, an assault—a situation she tried so often to re-enact with me. She spent the next two sessions trying not to tell me of a memory she had just recalled; of attending a birthday party as a little girl in India and fondling a dog; next day the dog became rabid and she had to have 14 days of painful daily injections against rabies, administered by a fat doctor who grabbed her by the skin of her belly and injected her in her abdomen. Clearly, in the transference, I was the most recent in the long line of attacking professionals she had so far encountered. You will recall that in the children studied sexual identifications also seemed to be adversely affected.

Mrs. A's material, in and out of the transference, was saturated with an intense, continuous sado-masochistic stance, and I think it is true to say that all her relationships carried this stamp. Underlying the sado-masochistic interactions, we could eventually reach the misery and poverty of the rejected, denigrated self. In a week after some six months of analysis, when I had been working hard but somewhat ineffectively on her angry despair and her excited victimization, she came to a session depressed but more accessible. Following yet another complaint about a pressurizing situation from a business associate, I again professed myself puzzled at her continuing need to experience herself at the centre of demanding, often sadistic objects, an experience that she desperately and continually tried to replicate with me. I suggested that, paradoxically, the pain of these situations gave her some sort of pleasurable, reassuring return that became a substitute for other sorts of close relationships. Mrs. A's response was: 'You see, I know it there, it's like being at home'. This led to our looking at her wish for the familiar, her fear of the unknown. Similarly, I suggested that her incessant, unremitting work pattern was painfully pleasing, protecting her from the possibility of any real pleasure. When later I tried to pursue this in terms of her experiences as a child, Mrs. A began crying pitiably, saying it was 'bad' for her to remember. She could not face remembering mother's rejection of her when she was sent to boarding school at the age of four. And she recalled that later mother frequently quarrelled with her older daughter and sometimes beat her, while she withdrew from Mrs. A in a more subtle sado-masochistic way. Mrs. A concluded that her mother had been 'almost mad' at times.

But her real mother had also, she felt, destroyed her relationship with father twice over: first when at the age of four she was sent away to boarding school after mother had an abortion (a memory that took some time to surface), and again when mother had, in Mrs. A's fantasy, killed father when she was seven. Her father's death amplified her earlier experiences of loss when father was frequently away and when she herself was dispatched to boarding school. Her amnesia about father seemed connected both with these losses and with the horror of being left with mother after his death, and thus it took over a year for her to recall him as an active, military man who commanded a fort, killed a scorpion and caught fireflies for her at the Taj Mahal and kept them for her in his pocket. She had a dream, calm and tender in tone, in which she—a small girl—sat looking out of the window while father painted nearby. But still the emphasis remained in the analysis on father's benign care of her. When Mrs. A was seven the family moved to England and father immediately became ill and died. Mrs. A claimed: 'Mother took all my feelings away', all her good memories and fantasies of father, and left her with the burden of mother's continuing depression, frequent sadistic attacks and the weekly obligatory visit to father's grave.

However, as we worked on the essentially pre-oedipal nature of her feelings for father, Mrs. A suddenly started an affair with a married man, an affair which gave her a lot of excitement and pleasure and allowed her to become orgastic for the first time in 16 years. At this point, the analytic material became more markedly oedipal: both in the transference and outside with her older sister, she experienced us as dangerous rivals who would destroy this relationship. Her resistance, always a hallmark of the analysis, became more entrenched and she precipitately broke off treatment from one day to the next. She did not respond to my efforts to bring her back into the analysis.

In retrospect, it seemed to me that, if she was to make a bid for the incestuous, oedipal father, it was a fight to the death in the transference between her and me, the dangerous mother; one of us had to die—either she would take another over-dose, or she had to kill me off by totally leaving me. The incestuous experience had assumed for her a reality of its own. Further, she could not tolerate the experience in the transference of having to acknowledge affectively the pain of remembering and knowing about her lost father, who had barely, if at all, become a real and consistent oedipal object for her.

## Second case illustration

Mr. B came into analysis at the age of 22, with the diagnosis of a severe character disorder with pronounced borderline and narcissistic features; there was sometimes a failure adequately to distinguish between reality and fantasy and his self-image vacillated between that of a malformed, unmasculine, faecal person and an omnipotent, brilliantly creative artist. He was a sculptor who particularly enjoyed handling and fashioning clay. At the beginning of his analysis, he described an aspect of his work that gave him much pleasure; it was to have in front of him an enormous block of wet clay, to press the whole of the posterior part of his naked body into the clay so as to leave a body outline; he would then embellish the imprint, giving it carefully fashioned limbs. Mr. B was born with a club-foot and was hospitalized for some months in his fifth year for surgical and orthopaedic treatment; he still walked with a slight limp. His body image, as portrayed in his sculpture, had a hermaphroditic quality and his genitalia were left completely ambiguous. Thus, his greatest vulnerability was in the area of his narcissistic feelings about his body and the self. A focus of the transference was his wish that I sit by him, love him, make him whole—that is, completely refashion his twisted, mis-shapen body. In the maternal transference, he was asking me whether I could accept his body (which in reality was only slightly malformed) or whether I would, like his mother, deny the existence of any damage. At the beginning of treatment, he suffered both from premature ejaculation and a failure to ejaculate at all. Again, we see the distortion in sexual identification.

Mr. B knew that his father had died when he was three years old but was unable to understand why so few of father's books and possessions remained in his mother's flat. He had no conscious memories of father but asserted in his first session that he had seen his father's ghost shortly after his death. Later, he did recapture some memories of being together with father, and we were also able to make certain reconstructions. Mr. B viewed his childhood relationship with his mother as idyllic for both of them and it was a painful experience for him as the analysis slowly began to uncover the flaws—for instance, his constant fear as he grew up that mother would find an alternative partner and abandon him, his anger with her for not giving him the special bodily care he wanted and for giving him a deformed body, her occasional eruptive rage towards him and, perhaps most importantly, her withdrawal and unavailability during her periods of depression. Mr. B idealized his father and maintained a paternal image that was benign and approving; punitive aspects of this image and his rage towards his father were denied. He quite consistently selected older men, usually from among his school and university teachers, as substitute paternal figures. He was not primarily homosexual in his orientation but, quite despairingly at times, tried to fashion these men into admired, idealized male objects. Inevitably, they were viewed by Mr. B as punitive and critical and he would pre-empt the escalating situation by abandoning them. The paternal introject was thus also hostile and rejecting and became crystallized into an archaic superego structure. An important internal object relationship, as it emerged, was of the enraged, yet confused small boy interacting with the disappointing, rejecting father. Relationships—with sexual partners, friends, and in the transference—were intolerable for him unless he could maintain an illusion of a two-person relationship; otherwise, the threat of exclusion, rejection and denigration became only too real for him.

In his first session, Mr. B clearly indicated that he wished me to share the couch with him; I understood this as expressing a wish for closeness and control, and it was a forerunner of variously expressed wishes for a unique one-to-one relationship. Mr. B quickly moved into an intense transference relationship: primarily, I represented the mother who would be both maternal and sexual to him; eventually too I represented the father who humiliated and disappointed him; sometimes too I was an undifferentiated father/mother. As the mother, he wished me to nurture and cherish him and also to gratify his infantile fantasies, particularly his scopophilic impulses. To protect himself—and me—from his infantile rage, he came to sessions late, was broodingly silent and between sessions and at weekends he would 'block off' (his words) myself and the analysis. At one point, there was a distinct ego regression; Mr. B became unable to look after his own body and he became dirty and smelly, wanting me to take over his entire bodily care. His disappointment and rage with me for not being the desperately sought-after masculine father with whom he could merge and identify also came under frequent scrutiny. He would, for instance, play with his open penknife as he lay on the couch, assuming that I was as frightened as he was of his own aggression.

It was not until the closing weeks of his analysis that mother could reveal to him that in fact his parents had never married and that his father had had another family, and thus had in reality not spent a great deal of the first three years of the patient's life with him. This knowledge, which hardly came as a surprise to either of us, seemed to facilitate further consolidation of the self as separate from the devouring mother and the idealized dead father.

Five years later Mr. B telephoned for an appointment. He was now 30 and married for the past year to a fellow student with whom he had established a relationship while in analysis. He felt he had to come back to see me, and he stipulated no more than six sessions, because he and his wife wanted to have a child. He was still uncertain about how he viewed himself (both his body and his self) and he did not know how to come to terms with further rationed pieces of information mother would occasionally give him about his father—for example, that after his birth, father had divorced his wife and did not marry the patient's mother but another woman by whom he had a child. His awareness of rejection by father was thus painfully experienced for the third time in his life. In our brief contact, it became clear that he was terrified that—like father—he would die in his thirties. More importantly, however, and hence his refusal to commit himself to more sustained and much needed further treatment, he still felt tied to mother and this despite his own relatively satisfying relationship with his wife. Thus, he was angrily confused and bewildered—his mother, he felt, told him half-truths about father and he could neither mourn him nor comfortably become a father in his own right; sometimes he still felt he had no choice but to take father's place in relation to his abandoned mother—for instance, he had stayed with mother for two days in order to do some decorating for her, and he had experienced his painting for her and her cooking for and care of him as an intimate erotic experience; and there was continuing confusion despite the partial success of his analysis—was he her regressed small child, her incestuous son still experiencing the original distorted oedipal fantasies or her grown-up son struggling to become a husband and father with his own adult partner?

## Conclusion

It is perhaps not purely a coincidence that both these patients took a certain constructive amount from their analyses—Mrs. A divorced her husband, set up her own small business, tentatively began to make contact with men and was, when she stopped coming to analysis, no longer immobilized by her manipulative and angry depressions; Mr. B maintained his relationship with a young woman and later married her and began a potentially successful career of teaching and making sculpture. But neither of them could pursue the analytic work further at an important point in treatment when incestuous oedipal material was emerging more distinctly and was available to be worked on centrally in the transference. It seems possible that patients who come from families where the father has been intermittently absent in childhood are capable through analysis of reaching a certain level—they are helped to make relationships, albeit with some pre-oedipal dominance, and they are often able to function well in their professional and social lives. It will be recalled that there was a similar pattern in our child cases. But there tends to be a protraction of the original narcissistic interference both in their self-investment and in their sexual identity; they are adhesively and ambivalently tied to the remaining primary object, and they seem to maintain a certain hopelessness about their adult capacities as partners and parents. A dimension of experience has been denied to them or distorted for them in childhood and, while analysis can go some way to offering them understanding of this deprivation, it cannot—predictably enough—make good the original damage. It was not until we had completed the child study and I then began to reflect on adult patients in a similar predicament, that I could begin to account more convincingly for an only partially successful outcome of their analyses. If nothing else, I have been alerted in the treatment of patients with such histories to be more cautious in my expectations and also to be more precise in my differential understanding of the pre-oedipal and oedipal transference.

## Summary

This paper discusses the effects on both child and adult when there has been a loss of the father through separation or divorce in the first five years of life. It is written with regard to the psychoanalytic treatment of individuals who have experienced such a loss of the father.

The first part of the paper deals with the developmental effects on the child from the viewpoints of the pattern of oedipal development, superego structuralization, identification and sexual identification, and the analytic treatment process. The second part gives brief accounts of the analyses of two adults.

It is proposed that while analysis of such patients may achieve a certain level of success, there may in some cases remain a relatively intractable degree of narcissistic interference and an impairment in their capacity to make an internal separation from the remaining primary object, the mother.

## Notes

1  This paper first appeared *Int. J. Psycho-Anal.*, 66: 311–320.
2  This study group consisted of Audrey Gavshon an myself as Co-Chairpersons, with Carla Elliott, Susan Vas Dias and Irene Wineman, I am particularly grateful to Audrey Gavshon for the work we did together on this topic.
3  In analysis with Audrey Gavshon.
4  Under the Directorship of Moses Laufer.
5  Such observations were made on these adolescents at referral, and not after therapy.

## References

Freud, A. (1965). *Normality and Pathology in Childhood*. London: Hogarth Press.
Freud, S. (1897). Extracts from the Fliess papers. *S.E.*, 1: 263–266.
Freud, S. (1910). A special type of choice of object made by men (Contributions to the psychology of love I.) *S.E.*, 11: 163–176.

Laplanche, J. and Pontalis, J.-B. (1973). *The Language of Psychoanalysis.* London: Hogarth Press.

Lebovici, S. (1982). The origins and development of the Oedipus complex. *Int. J. Psychoanal.*, 63: 201–215.

Loewald, H. W. (1979). The waning of the Oedipus complex. *J. Am. Psychoanal. Assoc.*, 27: 751–775.

Sophocles (1947). *The Theban Plays*, trans. by E. F. Watling. London: Penguin.

# 6

# OEDIPUS AT PLAY[1]

## Ken Robinson

### Oedipus and his family

The problem for Oedipus and his family was that they could not play. Had they been able to, he might not have ended up killing his father and enjoying an incestuous relationship with his mother. The story goes, of course, that his father Laius was so terrified by the oracle foretelling that Oedipus was destined to kill him that he tried to get rid of Oedipus at birth. His ankles were bolted and Laius and Jocasta order him to be carried to a remote location far from Thebes where he was to be left to die. The rest is tragedy. Oedipus is saved and taken to the childless Polybus in Corinth who raises him as his son. But not knowing of his adoption, and hearing of the oracle's prophecy, Oedipus is as fearful as Laius had been: he leaves Corinth so as not to murder Polybus. As he journeys towards his birthplace, Thebes, he meets and kills Laius at a point where symbolically three roads meet. A little further along he encounters the Sphinx, answers her riddle and thereby releases Thebes from her curse. As a reward, he is made King and given his mother, Jocasta's hand in marriage. They have children, live happily in a thriving Thebes, until another curse falls upon their kingdom. The oracle is consulted again and as its meaning unravels Oedipus has to recognise that he has unwittingly fulfilled its prophecy after all. Jocasta hangs herself, Oedipus blinds himself and banishes himself from Thebes forever.

## Freud's choice of Oedipus Rex, the play and play

Fear of patricide prevented Oedipus and Laius coming to terms with their inevitable rivalry within their family environment. The Oedipus myth tells the story of a dysfunctional family that acts on what should have remained wishes, and repressed ones at that. If someone turned up for a consultation and told anything like Oedipus's story, we certainly wouldn't think it normal. Oedipus is an oedipal wreck. So why did Freud choose the myth when he was concerned with normative development? I think part of the answer is that he did not simply turn to it to offer a useful mnemonic or to underline that creative writers had known about the Oedipus complex long before psychoanalysis came along. He turned to it in the form of Sophocles's *play*. For Freud *the play* is analogous to the dream as a wish-fulfilment, or to children's play. In dreams, we can satisfy our forbidden desires and wishes by hallucinating their fulfilment just as in play children can gratify their wishes, including the wish to be grown-up. Within the dream-state and play these satisfactions are experienced as *real*, really happening, even though only imagined. As Freud put it, the "hallucinatory wishful psychosis" of the dream-state "not only brings hidden or repressed wishes into consciousness; it also represents them, with the subject's entire belief, as fulfilled" (Freud 1917, p. 230). This is psychosis in the service of the ego, not psychotic. So too when we watch a performance of *Oedipus Rex*, we enter into the experience of the play to such an extent that it feels real even though paradoxically we are simultaneously aware that we are watching a play. We do not jump on the stage or shout out to try to intervene when we are confronted with horrendous suffering that in real life we might well try to prevent. And when we identify with the tragic hero our "enjoyment", in Freud's words,

> is based on an illusion; that is to say, [our] suffering is mitigated by the certainty that, firstly, it is someone other than [ourself] who is acting and suffering on the stage, and, secondly, that after all it is only a game, which can threaten no damage to [our] personal security.
>
> (p. 306)

In turning to the play *Oedipus Rex* to represent the Oedipus complex, Freud makes the point that the fulfilment of oedipal desires belongs *in the play* or *in our response to the play* as "the child's wishful phantasy ... brought into the open and realised as it would be in a dream" (Freud 1900, p. 264). In our development, it belongs *within play*. Although oedipal desires and fantasies are universally experienced, they are not normally acted upon. We dream of, or play at, their fulfilment, enjoy their satisfaction within the oedipal environment provided by our parents and later within the realm of literature.

Freud had already marked out children's play as a serious business and like Winnicott had used the language of illusion and play, illusion, as he put it, grounded in "the tangible and visible things of the real world" (Freud 1908, p. 144). Winnicott built on the paradox of something feeling to be intensely real whilst at the same time only being imagined to give us the concept of transitional phenomena (an intermediate area which is neither simply subjective nor objective). In play the child is preoccupied in a transitional space. He plays *in the world* but is also "in a world of his own". He plays with all seriousness in a make-believe world but knows at the same time that the objects manipulated to serve the illusion of his play are indeed objects. Despite the difference between Freud and Winnicott on illusion and play, they share a conviction that a capacity to entertain illusion and reality simultaneously, without one cancelling out the other, makes engagement in illusion and play possible—this is the essential point of Freud's version of Aristotle's tragic catharsis in his "Psychopathic Characters on Stage" (1942 [1905 or 1906]). In Winnicott's words: "*The intermediate area ... is the area that is allowed to the infant between primary creativity and objective perception based on reality testing*" (Winnicott 1971, p. 13). As the child develops, and sometimes within analysis as the patient develops, it is a capacity held within the environment until it can be experienced internally.

## Normative oedipal development

I want to emphasise that such deadly serious play is a central part of normative oedipal development. It is one of the strengths of Winnicott's concept of transitional phenomena, rooted in the infant's illusion that she creates the breast that is given to her, that it can be extended to later development and experience. Hence my title: Oedipus at play. We are used to the idea that children play at reading on the way to being able to read. We might equally say that they play at having very serious love affairs with their parents or their substitutes as they learn what it is to have a sexual identity and to bring together in one person their affectionate and sexual feelings in preparation ultimately for going on to establish a real loving sexual relationship outside the family. This seriously pretend love affair is not one-sided, though it is asymmetrical: the parents are required to play their part. Let me give a vignette of a little Oedipus at play.

### A family scene: Jamie

Imagine a mother, father and child, a boy, Jamie, who is about three and a half years old. Jamie is playing on his own, happily engrossed in his play and the father is in the same room. The mother enters. She takes in the scene, goes over to her husband and puts her arm around his waist affectionately. Together they watch their child for a few moments and then turn to each other. Without looking up Jamie seems to register his mother's presence. He emerges from play, looks towards his parents and for a short while he observes them. Suddenly, shouting "Daddy" the child runs towards his father and grabs him around the legs in something resembling a rugby tackle. He catches him slightly off balance and the two of them stagger away from the mother. Nothing in the external world prompts this dash at the father. The family group is now reconfigured: it is now the mother's turn to look on as father and son engage in aggressive play. As their aggression spends the boy cuddles into his father's leg and begins to suck on his thumb as his father gently strokes his hair. The mood is relaxed and somnolent. At this point the mother announces that she is going off to make coffee and asks her husband whether he would like a cup. When she returns father and son are sitting together at one end of the sofa looking at a book together. The father is pointing to and talking about the pictures in the book whilst his son listens intently even though together they present a languid scene. The father finishes the page they are looking at and tells his son that he is now going to sit and have his coffee with mummy who has moved to sit beside her husband. Once again the scene is reconfigured. When it shifts again it is because the boy squeezes in between his parents as they sit side by side. He nuzzles into his mother, levering his father away by pushing him with his legs as hard as he can. His father reminds him sharply that he is holding a cup of hot coffee and should be careful and then with mock-protestations moves away, touching his wife's neck tenderly as he does so, leaving her to his son. His son smiles. It is a smile that the father recognises from other scenes. When he arises first from bed in the mornings his son will often take his place. And when he says playfully (but no doubt seriously) "Hey, that's my place" his remonstration is met with undisguised triumph, and that same smile. His son also smiles in this way when he announces that he is going to do something which he knows he isn't supposed to do and looks to see how his parents will respond. And so it goes on. If we were to observe this family of three over a longer period, we might see each of them trying to find a way of dealing with the vicissitudes of their own impulses as they each evolve within a family.

In the very ordinary scene that I have described so briefly we have a snapshot of an oedipal drama, less dramatic than *Oedipus Rex* to be sure but an oedipal drama for all that. I could have reported more obvious material, like Jamie's anxious question to his mother on seeing her naked one day whether someone had chopped her willy off with a sword. But I have preferred this simple scene because it is a reminder that infantile sexuality is ubiquitous. Not only must the child find its own solution to the demands made by its impulses, its parents too must revisit their own oedipal past as it is reactivated in the present by their interaction with their child. If all goes well enough, they can revisit it and still provide an environment in which this child can play with the intensity that we see in Jamie.

## The Oedipus complex

I shall use this scene to comment briefly on the basics of the Oedipus complex before concentrating on the nature of the play involved.

The scene with Jamie and his family shows clearly the oedipal dimension which everyone knows about. The little boy seeks out his mother, nuzzles into her and fights with daddy, his favourite enemy. Although I have chosen a vignette involving a boy what I shall say applies equally to the girl (even though the detail and dynamics of the girl's development through the oedipal period are different). That is, the child wishes to possess exclusively the parent of the opposite sex and enters into rivalrous relation to the parent of the same sex. It is important not to turn the little child into an adult by construing his wish as simply a wish for sexual intercourse: it is more a matter of exhibiting masculinity or femininity so as to win the admiration of the mother or father in a bid for exclusive possession, though the child might have vague fantasies that foreshadow later desire for sexual intercourse.

It is equally clear that Jamie also wishes to take the parent of the same sex as his partner and enters into rivalry with the parent of the opposite sex. As well as splitting up the parents, Jamie's aggressive tussle with his father serves the purpose of discharging considerable sexual energy as well as aggression. There is a clear release of tension. In adult terms, the ensuing mood is distinctly post-coital. It is noteworthy how he moves from the charging young bull to being more passive, stroked by his father. Identification with the parent of the same sex is crucial to the child's developing identity, but the ability to take up both male and female roles through identification with both parents plays a part too in establishing this identity as both creatively experienced and reasonably secure even if still in formation. Several writers have identified this era "in which children of both genders experience fluctuating identifications and kaleidoscopically shifting erotic fantasy with parents of both sexes" as one marked by "transitional oedipal play" (Benjamin 1988; Davies 1994; Dimen 1991; Fast 1984; Gabbard 1994; Halberstadt-Freud 1998; Ogden 1987).

We are so used to thinking of the Oedipus complex in relation to early sexuality that it is worth emphasising that the development of sexuality is inseparable from the development of mind and the sense of a self as personally engaged in the world, capable of a creating the world as subjectively real. Indeed, we normally think of earlier development crystallising in the oedipal period. Jamie's progress through the oedipus complex goes hand in hand with his more general intellectual and psychological development. Jamie has a basic preconscious taxonomy of his world in place. He clearly acknowledges that there is a world independent of him which does not always fit what he wishes. He knows his numbers, one, two, three: me, them, us (me and him and me and her) and we three. He recognises generational differences (including the difference between big daddy and little Jamie). He seems aware of sexual differences: there is mummy and there is daddy. We see his capacity for delaying satisfaction as well as headlong pursuit of his wishes. And we witness his capacity to play in the area of transitional space. Theorists after Winnicott have explored further the two realities that the child comes to embrace: literal reality and pretend reality (Emde et al. 1997). Fonagy and

Target in particular have accorded play a central role in integrating the two into a sense of psychic reality and placed the consolidation of this integration in the oedipal phase (1996). This is the view from developmental psychology: from the inside, the child's capacity to experience the world as a "transitional object" is fundamental to his sense of being creatively alive. It is important to emphasise this more general development because where things go wrong in the oedipal period, especially where there is sexual abuse, this development can be undermined.

## Transitional oedipal play

Jamie is engaged in a form of "transitional oedipal play", transitional both because it is developmental and because it takes place in transitional space. In his playing we see a capacity for imaginative immersion in a pretend world without loss of his sense of reality. Jamie plays at being lover, rival, the absolute bees knees. To play in this way he needs his parents' help. He needs "flirting partners". I owe the phrase "flirting partner" to one of my patients whose father had disappeared from her life well before puberty and who had grown up without a significant substitute for him. In her analysis she went through a period of being very seductive towards me as her analysis kick-started arrested oedipal wishes. When later she reflected on how she had used me she told me that she had never before had a "flirting partner". Jamie also needs fighting partners. His father fights with him in a serious play fight, hard enough to allow Jamie to feel strong but not so hard as to humiliate him. And his mother is similarly able to enter into oedipal pretend with him. She allows him to usurp his father's place in bed beside her with that smile that says he is doing something he ought not to be doing, without making him feel foolishly small. On one occasion, he put her ability take him seriously to the test for as she came from the shower he was waiting for her on the landing outside the bathroom door. Wearing only his red Wellington boots and his father's old spectacles, he greeted her, in as deep a voice as he could muster, with: "Hello wife". By her own account she managed to keep a straight face and reply "Hello, Jamie-husband", a response that beautifully held both illusion and reality.

The parents have to manage the child's oedipal disillusionment too. The infant has already had to experience earlier disillusionments—weaning, being separate from but still needing a caretaker and so on—and now disillusionment is a fundamental part of the child's passage through the Oedipus complex. In the oedipal period, the child—we see it in Jamie—shows off as part of both exploring what it is to be a boy or girl, and beginning the process of establishing a relation to its own sexual body. Such exhibitionism is central to the oedipal child's playful seductive claims to exclusive attention. The parents under good-enough conditions meet his displays of bodily and mental accomplishments with pleasure, partly because of their own narcissistic investment in him as extra-special. Their response is crucial in laying the foundations of the child's self-esteem and his sense of having something of value to offer spontaneously to the world. Children play at seducing and possessing the parent as if they are grown up. It is the parent' task simultaneously to join the child in the illusion of play, as Jamie's mother does, and to disillusion. The little boy has to pass from the illusion "I am the big strong man that Mummy wants" to "I am strong enough for my age to feel good about myself. Daddy is big and strong. We do things together and one day I will be like him". He has to recognise that despite his seductions it is Daddy whom Mummy takes to bed with her and Daddy who helps Mummy to make babies. The little girl has to come to terms with the fact that although she might be the most beautiful princess in the world in Daddy's eyes, mummy is his queen. It is with her that Daddy makes babies. It is she who grows them inside her and who when they appear feeds them with her breasts.

In this way the parents hold a framework of reality within which the child can play and develop, just as the play *Oedipus Rex* offers a framework within which the members of the audience are free to explore their identifications. The outer reality of the parents' sexual relationship ensures that play, whether the play of seduction or rivalrous battle, remains play, no matter how intensely charged the child's play might be. This outer limit contributes to the growth and consolidation of internal constraints within the child. In Jamie budding internal constraint, an emerging super-ego, manifests itself in his smile. All this allows him to seduce and to triumph over his rival within the safety of play. The balance between omnipotent narcissistic satisfaction in the illusion of play and acknowledgement of disillusioning reality governs the degree of inevitable humiliation that the child has to experience in order to move on. Fear of castration is partly a fear that the disillusionment and humiliation will be catastrophic. It is noticeable in the vignette that the parents can both disillusion Jamie by firmly being the grown-up couple whilst at the same time smiling on him as he forms a couple with first one, then the other of them—though they too show jealousy when this happens. (The mother's making of coffee is a more subtle means of regaining her husband from his son's embrace than Jamie's rugby tackle, but it no less rivalrous for all that.) Just as the mother in infancy disillusions her child at a pace consistent with its developing capacity to tolerate frustration, so Jamie's parents let him down lightly.

## The transformative nature of play

The parents' capacity to support, engage in and hold their child's play is transformative, but, as Winnicott recognised, "playing is always liable to become frightening" (Winnicott 1971, p. 58). The hands that were pretending to be a crocodile become the frighteningly real crocodile and it is then the parents' job to hold literal reality, to disillusion the child and restore the "as-if" quality of symbolic play. In oedipal play the unconscious frightening scenario is that pretend seduction will become actual incest, or as in Oedipus's family that rivalrous patricidal wishes, which, as Hans Loewald recognised, are fundamental to the child's "urge for emancipation" from parental authority, will become actual patricide (1979, p. 757). In the oedipal phase the parents tacitly help their child to explore his emerging sexual fantasies, wishes and feelings whilst at the same time holding the reality of generational differences and the taboo on incest. Much of this is done silently, though on occasion it may be necessary to remind the child what belongs to the realm of mummy and daddy. The environment provides the child with a higher-level psychic organisation in the process of the child developing its sense of the relation of inner and outer. In analysis the analyst provides a similar environment.

How different the world of Jamie is from the world of Oedipus in the myth where fear of patricide, attempted filicide, flight and denial substitute for an environment (internal as well as external) that permits fantasies to be enjoyed, even if prohibited, without being acted on.

I have dwelt on the early phase of oedipal development but "transitional oedipal play" occurs again in adolescence when oedipal fantasies burst upon the scene with renewed force and peremptoriness.

The adolescent equivalent of the scene between Jamie and his parents would be a much more fraught and potentially disturbing affair for all concerned. The adolescent is not only driven by sexual and aggressive oedipal impulses but is now actually capable of begetting or conceiving a child by the parent of the opposite sex. The frightening aspect of oedipal play can feel all the more frightening, for both the adolescent and the parents. I do not have time for a comprehensive account of adolescence. I simply wish to emphasise the importance of oedipal play in the midst of the turmoil that it brings, its frightening aspect and the importance of the parents holding the frame and providing a continuing transformative environment.

## When the environment fails: Debra

So much for oedipal play in normative development: what about when things go wrong, as they did for Oedipus, where there is a family that cannot support oedipal play? What about oedipal wrecks? I shall outline an example to set beside Jamie. It is a case of a little girl who was sexually abused from when she between five and six years old. Her abuse was the polar opposite of oedipal *play*: the frightening aspects of play were actualised. In the scene I am about to describe Debra is about five or six. At this point she is the oldest of three children. Her mother is busy with the younger children, both boys, and her father sits in a chair at home reading the newspaper. Partly as a result of feeling to be supplanted by her brothers in a family where boys are preferred to girls, partly because her mother hates her, she desperately needs to be affirmed as worth something. On this occasion she plays at laying claim seductively to her father's admiration, showing off a ribbon in her hair as if she were saying: "Hey, look at me: put your newspaper down, I want your admiration now". As part of trying to seize his attention she puts her hand on her father's thigh. Instead of the sort of play that Jamie's parents engage in with him, her father, sexually aroused by his daughter, takes her hand and puts it on his erect penis. The illusion of her attempted play with him is shattered. Brutally disillusioned she ends up distressed, guilty and confused. This memory probably condenses other such scenes with her father, and maybe later scenes with both parents who were not only sexually perverse as a couple but involved their children—nine in all—in their perversion. Debra's memory may also contain mnemic traces of earlier traumatic experience with her mother. Her mother believed that she had been torn apart giving birth to Debra and therefore wished that Debra had never been born, so that it is unlikely that she would have been able to provide what Winnicott referred to as "opportunity for illusion" (Winnicott 1971, p. 14) in the earlier stages of Debra's life. Certainly, the father's abuse worsened and continued into adolescence whilst Debra's mother turned a blind eye. Debra tried to protect herself whilst being abused by conjuring up an autohypnotic state, a loop outside time, in sharp contrast to being lost in play.

In such an abusive scenario, the emphasis is not upon helping the child to come to terms with oedipal desires but upon the father's actual gratification of his sexual needs. Jamie's parents even if they are aroused, no matter what adult feelings or desires might be evoked in them, play *at the child's level*, at the level of what Ferenczi calls tenderness. When Debra's father abuses her, he takes her tender playful gesture and turns it into an adult overture. The result is in Ferenczi's terms "a confusion of tongues" (1933 [1949]). In Jamie's case the parents hold reality to provide a frame within which oedipal play can take place. In the case of Debra's abuse what should have stayed play and fantasy was turned into reality. And instead of play serving the development of internal constraints the result was confusion and guilt as the abusive father burdened his daughter with his own guilt. Finally, in contrast to the way that oedipal play feeds into the crystallisation of the child's intellectual and psychological development and the structuring of its mind, the trauma of abuse, at this stage of life, tends to destructure the mind, to fracture its taxonomy of its world, and to interfere with the development of psychic reality and the capacity to create the world as subjectively alive without losing touch with its objective reality. All this has consequences for the degree to which the child experiences herself as alive and authentic in the world.

## Debra's analysis

I saw Debra for analysis as a woman: not only had her experience severely diminished her capacity to trust, especially when she felt that someone was being kind to her, it had made her cling for dear life to what she took to be clear and real. She was radically afraid of the unexpected, of her unconscious, of her fantasies and of what I might do with them. She had not achieved the capacity to use her anxiety to take protective action and she lived on the edge of panic. She inhabited a world where symbols became what they symbolised. When one day, for example, a container of milk that she had been carrying in her briefcase spilt, the milk became semen and everything it touched had to be destroyed and the briefcase scrubbed out. If I ventured beyond the surface of her words to comment on the possible meaning of something that she told me I became her father unexpectedly changing what she offered me into something else for my own (analytic) gratification. She was unable to play.

As the analysis unfolded over many years it became a gradual process of Debra becoming able to use me as providing a safe framework in which she could come to tolerate, even enjoy, having feelings, thoughts, imaginings and fantasies, especially in relation to me, that could be seriously entertained without being experienced as frighteningly real. In other words, she had to learn to play.

Debra's relation to me in her analysis passed through several phases: initially I was a transference object in a psychotic transference, then a more trusted figure experienced as different from her transference objects, later a new developmental object in relation to whom she could explore development that had been foreclosed and finally I was simultaneously a transference figure and someone with whom she could think about her relation to that figure. Each of these stages involved a different form of play. (I am simplifying for the purpose of discussion: they were, of course, not quite so clearly demarcated from each other not least because she quickly regressed under the pressure of both external events and her analysis.)

## The phases of Debra's analysis: repeating vs. remembering

Debra first contacted me in a state of near breakdown with a precarious hold on the literal reality that she tried to cling to so desperately. I was doubtful about whether we would be able to work analytically together. All who enter analysis wish to change but to a greater or lesser extent bring resistance to change. In her case she desperately wished to change but her resistance was massive: it really was a matter of "better the devil she knew". The situation was worsened because she saw in me someone who sufficiently resembled her father for the resemblance to deepen her resistance: he was physically short and a well-known and respected figure within the local community of the caring professions. Freud (1914) made a famous distinction between being able to remember and having to repeat or enact our past. Before analysis Debra had repeated and repeated her relationship with her father in abusive relationships in a series of failed attempts at mastery. And now she sought to do so again, without knowing that she was repeating (Freud 1914, p. 150). She did this partly out of fear of change and partly because this was all she could manage by way of bringing her past into the analysis. But this time there was some hope, held by me for a considerable time, that her re-enactments could in time be understood as a form of remembering.

It is no easy task for any patient to use analysis to transform repeating into remembering because transference repetition takes place *in relation to the analyst*, the very person who at the same time is required to offer transformative help. Before such help could be accepted Debra had slowly to experience me as someone she could trust to be different from her father. In the early years of her analysis her erotised transference, psychotic and sadomasochistic, rendered her more terrified than trusting—so much so that I continued to question whether it was unreasonable to hope that analysis was possible. Debra had, however, achieved much in her life, as mother and professional, she had hung onto her achievements and was still consolidating them. It seemed to me possible that her erotised transference contained within it both an attempt to triumph masochistically over her trauma and, as part of such mastery, a sadistic desire to degrade me and destroy the analysis (Cf. Blum 1973). In this I saw a glimmer of healthy refusal to surrender.

## The playground of the transference

Freud recognised that such repetition in transference within the consulting room involves a form of play: he wrote of "the transference as a playground" as creating "an intermediate region between illness and real life through which the transition from the one to the other is made" (1914, p. 154). Building on his foundation Ella Sharpe, Winnicott and Loewald amongst others have helped us to understand further the dynamics of what happens in this playground. For Ella Sharpe transference is an "unfolding drama": the patient casts the analyst in various roles as she replays her past, both "real and phantastic" in relation to him (1930, pp. 376–377). Later analysts have expanded on the importance of the analyst being able to be alive to and to use the feelings generated in him by having these roles thrust upon him (see, for example, Sandler 1976). It is part of the intensity with which the patient makes this transference that the analyst who tries to be empathically in touch with the patient's world not only occupies the role of past figures but experiences thoughts and feelings appropriate to those figures, as if he were those figures, without himself enacting them in relation to the patient. No matter how tough it might be to grapple with some of the feelings evoked in him by being responsive to the role demanded of him by the patient's transference, he knows that all this helps him to understand the patient from the inside.

All this happens unbeknown to the patient. It is part of the asymmetry of the analyst-patient relationship that the playground is initially located internally in the analyst. From the analyst's vantage point the past is replayed under controlled conditions, in a "set situation", but it can take some time for the patient to enter into a form of play in which both analyst and patient co-operate to experience the past as alive and real in the intermediate space of the consulting room. It is only when the patient can experience the transference as a playground, a potential space (like a dream or play) rather than actually real, that collaborative play is possible (Winnicott 1971, p. 56). The patient has to learn to play if she doesn't yet have that capacity. Until she does the analyst must be able to play in his own mind with the meaning of the enactments and hold the frame in which collaborative play might become possible.

I am distinguishing what it is like from the side of the patient and the side of the analyst because for some considerable time Debra, caught in a stagnant past, cast me as her abusive father or careless perverse mother in her drama. She could not yet enjoy the luxury of "the playground as transference". I was left to recognise silently the roles that I occupied in her mind without acting on them. As Sharpe put it "we accept the rôles in order to analyse them, but we cannot analyse them if unconsciously any rôle becomes psychically our own" (1930, p. 378). Listening, abstinence, neutrality, patience and disciplined waiting: these were important ingredients in Debra's analysis in the time that she was slowly settling into becoming less fearful. In his paper on the neutral position, Ron Baker has described the effect of the analyst waiting and not enacting under provocation from the patient. The analyst's refusal to enact has the force, he thinks, of an implicit transference interpretation. It silently disconfirms the patient's distorted perception and as such establishes the analyst as a potentially new object different from transference objects (1993, p. 1229 and 2000, p. 143). The analyst, in Winnicott's terms, places himself *"outside the area of subjective phenomena"* and as such is available to be used when the patients can manage it (1971, p. 102). I believe that this is partly what happened with Debra, but it was also, I think, that she grew to experience herself as in the presence of someone able to perform functions that she was as yet unable to perform herself. As I attended to the thoughts and feelings evoked in me in accepting the roles that she projected on to me, I was able to immerse myself imaginatively and empathically in her subjective fantasy world *without loss of my sense of reality.*

## From one-sided to co-operative play

In the early stages of our work together play, then, was one-sided and not co-operative. Over time this shifted as my silent understanding of her had a cumulative effect. Having begun to experience me implicitly as potentially different from her transference objects, Debra began to treat me as a new developmental object, as a "flirting partner". She began to entertain the developmental illusion that I was her exclusive love object. The phrase "developmental illusion" is Rita Tähkä's. It usefully distinguishes the transference illusion from the developmental illusion and it locates the latter as emerging from "the relationship between the emergent 'developing child' in the patient and the analyst as its new developmental object" (Tähkä 2000, p. 73). Because of anxiety about boundary violations in our work as analysts, I think that we can sometimes be over-cautious about how to respond to erotic feelings directed towards us. They may feel all the more problematic when we cannot simply categorise them as transference. But where those feelings are part of a developmental trajectory set in motion by the analysis they need to be nurtured just as Jamie's parents nurtured his. They need to be accepted, respected and given proportion. In such transitional oedipal play two people play together and the patient's preparedness to play implies trust (Winnicott 1971, p. 60). They play within an asymmetrical relationship, the parent/analyst providing transformative higher functioning. As with Jamie's play, it was not yet appropriate to interpret Debra's play: my task was more to manage it tacitly, recognising the vulnerability it brought with it.

It is essential when providing a framework in which oedipal play may happen that the analyst is neither afraid, nor narcissistically excited, to be a developmental oedipal object. It is also essential that he is alert to being used in this way because if he is not the patient may lose heart, experience her oedipal desires as too dangerous to deal with, or feel that she must make more and more determined efforts to make an impression. What needs to be offered is firm holding of the situation on the model of the parents' holding.

## Dreams as a gift and a challenge: the difficulty of accepting a new developmental object

But change is not easily embraced. The child taking her first steps is poised to crawl if movement forward becomes too scary and so it is with all later development. As Debra was developing a relation to me as a new developmental object she also provided herself with an escape route back into her earlier frightening transference. At the same time she set me a test: was I in truth a new object or was I really the same old abusive figure she had earlier cast me as? After a long period of being unable to remember or report any dreams she began to bring dreams to her analysis. For her, remembering dreams at all was an achievement and reporting them all the more so. She brought them rather proudly and flirtatiously as gifts, with an implicit invitation for me to comment on them. But they were invariably dreams which on the surface had a clear sexual dimension that she seemed oblivious of. She found it difficult, if not impossible, to associate to them and left it to me to make something of them. But if I drew attention to their sexual content, or offered thoughts about it, the result was disastrous, because Debra became terrified of me. Once again I became her abusing father, who took her gesture, turned it into something else and forced his sexual interest upon her. Erotised transference was an attractive alternative to stepping out on the new developmental path of oedipal play.

I took to keeping to myself my thoughts about the content of her dreams and how she was using them and simply accepted them as attempts to elicit my admiration (as her showing off her ribbon had been). I took an interest in when she had dreamed them, commented on how vivid they were and found other ways of valuing them without interpreting them. Over time she brought dreams less and when she did bring them they were less seductively sexual.

She began to tell me more of her achievements in the previous day. Sometimes she brought bits of writing to show me, sometimes photographs and once a poster that she had designed for her church. She was becoming more able to use me as a figure different from her father, a figure in relation to whom she could develop rather than traumatically repeat. Of course there was a danger in treating her dreams in this way that she might think I could not handle their sexual content, but I was encouraged by the fact that as her reports of dreams became less frequent there was still an atmosphere of flirtatiousness. It was an atmosphere that it would have been no more appropriate to comment on than it would be to tell ones child that she is using you developmentally. In fact, it would, I believe, have inhibited development.

## Testing boundaries

Then came a phase when emboldened by getting my attention she demanded ruthlessly that I be exquisitely attuned to her needs and moods at all times. Her flirtatiousness became more overt. When I coughed in a session she was furious. How could I cough and have my mind wholly on her? Next, she challenged the boundaries of the analysis, turning up in inappropriate places where she had a good chance of seeing me and she became fiercely rivalrous towards other patients and my family. By this time, however, it had become more possible to take up her demands with her and now I had to set firm limits. Her attempts to blur the boundaries of analysis made her very anxious, put her back on the edge of panic, but the emphasis had now shifted, from fears associated with being a passive victim, to anxiety that she would experience such peremptory desires that she would act on them, that, for example, as she entered the consulting room she might throw her arms around me or that at the end of a session she might so wish to remain that she would refuse to leave. Only secondarily did she worry that I might not be able to withstand her and join her in a boundary violation. Setting limits diminished her anxiety and made the consulting room a safer place to be in. I was called on to join in her play whilst holding an outer reality, much as Jamie's parents did. In this way she had to experience oedipal disillusionment: we could be analytic partners but not sexual partners. Only later could we begin to be able to work "in the overlap of two areas of playing, that of the patient and that of the therapist"

(Winnicott 1971, p. 44). Then we could return to the scene with her father in transference without her losing her sense of transference as an illusion: we were at last in the playground together.

Of course, there were ups and downs in Debra's analysis, times when it felt that any gains had been lost. It would never be possible to undo all the damage caused by her abuse, but I hope Debra's case goes some way to showing what happens when the capacity for oedipal play is undermined, how analysis might help and how important oedipal play in relation to the analyst is in the course of a new development.

As Oedipus's destiny inexorably unravels Jocasta reassures him with tragic irony:

> Many a man before you
> in his dreams, has shared his mother's bed.
> Take such things for shadows, nothing at all.
>
> (Sophocles 1984)

The incest that should have remained "shadows" has actually happened. So too it had for Debra, foreclosing the possibility of oedipal play. It fell to analysis to try to make possible that play in the hope of intervening between her and what seemed her inevitable fate: to continue to repeat her trauma *ad infinitum*.

## Note

1 An earlier version of this paper appeared in *Revue Psychoanalytiká Psychoterapie,* 15 (2013): 67–79.

## References

Baker, R. (1993). The patient's discovery of the psychoanalyst as a new object. *Int. J. Psycho-Anal.*, 74: 1223–1233.

Baker, R. (2000). Finding the neutral position. *J. Am. Psychoanal. Assoc.*, 48: 129–153.

Benjamin, J. (1988). *The Bonds of Love.* New York: Pantheon.

Blum, H. P. (1973). The concept of erotized transference. *J. Am. Psychoanal. Assoc.*, 21: 61–76.

Davies, J. M. (1994). Love in the afternoon: a relational reconsideration of desire and dread in the countertransference. *Psychoanal. Dialog.*, 4: 153–170.

Dimen, M. (1991), Deconstructing difference: gender, splitting, and transitional space. *Psychoanal. Dial.*, 1: 335–352.

Emde, R., Kubicek, L. and Oppenheim, D. (1997). Imaginative reality observed during early language development. *Int. J. Psycho-Anal.* 78: 115–133.

Fast, I. (1984). *Gender Identity.* Hillsdale, NJ: The Analytic Press.

Ferenczi, S. (1949). Confusion of the tongues between the adults and the child. *Int. J. Psycho-Anal.*, 30: 225–230.

Fonagy, P. and Target, M. (1996). Playing with reality: I. theory of mind and the normal development of psychic reality. *Int. J. Psycho-Anal.*, 77: 217–233.

Freud, S. (1900). The interpretation of dreams. *S.E.*, 4 & 5: 1–627.

Freud, S. (1908). Creative writers and day-dreaming. *S.E.*, 9: 141–154.

Freud, S. (1914). Remembering, repeating and working through. *S.E.*, 12: 145–156.

Freud, S. (1917). A metapsychological supplement to the theory of dreams. *S.E.*, 14: 217–235.

Freud, S. (1942 [1905 or 1906]). Psychopathic characters on the stage. *S.E.*, 7: 303–310.

Gabbard, G. O. (1994). Sexual excitement and countertransference love in the analyst. *J. Am. Psychoanal. Assoc.*, 42: 1083–1106.

Halberstadt-Freud, H. C. (1998). Electra versus Oedipus: femininity reconsidered. *Int. J. Psycho-Anal.*, 79: 41–56.

Loewald, H. W. (1979). The waning of the Oedipus complex. *J. Am. Psychoanal. Assoc.*, 27: 751–775.

Ogden, T.H. (1987). The transitional oedipal relationship in female development. *Int. J. Psycho-Anal.*, 68: 485–498.

Sandler, J. (1976). Countertransference and role-responsiveness. *Int. Rev. Psycho-Anal.*, 3: 43–47.

Sharpe, E. F. (1930). The technique of psycho-analysis. *Int. J. Psycho-Anal.*, 11: 361–386.

Sophocles (1984). *The Three Theban Plays*, trans. Robert Fagles. London: Penguin Books.

Tähkä, R. (2000). Illusion and reality in the psychoanalytic relationship. *Scand. Psychoanal. Rev.*, 23: 65–88.

Winnicott, D. W. (1971). *Playing and Reality.* London: Tavistock Publications.

# 7

# FEMALE MASTURBATION IN ADOLESCENCE AND THE DEVELOPMENT OF THE RELATIONSHIP TO THE BODY[1]

## M. Eglé Laufer

It has always been noted by analytic writers from Freud onwards that the attitude women have to masturbation differs from that of men. Freud remarks, for instance, that whereas a man would probably not hesitate to use masturbation when no other means of sexual gratification are available to him, a woman would be less likely to do so. The difference is even more marked if we look at the period of adolescent development, since we know that masturbation plays an essential and positive part in the move towards normal adulthood for adolescent boys, while it does not seem to have the same essential role in the adolescent girl's sexual development. When discussing these observations, Freud traced the reasons for the absence of masturbation in the sexual activity of the little girl to the original experience of her disappointment in the size of her genitals when she begins to compare them with those of the boy. This explanation has been, and still is, the cause of much disagreement amongst analysts and others.

But, by keeping the discussion focused on whether or not the girl's sexual development is primarily determined by her penis envy and its consequences, an important issue has been left unresolved. What is the role played by masturbation in the normal development of the little girl and in the life of the adolescent girl and adult woman? Is it, in fact, normal for the girl to give it up or, as some analysts seem to imply, is its lack in an adolescent girl or a woman indicative of earlier repression—one that analysis should succeed in lifting? I have often heard it reported in clinical descriptions that a female patient had 'become able' to masturbate. Rarely have I seen it questioned whether this is a sign of a normal, progressive move and, if not, what the meaning of it might be and what is being communicated to the analyst by such information. It is my intention to attempt to answer some of these questions.

In order to do so, I first want to examine the significance of that period of infantile sexual development that Freud (1905) in 'Three Essays' called the first phase of masturbation. He is not specific about dating this period but, inasmuch as he equates the second period with the oedipal phase, it seems safe to include all the pre-oedipal period in this first phase. What I want to show is that it is in this earliest phase of masturbation that the relationship to the body is formed, and that this relationship is originally expressed, and later symbolically experienced, in the relationship of the hand to the body. Freud placed enormous emphasis on Lindner's observation that the infant's thumb-sucking has an erotic component because this provided Freud with the basis for his theoretical formulations concerning the developmental significance of masturbation in the total spectrum of sexual activity, and thus for extending the concept of sexuality beyond that of genital sexuality. He showed that the erotic satisfaction experienced by the infant in thumb-sucking implies the existence of an oral sexual drive with the breast as its object, and that the mother (in her function of caring for the infant's body) acts both as seducer and frustrater of the child's other libidinally determined wishes (such as being held, kept warm and fondled). The breast is first experienced as a frustrating object through the experience of its absence, and it is this aspect of the breast which the infant is able to negate through finding that a part of its own body can be used to create the absent object and, in this way, to undo the frustrating experience. The significance of the simultaneous nature of the infant's experience of two separate parts of its own body for the formation of a separate body image has been discussed by Hoffer (1949).

But I would like to place the emphasis on another aspect of the significance this experience holds for the infant, that is, on the infant's experience of its own body as having the capacity for gratification.

The relationship that is represented by the activity of the thumb in relation to the infant's mouth repeats and becomes identified with the mother's active satisfying relationship to the infant. Subsequently, the activity of the whole hand in relation to the child's body is a repetition of the experience of the activity of the mother's hand in relation to the child. All masturbatory activity contains the duality of both an active and a passive experience. During this first phase of masturbation, while the infant is progressively experiencing its body as separate from that of the mother, the activity of the thumb in relation to the mouth, and later of the hand to the body and genitals, provides the basis for the identification with the mother's activity in relation to the child's body. This enables the child to undo the experience of separation by feeling more in control of the satisfaction of pre-oedipal wishes through the use of its own body. We know, from work with children, that a delicate balance exists between the continued ability to use the body actively as a means of experiencing it as a source of satisfaction and a sense of autonomy, and the masturbatory activity which is used as a defensive means of dealing with real deprivation. But by taking into account the unconscious identification of the hand with that of the mother's, the conflict for the little girl regarding masturbation becomes clearer.

By limiting our observations to female masturbation, an important difference which exists among female children, adolescent girls and adult women can be taken into account. We know from clinical observation that only some girls or women masturbate; the difference between those who masturbate and those who do not can be defined more specifically as being between those who use their hand to touch their genitals and those who do not. Those writers who use clinical material to show that little girls use different means for obtaining sexual excitement (such as thigh pressure or faecal retention), and who conclude that there is no basic difference in the significance of masturbation in female and male development, do not take sufficiently into account the significance of this existing difference. I see this avoidance of the use of the hand for masturbation by some women as that which characterizes the difference between male and female. This does not mean that there are no boys who avoid touching the penis for masturbatory purposes but, in the case of boys, it is always a sign of severe disturbance in normal development.

In his paper on 'Female sexuality', Freud (1931) points out that the girl's relinquishing of masturbation—which he saw as occurring

## Female masturbation in adolescence

at the end of her long period of attachment to her mother—could not be viewed simply as a result of prohibitions coming from the external world. Prohibition, he pointed out, can lead to a defiant need to cling to an activity as easily as to its relinquishment. Freud's explanation was that it must therefore be internally determined, that is, by the child's experience of disappointment with her own body. Irrespective of the unconscious content of that disappointment, this observation has been confirmed and reported by analysts in their own clinical work with children and adults. But it seems less clear why this disappointment is expressed by the avoidance of touching the genitals. To explain, as Freud did, that the satisfaction which the girl obtains is no longer sufficient because of the fantasy of what she could be experiencing if she had a penis seems unconvincing to many analysts. It can be understood instead as the giving up of an active relationship to her own body when she is forced to become aware that she is not able to undo the frustration of her wishes through the activity of her hand. Until that time the hand has served as a means of being able to identify her activity with that of her mother. When she is forced to recognize that she cannot fulfil the wish of identifying her body with that of the mother as, for instance, by being able to produce a baby of her own, the activity of the hand becomes a source of anxiety for the little girl. The hand, instead of being able to be identified with the gratifying object, is now potentially identified with a depriving and frustrating one, this being so since the little girl no longer feels that she can satisfy her wishes through its use.

The implication of such a view seems to be that the continued use of masturbation beyond the oedipal phase in the girl is defensive against the underlying anxiety aroused by the impulse to reject or hate her body as a source of disappointment and frustration. The continued effort to experience the body as a source of gratification via masturbation may enable the girl to maintain a defensive idealization of her own body, but at the expense of maintaining the repression of her hostility towards the mother and a denial of the disappointing reality of her own body in comparison to that of her mother.

From a developmental point of view, everything I have said up to now about the basis for the girl's relationship to her body seems equally true for the boy. The difference in the time taken by the little girl before she turns away from her exclusive attachment to the mother can be explained by the encouragement given to the little girl, through her own observation of having a similar body to that of her mother, to cling to the expectation of being able to identify with all her mother's activity for much longer than the boy.

Although I have suggested that the final wish which is experienced as a source of frustration for the little girl is for a body which can produce a baby and not necessarily for a body that includes a penis, I do not see this as the essential issue. A central issue of the pre-oedipal period is the conflict between activity and passivity, and the need for the child to establish an active role towards the mother as a means of becoming separate from her (Mack Brunswick 1940). In discussing the significance which masturbation has to the development of the relationship the child has to its own body, I am concerned here in showing how the activity of the hand in relation to the body permits the child to feel that the body is capable of providing a source for the experience of satisfaction independently of the mother. I am less concerned here with the actual content of the fantasy or wish. My experience within the transference of analysing female patients has often confirmed this view. The patient's experience of the transference is of a hostile, depriving mother who withholds that which would enable the patient to become like the analyst. The suspicion is that the analyst does this in order to keep the patient helpless and thus to force her to remain passively dependent on the analyst.

The effect of puberty on the girl, according to Freud, is to set in motion a renewal of the repression of masturbation. The implication is that the girl reacts to puberty as a confirmation of her lack of a penis. If the relationship to her body has followed the path I have described, that is, that it includes the acceptance of her body as one which is not able to replace totally the mother's as part of the oedipal resolution, such an explanation for the repression of masturbation following puberty no longer follows. Puberty now fulfils the old wish of having a body that is able to produce a child. I would see the anxiety aroused at puberty due to other factors, and which once more lead to the avoidance of the use of the hand by the girl in relation to her own genitals.

Inasmuch as the hand is unconsciously identified with the caring and gratifying aspects of the mother, the experience of sexual pleasure through the use of the hand could unconsciously be experienced as the fulfilment of the wish to be passively gratified by the mother.

## Female masturbation in adolescence

But the emergence of this wish into consciousness opens the way to the active seeking of a homosexual object choice and can potentially interfere with the choice of a male sexual object. Fantasies of actively caring for or of rescuing the mother and, in the transference, the analyst, as can be observed in the analysis of many female patients, are evidence of the need for an active identification to defend against the passive wishes when they are aroused in the transference. But for the female child who continues to use masturbation both as a means of maintaining an active identification with the mother and of denying the reality of the inadequacy of her own body, puberty poses a new threat. In order to maintain the defensive struggle in relation to her body through masturbation, the girl now becomes vulnerable to being forced into making a homosexual object choice. At the same time the identification of her pubertal body with that of her mother's makes the need to maintain the idealized relationship to her own body ever more urgent. This then acts as a means of protecting herself from the emergence into consciousness of the hatred related both to her mother's body and to her own.

This particular aspect of puberty—the meaning to the girl of having a body which is identified with that of her mother'—is of crucial importance in the future development of her relationship to her own sexual body. It is something which is frequently not given sufficient importance when considering difficulties in female sexual development. If the need for the renewed suppression of masturbation following puberty is understood as an avoidance of the use of the hand for masturbatory purposes, rather than just as the suppression of masturbation, it follows that what is being avoided is the depriving and frustrating potential which is unconsciously felt to be contained in the activity of the hand in relation to the genitals which are now identified with the mother's sexual body. Some analysts have used their clinical observations to show that adolescent girls do in fact masturbate and have stated that, even if they do not masturbate consciously, these adolescent girls are denying their awareness of the way in which they use other activities, seeming to imply that there is no basic difference in the significance which masturbatory activity has for the male or female adolescent. I feel that there is a basic difference—for the boy, it is part of his progressive move of separating and differentiating his body from that of the mother's, while for the girl the same activity can be experienced as forcing her to submit to the identification of her body with that of her hated mother's body.

It is only by taking into account these meanings that masturbation can have for the adolescent girl, that the nature of the anxiety aroused as a result of puberty can be properly understood. It is these anxieties that help to explain the intensity of the struggle that exists for some adolescent girls against masturbation, and which may result in the compelling need to attack their bodies actively with their hand. The choice of the wrist or arm as the area for attack can then be understood as part of the effort to control the hand by symbolically cutting it off from the body. From my own clinical observations, the impulse for self-cutting always occurred at times when the patient experienced a fear of giving in to the regressive wish to be passively cared for; the self-damage was preceded by an outburst of uncontrolled hostility against the mother, the sexual partner or the analyst.

## Clinical material

The clinical material which follows is presented in order to make my meaning clearer, rather than as proof of the conclusions which I have described. The importance of clarifying the issue of the significance of masturbation for women lies in its clinical application.

## Case 1

A young married woman anxiously said at the start of her analysis that she hoped that I would not try to make her feel guilty about masturbating. Her husband knew of it and they both felt there was nothing wrong with it. She said that she would resent it very much if I created a problem about it. Despite this effort to avoid feelings of resentment being experienced by her in the analysis, she experienced the first period of her analysis as overwhelmingly frustrating and the analyst in the transference as totally depriving. After becoming involved in a new heterosexual relationship, she told of having masturbated with the accompanying angry thought: 'Now I can do without you!' after having felt disappointed by sexual intercourse. Consciously she was angry with her boyfriend, but the person being attacked in her fantasy could clearly be understood in the transference to be related to me representing both her mother and a sexual woman with whom she wanted to compete. The patient, before starting this new relationship, had become very anxious when the close relationship she had to a woman friend had led to some physical contact. She had been both excited and frightened by the experience because it made her consciously aware of her fear that she might be sexually abnormal. This fear could be related to old feelings about her body, her hatred of it and her fear that it was damaged and that she would be unable to have a child. In the analysis this fear could be linked to much earlier feelings and fantasies related to earlier deprivations of not having been wanted as a child by her mother, and subsequently of feeling that her mother wanted her to be injured and unable to have children. The regressive pull of the wish to experience the mother as gratifying, which was repeated in the analysis, was determined by the intensity of her old disappointment and anger and her fear of having to submit to the fantasied, punitive, pre-oedipal mother.

She had masturbated actively throughout her childhood and at times when she knew she might be discovered by her mother. In adolescence her hostile, demanding behaviour was expressed in delinquent acts outside the home, while the regressive wish to be gratified by the mother was expressed in a fantasy that her mother was forcing her to offer herself sexually to a man in return for money which she would then have to give to her mother. This fantasy expressed her wish to feel that her mother was responsible for her sexual activity, and that her wish was not to destroy her mother but instead to help her live. This fantasy was repeated during her analysis in a dream that the patient had during the night after having masturbated. *She had dreamt that the analyst was suggesting that she should work.* Although the impulse to masturbate was related to feelings of frustration in an ongoing heterosexual relationship, the fantasy that had to be denied was the homosexual one of being gratified by the mother or the female analyst which she needed in order to defend against the anxiety of wanting to attack her own body as the source of the frustration.

## Case 2

A similar fantasy was reported by an older married woman patient. She had always felt very anxious that she was sexually abnormal because the only way in which she could become sexually aroused by her husband was through the creation of a fantasy (while she was having intercourse) of an old repulsive woman watching her being forcibly raped by a man and scolding her for resisting him, while encouraging the man to humiliate her even further. In this way she could allow herself to enjoy intercourse through the fantasy of giving in to the wish to be cared for by her mother, while feeling at the same time that through needing to use this fantasy, she was proving herself to be abnormal.

This patient brought no memories of having masturbated as a child. But she remembered with a great deal of guilt that she had such violent fights with a younger brother that her mother was afraid of leaving her alone with him. She also recalled that her mother used to beat her as a child. Thus, her sexual fantasy could be understood as a wish that her mother, represented by the repulsive woman in the fantasy, was still in control of her body because sexual excitement for her was identified with uncontrollable violence against her mother's babies. Her own hatred of her body for containing this violence was expressed in the transference by her feeling that I must be disgusted by her sexual fantasies, that I hated her, and that I therefore also hated her body, The woman in her fantasy was old and repulsive in order to defend against recognizing her wish for a young attractive woman to caress and who would want her body. In this way she could feel free of her own hatred of it and of the need to hurt and attack herself as she felt she did in intercourse through having such a fantasy. During her adolescence this patient had also become frightened when a close relationship to a girl threatened to develop into a homosexual one. In the transference what could be seen was the renewal of this wish in her demand that I should love her body and caress her because she felt it was the only way she could undo her own hatred of her body. My failure to do so was felt by her as proof of my disgust for her.

This case shows how the actual experience of her mother beating her had become part of her own masochistic relationship to her body and was represented in her fantasy by feeling forced to put her body into the position of being humiliated and hurt by a man. As a child, while avoiding touching herself, her fear of what her own hand would do to her body if she did touch herself by masturbating was expressed in her violent attacks on her brother. After puberty her wish for a loving, caring hand of another woman to touch her and thus make her body feel lovable became the only means by which she felt she could control the violence she was afraid she could direct against herself.

## Case 3

After seeing me for an initial interview, this patient, a married woman, told me of a dream where I was identified with a woman with whom, in reality, she had felt uncomfortable.

She had suspected this woman of homosexual tendencies because of the way in which the woman would touch her every time they met. In her analysis she talked of waking up at night and finding her hand touching her genitals. This made her feel terribly anxious and ashamed in case she might have masturbated in her sleep. She could only relieve her anxiety by going to urinate. If she was able to urinate it indicated to her that she had only been woken by the need to urinate and not because she had been secretly masturbating.

She had had a very lonely, isolated childhood with no memories of any pleasurable experiences shared with her mother. Her first anxiety attack had occurred in early adolescence during her first prolonged absence from home. She had found it extremely difficult to urinate and she was convinced that she would have to return home because she believed she needed the presence of her mother to urinate.

Her fear in experiencing anxiety about needing to urinate was related to the fantasy that her mother had deprived her as a child of a strong body which would have enabled her to feel brave, like a man, instead of being anxious and thus like her mother, a woman. The identification of her hand with the deprivation she felt she had experienced from her mother, made her consciously terrified of touching her husband's or her children's genitals.

At adolescence the need for her mother to be present so that she could urinate, represented a breakthrough into consciousness of the masturbatory meaning urination had for her. The wish was to experience her need to urinate as still being the responsibility of the mother and something that she could share with her. Only in this way could she feel that her wish to attack her mother's body could remain controlled. Later I learned that if she urinated in strange lavatories, she always did so standing up because of her fear of contamination. Therefore, her fear that she would have to return home to her mother also expressed her need to give in to her mother in order to maintain her fantasy of being able to be like a boy.

## Comment

These clinical examples show that the need to suppress masturbation during adolescence is closely linked both to the fear of bringing into consciousness the passive homosexual wishes, as well as to the anxiety aroused after puberty through the potential of living out the destructive aspects of these fantasies against the mother's body. Each of the patients had formed an intense relationship, either with another girl or an adult woman, during their adolescence. From their account and subsequent reconstruction within the analysis, these relationships had represented symbolically the living out of mutually gratifying and exciting masturbatory activity—something which is part of the normal development of adolescent girls. What was significant in these patients, however, was that they had all broken off these relationships precipitously at a point where some external event had made the patient feel that the other girl had been harmed or had suffered as the result of their shared activity. This can be understood as further evidence that the conflict which exists around the use of normal means of masturbation for the adolescent girl is linked to the intensity of the need to experience her body as lovable through feeling it as capable of being a source of gratification; the anxiety which is aroused by the experience is because it makes conscious the destructive capacity of the adolescent girl's activity. This explanation also makes it possible to understand the tendency, seen in many seriously disturbed adolescent girls, to actions which result in physical damage to their own bodies.

I am aware that I have made no mention of the father nor of the oedipal situation or accompanying fantasies of the girl. The reason these have not been discussed is that I was trying to find an answer to why masturbation does not appear to be as available to the girl for the purpose of experiencing and integrating these fantasies as it is for the boy. The theoretical considerations and the clinical material I presented were chosen to show why I think the reason for this difference can be found in the early development of the relationship to the body that takes place in the interaction with the mother's care of the child's body and its subsequent development as the result of puberty. In the oedipal situation, where the girl experiences her mother as hostile and envious of her relationship to her father, the hand is now feared as potentially damaging to the girl's genitals because it has already become identified with a hostile, depriving attitude towards the girl's body. The boy's fear of castration can, however, remain externalized on to the father and thus masturbation remains a possibility.

How normal, then, should we regard female masturbation? I have tried to show that the need to masturbate can be viewed as containing a defensive need to experience the body as gratifying and idealized in order to feel in control of the hatred of the body that is aroused through the experience of frustration or disappointment. Inasmuch as the activity of the hand is still attached to the wish to re-experience a relationship to a woman, to replace the pre-oedipal mother, it opens the door to the search for a homosexual object to help defend against the destructive wishes directed at the mother's body and now her own sexual body.

## Summary

The significance of the role played by masturbation in the female is examined from a developmental point of view in order to question the assumption, often made, that female masturbation has the same normal significance as masturbation for the male. In order to do so, the difference between attitudes to male and female masturbation is defined as a difference in attitude to the use of the hand for masturbatory activity and is related to the observation that it is that activity that female children give up post-oedipally and again in post-puberty. The unconscious meaning of the hand, as identified with the mother's active handling of the child's body, is examined to show that masturbation is needed by the child to internalize a positive narcissistic cathexis of the body as well as a means of separating from the mother's body. The continued use of the hand during adolescence and adulthood by the girl or woman is then seen as a defensive means of maintaining a positive relationship to her own sexual body once the girl's body has become identified with that of her mother. The failure of this defence when used by the girl as a means to maintain a positive relationship to her own sexual body is seen as leading to the unconsciously determined need to attack her body, as can be observed clinically in those adolescents who physically attack their body.

## Note

1  This paper first appeared in *Int. J. Psycho-Anal.*, 63: 295–302.

## References

Freud, S. (1905). Three essays on the theory of sexuality. *S.E.*, 7: 123–246.
Freud, S. (1931). Female sexuality. *S.E.*, 21: 221–244.
Hoffer, W. (1949). Mouth, hand and ego-integration. *Psychoanal. St. Child*, 3/4: 49–56.
Mack Brunswick, R. (1940). The preoedipal phase of the libido development. *Psychoanal. Q.*, 9: 293–319.

# 8

# MODES OF COMMUNICATION—THE DIFFERENTIATION OF SOMATIC AND VERBAL EXPRESSION[1]

Rose M. Edgcumbe

Psychoanalysts have been interested in the communicative aspects of somatic manifestations ever since Breuer and Freud (1893–1895) defined hysterical conversion as "the transformation of psychical excitation into chronic somatic symptoms" (p. 86) and discovered that such symptoms disappeared when the traumatic events which had provoked the excitation were remembered, and when the accompanying affect was aroused and put into words. In their abreaction technique talking served as a substitute for action. Psychoanalysts are sometimes accused (rightly) of taking an over simplistic view of somatic symptoms and of psychosomatic disease in that they concentrate on interpretation of unconscious conflict and ignore other factors. Freud himself certainly did not take such a simplistic view. He distinguished between "actual" neuroses with a physical cause and psychoneuroses with functional symptoms (1896, 1898). He further distinguished between symptoms which begin as symbolic somatic expressions of psychic states of mind and those which may be originally unrelated to the trauma and only fortuitously become associated with it (1893–1895). Such symptoms may derive from actual organic conditions, from motor phenomena expressing emotions, from the overflow of excitation such as restless movements in the attempt to overcome pain, or from attempts at inhibition of sound or movement. Freud (1912) was also aware of the complex interactions between individual life experience and predisposition.

At present even to keep up with the emerging literature on psychosomatic medicine is quite an onerous task. Fortunately, there are several good summary papers available. Lipowski (1977), for example, gives a good overview of present-day psychosomatic medicine, which he defines as a scientific discipline concerned with the study of the relationships of biological, psychological, and social determinants of health and disease; and as a set of postulates and guidelines embodying a holistic approach to the practice of medicine. Noting the waning influence of psychoanalysis on psychosomatic theory, he states that ideas of individual psychodynamics are today supplemented by interest in many social and ecological factors. Lipowski takes the view that in all the current research one core assumption is that man's symbolic activity, subserved by cerebral structures and functions, influences organismic processes at all other levels of organization down to the cellular level. Another set of core assumptions, which has particularly interested us at the Hampstead Clinic, is concerned with the role of enduring psychological and physiological tendencies to react to specific stimuli with individually specific patterns of cognitive, emotional, behavioral, and physiological responses. These are partly inborn, partly learned, and are subject to modification and self-control. Developmental and environmental factors, especially those occurring during early development, help to shape future patterns.

In this paper I offer a few ideas from a psychoanalytic point of view, which may contribute, in particular, to the understanding of the way in which early development and environmental factors influence future psychosomatic patterns. We believe that early understanding and communication between mother and baby have an important role to play in the organization of somatic and psychic experience; in the individual's ability to contain, manage, and adaptively express feelings and reactions to somatic and psychological events and situations; and in structural development, which includes the capacity to create representations or symbolize such events and situations.

Over the years a number of Hampstead study groups have been interested in various aspects of communication.[2] Many years ago Anna Freud raised the question of the intentionality of analytic communication. She was concerned that therapists too often assumed that the child meant to tell them something, when the child was only playing out his own fantasy or reacting to some experience without necessarily wishing, even unconsciously, for the therapist to understand his thoughts and feelings. This, of course, is a point of considerable technical importance in the analysis of patients of any age.

Although the patient may not mean to communicate, the analyst may nevertheless understand and begin to recruit the child's fantasy or play activity into the service of communication. We use such unintended clues with our adult patients as well, but we find great variations in the extent of our success in eliciting the patient's wish to communicate or interest in his own communication.

In an earlier paper I put forward the beginning of a developmental line for language, which centered on reciprocal communication between infant and mother (Edgcumbe 1981). I expressed the view that variations in development were partly dependent on constitutional endowment but partly, and importantly, on the mother's capacity to tune in to the infant, giving meaning to the infant's various forms of discharge of tension, reactions to inner experiences, and perceptions of the external world. In a recent paper on an adult patient I drew a comparison between this task in the mother-child relationship and the analyst's task in the analysis of some severely disturbed patients who had communication difficulties (Edgcumbe 1983). My patient had difficulties in thinking which went far beyond the neurotic interference arising from repression and other defenses with which we are familiar. She seemed totally unable to think consciously about anything emotionally important; she could not talk to me, nor could she talk to herself. She seemed to lack any awareness that talking and thinking were useful activities either for purposes of communication with people or for sorting out and connecting up her own experiences. She had never, so far as she could recall, been able to talk to her mother. When she began to think for herself, it was at first always in the form of a conversation with me. Her disturbance of thinking was accompanied by a marked inhibition of affects and by a number of psychosomatic symptoms which seemed to be her only means of tension discharge. From one point of view her somatic symptoms could be seen as her only means of communication, but she certainly did not intend to communicate. It is this sort of patient that points up the link between issues of language and communication and psychosomatic phenomena.

A number of analysts have studied this area in their adult patients. McDougall (1974), for example, stresses the role of parents' unconscious fears and desires in limiting the child's capacity to create symbolic structures upon which self-object separation depends. She distinguishes, as Freud did, between hysterical symptoms which, being based on fantasy and conflict, "tell a story" and psychosomatic symptoms which are devoid of symbolic meaning. She stresses that though fantasies may subsequently become linked with such psychosomatic symptoms, they are not their cause. Psychosomatic transformations are signs rather than symptoms: they bring messages from the body but do not symbolize it.

McDougall regards the psychosomatic patient as having a defect or failure of development: the lack of mental representation of the body as an object for the psyche, and the failure of emotional and physical pain to achieve mental representation, so that affect cannot fill its role of linking psyche and soma. She points out that interpretations may be meaningless to such patients since they have no appropriate symbolic representation with which interpretation can link.

Krystal (1978) takes issue with McDougall over the question whether there is an actual defect or absence of capacity for representation. He favors the notion of regression in functioning and externalization of superego. Krystal's thesis is that the child regards body functioning and body care as belonging to mother/god/doctors/fate at a time in development when magical thinking prevails. To take it over, therefore, is a terrifying, guilt-and anxiety-provoking responsibility. Individuals who have failed to accept such responsibility continue to feel it is up to the object to take care of them and make them feel good. When this is not achieved, they rage against unfairness. The wish to get better is opposed by the stronger fear of taking over the self-caring function. Krystal suggests that the idea of a defect which must be repaired by the object is the patients' theory of what is wrong with them, but the failure to take over or develop the self-caring function is defensive rather than due to a developmental absence of the function. Krystal and McDougall both stress the role of the mother in facilitating early communication between child and mother, upon which depends the development of symbolization and thinking, the acquisition of language and the desire to communicate, affective development and differentiation, psychosomatic unity, and the self-caring function.

We have looked at some aspects of normal body-mind development; analysts are used to thinking in terms of a gradual shift from somatic to psychic modes of discharge and the gradual supplanting of bodily by mental pathways. Anna Freud (1974), for example, outlining the developmental line from physical to mental pathways of discharge, says:

> ... during the whole of the first year, while psychological life expands, the access between body and mind remains an easy one. Every upheaval in the bodily sphere causes mental distress, crying, etc., while every mental upset such as shock, frustration, anxiety causes physical upheaval. This truly psychosomatic period comes to an end as, with advancing age, more and more mental pathways open up for the child and the discharge of mental tension is allocated to them. In the second year the use of the mind for the purpose of tension discharge increases considerably until, approximately in the third year, due to the perfection of secondary process thinking and speech, the division becomes decisive, mental excitation from then onward being discharged mentally and bodily excitation physically....
>
> [Exceptions to this smooth progress occur because] repressed libidinal fantasies and aggressive impulses find the way blocked to psychological expression and for this reason continue with, or regress to, physical discharge in the form of psychosomatic or hysterical manifestations.
>
> (p. 65)

In its present form this developmental line seems to us oversimplified in that the shift and the separation of mental and physical processes are never so complete in normal development. We are trying to elaborate the line to show, on the one hand, the continuing normal use of a degree of somatic expression, and, on the other hand, the diverging line of mental expression, both of which develop out of the normal, undifferentiated, psychosomatic expressions which come naturally to the child in the first year of life. Along with many other workers, we question the usefulness of continuing to think in terms of a body-mind dichotomy. It might be more appropriate to emphasize the unity or interaction of body and mind and the relative balance between them which results in normal or abnormal development.

A central aim of analysis is to help patients verbalize rather than somatize or enact. On the other hand, we do not regard it as healthy to go too far in the direction of substituting thought for feeling or action. The intellectualizer may be just as disturbed as the somatizer.

Language develops out of a wish to communicate with the object and to explain to oneself about two main things: what one is experiencing; and what one does, wants to do, or have done about it. Body language serves as well as verbal language for dealing with basic infantile experiences and needs, but verbal language is increasingly required for more complex experiences and more sophisticated reactions and needs.

I have previously discussed (1981) the mother's role in recruiting the baby's earliest gestures, noises, and facial expressions into the service of verbal communication, by treating them as if the baby intended to communicate. Thus, they give value to the baby's expressions. Mothers who ignore, misinterpret, or react inappropriately to these early precursors of communication in the child may discourage or retard the development of the child's wish and ability to communicate verbally.

I now postulate that as part of this process the mother recruits the child's somatic expressions and reactions into the service of communication first of all by responding appropriately though not necessarily verbally, for example, knowing whether the baby's crying or thrashing about indicates that he is hungry, wet or cold, or lonely, and hence in need of feeding, changing, or cuddling. Next, she begins to recruit such signs from the baby specifically into the service of verbal communication by herself, putting words to the child's somatic expressions or feelings and ideas. "You're hungry, aren't you?" or "Are you uncomfortable?" or "You want some attention, don't you?" If the mother is unable (whether for reasons in herself or the child) to respond appropriately to the child's somatic manifestations, the wish to communicate and the expectation of being understood may be stunted in the child. If the mother continues to respond mainly in physical ways rather than by verbalizing, the child's ability to talk and think in words may be hindered. Somatization may become the only means of communication acceptable (in the child's unconscious view) to the object, so that body language retains a more prominent place than verbal language in the child's repertoire of communication. At the other extreme where words are used to "talk away" feelings (physical and emotional), the child may become unable to use even age-appropriate forms of somatic discharge, like crying, or to be aware of feelings.

What I am talking about here is the role of early interaction between infant and mother in the building up of the capacity for mental representation or symbolization, which can then be used further for communication with both objects and oneself, i.e., thinking, self-awareness, organization of feelings and experiences.

Greenspan (1982) discussed the problem of "awareness" and mind-body relationships as issues to be understood in a relative sense within the context of a continuum of different levels of learning. He thinks we should move away from the concept of mind-body dualism and consider a range of bodily and mental phenomena attributable to different levels of learning.

He suggests that the earliest level is somatic learning; the basic, early "fitting in" of child and mother, when somatic patterns are organized, and the infant develops some ability to regulate bodily states and cycles, e.g., of sleep/wakefulness, self-consoling, etc. Somatic levels of awareness and intelligence are based on this early learning. Next comes consequence learning, giving some awareness of means and ends and allowing more flexibility in adapting to the environment. Learning by internalization is a transitional stage in which the infant learns to discriminate significant others more clearly. This leads to an increase of imitative behavior and an increasing capacity to combine known schemes into new, more complex forms of behavior. This transitional phase (which I would view as deserving far more emphasis than Greenspan gives it) leads into a third level, representational-structural learning, with a capacity for new levels of organization: identificatory behavior, sense of self, person, and object permanence. The capacity for psychological representation leads to potential for a new order of intelligence and a growing ability to elaborate ideas and fantasy (symbols), reality orientation in the cognitive world and in the emotion-laden interpersonal realm. Greenspan believes that once the representational capacity is established, conflicts may lead to compromise formation and specific symptoms which are highly symbolized and relate to unconscious meanings. But there may be a group of patients who cannot perceive, elaborate, or transform certain types of somatic patterns of sensations at the representational level. If there is not access to the level of meanings, bodily sensation may be experienced as strange, frightening, or confusing, like external dangers. If there is no meaning, no adaptive action can be taken.

I suggest that there may be a range of disturbances of this developmental process, the worst of which may result in what amounts to a structural defect of the sort McDougall describes, a virtual absence or at any rate complete nonfunctioning of a capacity to create mental representations of one's own body or of physical and emotional pain and other feelings, so that the connections between psyche and soma cannot be perceived or understood. In less severe cases the capacity may be better developed but interfered with in varying degrees of severity and in various ways. This range of disturbances is illustrated by some of our child patients at Hampstead.

First, I briefly describe two children who illustrate the more severe form of defect. In one, the developmental failure seems mainly attributable to the mother's state; in the other, to the child's.

Susan was a child in whom the wish and ability to understand and communicate about herself was stunted in the extreme, largely it seems because of difficulties in her mother. Susan was verbally articulate, but for the most part disinterested in her own inner life. She was the only surviving child of a woman with a distressing obstetric history of innumerable miscarriages and stillbirths, who managed to carry to full term only by dint of spending months in the hospital. She had given up hope of having children and said she no longer wanted the baby. The well-baby clinic notes contain repeated remarks on the mother's anger, depression, lack of enjoyment in Susan or interaction with her. She rarely cuddled the baby, mostly holding her at a distance on the edge of her knee, and expressed disgust at her messiness. She talked to the baby in a distant, inappropriate way. Reports comment on the baby's quiet, often apathetic state; she is described as dejected or subdued. Occasionally they note the baby's responsiveness to her mother or attempts to engage mother's attention; but on each occasion Susan quickly ceased her attempts when her mother did not respond. Initially Susan was lively and responsive with the well-baby clinic staff, who played and talked to her, while they undressed and examined her. As she grew older, however, reports note her aimlessness and lack of concentration in play.

Speech developed apparently normally, but when at age 12 years she was eventually referred for treatment, it became apparent that she talked about intellectual matters and events, but not about feelings, hopes, or wishes, except for her determination to do well at school. Both parents were intelligent but had been prevented by economic circumstances from studying, and they were determined that their daughter should fulfill their ambitions. To this end they valued educational achievements above everything and disregarded the importance of feelings, dealing with them by an insistence on mastering activities.

In infancy a series of illnesses are noted, including colic, frequent colds, and earache; later Susan suffered from diarrhea, beginning about the time of toilet training, and wetting and nightmares when she started nursery school. Repeated attacks of tonsillitis, bronchitis, and ear infections led to tonsillectomy and adenoidectomy at age three. Susan seemed happier after spending a week in the hospital with her mother, and soon thereafter developed attacks of bronchospasm, to which her mother reacted with anger, seeing them as bids for attention. Susan went on to serious asthmatic attacks, sometimes requiring hospitalization. She had occasional convulsions associated with feverish illnesses. It seemed that while some of Susan's minor symptoms may have been predominantly psychological in origin, she also had serious physical illnesses which were probably exacerbated by the family's psychological difficulties. The well-baby clinic staff felt that the parents denied even serious illness to a pathological extent and could not consider the psychological implications of Susan's bodily symptoms. Hence, they refused offers of psychotherapy until her life was in danger. In addition to her somatic symptoms, Susan was also accident-prone, in a way which appeared to start as a result of her parents' neglect, but subsequently became an expression sometimes of her own destructive rage, sometimes of her failure to see causal links and profit from experience. The baby clinic had noted mother's clumsy handling when Susan was an infant; and various minor accidents were reported throughout childhood. Her hospital notes record a series of road traffic accidents, three of which required outpatient treatment, until at age 12 she suffered multiple injuries to her head, shoulder, and ribs. This time the parents were sufficiently worried to seek psychotherapeutic help because of Susan's unusual reaction after this accident: she became tense and miserable, passive, and not helping herself. The preoccupation with death and disease which she had had for some time now became pronounced. Clinic staff were concerned about the psychopathological implications of her accident-proneness and her failure to avoid situations which could exacerbate her somatic symptoms.

By this time, Susan herself was set against the idea of psychotherapy, and it was clear that she saw no value whatever in talking about her feelings and experiences. She came reluctantly for non-intensive therapy, and although she did make a relationship, her therapist found it difficult to engage Susan's interest in her own inner life. It was possible to counteract the self-destructive tendencies to some extent by working on areas which could raise the child's self-esteem and therefore somewhat increase her wish to care for herself. In the main, however, Susan took to extremes the family use of defensive denial and isolation, unable to recognize cause-and-effect relationships. For example, she brought on a severe asthma attack by playing in a haystack, but until her therapist talked about it with her she had quite failed to see the connection between this enjoyable activity and her illness, although she knew she was allergic. That is, as with my adult patient, Susan suffered not only interference with her ability to communicate with objects, but a disruption of her own thinking and understanding of herself. She demonstrates an extreme stunting of the development and differentiation of affects and of somatic and psychic modes of expression; and her parents seemed to have played a significant role in this development.

In another child, Joan, her tendency to somatize was due in part to early experiences of bodily pain. She had a bone disease, in which inflammation caused her pain whenever she was held or handled. This began at age five weeks and meant that the regular episodes of daily bodily care, which for normal infants are times of pleasurable interactions with mother and provide the basis for the development of communication, were unpleasant for Joan; loving cuddles were precluded, and the mother had to help in painful and frightening medical procedures and investigations. Thus, in this case the mother-child relationship was distorted by the child's bodily illness; and her analysis revealed a deeply ingrained view of her mother as an attacker. Both in her real relationship to her mother and in the transference to her therapist, she constantly felt attacked and retaliated with extreme verbal and sometimes physical abuse.

She was her mother's first child, and Mrs. B. told her own worker that she thought she would have had difficulty mothering her first child whatever the circumstances, because of her own deprived upbringing. But she felt particularly helpless and inadequate in the face of this baby's irritability and misery, which for several months could not be relieved. At five months Joan was put on steroids which cured the disease by about 24 months, but in the meantime bloated and immobilized her. This interference with mobility restricted her capacity to discharge excitement or aggression, especially to displace it away from mother. In later years she showed a marked weakness in ego control of drive activity. Joan became able to walk only after the steroids were discontinued when she was two.

When Joan entered analysis at age 11, she and her parents were engaged in battles over many issues of daily living, since Joan easily felt slighted or unfavored and reacted with rage. She envied the good relationship between her mother and younger sister, who was a much easier, cuddly baby, more rewarding for the mother. Joan's parents were far more aware of psychological issues than Susan's, but still the family pattern was to deny anxiety or concern about illness and to promote a "stiff upper lip" attitude.

When Joan unwillingly began treatment, she, like Susan, had no wish to communicate with her analyst about her inner world, no awareness of problems in herself, no wish for insight or exploration, no sense of achievement in understanding. She spent most of the first two years blaming and abusing her analyst. Verbalization of affect and interpretations of conflict had little meaning for her, and she denigrated her analyst's attempts to think about her or make sense of her experience. Externalization and projection were favored defenses so that she felt attacked whenever her analyst tried to show her own contribution to events. She could never admit to being worried or upset: she could only be in a rage with someone who crossed her or dismiss the event as unimportant; she also had frequent minor illnesses such as colds, hay fever, and boils, but usually could not recognize that she was ill. Thus, it fell to her analyst to turn these various expressions of psychological or somatic states into communications by sorting out whether she was physically ill or in a bad mood, a service for which Joan was not grateful, though the minor illnesses did diminish in frequency. It took prolonged experience of her analyst as a person who cared about her well-being and made strenuous efforts to understand and ameliorate her somatic and psychic state, before Joan could begin to shift from her initial suspicious and hostile attitude. It became clear that she was in conflict between a strong wish for passive dependence and care (of which she felt she had been deprived) and an equally strong belief that her needs could not be met because she was so damaged. Because of the eventual availability of conflict Joan, more than Susan, could slowly be drawn into the beginnings of a treatment alliance in which she first used the analyst as ego auxiliary and subsequently moved on to a more active role in exploring her own inner world.

Joan's mother, unlike Susan's, was not so emphatically averse to understanding her child. Also, Joan's father could often mediate between mother and child in a way that facilitated understanding between them, whereas Susan's father was even more aloof than her mother. This may account for the fact that Joan still retained some hope of being understood, and this could be elicited in therapy so that communication could begin around her somatic symptoms and physical enactments, and then shift to more verbal modes. In her case the analyst could recruit behavioral and somatic discharge phenomena into the service of communication, whereas Susan remained disbelieving of the usefulness of such attempts. But both children illustrate the failure to develop the wish or ability to communicate with their objects or within themselves about their experiences, needs, and wishes. Both tended to express all forms of excitation in a relatively primitive way.

In other cases, there is a move forward from the primitive discharge mechanisms. Mental representation and organization of experience and the wish to communicate with the object do develop, but the abilities are limited or distorted in some way.

We are all familiar with the kind of split between verbal and somatic communication that can occur especially in obsessional patients. John, for example, was a highly articulate 14 year-old when he started treatment, who delighted in talking about himself and investigating his own motives and past history; but much of this was intellectualization, divorced from real feelings. When the crunch came, anxiety was usually expressed somatically in feeling sick or having headaches or fever. He had in fact been referred because total school failure had eventually developed after years of missing odd days because he felt the only way he could get attention for his anxiety or distress was to say, "I feel ill". In his case the choice of somatic pathways had been heavily influenced by his father's having a dangerous heart condition, which meant that the children had to learn to be quiet and considerate, undemanding and unaggressive for fear of causing father's death and in order to free mother to look after father. John's normal processes of masculine identification played a large part in his taking over the role of sick member of the family after his father had an operation when John was 12, which suddenly and unexpectedly changed the father from a potentially dying man to a healthy one.

Many patients attempt, as John did, to "talk away" their trouble, especially if they come from families which place emphasis on the importance of verbal explanations rather than physical reactions, comforting or restraint. Like Freud and his patients, they discover that abreaction through talking only works if the appropriate affects are aroused, linked with the experience, and then contained or defended in some other way than discharge through physical symptoms. Without this, the talk merely serves to increase the split between experience and affect, between ideas and feelings.

In many cases verbalization of affect plays a major role in the reduction of somatic symptoms. William, for example, suffered from bad headaches, including migraine. When he began analysis at age nine, he was unaware of the connection between experiences which acted as precipitating causes and the resulting headache; nor was he aware of the feelings aroused by these experiences. Unlike Susan and Joan, he was able very quickly to respond to the therapist's efforts to understand him. His disturbance was primarily neurotic, and analysis of his defensive denial of affects and repression of the links between experiences and feelings was effective in reducing his headaches. He realized that if he knew what was upsetting him, and if he cried or experienced the appropriate feelings, his headache was less likely to develop into migraine. He became able to use the first sign of a headache as a signal to think about what was distressing and could in this way prevent a migraine from developing; i.e., his symptom achieved mental representation and acquired meaning in his inner world; it was no longer simply a somatic expression of tension.

William's birth was difficult, and there were early feeding disturbances including quite severe vomiting and pain. These early body problems may have reinforced a tendency to somatize both because of the painful experiences, and because they served to focus mother's attention on him since she felt obliged to respond to his physical needs, although she was depressed and disappointed in her baby. Neither parent could easily tune in to William's feelings and other needs. Their relationship was deteriorating, they separated when he was three, and both had further relationships. Both were preoccupied with their own needs and difficulties, and William was subjected to many upheavals and changing circumstances. When in analysis his headaches began to give way to feelings, his rage, disappointment, loneliness, and helplessness were particularly important; the most frequent triggers for these were actual or anticipated separations, disappointments, and rejections by his parents or their substitutes. Later sexual fantasies and masturbatory activities emerged as triggers for anxiety, states of helplessness, and fears of failure. William seemed not to have developed the capacity to recognize, experience, and contain his own feelings, probably because he received no help in this task from his parents, so that he felt as helpless to control himself as he was to control external events. His tendency to collapse helplessly, "like a jelly", as his mother said, in the face of any kind of difficulties, had resulted in failure at school. This factor was as important as his headaches in his mother's decision to refer him for help. A significant achievement in treatment was his ability to differentiate between external events he could not control and internal events over which he could gain control, so that he began to take more active responsibility for himself.

In William's case, the choice of somatic rather than verbal communication was probably due to a mixture of factors: constitutional, identificatory, and environmental. In other children, it is more obviously influenced by a physical condition, as in the case of Katie who had infantile eczema of such severity that she would have had prolonged stays in the hospital had her mother not been a doctor able to treat her at home. In some respects, the eczema increased the closeness of mother and child, due to Katie's need for bodily care. At the same time this kept Katie dependent, and there was delay in many areas of development. In particular the diagnostician thought the eczema had kept open primitive discharge pathways to the extent that affects were still experienced in somatic terms and not as mental representations. Katie, at age five, readily engaged with her analyst in cooperative efforts at understanding herself. There were dramatic examples of her rash flaring up in reaction to some distressing experience, and then being visibly reduced by verbalization of feelings and interpretation of conflict. Her analyst had embarked on the treatment not expecting to cure the eczema, only to deal with the psychological sequelae, and was therefore surprised at the degree of long-term improvement which was achieved. Even the old scarring from deep lesions was reduced, and bad rashes became infrequent. What became apparent in Katie's treatment was that while she and her mother were able to talk and think together about many things, the eczema itself was too painful to be spoken of. At bathtime the mother could hardly bear to look at Katie's scarred body, and Katie felt her rash made her repulsive. She tried hard, and often with success, to be a big girl, brave, uncomplaining, clever, talented, not showing babyish feelings. Her eczema was unspeakable, and her feelings about it had to be hidden; but they did exist.

Only when she had developed considerable trust in her analyst could she demonstrate her eczema by scratching and crying. Katie's mother could not bear to watch this, but the therapist put words to the physical and mental pain and to the fears of being ugly and unlovable, as well as touching and comforting the child physically. Putting words to the pain helped to give it representational status in the child's inner world, so that she could develop more adaptive ways of dealing with it. Katie's mother could also be helped to overcome her own distress and join in the exploration of feelings and ideas about the eczema. Katie's analysis also dealt with issues common in young children, among which conflicts over aggression were especially important for Katie. She developed into a well-functioning schoolchild with good family and peer relationships, but she retained a tendency to regress under stress, particularly at times of separation and fear of her own or the object's anger. Her mother reported that she would then have an attack of eczema, asthma, boils, or a bad cold, and would temporarily lose her ability to verbalize. But her mother's understanding of the situation could help Katie return to verbalizing. It seems that Katie's eczema had caused a specific defensive interference with some areas of mental representation and communication, but her basic capacity was intact. Her physical condition also created a vulnerability to regression to somatic expression of affect.

I hope that these cases have served to illustrate some of our ideas about the role of development of bodily and verbal communication between child and mother; the range of effects of interferences with this interaction on later development, and the way such difficulties are manifest in treatment.

I have assumed that one of the first differentiations the infant has to make with the help of his mother would be between the experience of something happening and his responding to it. Subsequent differentiations would involve differentiation of experiences into somatic and psychic; reactions, too, would first differentiate into somatic and psychic, with further subsequent division into thought, feeling, action, etc. But two main forms of expression continue: the bodily and the verbal; their conversion into modes of communication, "languages", depends on their acquiring value within mother-child communication and representation in the inner world. Body language comprises somatic symptoms and physical actions, verbal language includes the various levels of thought and some levels of fantasy; other fantasies, which remain nonverbal, and emotions perhaps always continue in normal development to bridge the gap between the bodily and the mental.

Analysts have long been used to working with neurotic patients whose conflicts are expressed in somatic symptoms or bodily actions, which can relatively readily be converted into verbal and affective expression as long as the patients retain the wish to communicate with the object and to understand themselves, and the belief in the object's interest and goodwill towards them, so that communication is experienced as having value and purpose. Those patients who do not retain or have not developed this wish and belief present much more difficult technical problems and have developmental disturbances more far-reaching than simple neuroses. They force us to become aware that psychosomatic differentiation is not a simple process of shifting from somatic to psychic modes of expression and representation; rather, it is a more complex development in which only the relative emphasis normally shifts, while links between psyche and soma are maintained. Too great disconnection of psyche and soma, or too great emphasis on one or the other, produces various forms of disturbance.

## Notes

1 This paper first appeared *Psychoanal. St. Child*, 39: 137–154.
2 Most immediately, the paper derives from discussions in two study groups on Language Development and Emotional Disturbances Expressed via the Body, both chaired by the author. Members of these groups and contributors of material include: J. Boutall, M. Burgner, A. Gavshon, B. Grant, C. Lament, D. Luciani, S. Marans, F. Marton, S. Melzak, E. Model, T. Nyhamar, R. Oldeschulte, E. Phipps, D. Roditi, J. Szydlo, S. Vas Dias, D. Wills. Antecedent groups include the Psychosomatic study group chaired by C. Yorke; the Index study group chaired by J. Sandler; a concurrent group on Developmental Disturbance is chaired by H. Kennedy.

## References

Breuer, J. and Freud, S. (1893–1895). Frau Emmy von N. In *Case Histories from Studies on Hysteria*. S.E., 2: 48–105.

Edgcumbe, R. (1981). Toward a developmental line for the acquisition of language. *Psychoanal. St. Child.*, 36: 71–103.

Edgcumbe, R. (1983). On learning to talk to oneself. *Bull. Brit. Psychoanal. Soc.*, 5: 1–13.

Freud, A. (1974). A psychoanalytic view of developmental psychopathology. In *The Writings of Anna Freud*, Vol. 8. New York: International UP, 1968, pp. 57–74.

Freud, S. (1896). Heredity and the aetiology of the neuroses. *S.E.*, 3: 141–156.

Freud, S. (1898). Sexuality in the aetiology of the neuroses. *S.E.*, 3: 261–285.

Freud, S. (1912). Types of onset of neurosis. *S.E.*, 12: 227–238.

Greenspan, S. I. (1982). Three levels of learning. *Psychoanal. Inq.*, 1: 659–694.

Krystal, H. (1978). Self representation and the capacity for self care. *Ann. Psychoanal.*, 6: 209–246.

Lipowski, Z. J. (1977). Psychosomatic medicine in the seventies. *Am. J. Psychiat.*, 134: 233–244.

McDougall, J. (1974). The psycho-soma and the psychoanalytic process. *Int. R. Psychoanal.*. 1: 437–460.

# 9

# THE SOMA AND THE BODY
Navigating through the countertransference

Marina Perris-Myttas

### Setting the scene

In this paper, I would like to consider the body and the soma in terms of what I have come to experience as their distinctive presence in the work of analysis. I will discuss their intimate connections, as well as their substantial differences. The distinction between the soma and the body raises several questions: how do they interrelate and partake in the formation of the psychic world? Is the soma only the concern of medical sciences or is it relevant to psychoanalysis? These questions, in their gravity, complexity and philosophical nature, lie at the core of psychoanalytic theory and praxis and will be considered in this paper on a clinical and theoretical level.

I am particularly interested in the exploration of the countertransference, in both its narrow sense and in the broader sense described by Paula Heimann (1950), which is the main use of the term in this paper. Indeed, Heimann following Freud (1915b) suggests that "basic assumption is that the analyst's unconscious understands that of his patient. This rapport on the deep level comes to the surface in the form of feelings which the analyst notices in response to his patient, in his 'counter-transference'" (p. 82).

With this definition as my starting point I have here developed my thinking about the inter-relationship between the libidinal body and the soma as they emerge in the analytic process.

I will start by giving two brief vignettes from the initial consultations of two patients. In presenting these vignettes, I wish to draw attention to the strikingly different textures of my first countertransference responses in the opening moments of these patients' analyses.

### Initial impressions: Zoe and Liona

Zoe came to see me in her early thirties. She presented herself in a deliberately attractive manner, dressed in a way that revealed her well-shaped body. She had a seductive presence, while talking to me about her "suffering body" and criticising herself for being unstoppably preoccupied with "aches and pains". Her mind was full of worries about being struck by lethal ailments. While talking to me she ran her hands over the front of her body, stroking and caressing it, mainly her tummy, in order to "show" me where the pain was. "I have had all sorts of investigations, there is nothing wrong with me, but still I cannot leave my body alone", she said.

For the first couple of months I found it hard to listen to Zoe's words. My attention was drawn to her body. I started to realise that my patient was reaching out to me by communicating almost exclusively through her body: her posturing, her gestures, particularly the continuous movement of her hands and intense eye contact, which at times came with a "knowing smile". All this was much louder than any of her verbal communications. In my countertransference, I myself "could not leave her body alone" either. I felt captivated by it in a very concrete way. I felt, I was being seduced away from my analytic listening to a place where I was concretely "watching" her gestures and bodily posturing, as if I was a spectator of a dancer, and I found myself, disturbingly, keeping away from the suffering young woman who came for help.

Liona, the second patient, introduced herself by saying, "I am here because I find life impossible". She was in her thirties, she had a three-year-old daughter and was single. She was dressed—or covered, I should say—in black, and inescapably anxious. She had a long history of somatic illnesses, mainly gastrointestinal disturbances and eczema, which she had suffered since childhood. Liona was the only child, born within the first year of her parents living together. Her mother was very young and inexperienced. "I was still playing with my dolls when I had you", she had said to my patient, "I was excited,

## The soma and the body

but I did not know what to do with you". Liona herself had a troubled adolescence. "Getting on with boys was difficult, I never liked the sexual thing. I still don't".

Liona expressed a strong enthusiasm for the analytic work from the very beginning, in particular for the setting, and she quickly wanted to come "every day". In my countertransference, I felt apprehensive about offering her five sessions a week, feeling that it might be "too much", but five sessions a week would certainly fall short of the "coming every day" that she was asking for.

With five sessions a week, Liona's anxiety subsided and I was swept into her narcissistic aura, where she and I were experienced as one ideal, one wonderfully potent entity. Her thirst to establish oneness was for me reminiscent of what Marty has described as the 'Allergic Object Relationship' (Marty 1958). I became steadily aware that I, as her object, was not allowed to be a separate entity. I felt invaded in a rather concrete way: for instance, I was struck at times that when she mentioned the name of her daughter, I found myself changing it in my mind to my daughter's name. I was perturbed by these episodes, which I felt as an intrusion that I could not protect myself from. Later in the analysis I came to think of this early experience as the precursor to the much more powerful invasion. I felt, a kind of somatic "transmission", which occurred a few years into the analysis.

I hope these brief vignettes give a flavour of the different textures of my two countertransference responses. Despite their differences, my responses were also strikingly similar in the way they were evoked at that initial contact: outside the realm of verbal communication, of fluid associations and psychic representations.

### Theoretical framework

Current theoretical developments in psychoanalysis support the core principle of Freud's metapsychology that the libidinal body, as the locus of psycho-sexuality, emerges from the movement of the drives, which means that the body is itself reached by the unconscious processes and by psychic representations.

### The soma and the body

In his 1915 paper "Instincts and their Vicissitudes", Freud seems to allude, to some demarcation between the somatic and the body when he describes the somatic as the place of origin of the drive. In his celebrated definition of the drive, Freud writes:

> If now we apply ourselves to considering mental life from a *biological* point of view, an 'instinct' appears to us as a concept on the frontier between the mental and the somatic, as the psychical representative of the stimuli originating from within the organism, and reaching the mind, as a measure of the demand made upon the mind for work in consequence of its connection with the body.
>
> (1915a, pp. 121–122)

As I understand it, Freud postulates that the stimuli originate from within the organism. A process is then initiated and through its unfolding a demand for work is eventually placed upon the mind. It is in the meeting of this demand that the drive is constituted as the psychic representative of the somatic.

André Green depicts the onset of this process very eloquently when he describes "the stimuli originating from within the soma" as the "mooring of the somatic". It is my understanding that, following Freud, Green sees the soma as there from the beginning: the soma is the actuality of the organism from which excitation originates. Green, moreover, contends that the somatic excitations initially reach the mind at this "first zone of transition, which I consider to be absolutely fundamental, which is the somato-psychic barrier: no one speaks about it, but it is of cardinal importance" (Green 2010, p. 40). In my opinion, following on from this 'first zone of transition" during *unobstructed development*, comes "the demand made upon the mind" and the constitution of the drive: somatic excitations meet with perceptions and memory traces, the libidinal body comes into being and the unfolding of the psychic world is inaugurated. Our knowledge of such processes leaves a lot to be desired, but what is important, at this juncture Green advocates, is "to consider the drive in this position; it designates the "psychical representation of the stimuli within the body" (Ibid., p. 40).

I would like to open a parenthesis here to consider the notion of "unobstructed development", which depends on the quality of the mediating, primary object that is of vital importance: the mediating object can obstruct or facilitate the quality of the transition from the somatic excitation to the constitution of the drive, along with the coming into being of the libidinal body and world of representations.[1] The mediation can be facilitating or hindering depending on the psychic givens and responsiveness of the primary object.

In the fifties in his book, *Through Paediatrics to Psychoanalysis*, Donald Winnicott brought to the fore the significance of the primary object. Here, Winnicott introduced his notion of the "good enough" mother who, in the state of "primary maternal preoccupation", allows for the "going on being" of the infant and keeps him safe from intolerable impingements, starting from the time of absolute dependence. For the infant, if all goes well, this "maternal provision" will allow, for non-obstructed development, first and foremost by securing the psyche-in-dwelling-in the soma, a developmental achievement itself.

Following Freud, Winnicott turns his attention to the individual's psychosomatic existence. Winnicott invites us to attempt to:

> ... think of the developing individual, starting in the beginning. Here is a body, and the psyche and the soma are not to be distinguished except according to the direction from which one is looking. One can look at the developing body or at the developing psyche. I suppose psyche means here the *imaginative elaboration of somatic parts, feelings and functions*, that is of physical aliveness.
> (D. W. Winnicott 1975, p. 244)

Winnicott further defines the 'mind' as "no more than a special case of the functioning of the psyche-soma" (Ibid., p. 244). This designation of the mind evokes, in my opinion, Freud's notion of the drive, or rather the process of the drive's constitution, along with its concurrent creation of the mind in exerting its demand. Green draws on both Freud and Winnicott to bring together the drive and the object:

> The concept of the drive is unthinkable without the object. The proof of this is that the object is part of the drive assembly. Furthermore, the object thus conceived always implies an object that is external to this assembly and independent of it at the outset, ensuring functions of survival.
> (2002, p. 64)

In analysis, the drive—manifested through its exponent the affect, and developed in relation to the object—is experienced in the economic dimension. The economic perspective, which was the last, following from the topographical and the dynamic, to be considered by Freud, "endeavours to follow out the vicissitudes of amounts of excitation and to arrive at least at some *relative* estimate of their magnitude" (Freud 1915b, p. 181). The economic dimension is expressed in "the characteristic of exercising pressure [which] is common to all drives; in fact, it is their *very* essence" (Freud 1915a, p. 122).

From Freud's second model of the mind onwards the force of the drive can be considered to be that of the alloy of Eros and Thanatos arrived at through the processes of binding (Freud 1923). Working with this force is deemed to be of paramount significance for analytic practice (Freud 1937). This is particularly the case when we work with patients who communicate through their libidinal body, and even more so with patients who are affected by somatic illnesses (Aisenstein 1993).

The distinction between the soma and the body has become a central theme in contemporary psychoanalytic discourse. The Paris School of Psychosomatics is dedicated to the study of the economy of the drive movements towards structure or disorganisation. They have developed the theory and practice of psychoanalysis by focussing on work with physically ill patients, where the somatic is the protagonist of the analytic scene. The Paris School of Psychosomatics developed the concept of 'somatisation processes' (somatic regression and somatic disorganization) to describe and study the evolution of processes which occur in some physically ill patients, where "the mental apparatus" switches off and "the somatic reaction had kicked in, more or less totally, substituting for the psychical reaction" (Smadja 2005, p. 32). These processes are understood to arise from an excess of excitation whose quantity prevents representation and psychic working through. The distinction between the body and the soma, as it emerges in the work of analysis, is remarked upon by M. Aisenstein:

> In analysis when patients are in health, the analyst works with the libidinal body. At the time of physical illness however, the analyst has to do deal with both the libidinal body and the suffering soma permeated, as it is, by somatic excitation which has lost its quality of drive and therefore its connection with representation.
>
> (personal communication)

André Green has also argued for the distinction between the soma and the body, underlining the essential differences between the two:

> The body is the libidinal body, in the broad sense (erotic libido, aggressive libido and narcissistic libido) whereas the soma refers to what is known of the biological organisation. It is quite conceivable, moreover, that the latter can cut itself off from the libido and the unconscious, as Marty maintains. Generally speaking, in analysis, it may be considered that we are *always* dealing with the body. Even when there is a somatic disorganisation! Can we deal with the soma directly?.
>
> (2010, p. 37)

I think that Green's question calls for other more specific questions to be considered. One might ask what does Green mean by "deal"? Can the soma enter the reciprocal exchange between the analyst and the analysand, which constitutes the psychoanalytic treatment? And by what means?

I will now turn to these questions and grapple with them through the lens of clinical practice. In my view, raising these questions is critical for our work with patients suffering from what Szwec calls "a somatically ill body" (Szwec 2010, p. 164), including patients who, as they sometimes do, fall ill during the analysis. Falling ill while in analysis may reflect a somatization process, during which the patient's representational capacity suffers, and the reciprocal psychic exchange with the analyst may come to a halt. When this happens, as it did with Liona, the analyst may experience and endeavour to grapple with the vicissitudes and magnitude of excitations, which might be communicated, I am suggesting, at the somatic level.

Here the work of the countertransference is particularly critical, and it may be the main way the analyst has of reaching the patient (Aisenstein 2017; Miller 2014). Experiencing and working through the countertransference, I argue, provides the primary way for the analyst to gauge the magnitude of the excitations. In so doing, the economic dimension of the drive and affect is assessed, and the patient is reached "despite", or even through, we may think, the somatic regression. From this vantage point, I propose that "dealing" in analysis occurs at different levels. It partly means working in the transference and countertransference. When patients fall physically ill, at times the analytic exchange can be experienced as mediated through the actuality of the somatic processes in a rather direct manner—through the concrete transmission and induction of the somatic experience of the physically suffering patient to the unconscious of the analyst. I consider that this kind of communication can be a possible manifestation of what Freud describes as "… a very remarkable thing that the Ucs. of one human being can react upon that of another, without passing through the Cs" (1915b, p. 194).

Led by such unconscious experience, and focusing on the economic dimension, the analyst can carefully gauge the level of affective intensity that can be tolerated by the patient, while taking care to avoid the risk of a possible deepening of the somatic regression. When lived and worked through, this kind of countertransference enables, in my experience, what Green refers to as speaking to the soma "through the voice of the body" (2010, p. 37), whilst the psychic world gradually becomes infused with the presence of affects and representations. Analytic work with the economic dimension in mind can open the way to the reversing of the somatic regression and gradually returning to the analytic work within the psychic field.

I will now move on to explore the different quality of the presence of the body and of the soma in analysis, by focusing on the diverse countertransference in the two analyses.

## Zoe: painful longings

Zoe's fears of possible illnesses subsided during the first six months of analysis. The presence of her body and her absorption with it, however, remained at the centre of her communications. There was, nevertheless, a shift in their quality. Zoe became filled with excitement about her sexually "alluring" body. I felt urged to join in her homosexual call by "watching" her body. This allowed me little space for reflection, and I found I had moved away from my analytic listening and reverie. I felt relieved at the moments when I could recover some ability to both be present in my experience with the patient and retain my analytic capacity. When I could manage that, my mind went back to Zoe's early years: she was two-and-a-half when her mother "left home" to attend to her own much younger sister who had become critically ill, and she stayed away for more than a year. (Zoe's mother was 17 when her sister was born.)

When Zoe's mother went away to look after her sister, Zoe was left with her father and paternal grandmother. Her mother's absence was traumatic for Zoe. It was my overall countertransferential experience, as I have described it up to now, that led me to form the first idea that the trauma was registered at a bodily level. I was to "watch" her excitement with her body and her pleasured expressions. Was she, unconsciously, eliciting her mother's gaze, which she had early on, desired and enjoyed but traumatically lost when her mother left? Was this her way of pointing for us both to the traumatic experience she had sustained?

At times, Zoe would refer to dreams, "but not dreams really". One day she said, "Last night I had a near-dream. I was dreaming half-awake, actually touching myself, down there. I was left with an "old taste" in my mouth. I woke up feeling alive with a sense of satisfaction all over my body. It was so fine. There are no words for it".

I was left with images and alert to her bodily sensations, and I felt myself in some kind of formal regression, unable to find words to communicate to her. Was the presence of her body overtaking her spoken communications in such a way that dominated my countertransference, leaving me speechless? Only after the session did I notice the connection of the genitals to the erogenous zone of the mouth in terms of her narration in the autoerotic "near-dream"—the "old taste" in her mouth. The presence of eroticised orality, as the dominant thread of her psychosexuality, was shaping the transference, manifested as it was, through bodily communications. A defensive function was served as well: she was keeping the object close through sexual excitement, while keeping at bay her needs for terrifying dependency stirred up by the presence of the object.

In pointing to these instances from Zoe's analysis, I want to emphasise that my patient's bodily impulses were at times in excess and so uncontained in her mind that even dreams were aborted and turned into action, an action which, albeit in very different ways, was taking place both in her night experiences and in the sessions. Furthermore, and in regard to the distinction between the body and the soma discussed above, Zoe's action within the "near-dream" was not the "acting-in in the body" (Aisenstein 2006, p. 2) that we see in patients affected by somatic illnesses. It was rather an action *on her own body*, an "acting–out" of feelings, for which there were "no-words", through her body.

With time, and as I was able to work-through the conscious and unconscious dimensions of my response of "watching" her body, Zoe started to bring real dreams, and threads of symbolization became increasingly present. This opened the way for early experiences to start emerging in the analytic scene, which came into focus through the way they shaped the movements of the transference and countertransference. For instance, there was one time when Zoe said she felt joy after the session she had two days ago. Then she went home, and as she was preparing food for her herself she was "talking" to me in her mind. "You were with me, I felt calm and very pleased". "Strange", she continued,

> I do not remember almost anything from the time when my mother was absent. But yesterday evening I had the thought that when my mother left I lost the world I was living in: that's the only way I can speak about it.

Through tears she talked about missing her mother, "all her life". She talked of craving her mother's warmth and soft skin when she was held in her mother's arms.

> I took to sucking my thumb, I was doing that for years. Then much later, I was holding on to my genitals to put myself to sleep like I was trying to fetch myself in a new warm world of my own creation.

I thought of her mother's extensive absence as the traumatic loss of the paradise which she had experienced in the early relationship with her mother. It was at a much later time that there emerged in the analysis the rage and murderousness that this loss fuelled, split off as it was into a grandiose omnipotence, defensively erected to protect her from the experience of loss. But at the time I am speaking of here, listening to Zoe brought to my mind E. Laufer's thoughts presented in her paper: "The female Oedipus complex and the relationship with the body", in regard to the consequences of very early experiences in the infant girl's life:

> The way I have understood the significance of the earlier phase [pre-oedipal years] is that it is the period in which the relationship to the girl's own body becomes established. The decisive factor is the extent to which she is left with a narcissistic libidinal cathexis of her body, rather than vulnerable to her self-destructive impulses, because the predominance of a narcissistic cathexis will

help her to negotiate possessing a female body and becoming a mother who can enjoy her child's body.

(1993, p. 70)

## Liona: eruption of the somatic

As the analysis progressed Liona was finding life less "impossible"; she was creative in her work, she struggled less in her relationships and stayed free of somatic ailments. There was, however, an ever-present sense of brittleness, which at times immobilised us both.

The unfolding of dynamics in the transference made me think of the internal situation described in Glasser's core complex where:

> ... since the mother is considered to be annihilatory she will provoke an aggressive reaction which is aimed at totally destroying her. But she is, after all, the (only) object which can gratify the infant's needs. Thus, the infant is confronted by an irreconcilable conflict of opposites.
>
> (1993, p. 218)

However, notwithstanding the exploration of such dynamics in the transference, there was a little movement in this area. Liona's use of her analyst as her object, undifferentiated as it remained, had always, as its core and deep characteristic, what Marty has described as the incessant and unrelenting effort of the patient to approach the object so that merging with it will become possible (Marty 1958, p. 99).

With time, the sense of an infantile traumatic past emerged in the analytic scene, suggested through the deficiency of the coming together of affect and representation. For instance, towards the end of a session in which Liona was extremely anxious about her daughter running a high fever, she said that she was woken up the night before by a "terrible migraine". I said that it seemed to me that her intense worry about her daughter's fever the night before gave her a migraine. I received a sharp and cutting response back: "No, I do not think so". "Anyway", she immediately added in an anxious manner, "I always felt I exist from the neck up. I am here for you to fix my head, this would be enough and I shall be grateful". I was dumbfounded. It appeared that my intervention failed to facilitate associations and feelings to emerge, other than anxiety.

Still feeling at a loss after the session, the term "counter-transference on edge", came to my mind. M. Aisenstein suggests this often occurs with psychosomatic patients. Faced with a poverty of associations, of representations and ideational content, "the analyst is compelled to listen to the inaudible, to construct and invent, where affect is involved" (Aisenstein 2013, p. 178).

I sensed the fragility of the patient that I had on the couch. And at times was remembering that "by inviting the patient to lie on the couch and say whatever comes to mind, within a setting where rules are determined by the analyst, the relationship with the primordial object is brought forth" (Perelberg 2008, p. 132). Were we, patient and analyst, at a moment of the ascendance of utter helplessness that often proclaims the presence of infantile trauma? I had the image of disconnected threads and the uneasy feeling of a deep severance between the body and the mind.

Seven years into her analysis when Liona was submitting her Ph.D. proposal, and she told me that, "if it gets accepted it would be the beginning of the end of my analysis". This first perception of a loss functioned, it seemed, as a rupture in her still active unconscious belief in our idyllic oneness. A few months later she started changing. She was experiencing, I thought, a vague threat of impending loss, which I sensed she could not find a way to think about. She became increasingly detached both from me and from herself. Her communications became factual, mostly about the logistics of putting together her proposal. She was talking about "life becoming colourless".

I sensed a mounting underlying anxiety, while other feelings were disappearing. It seemed that at the prospect of the upcoming end of the analysis, under the sway of the transference, split-off early experiences of the traumatic loss in the order of primary narcissism were returning and were repeated in analysis. Liona fell physically ill. She started having gastrointestinal problems, she was aching, and had severe diarrhoea on a daily basis. She was falling ill following the path of a "somatic regression".

In her adolescence, Liona had suffered from irritable bowel syndrome and her symptoms were coming back. "I check when I go to the toilet to see if the "black colour in my faeces comes back". I knew that when she was 16 the "black colour" was followed by the finding of internal bleeding and horrendously painful episodes of gastric spasms. Liona began to remember all the intrusive tests she had to go through, and the pre-cancerous state that was diagnosed. "This is what my doctor thinks goes on now as well", she said. In sharp contrast to her factual and detailed narration, I felt left "in the dark": she was no longer "talking" to me.

I then started to observe myself oscillating in my countertransference. With hindsight, I came to think that I was experiencing my patient in an almost "actualizing" manner (Sandler 1976, pp. 43–44). In my identification with her, I was oscillating between not keeping her in my mind, and at other times anxiously waiting for her. Through this experience, I could sense that my patient, who faced a perceived loss—a feeling which was at that point escaping representation—was de-cathecting me as her object. An absence of psychic elaboration prevailed in Liona, while my own capacity for analytic thinking was also overwhelmed.

As Liona filled the sessions with her somatic experiences, I started having stomach and intestinal cramps, and I often felt an urge to interrupt the session and go to the toilet. I was feeling quite sick. My somatic "re-action" was, I thought afterwards, the outcome of a transmission: the excitation which originated in the patient's somatically ill body was received by her analyst through the somatic reactions in and outside the sessions. During this time, when I was not feeling pain and suffering in my own body, I felt shaken, unable to represent to myself what was happening to me.

Marty's early reflections on the analyst's countertransference when encountering physically ill patients, were coming to my mind. Marty, as quoted by Aisenstein writes:

> A twofold identificatory process develops in the [analyst]; on the one hand, he experiences, personally through identification with his patient, the fragmentation of his body and the alteration of his self-image; and, on the other, he is subjected to a movement of identification on the patient's part that attacks the quality of the psychoanalyst as object, and thus undermines his sense of alterity or otherness.
>
> (Aisenstein 2017, p. 53)

One Monday morning, just before the end of her session, Liona said that she had been very anxious about coming to her session that day. She did not want to see me. Drawing on the force of the experience of my physical state the previous week I said, "You were anxious about what impact you had on me last Friday, you feared I became undone and I would not be here for you today". I felt the fragility of her affective state as I was talking, and I worried about the effect on her tenuous psychosomatic balance. She remained silent, but then I saw her body relaxing on the couch. I thought I might have managed to stay close to the force of the drive movement and gauge its economic dimension in a way that enabled a facilitating exchange between us. But it remained to be seen.

She called before her next session, which was on Tuesday evening, to say she was too ill and exhausted to come to see me. Could we speak on the phone? I agreed—which was a questionable response. She told me that most of the bowel investigations came back negative, but that last night she had found a lump, a "mass" in her breast. It was a cyst which she had aspirated immediately. "I am waiting to hear now, the consultant said that there was black blood coming out of the aspiration. This waiting is killing me", she said in a calm voice which impressed me. I was relieved to hear that she was able to wait, albeit with great difficulty. She continued: "will this 'mass' be malignant? All these things: the proposal, the interview, my gut problems, now this 'mass'"". I felt relieved at hearing her refer to the proposal; she was making a link between her illness and her sense of impending loss.

> I said, "A mass of thoughts and feelings that cannot be fathomed".
> Liona: "The blackness moved from one place to another".
> "And black is for mourning", I replied.

I heard her crying. Eventually she said, "I was not sure that you would still be here today".

The "mass" was not malignant and after this came a very productive time in the analysis, albeit very painful, as her early maternal trauma, which had shown some signs in the past, was becoming increasingly present. She was full of anxiety, but this time the anxiety was not diffused and generalised. On the contrary, it was attached to future prospects that would leave her unprotected. She feared, for instance, that something would "fall apart" in her car and she would find herself "stranded" and maybe attacked in the street on her way to analysis. This was a fear which we were later able to connect with her fear that I would speak with words that were "cutting and damaging" to her: she would find herself unshielded in the face of this danger. One day she brought the following dream:

> "I was in a rather dark room, looking at a little baby girl. There was piercing on her navel, the skin was red, I could not stand it. I was looking at her face, I thought she was numb. I started screaming, "who is doing this? She is too little for this". I woke up in terror. When I feel asleep again and the dream came back, I could not get rid of it". After a pause she added "I was impressed that I screamed so loud, but glad I did!"

While suggesting some symbolic capacity, the dream also reveals the tenuous quality of Liona's network of representations: it becomes a nightmare and points to primary trauma. Nightmares arise when the dream work is not strong enough to contain the excitation present in the dreamer, and the sleep then gets disrupted. And yet she could not avoid her dream, even as it started turning into a nightmare. As she began falling asleep again her dream kept coming back, kept turning into a nightmare and returning. It kept coming back to deliver its message, I thought.

Working on the dream while living through the rage and terror that the piercing was, at that moment, happening all over again in the analytic relationship, we arrived at the idea that the piercing was a repetition, signalling the way her unconscious was taking her and us both back to a time of trauma—a trauma whose origins led me to think of Ferenczi's "Confusion of Tongues between the Adult and the Child" (Ferenczi 1949).

Ferenczi's thoughts, in my view, reverberate in Winnicott's notion of early maternal impingements which disturb the psyche-indwelling- in the soma as well as in Laplanche's notion of traumatic "untranslatable messages": messages conveyed through unconscious processes in instances when the adult is overcome by the excitation the child's body arouses in him (Laplanche 1997). Dejours takes this notion a step further when he suggests that when the translation of the adult's message breaks down, the experience remains "recorded as that of a torrent of excitement in the body that leads to a destabilization, indeed a rupture of the ego, of the ego that is in the process of being formed" (2010, p. 201). The integrity of the ego is threatened.

In all of these theorizations, the adult's uncontained libidinal unconscious emits untranslatable messages which become inscribed in the infant's body "as a torrent of excitation" and as such remain un-representable.

Returning to my patient, my understanding is that mother's holding gestures were experienced as physical violations, which were symbolized in the dream by the "piercing": a violent intrusiveness which has permeated the transference and countertransference in different forms and intensities throughout the analysis, including in the somatic transmission. The image of the tender skin of the navel came to my mind and with it, the tenderness of the primal connection between the mother and her infant. The site of the trauma seemed to be in that very connection, symbolized, one might think, by the evocation of the umbilical cord being pierced. Further the piercing, brought to my mind the possibility of infection, and the anxious tenacity with which, some years ago, she declared that she could only exist from the neck up.

I said, "You speak of scarring on the infant's body, there is a fear of an infection that can fester and endanger life".

"Endanger the life of senses and feelings", she said.

This early scarring was at the root of the disconnection between my patient's mind and libidinal body, and the related serious blockages in the unfolding of her psychosexuality, and at the same time served as a fertile ground for the somatization. The work that followed allowed for the creation of meaning and facilitated the re-integration of the somatic event into the chains of associations, opening the route for psychic elaboration. With time, the deepening of our understanding and further elaboration of the early trauma became possible. Towards the end of the analysis we saw the first signs of some restoration of Liona's psycho-sexual life through her dreams and changes she brought about in her external reality.

## Discussion and closing comments

I would like to consider the similarities and differences of what emerged in the work with the patients I have discussed in this paper. In both analyses we arrived at the early traumatic experiences of the patients, which emerged in the après-coup of the transference in its articulation with the countertransference. Further these experiences were elaborated, primarily, by working through the different textures of the countertransferences.

In 'Sketches for A Preliminary Communication', Freud defines trauma as an experience that overrides the capacity for psychic elaboration (1893, p. 154). In both analyses, there emerged an early trauma with harmful consequences for the patients' capacities for psychic functioning. However, the timing, nature and effects of these traumas, as they emerged in the après-coup of the transference through dreams and associations, were very different.

With Zoe, the reverberations of her mother's extended and traumatic absence and its damaging consequences were manifested in her way of relating to her female body. Zoe's traumatic experience of the extended absence of her mother at the age of two came after her satisfactory first two years of life when the narcissistic cathexis of her body was established. With her mother's extended absence, Zoe seemed to have taken her own body as her new object—as the recipient of her erotic, aggressive, and narcissistic libido, in order to keep at bay the fragmentation that the traumatic loss of her mother's presence might have brought about. The development of her psycho-sexuality, however, remained infiltrated by autoeroticism and prematurity. Still in all its fragility, her sexuality became the locus of her ego integration. The demands of adult sexuality, however, and the prospect of taking full possession of her female body, led to defensive hypochondriac preoccupations with physical ailments, which had the painful and paralysing effects she displayed when she arrived in analysis.

Zoe's transference was marked by the tenacity of her desire, unconscious as it was, not to relinquish the primary libidinal tie with the mother. This transference, albeit at times expressed primarily through her bodily communications, remained "the lever of psychoanalytic action" (Green 2002, p. 260). In the main, I was experienced as her object separate from her, summoned by her psychic call, predominantly through the actual presence of her body. This bodily communication however, remained infused by representations and preconscious activity, throughout her analysis.

With Liona, my construction would be that the trauma originated in early infancy disrupting the process that Winnicott describes as psyche-in-dwelling-in the soma—the moment at which 'the psyche ... means the *imaginative elaboration of somatic parts, feelings, and functions*'. Considered from the angle of Freud's metapsychology, Liona's trauma is also to be rooted in infancy; at the time of primary narcissism and has impeded the constitution of the drive, and the development of psychic representations.

Liona's child-like mother seemed to have been unprepared for her own sexuality and for motherhood. She might have been unable to "accept and contain her own instincts at the same time, to be able to awaken the child to instinctual life", and to "enable him to recognize his own instincts in her, to feel that she can be used as a receptacle for them, so that they can be returned to him in a more acceptable form" (Green 1997, p. 245). On the contrary, her mother came across as being overwhelmed by her baby's bodily call, finding it at times impossible to contain her own erotic and sexualized aggressive impulses. I suggest that the un-translated maternal messages remained inscribed in Liona's infantile body, as an inundation of traumatic excitation which overwhelmed her capacity for psychic elaboration. Instead, the influx of excitation left representational gaps in Liona and a seriously compromised capacity to tolerate her affectivity and in particular the feelings of loss.

Over the years of Liona's analysis there was movement in psychical activity, which was shaped by and shaped the transference. With the first perception of loss however, as the related feelings were about to emerge in the transference, their unfolding came to a halt, the transference lost its levering function and the analytic scene became filled with pervasive, diffused anxiety, which accompanied the advent of somatisation. The communication, from unconscious to unconscious was unfolding in action: not an acting out, but an acting-in in the body, which as previously suggested, characterises somatic regression.

As I have described in the clinical material presented, the texture of my countertransference was fundamentally different with each patient. In Zoe's case, the countertransference was predominantly the feeling of being seduced, and was a response to the communications from my patient's libidinal body. Experiencing her bodily messages often left me speechless, but I always maintained some capacity for the psychical elaboration of my own reactions, whereas this was not possible at the time of somatisation in Liona's analysis.

Indeed, I was then in a very different countertransferential landscape, where it was hard to find my bearings and sustained the experience of being invaded. I understood that this feeling arose from my unconscious perception of the somatic excitation that permeated my patient's suffering soma. This excitation—a disqualified drive with no connection to representation—I registered at a somatic level, in the somatic symptoms I developed, albeit transient ones. At that time the soma became present in the analysis. Working thorough this countertransference experience had summoned, I believe, the infantile trauma in the analytic scene for us to work on.

To conclude, I will return to my opening question: is the somatic relevant to psychoanalysis, or is the soma the exclusive concern of medical science? Clinical work with physically ill patients, as happened in my experience with Liona, seems to suggest that we can find ourselves encountering, "dealing with", somatic processes directly through our countertransference, shaped by the economy of the movements of the drive. Working through the countertransference can help us arrive at a place where we can speak to the soma "through the voice of the body". The recognition and working through of different textures of countertransference, as presented in my two cases, not only suggests the possibility of working with patients who suffer from a somatically ill body, but also brings to the fore the real nature of the distinction between the body and the somatic processes as they emerge in the work of analysis—a distinction which might open up further explorations in the field of psychosomatics and help enrich our practice.

## Note

1 The metapsychological understanding of the complexity of the transition from the somatic excitation to the constitution of the drive is, for some psychoanalytic writers, a fertile ground for further investigation. There are other psychoanalytic thinkers, however, most importantly W. Bion (1984), for whom the issue of this transition ceases to be of concern since the concept of the drive has not found a place in his metapsychology (Perris 2019).

## References

Aisenstein, M. (1993). Psychosomatic solution or somatic outcome: the man from Burma – psychotherapy of a case haemorrhagic rectocolitis. In *Reading French Psychoanalysis*, eds. D. Birkstead-Breen, S. Flanders and A. Gibeault. London: Routledge, pp. 463–476.

Aisenstein, M. (2006). The indissociable unity of psyche and soma: a view from the Paris School. *Int. J. Psycho-Anal.*, 87: 667–680.

Aisenstein, M. (2013). Drive, representation and the demands of representation. In *Unrepresented States and the Construction of Meaning: Clinical and Theoretical Contributions*, eds. H.B. Levine, G.S. Reed and D. Scarfone. London: Karnac Books, pp. 175–188.

Aisenstein, M. (2017). Countertransference and transference with somatic patients. In *An Analytic Journey*, ed. M. Aisenstein. London: Karnac Books.

Bion, W. R. (1984). A theory of thinking. In *Second Thoughts: Selected Papers on Psycho-analysis*. London: Karnac Books.

Dejours, C. (2010). Body and sexuality. *Bull. Eur. Psychoanal. Fed.*, 64: 200–201.

Ferenczi, S. (1949 [1932]). Confusion of the tongues between the adults and the child—(The language of tenderness and of passion). *Int. J. Psycho-Anal.*, 30: 225–230.

Freud, S. (1893). Sketches for preliminary communication. *S.E.*, 1: 145–154.

Freud, S. (1915a). Instincts and their vicissitudes. *S.E.*, 14: 119–140.

Freud, S. (1915b). The unconscious. *S.E.*, 14: 159–209.

Freud, S. (1923). The Ego and the Id. *S.E.* 19: 1–66.

Freud, S. (1937). Analysis terminable and interminable. *S.E.*, 23: 209–254.

Glasser, M. (1993). 'The weak spot' – some observations on male sexuality. In *The Gender Conundrum: Contemporary Psychoanalytic Perspectives on Femininity and Masculinity*, ed. D. Breen. London: Routledge, pp. 212–227.

Green, A. (1997). *On Private Madness*. Madison: International Universities Press.

Green, A. (2002). *Psychoanalysis: A Paradigm for Clinical Thinking*. London: Free Association Books.

Green, A. (2010). Thoughts on the Paris School of psychosomatics. In *Psychosomatics Today: A Psychoanalytic Perspective*, eds. M. Aisenstein and E. Rappoport de Aisemberg. London: Karnac Books, pp. 1–46.

Heimann, P. (1950). On countertransference. *Int. J. Psycho-Anal.*, 31: 81–84.

Laufer, M. E. (1993). The female Oedipus complex and the relationship to the body. In *The Gender Conundrum: Contemporary Psychoanalytic Perspectives on Femininity and Masculinity*, ed. D. Breen. London: Routledge, pp. 67–81.

Laplanche, J. (1997). The theory of seduction and the problem of the other. *Int. J. Psycho-Anal.*, 78: 653–666.

Marty, P. (1958). The allergic object relationship. *Int. J. Psycho-Anal.*, 39: 98–103.

Miller, P. (2014). *Driving Soma: A Transformational Process in the Analytic Encounter*. London: Karnac Books.

Perelberg, R. J. (2008). *Time, Space and Phantasy*. London: Routledge.

Perris-Myttas, M. (2019). Drives and affects. In *Experiencing the Body: A Psychoanalytic Dialogue on Psychosomatics*, ed. J. Press et al. London: Routledge, pp. 9–31.

Sandler, J. (1976). Countertransference and role-responsiveness. *Int. R. Psycho-Anal.*, 3: 43–48.
Smadja, C. (2005). *The Psychosomatic Paradox*. London: Free Association.
Szwec, G. (2010). The capacity to say no and psychosomatic disorders in child. In *Psychosomatics Today: A Psychoanalytic Perspective*, eds. M. Aisenstein and E. Rappoport de Aisemberg. London: Karnac Books, pp. 163–180.
Winnicott, D. W. ([1949] 1975). Mind and its relation to the Psyche-Soma. In *Through Paediatrics to Psychoanalysis: Collected Papers*. London: Hogarth Press.

# 10

# PREGNANCY, MISCARRIAGE AND ABORTION. A PSYCHOANALYTIC PERSPECTIVE[1]

## Dinora. Pines

Despite a growing interest in the psychoanalytical understanding of pregnancy there is as yet no literature regarding spontaneous abortion or miscarriage, although some attention has been paid to planned abortion. Analysis of women patients who have miscarried often reveals their sense of loss, prolonged grief and unresolved mourning many years after this event.[2] Analysis of these women frequently reveals a longstanding depression, a loss of self-esteem and hatred of their female bodies which do not bear live children as their mothers did. Their self-representation is damaged.

In this presentation I shall discuss miscarriage, i.e. spontaneous abortion, and planned abortion, their psychological antecedents and consequences. In both situations young women become pregnant, enter a normal further developmental stage of the life cycle, but are unable to continue their pregnancy to become mothers and bring a live child into the world. Thus, spontaneous abortion is frequently a threat to normal first pregnancy. The medical reasons are often difficult to diagnose and treat and do not necessarily recur in subsequent pregnancies. Most occur during the first trimester of pregnancy when the pregnant woman consciously experiences the developing foetus as an integral part of herself. Her dreams may reveal other aspects of unconscious fantasy and anxiety, such as whom the foetus represents, and who has fathered the oedipal girl's baby in a forbidden guilt-laden intercourse.

In analysing women's dreams, I have been impressed by the influence of physiological bodily changes on psychic life. Dreams may reflect a woman's bodily hormonal change during a menstrual cycle. Mind and bodily changes influence each other in a woman's monthly and developmental cycle and the intimate link between them allows a woman unconsciously to use her body in an attempt to avoid psychic conflict. In considering women patients in my practice who have had miscarriages, I have come to speculate on some possible unconscious reasons for some spontaneous abortions, factors that might be considered in which analysis could be helpful. A first pregnancy, a move from childlessness towards parenthood, is a time of emotional and psychological upheaval. Yet it is a normal developmental phase despite the emotional crisis it provokes, and a valuable time of emotional preparation for motherhood. During pregnancy, particularly first pregnancy, conflicts belonging to past developmental stages are revived and the young woman has to achieve a new adaptive position within her internal and external worlds. We may therefore view first pregnancy as a crisis point in the long search for a feminine identity and as a point of no return.

Pregnancy is an important phase in a woman's life-long task of separation and individuation from her own mother (Pines 1982). Childhood wishes to identify with a primary object, namely the powerful pre-oedipal mother are foreshadowed in play and fantasy long before there is any possibility of parenthood. A little girl's gender identity is established in early childhood and a young girl's sexual identity largely resolved by the end of adolescence. At this point the adolescent's physiologically mature body forces an important stage of separation and individuation upon her. The intense revival of sexual feelings drives the young girl towards her first intercourse, which confirms her right to take responsibility for her sexuality and ownership of her adult body as distinct from that of her mother. Her mother's ownership of her daughter's body has now ceased.

However, pregnancy, the next stage in a woman's life-cycle, offers an adult woman a further stage of emotional identification with the pre-oedipal mother. The unseen foetus, concretely within her body, enables her to re-experience a feeling of primary unity with her mother, and at the same time to identify narcissistically with that same intra-uterine foetus, as if it were herself in her mother's body. Such a symbiotic state in the future mother may well activate intense ambivalent feelings both to the foetus and to her own mother. For a young woman whose experience with her own mother has been "good enough", the temporary regression to a primary identification with a generous life-giving mother as well as with herself, as if she were her own infant, is a pleasurable developmental phase. For others, where ambivalent feelings towards the mother have been unresolved, or where negative feelings towards the self, the sexual partner or important figures from the past predominate, the inevitable regressions of pregnancy facilitate the projection of such feelings on to the foetus. Thus, the foetus may already possess a negative prenatal identity in the mother's mind long before the birth.

In a first pregnancy the young woman has two alternative means of resolving psychic conflict. The foetus may be physically retained, given life and cocooned or may be physically rejected as in miscarriage and abortion. A mother may thus either facilitate life and motherhood or destroy them both. Unfulfilled pregnancy and the failure to produce a live child, either because of unconscious reasons for spontaneous abortion, or conscious reasons for planned abortion, will affect each patient individually. Interaction between fantasy and reality in the pregnant woman's mind will affect the emotional outcome. For some women, from the moment that pregnancy is confirmed, the foetus is invested, in conscious fantasy and daydreams, or in unconscious fantasy and night dreams, with the physical appearance of a baby and even with a sexual identity of its own. These women look forward to becoming good enough mothers as they had experienced their own mothers. Miscarriage for them is a painful loss as if a full-term baby had died and has to be mourned.

Other women regard the foetus as a part of their body which can be dispensed with as easily as an inflamed appendix. Their conscious wish to become pregnant does not have motherhood as its ultimate goal. Pregnancy for them may be an unconscious means of confirming a female sexual identity or adult physical maturity. The foetus is not represented as a baby in fantasy, dreams or reality but rather as an aspect of the bad self, or as a bad internal object that must be expelled. Analysis of such patients reveals an early relationship with the mother which is suffused with frustration, rage, disappointment and guilt. Loss of the foetus either by miscarriage or abortion is experienced as a relief, rather than a loss, as if the continuing internal bad mother had not given permission for the child to become a mother herself. It is possible that the pregnant woman's unconscious anxieties connected with the fantasy of the foetus, representing a

## Pregnancy, miscarriage and abortion

bad and dangerous aspect of the self or of her partner, may be a contributing factor to the stimulation of uterine expulsive movements, which end in miscarriage. The analyst is experienced as this malign internal mother in the transference. Analysis of these aspects of psychic life may enable a woman to maintain her pregnancy and become a mother herself.

Freud's predominant attitude towards motherhood was that the mother's first child was the extension of her own narcissism, and thus her ambivalence towards her living child would be positively resolved. Her child would feel wanted and loved. Her love for this living child would elicit guilt about her negative feelings and prompt her toward reparation. However, Freud also acknowledged maternal ambivalence and the difficulty for a mother in having a surviving yet unwanted child. "How many mothers, who love their children tenderly, perhaps over-tenderly ... conceived them unwillingly and wished at that time that the living thing within them might not develop further!" (1916, p. 202).

Clinical experience leads us to recognize that ambivalence, whether latent or manifest, is present in all parent-child relationships and much depends on the relationship between the biological parents and with their future child. The biblical myth of Moses, the Greek myth of Oedipus and the Celtic legend of Merlin, all babies abandoned by the parents after their birth, illustrate the universality of this theme. Clinical experience bears out the universality of the temptation to be physically or emotionally cruel to a helpless demanding baby or to a difficult growing child. This universal parental dilemma may be highlighted in our counter-transference feelings when a patient's behaviour may run counter to our personal standards of morality. In these circumstances, particularly with perverse or sadistic patients, the neutral stance of the analyst may be particularly difficult to maintain. The analyst may have to monitor his own position in order to withstand the temptation to take on the role of the parent who judges and maintains standards of morality for the recalcitrant child.

I shall illustrate my view regarding the universal dilemma of maternal ambivalence and its varying solutions by presenting material from three patients. The first patient was a victim of the Holocaust, and her traumatic experiences led her to miscarry several times. The second patient had an extremely difficult relationship to her own mother and, despite a conscious wish to have a child, analysis revealed her unconscious ambivalence towards the foetus but also helped her not to miscarry. The third patient had intentionally aborted three pregnancies and felt relieved when her menopause approached and she could no longer be pregnant.

## Clinical illustration 1

Mrs. A was a survivor of the Holocaust. One week after her first period had started she was sent to Auschwitz. Her parents perished there. After her release from the camp, Mrs. A emigrated to England and married. Her periods returned irregularly. Mrs. A longed to become pregnant and bring a new life into her new world which was no longer dominated by sadism and psychic and physical death. For her, as for many survivors of the Holocaust, babies represented the restoration of normality from a psychotic world and the re-establishment of family life. Unconsciously, Mrs. A's future children were to replace her dead parents. Mrs. A, who was desperate to have a child, joyfully became pregnant several times, but each time miscarried. Each miscarriage was physically unbearable. She took a long time to recover physically and frequently remained huddled under her bed covers in a darkened room.

Mrs. A was living in her present reality, as well as in the past reality of Auschwitz where she had spent so much time hiding under her ragged bed covers. Her past had not been integrated and mourning for the murdered past objects had not been achieved. Two vital aspects of emotional identification in pregnancy were impossible to achieve; identification with her own mother and identification with the foetus as if it were herself. Although Mrs. A had seen her dead mother's body she could not let her die in her mind and thus mourn her, for that involved her own guilt at surviving her. Identification with the foetus as a representation of herself was too traumatic to bear. Her wish to become pregnant also contained Mrs. A's unconscious wish for rebirth and for a new self. Yet there was no viable alternative in Mrs. A's mind for a murdered mother and a traumatized child. Thus, while pregnancy satisfied her wish to become a mother, miscarriage enabled her to avoid her own mother's fate and spared her unborn child from the fate that had been her own. Analysis enabled Mrs. A to begin mourning her past and to fight for her right to emotional survival. Her acceptance of her analyst as being a strong life-giving mother in the transference encouraged her to bring new life into a safer world. Mrs. A eventually had a family of three children, although she never forgot the age that the miscarried babies might have been had they survived.

## Clinical illustration 2

Mrs. B had married late in life, and consciously longed to fulfil her childhood wish to have a child in the short time that was available to her before the menopause. She was the only daughter of a professional woman who devalued her own femininity and that of her little girl. Mrs. B's mother doted on her two elder sons and constantly praised their physical and academic achievements, while Mrs. B's own achievements appeared to her to remain unnoticed. Mrs. B's father was ill and retiring, so that the mother's idealization of her sons influenced the solution of her daughter's oedipal conflict. Mrs. B knew she wanted to be a boy throughout her childhood in order to gain her mother's love, as her brothers had done. Her quick intelligence enabled her to achieve high academic rewards, which eventually gained her mother's admiration, but Mrs. B's femininity and pleasure in her female body remained unsatisfying to her, since her mother had not valued it or her own. However, for several childhood years a secret relationship with her younger brother, consisting of mutual masturbation, had enabled her to enjoy giving and receiving sexual pleasure with a male which raised her self-esteem. Nevertheless, the underlying difficult early relationship with her mother, in which she felt neither of them to be satisfying or satisfactory to each other, led to an unstable basic sense of well-being and narcissistic difficulties, which Mrs. B attempted to solve by a series of heterosexual relationships. These were physically satisfying but emotionally painful. Her first lover was old and gentle, as her father had been, and those who succeeded him were younger and treated her badly and scornfully, as her brothers had done.

During the course of her analysis, Mrs. B's initial transference feelings towards her female analyst, originally seen as the projected terrifying powerful mother of her internal world who could neither give nor receive love, were modified. A warmer and easier relationship both with her mother and her analyst ensued. Mrs. B, now more capable of giving and receiving love, found a caring partner. She married him and became pregnant. Consciously she was delighted and yet it became clear as the pregnancy progressed that she remained unconsciously ambivalent towards her future child. She did not look after her own health nor that of the foetus which the scan had revealed was a boy. The earlier conflicts and difficulties that appeared to have been previously worked through in her analysis re-emerged during her pregnancy, as if the new identity of future mother to a child threatened her old identity. Her mother showed no enthusiasm for her daughter's pregnancy. Several times Mrs. B bled but would not rest in order to save her pregnancy.

A dream, after a short break when I had cancelled three sessions, revealed her conflict.

> In the dream she was walking with her mother and felt she was in danger of miscarrying. Her mother said nothing could be done, but Mrs. B knew that she must hurry to the hospital where the doctor would save her baby. Her mother said there was no point and did not help her or give her permission to bear a living baby.

Mrs. B knew that the hospital doctor represented her analyst whose positive response to her pregnancy reinforced her husband's confirmation of herself as a woman. Analysis had shown her that something could be done in the past and she was impatiently waiting for her analyst to return. Mrs. B did not miscarry in reality.

As her pregnancy proceeded and the reality of the kicking baby inside her impelled her towards her new identity, a series of dreams revealed the compelling re-emergence of her analytic themes.

> In the first dream she was applying for a new passport; in another she was at a swimming pool where the big boys were rough with a little boy and pushed him under the water. Another woman jumped in and saved him. Mrs. B was relieved to see him alive.

In her associations Mrs. B remembered being pushed under water by her brothers when a woman nearby had shouted and made them stop. She was dismayed that even in her dream it had to be her analyst who saved the boy foetus and not herself, as if she was identified with the mother who did not save her. She was relieved that her ambivalence could be calmly accepted by her analyst, her unconscious guilt made conscious, and her pregnancy kept safe. In other dreams Mrs. B's childhood envy of her brothers came to the fore.

> She dreamt that she was a hermaphrodite and allowed herself to remember that, as a small girl, she had thought of herself as brain-damaged small boy.

This new material enabled a further working through of her ambivalence towards boys and towards her unborn baby boy. Finally, it became clear that for her the unseen foetus was an oedipal child, and thus evidence of her fantasized incestuous relationship with her brother. Resolution of so much unconscious guilt during the course of her pregnancy has helped Mrs. B to become a good mother to her baby boy, with whom she is closely identified.

## Clinical illustration 3

My final case illustration[3] concerns a patient whose conscious negative feelings towards her mother and her own motherhood and mothering were enacted in planned abortions. Yet each time pregnancy confirmed that her feminine identity was important to her.

Mrs. C was the eldest of a large family. Her father, a passive and retiring man, had died when she was 14 years old and she was shocked when her mother, a vigorous, attractive woman, married her lover immediately after her husband's death. Mrs. C's separate emotional needs and ambitions were never acknowledged by her mother, although she had always cared for her daughter's body. Her mother had told her that it had been a long and hard labour when she was born, since her body was too big for her mother to give birth to her easily. She told her repeatedly what a bad child she was and finally angrily told her that even in the womb she had defied her, when she tried to abort her during pregnancy. She was thus left with an image of herself as a bad child and with a potentially murderous internal mother. These stories had reinforced Mrs. C's feelings that her body and her character had never satisfied her mother.

Adolescence enabled her to find an alternative way of dealing with her painful situation. By using her physically mature body and her adolescent sexuality, she could bypass the painful affects of mourning her father's loss as well as the narcissistic rage evoked by her mother's involvement with her lover. Her relationships with boys provided her with the regressive, primitive satisfaction of the mother-baby relationship, in which she sought the comfort always denied her by her mother. Mrs. C's mother was angry at her daughter's attempts to separate from her and contrived to make her feel guilty. Eventually the situation became so intolerable that Mrs. C made an abortive suicide attempt. The policeman who saved her and took her back to her mother severely reprimanded her and told her that she was her mother's property until she was 18 and had no right to kill herself. This confirmed her conviction that her body belonged to her mother and was not her own.

Mrs. C's relationships with men were always stormy as they had been with her mother and she unconsciously provoked them to violent anger, although she herself showed none and felt she was their victim. She could thus break off and abort each relationship. In this way she was, in fantasy, not only the baby who has to cling on to keep alive but also the mother who had to abort the foetus in her turn. The fantasy of clinging to life, in spite of her powerful mother's attempt to abort her, had become the basis of a narcissistic, omnipotent fantasy which she enacted by making decisions of life and death for the foetus.

During the course of her analysis, Mrs. C disclosed that she had had three planned abortions during her adult life, and that she had each time become pregnant with a man whom she had seduced into the relationship. Shortly after aborting the foetus she aborted the relationship with the man and repeated this pattern when she aborted two previous attempts at therapy. It emerged during her analysis that the emotional closeness with others, in which she sought and regained the earliest pleasure of the symbiotic, mutually satisfying relationship with her mother, also revived primitive fears of merging, since her mother could not recognize her as emotionally separate with needs of her own. Emotional separation from her mother was not achieved. Once her sexual identity and separateness from her mother's body had been concretely established by a pregnancy, she could abort the foetus as if it were a meaningless part of her body. Yet Mrs. C remembered the dates at which these foetuses would have been born and how old they would have been.

We gradually understood Mrs. C's unconscious use of her body to seek revenge on her dominating mother. Her sexual exploits were enjoyed with black men, whom her mother disapproved of, and were designed to use her body as if it were an extension of her mother's and thus subtly to humiliate her mother. Mrs. C's mother frequently criticized and reproached her, saying, "how can your body which was once in mine, feel anything for a man I cannot tolerate?" In this way we could see that Mrs. C's mother reciprocally shared her daughter's fantasy of not being bodily separate from her. We understood that by aborting the foetus, her relationships and her previous attempts at analysis, Mrs. C had felt herself to be even more grandiose and omnipotent than the bad and murderous aggressor-mother with whom she was identified.

Mrs. C's use of her body was also subtly reflected in the transference. Interpretations that showed understanding aroused her fears of fusion with me and she used her body, in order to remain separate from me, by having intercourse with her lover before every analytic hour. In this way the excitement of good emotional closeness with me and the fear of merging was defused by a physical experience of orgiastic fusion with a man. Each time I had hope of creating a healthy analytic baby Mrs. C was impelled to abort it. This was reflected in Mrs. C's work, where she could create lively ideas which she felt obliged to pass on to others to fulfil. In this way her inability to produce a live baby was complemented by her inability to allow her brain babies to grow. She projected her destructive wishes on to the outside world in which every reader was the critical, sadistic, aborting mother with whom she felt fused in her internal world.

Mrs. C was relieved when her menopause approached and she could no longer become pregnant.

## Conclusion

Women who miscarry or consciously abort a foetus may have unconscious difficulties in identifying with a generous representation of their own mother and her capacity to mother. For the nutrient mother may be seen as a Janus like figure; on the one hand a powerful generous nourishing life-giving object or on the other her fantasized opposite face, the witch-like murderous mother, who will bring retaliation to bear upon her daughter. Difficulty in integrating these two polarized aspects of the mother and her mothering into that of a "good enough mother", may lead to a negatively ambivalent relationship between mother and daughter, to difficulties in emotional separation and identification with the murderous mother and infanticide, rather than towards identification with the positive nurturing mother that gives life to her child. Fathers of these women may often have been dead, absent or emotionally detached, unable to influence the difficult relationship between these mothers and daughters.

These women may have unconsciously somatized their childhood emotional difficulties by using their bodies to avoid unconscious affects and fantasies which have felt overwhelming to the young child's ego. Thus, for some women, the small girl's wish to bear a child in identification with the fertile mother may be difficult to fulfil, since the child's early sexual wishes and fantasies are invested in a forbidden object; mother's sexual partner. In the child's psychic reality, the oedipal wishes have become so traumatic and guilt-laden that they remain unconscious, unacknowledged and unresolved in adult life. They are therefore unavailable in adult heterosexual relationships, although the pervasive ill-defined sense of guilt may lead to an unconscious need for punishment, such as masochistic submission to a sadistic partner, or to self-punishment by miscarrying a longed-for pregnancy. The pregnant woman's normal ambivalence towards the foetus and whom it represents may be reinforced by the small girl's unacknowledged and unresolved guilt-laden wishes towards a forbidden sexual object.

Spontaneous abortion which denies life to the foetus may provide a psychosomatic solution to this psychic conflict. If the patient is in analysis during pregnancy, analysis of her conflicts may in some cases lead to a successful pregnancy and to the birth of a baby.

## Summary

This paper examines some of the unconscious reasons that may lead to unfulfilled pregnancy, either by means of spontaneous abortion, or by conscious planned abortion. During pregnancy the universal dilemma of maternal ambivalence towards the foetus and whom it represents may be strongly influenced by unresolved conflicts and anxieties belonging to earlier stages of a woman's psychic development. Spontaneous or planned abortion, which allows the woman who has become pregnant to deny life to the foetus, may provide a psychosomatic solution to this psychic conflict.

## Notes

1 This paper first appeared *Int. J. Psycho-Anal.*, 71: 301–307.
2 It should be noted that one first pregnancy in four ends in miscarriage.
3 I have described this patient more fully elsewhere (Pines 1982).

## References

Freud, S. (1916). Introductory lectures on psycho-analysis: lecture XI the dream-work. *S.E.*, 15: 170–183.

Pines, D. (1982). The relevance of early psychic development to pregnancy and abortion. *Int. J. Psychoanal.*, 63: 311–319.

# 11

# MASCULINITY, FEMININITY AND INTERNALIZATION IN MALE HOMOSEXUALS[1]

## Mervin Glasser

In a book I was reading I came across the following letter:

> My darling heart (perhaps an unfortunate phrase – but I can't use any other) I feel I must write a squiggle which I couldn't say on the telephone without bursting into those silly tears – I do love you so terribly. I had to switch off... because I couldn't [bear] anything after [the song] 'how long, how long'. How long? – only till Dec. 20th – I think I can just bear it. But I love you, I love you, I love you.[2]

Were people not primed by the known topic of this paper, I think they would assume that this letter was written by a woman to her lover. In fact, it was written by the composer Benjamin Britten to his partner, Peter Pears.

This characteristic of homosexuals leads us directly into a considerations of their fundamental make-up particularly in regard to their sexuality and all that it reflects. Is there, it might be asked, a third sex? But we are immediately beset by difficulties in looking for general answers because of the heterogeneity to be found in homosexuals. Not all homosexuals are effeminate; and even if we were not focusing on this particular feature, the diversity is great.

To return to Benjamin Britten and the question of the 'femininity' of some homosexuals: what is it that makes a male, seemingly

## Masculinity, femininity and internalization

normal in all other respects, be woman–like when it comes to his sexuality? Most of the attempted psychoanalytic answers involve the contribution of a fundamental, universal bisexuality. Although this is a fundamental tenet of Freud and of great interest and relevance I shall focus on another perspective.

Considering the 'femininity' of some homosexuals a little more closely we can see that they are not *really* womanlike. This type of homosexual is not being like the transvestite trying in his complicated way to achieve the bodily and psychological state of experiencing being a woman temporarily; and he is not being like the transsexual who is convinced he is a woman in a man's body and seeks psychotically to transform himself into a woman, asking for castration. There is no loss in the homosexual of the significance of castration anxiety. One would never mistake a homosexual for a woman. In fact, considering the seemingly most effeminate, the so–called "camp" homosexual, his mincing speech, manner and behaviour leads him to look like a *parody* of women.

To look then for genetic or biochemical explanations of such a homosexual's "femininity" is a response to the wrong question. The whole issue of a genetic or constitutional basis for homosexuality is one I cannot take up here except to quote from the lecture to the Applied Section [of the British Psychoanalytical Society] by Richard Horton (1996), which so convincingly challenges the genetic and organic studies which claim that they have established that homosexuality is biologically determined:

> The issue [is] ... (he states) ... that of how much genes can be held directly accountable for determining behaviour. And sexuality in particular. And, to be more precise, what aspect of sexuality? Our fantasies, our courtship behaviours, our ability to be aroused, our preference for men or women, or to fair or dark skin, or hair? Here, the complexities show how the notion of "cause" is nonsense. There may be a gene or a collection of genes that govern the development of the penis or the vagina, just as there are genes for the lungs, larynx, mouth, and speech areas of the brain. But we would laugh at the notion of a gene for "talking", and so we should... be equally sceptical of claims for genes or a collection of genes determining, in a predictable way, sexuality or sexual preference.

In any case, homosexuals being such a heterogeneous group, it is difficult to regard all of their sexual qualities as resulting from a special gene or a particular centre in the brain, or from a specific psychodynamic factor. We can only agree with Horton when he states:

> I would argue, though it remains to be proved, that one's sexuality emerges from a collision of forces but exactly how it will emerge is unpredictable, though it may be, in some sense, deterministic ... We do not need to impose a "cause" to know that sexuality is a fundamental characteristic of the concept, "to be human". But also, the notion of sexuality has synthetic properties since sexual preference clearly does have antecedent events that influence its eventual expression.

Homosexuality is deviant in the statistical sense; and of course, deviance is not in itself indicative of psychopathology and certainly does not automatically warrant social condemnation. The perspectives given by studying other cultures is an interesting one, but even cursory study shows it to be a complex issue which cannot be pursued in this paper. Suffice it to say that it does not meet our concern to identify the specific characteristics of homosexuality.

We may thus turn to considering homosexuality from a psychological and particularly a psychoanalytic point of view. I must immediately say that it too will not provide us with a final answer to which we can turn with relief. So, what then can psychoanalysis contribute in its own right to the explanation of the phenomenon of homosexuality? Clearly the answer to this question must be in multifactorial terms and one cannot do justice to them all—in fact to any one of them!—in a single paper. I have therefore chosen to limit my discussion to one particular aspect embodied in the title of this paper.

I would like, then, to start by considering further the type of homosexual who conducts himself in a way which caricatures women. Because he presents himself so openly and invites comment, it will be easier, perhaps. to identify elements writ large in him which are more subtly operative in other homosexuals. What leads him to adopt this peculiar manner of leading one to link him with femininity and yet at the same time express hostility to women?

When I have been able to explore the psychodynamics of such individuals, I have found that they shared a developmental conflict with the rest of humanity but the attempted solution to that conflict followed the same course as those suffering from perversions.

The conflict is inherent in the *Core Complex* which I have come to regard as a universal developmental feature. This complex is made up of interacting elements. These are, in brief:

1. The fantasy of *fusion* with the idealized mother as a means of meeting the person's (originally the infant's) deep–seated longing for satiety and security. In this context we may describe it as the fantasy of ultimate narcissistic fulfilment, or the fantasy of primary narcissism.
2. The mother is, however, a split figure for she is also regarded as relating entirely narcissistically to the subject: she is conceived of as either:

    a) *avaricious*: so that fusion inextricably involves complete and permanent incorporation and thus annihilation of the self-expressed in such ideas as engulfment, envelopment, intrusion, possession and so on;
    or
    b) *indifferent*: to the needs (particularly the emotional needs) of the subject, paying no attention to them or having no wish to recognize, comprehend or appreciate them. This often involves, and is always experienced as, rejection.

3. The consequent *annihilation anxiety* provokes two, concurrent defensive responses, namely:

    a) *narcissistic withdrawal* in pursuit of safety and self–sufficiency. But this leads to *anxieties of abandonment and disintegration*, with attendant states of isolation, depression and deprivation of narcissistic supplies. In consequence there is the intense wish for secure gratification and protection and containment of aggression (see below), which is to be achieved through eternal fusion with the idealized mother (i.e. this part of the core complex involves a vicious circle);
    and
    b) *self-preservative aggression* which has the aim of totally destroying or negating the dangerous, annihilatory mother. This leads to further anxieties of the total loss of, or rejection by, the mother.

4. The mother's indifference leads to responses similar to those detailed above in reaction to the annihilatory and abandonment anxieties (and they are of course intermingled clinically). They are:

   a) *narcissistic withdrawal* from the painful situation, with feelings of low self–worth, loneliness and misery; and
   b) *self-preservative aggression* which aims to destroy the 'ungivingness' of the mother. (We can appreciate how close this reaction is to rape.)

5. Since the withdrawal and aggressive responses are concurrent, the *aggression is also turned onto the self.*

The subject is thus caught between the conflicting impulses to engage intimately with the object, on the one hand, and, on the other hand, both to seek to destroy the object and to get to a safe distance from it. In my view this is a conflict which every infant experiences and the solution or attempted solution of it plays a significant role in the aetiology of different psychopathological conditions, as well as in "normality".

In my therapeutic work with homosexuals there is one developmental feature which they all have in common and that is the way they attempt to solve these conflicts of the core complex. namely, the sexualization of the destructive aggression towards the mother, thus converting it into sadism. This protects the mother and makes the relationship with her viable; but it is at the cost of the relationships being fundamentally and inescapably sadomasochistic and never allowing true intimacy. This generalizes to all relationships, including of course, the transference relationship. It is relevant to state that my clinical experience has led me to identify all the same features that I have detailed in the nosological group known as the perversions.

Some clinical material concerning Mr. C illustrates these features. His favoured form of sexual activity was what is known amongst homosexuals as "hole-in-the-wall" contacts. He would visit public lavatories and go to a cubicle in the wall of which was a hole at the appropriate height. A man in the adjoining cubicle would stick his penis through the hole and Mr. C would carry out fellatio. In this way he could try to meet and reconcile the opposing needs of the

## Masculinity, femininity and internalization

core complex to engage intimately with the object and yet maintain a safe distance from him: having the penis in his mouth, including ejaculation, of a man who is a complete stranger and whom he will never see.

Of course, sexualization operates in the transference, sometimes vividly:

> In a session Mr. C talked about his mother's recent visit to London. He complained about how unforthcoming she was: she said she'd come down to London to do some shopping and to see him at the same time. Why did she have to make that excuse? Why couldn't she just have phoned and said she wanted to visit and he'd have said 'Yes' or 'No' and that would've been that? Why didn't she say how much she had enjoyed it without his having to ask her? And why couldn't she show any pleasure at seeing him? His mother and father, for that matter were so ungiving!
>
> I commented that he had expressed these feelings to me often enough before for me to know how strong and important they were to him. But I owed it to him to be a bit questioning because, firstly, he had talked about how he couldn't stand her to come close and how he therefore pushed her away; and secondly, I had an impression that made me ask whether she actually was as unforthcoming as he said. He reacted quite angrily complaining that his mother was suffocating: she was like a spider on his face and he illustrated this by putting his hand with spread–out fingers over his face. I pointed out that he had expressed his disappointment about his mother at the beginning of the session but he evidently had to keep her at a safe distance because he found her closeness threatening and so he had to find reasons to be annoyed and rejecting. He responded with some sadness that he knew this to be true but what could he do about it? Later in the session, when the material returned to his referring to his 'spidery' mother, I said we could consider that the feelings he attributed to his 'spidery' mother were actually his own feelings. I focused on his greed quoting the way he ate chocolates to excess and with great frequency. I also quoted his preferred form of sexual activity, namely his 'hole-in-the-wall' fellatio. He tried to get away from thinking about his greed and, because I felt it important to get him to at least consider what I had put to him, I brought him back to it: and included referring to material from previous sessions

to demonstrate that he experienced me as 'spidery'. He said that what I was saying was very disturbing: he felt dizzy and the lights on the ceiling seemed to be swaying. He wanted to make me shut up. He wanted to turn round and seduce me by carrying out fellatio on me so that I wouldn't go on saying what I was saying.

As I stated above, I have found clinically that the homosexual shares these features with those suffering from perversions, but I should stress at this point that it must not be overlooked that I am referring to *patients* and that there may be many homosexuals whose basic make–up—whose solution to the core complex problems—is different. After all, it would be absurd for me to characterize all heterosexual people on the basis of my clinical understanding of heterosexual perversions.

The core complex pervades the whole psychic structure and thus affects identificatory processes; and I would like to concentrate on this. There is some ambiguity and confusion in the usage of the various terms associated with the processes of internalization. I use *identification* to refer to the incorporation of the object–representation, or an aspect of the object representation, into the self-representation so thoroughly that its separate origin is no longer recognized. Through identification, characteristics of the object become that of the subject.

For other processes of internalization in which the object or parts of the object are established in the internal world but do not become part of the self-representation, I use the terms "internal objects", "introjects" and "object-representation" as synonyms.

Often, we conceive of these processes too crudely, as if what is internalized is a complete reproduction of the object and thenceforth a homuncule sits in the psyche relating to the self. In fact, it seems self–evident that what is internalized are contemporaneously relevant aspects of the object or more precisely, aspects of the object as they feature in the subject's relationship with the object—the *meaning* of the aspect concerned. What is internalized is a quality relevant to the subject's internal dynamics, something which will help to re–establish psychological homeostasis. When we observe father and son and see, let us say, how much the son's gait resembles that of his father, it is not simply a mechanical reproduction of the father's way of walking that the boy incorporates; it is the subtle or not so subtle intrapsychic meanings that the walk expresses, that is, meanings that the son can exploit for his own internal dynamics.

The process of identification is complex. Some features come to acquire, in addition to their internal object relations meaning, an impersonal, functional quality: in addition to contributing to attributes of the self. they are transformed into operations of the ego. They thus contribute to psychic structure rather than psychic content. A little boy may initially relate to his tying his shoe–laces as acquiring his parents' or older siblings' capabilities (with all that that. implies) but eventually it ceases to carry that meaning and simply functions as an ego–ability; and later he will use it, say, when he ties knots in the stitches in a surgical operation. I am thus distinguishing two components of the process of identification, the one bringing about changes in the self–representation and the other providing acquisitions to the functioning of the ego.

This differentiation has a significant clinical application to the homosexual. In the first place, we find that the identificatory process resulting in modification of the self is substantially impaired by core complex anxieties operating in the internal world: any move towards the incorporation of the internal object into the self is reacted to as if the internal object would take over the self thus threatening the annihilation of the self. Consequently, this is resisted and since, as Freud pointed out. a substantial contribution to the make–up of the self comes from identifications, to the extent that this is obstructed, the homosexual patient suffers from a lack of a substantial identity and will complain of symptoms related to the paucity of his self, such as an inner emptiness and an ignorance of his true identity.

The internal object is thus kept at arm's length from the self but not rejected. The relationship to the internal object is a sadomasochistic one. This may be most easily observed in his relationship to his superego. This is too extensive a subject to go into here, so I limit myself to the comment that to say, as some psychoanalysts have done, that the homosexual has no superego is simply nonsense.

The second component of identification, that involving structuralization, does not suffer this fate, perhaps because it has been impersonalized. Many homosexual patients may be seen to have a well-functioning ego in many respects. We may thus observe a contrast between his distorted faulty object relations and his operating competently in other fields, such as in his work.

For example, Mr. E, a young, very tense and unhappy homosexual whom I saw for a short period was evidently outstanding in his work for a merchant bank. One of the consequences of this was that he had the finances to spend the weekends as he did. Every Friday afternoon he would fly by Concorde to New York. On Saturday night, high on alcohol and amphetamines, he would dance and have sex promiscuously all night at a homosexual club, wake late on Sunday morning, exhausted and hung over, catch the Concorde on Sunday afternoon and be back working efficiently on Monday morning. (It is not surprising that he broke off treatment after a few weeks.)

It seems to me that it is this double process involved in identification that is responsible for what is regarded as "splitting" in such patients. This is different from the splitting of the self that is evident in the more seriously disturbed homosexual patients, those suffering from suicidal depression or paranoid functioning close to psychosis—in addition, they are so embroiled in their more primitive conflictual internal object relationships that they are prevented from carrying out the identificatory processes leading to structure, described earlier. Perhaps the breakdown of the functional ego is most concretely to be seen in the catatonic schizophrenic.

Because, as discussed above, the homosexual patient suffers from a lack of a substantial identity, he has to resort to *simulation*, as I have called it (Glasser 1986). In this process the subject, like a chameleon, acquires features of whatever object he is with, but these are as easily dispensed with as they are taken on—a feature of the "as if" personality (Deutsch 1942). In the "false self" personality (Winnicott 1960), simulation is used in the deceptive compliance aimed at keeping the object at bay. In this process of simulation even the subtle characteristics of the object are assimilated but, since they are not serving their original psychodynamic purposes, there is a lack of substance and stability to the person's personality.

I am now in a position to return to the focus of my discussion, that is, the sexual identity of the homosexual. The type of homosexual whom I identified by his caricaturing of women shows up the psychodynamics most vividly. What we observe is that he is often seemingly very attached to his mother and appears to get on well with women. We learn from his therapy that he sustains his relationship to his mother by his feminine simulation and his sadomasochism: by being like her he can reach for attention and interest serving his mother's narcissistic need. It may also be that there is some connection of this with the primitive equating of identification with love. However, at the same time in his caricature of

## Masculinity, femininity and internalization

women, ultimately his mother, he is actually being revengefully very cruel and denigratory.

In his sexual behaviour he tends to be the passive, masochistic subject (seemingly in identification with her) and at the extreme he seeks to be treated brutally and degradingly. His analysis shows this also to be a way of expressing his sadistic feelings towards his mother using his body to represent her and his sadistic partner to carry his brutality. So, beneath his often engaging, chatty, camp manner and his sharp humour is a deeply unhappy man, unable to sustain relationships or obtain any deep gratification from them. Internally he is characterized by a lack of any substantial self–esteem.

Of course, not all effeminate homosexuals are like this type. Another type does not have this mocking quality but expresses more or less subtle feminine elements in the way he conducts himself, physically and socially. Psychically, too, there is a feminine quality to his personality. Benjamin Britten is an illustration of this type.

Mr. D, for example, was a mild–mannered, gentle, soft–spoken, submissive man who quickly introduced a masochistic way of relating to me. He would apologize when it wasn't required, express himself grateful for my interest in my continuing to see him, and so on.

This masochism manifested itself in his sexual activities. He was the receptive participant in the anal intercourse which took place whenever his partner wanted, but the partner had no compunction in leaving him frustrated when he did not feel like it. This sadomasochism was also frequently evident in their relationship. The partner was socially and educationally lower than him, lived off him, ruled the home, drank heavily and was very aggressive when drunk.

Mr. D's family had been dominated by his powerful father who had built himself up to be a prominent businessman. From childhood the father regarded him with contempt and once said to him "I sometimes wonder if you have any balls".

He felt that both his parents were remote in his childhood and that he was always made to serve the needs of others. His mother related to him in a way which demanded his meeting her needs. He was told by an aunt how, when he was a little boy, his mother enjoyed dressing him up in girl's clothes and laughing at him. He felt that being homosexual was like being a cripple and that his mother was to blame for this. He often felt as if he could attack his mother violently or even murder her.

Some of the subtleties of this could be seen in the transference: He started a session by reporting two dreams:

Dream 1: The police were conducting a house-to-house enquiry over a murder. They were coming closer and closer to him. He felt intense fear: *he* had committed the murder! He had hidden the body either by burying it behind a fence or by putting it in the boot of a car.

Dream 2: He came into a house and was greeted by his maternal grandmother sitting in a chair. He went to sit in another chair but she said, "Your place is here", pointing to a darkish area next to her. He saw that it was a coffin drawing him into it like a magnet.

His interpretation for both dreams was that they referred to the killing of part of himself.

He went on to talk about how he was being strongly affected by our meetings: they had become a process of his finding in himself things he didn't want to. He had discussed lots of things he had never talked about to anyone else. He said he was extremely frightened of what the analysis would cause him to learn about himself. He added that he was pleased I found him "interesting" enough to want to treat him.

A little later he told me of a third dream:

Dream 3: A huge wave was curling over him, engulfing him.

He went on to say that he had felt very depressed over the weekend. He was scared to come to the session today. He talked about how his being so active at work was a deception, his real self was very passive, he just let things drift: the treatment was his giving himself to passivity. I suggested that he was using the same deception with me but in reverse: he dealt with his rage and anxiety by seeking to deceive me into believing his passivity. I quoted how he spoke about "how pleased he was that I found him 'interesting' enough to want to treat him" and how his real self was very passive, he just let things drift: the treatment was his giving himself to passivity".

This material illustrates the homicidal intensity of his aggression hidden behind his evident absence of "balls", a murderousness which he feared I would uncover through my house-to-house search of his psyche. His feminine simulation was thus an elaborate defence against any recognition of his intense aggression by either him or me. The stimulus to such feelings was his terror of being engulfed by the wave/mother/me (and grandmother in Dream 2).

That this homosexual submission is a deception is embodied in his telling me in another session how he thought of the vagina as a Venus fly–trap plant (and he remembered his fears of the vagina dentata). He compared his rectum to this plant when he went on to say that the most enjoyable part of anal intercourse was gripping his partner's penis with his anal sphincter and thus getting power over it and being able to break it off when he wanted to. This was in the first place understood in oedipal terms, that is, as a gratifying but ambivalent fantasy not only of obtaining the intense attention of his father/analyst, but also of castrating him (he had told me of a memory of seeing his father's penis and being impressed by its largeness).

The session went on to indicate a deeper, core complex meaning to this material. His talk of his identifying his rectum with the vagina's Venus fly–trap nature led us to recognize that he converted himself into his consuming mother imagining that he consumed the penis/person with his anal mouth, denigrated him into worthless or disgusting faeces, and then excreted him (thus, incidentally, reassuring himself that what goes in must come out!). The clinical material supported our expectation that his passive, submissive femininity was based on a representation of his mother who behaved deceptively in *her* submissive, placatory manner to his dominating and bullying father and whom he saw, when walking into the parental bedroom, accepting his father's large penis in their violent intercourse.

The point I wish to emphasize is that, looked at from this perspective, what we learn from patients is that there is nothing about the homosexual which is truly feminine. Although with Freud we must regard him as sharing with the rest of humanity an intrinsic bisexuality there is little to indicate that it is playing a more substantial role in the psychodynamics discussed above than can be seen in the heterosexual individual.

The extensiveness and complexity of the subject is highlighted when we realize that I have up to this point only dealt with essentially one aspect, internalization, of those homosexuals who display a supposedly feminine quality.

In turning to the consideration of the part played by internalization in the apparently masculine homosexual, I quote from another letter, this time from Peter Pears to Benjamin Britten:

> My darling Ben
> It was marvellous to get your letters ... I don't suppose you'll get my last letter for a bit, as I sent it care of Goldberg .... I only hope he doesn't open it, as my letter was compromising to say the least of it! You poor little Cat, frozen to death in 12 degrees below zero weather I do hope it's not quite so cold now.... I was so sad that you were so depressed and cold I wanted to hop into a plane and come and comfort you at once. I would have kissed you all over and then blown you all over and then... and... and then you'd have been as warm as toast!

And further on in the letter he writes:

> H. imagines [Ralph] will fly straight to you (grr!), you little much too attractive so–and–so.... Everyone [misses you] except me, and of course I don't care a brass farthing how long you stay away, because if you stay away a day longer than Wednesday I'm going to come and fetch you. wherever you may be, and as long as I'm with you, you can stay away till the moon turns blue.

And he finishes his letter by writing:

> I shall never forget a certain night at Grand Rapids. Ich liebe dich, io t'amo, jeg elske dyg (?), je t'aime, in fact, my little white–thighed beauty, I'm terribly in love with you.

If we weren't informed to the contrary. we would unhesitatingly assume this letter was written by an adoring, rather randy, virile man to his woman lover. What is responsible for Peter Pears being so different in this respect from Benjamin Britten? And how is he to be distinguished from a heterosexual man?

You will remember that earlier I expressed my view that the core complex was something which every infant experienced and the "solution" or attempted solution of the intrinsic conflicts played a substantial role in the aetiology of different psychopathological conditions, as well as in "normality". For "normal" development to take place the role of the father is essential. You will remember that the infant has to struggle with the consequences of his profound involvement with his mother. With the interaction with other factors, the future homosexual's solution was to sexualize the intense, destructive aggression converting it into sadomasochism. The infant who is going to develop normally takes another course which depends on a triadic set–up to displace the dyadic one, that is, it depends on the availability of the father as an object to be internalized and subsequently identified with. In this way, the infant is provided with an alternative object at least partially to gratify his needs for security, protection, feeling loved and so on. The father is also able to be used as an ally in his struggle with the possessive/invasive mother. (This indicates the complexity of the normal Oedipus complex that is to follow as well as some of the meaning of the negative Oedipus complex.)

The infant who is to become a 'masculine' homosexual makes partial use of both these lines of development. He is able to avoid the loss of his mother partly on the basis of dealing with his aggression by sexualizing it and partly by internalizing his father. However, because the core complex anxieties are generalized to all objects, the internalization of the father leads to a mixture of true identification with and simulation of the father.

Although such developments are to be observed in the psychoanalytic treatment of such homosexuals, difficulties in this conceptualization are raised when it is recognized that the classic family constellation of the homosexual—an intensely involved, dominant, powerful mother and a father who is emotionally remote or sometimes contemptuously rejecting if not violent—may equally be observed in the family circumstances of both the effeminate and masculine homosexual. In my experience, with this type of homosexual patient, the father is a positive presence in the family dynamics even if he is geographically absent or manifestly uninvolved with his family; the father, and sometimes the grandfather (Ogden 1987), exists in the mother's mind. The father's "presence" is implicitly or explicitly recognized to be so by all the members of the family.

In Peter Pears' childhood, for example, his father, who was a civil engineer, worked mainly overseas—Africa, South America, Burma, India—as a builder of roads and ended his career as chief engineer and company director of the Burma Railways.

Peter Pears said "My father, of course, I hardly ever saw ... He cannot, I think, have been there when I was born... I always did feel as though I never saw my father until he finally retired". He was then 13 years old.

His mother joined her husband overseas from time to time. Tending to deny her absences, he talked of remembering his mother as left alone in England "in charge of the family... my constant companion". I was very close to my mother, he said, "... a very sweet woman. I only realized later that she had quite a sharp side to her. I thought she was soft and cuddly". Illustrated by his giving expression to oedipal type jealousies and antagonism, we see that his father was very much present in Pears' psychic world.

Mr. F can serve as a representative of this kind of patient. He was a school–teacher who came to treatment saying he wanted to be freed of his homosexuality about which he was guilty and ashamed. He claimed he was bisexual, quoting on the one hand his attraction to men and boys and on the other hand his attraction to women and the fact that he had enjoyed sex with both. His appearance and manner betrayed no femininity and I felt sure that had I met him in social circumstances it would not have crossed my mind to doubt his heterosexuality. But, he told me, when he was in the company of his homosexual friends, he could "camp it up" easily and freely an illustration of the use he made of simulation. The character of his sexuality can be judged from the following extract from a session:

> In reaction to a comment I had made about his need to feel he could control me, he told me that although he was listening his mind wandered to (to quote him) "images of fucking men their buttocks the cleft the man's gasp or groan when I penetrated him. I thought of lifting myself up so I could see my penis going in. It is lust not love the person doesn't matter". He added: "One of the things that's good about fucking a man is that you can't see who you're fucking".

The process in this patient was found to have the following steps: the active buggery is a reactive move from seeking passive penetration from the powerful mother, in anal and phallic terms. This 'reactive move' is facilitated by a simulation of his mother whom he perceives as active, domineering, penetrating to the point of his negation. The fear of penetration, which has both castrative and annihilatory dangers, derives from the original wish to be filled by the mother. Again, we see core complex considerations playing a dominant role in the psychodynamics of the homosexual patient. There was little or no material to point to an identification with father, although we would expect it to become perceivable in due course. His evident heterosexual involvement with women was found to be simulatory in nature and it is relevant that the outcome of his treatment, which was psychoanalytic psychotherapy. was that it helped him to be able to accept his homosexuality: he consequently became much more relaxed and more evenly functioning.

## Conclusion

In considering the complex and elaborate psychodynamics of homo-sexuality, I have carefully by–passed many fundamental issues such as the issue of bisexuality, the role of narcissism, the part played by his relationship to his body, the Oedipus complex, homosexuality as defence against psychosis, and so on. Not one of them, much less all of them, could be dealt with adequately in the course of a single lecture. Instead I have confined myself to considering the "masculinity" and "femininity" of the homosexual and even then only in respect to the contribution of *internalization* to this. Even in this respect we have seen that I have not been able to do the subject justice because of the wide variation to be found amongst homosexual patients. It is a matter for more elaborate exploration and discussion to consider to what extent what we see in such patients applies to homosexuals in the community who do not feel the need to come to us for help.

## Notes

1  This paper first appeared in *Bull. Brit. Psychoanal. Soc.*, 32(11): (1996).
2  This and other quotations are extracts from letters quoted in Headington (1992).

## References

Deutsch, H. (1942). Some forms of emotional disturbance and their relationship to schizophrenia. *Psychoanal. Q.*, 11: 301–321.
Glasser, M. (1986). Identification and its vicissitudes as observed in the perversions. *Int. J. Psychoanal.*, 67: 9–17.

Headington, C. (1992). *Peter Pears, A Biography*. London: Faber and Faber.

Horton, R. (1996). The alchemy of desire. Paper read to the Applied Section of The British Psycho-Analytical Society. Unpublished.

Ogden, T. H. (1987). The transitional oedipal relationship in female development. *Int. J. Pyschoanal.*, 68: 485–498.

Winnicott, D. W. (1960). Ego distortion in terms of true and false self. In *The Maturational Process and the Facilitating Environment*. London: Hogarth Press, 1965, pp. 140–152.

# 12

# DOUBT IN THE PSYCHOANALYSIS OF A PAEDOPHILE[1]

Donald Campbell

### Introduction

Here are Mr. Smith's first words from his first session: "There was a memory from 12 or 13 of a lover, a doctor or psychiatrist. Sucking a penis. Swallowing semen. But no name. Details, but no name. Strange. Not forgetting, just not there to forget". After a pause, he continued:

> Abuse at 2 to 3, 6,8 to 9, 12 to 13. I discovered last year I can write right-handed. It was the healing massage. I got in touch with deadness in my left side. All my thoughts are on the right side. Pain, anger and confusion are all on the right side. When I was three I broke my leg. Had my right hand, I mean right leg in a leg iron for a year. Buggered by boys. I masturbated the gardener with my right hand. It's numb where I touched his pubic hair. Touching my mother's hair. It's as though memories are stored in my body. Once I retrieve the memories …the physical se-se-se-sensation goes away.

In his first rush of fragmented associations, Mr. Smith seemed to be defensively pushing me back while communicating an experience of abuse that was sensorially stimulating, emotionally overwhelming and mentally confusing. I assumed that, through a process of dissociation,[2] Mr. Smith had effectively severed the links between real or imagined events and their emotional significance (Davies and Frawley 1994, p. 62). After a lengthy silence, Mr. Smith confessed he had been disturbed by the emergence of fragments of memory during a recent course of massage therapy. He told me that he wanted an analysis to find out if he "could do something without knowing it". I soon learned that this lack of specificity was typical of Mr. Smith; he would partially expose a significant thought, treat it as impermeable to interpretation, and, often, never mention it again.

I was bewildered and intrigued by Mr. Smith. I was also touched by his suffering and respected the effort he was making to retrieve his past and make sense of it. He appeared to sense the depth and complexity of his disturbance, and although it was clear an analysis would be difficult for both of us, I felt there was a possibility he could benefit from it. My view was influenced by my experience at the Portman Clinic[3] treating paedophiles, many of whom made significant gains with psychotherapy.

I begin my account of Mr. Smith with his first words to convey some of the sense of disorientation our first interaction provoked in me, a disorientation that would continue through the course of our analysis and would lead to the ideas expressed here about the connection between paedophilia and doubt—which I break down into three distinct categories: *honest, inherent,* and *sadistic.* This paper is, in part, an attempt to reduce my confusion by increasing my understanding of Mr. Smith and, in turn, deepening psychoanalytic understanding of other paedophiles, particularly ones who report being abused as children and admit to abusing children.

Questions of doubt—as I will discuss them in this paper—are inextricably linked to questions of trust, and Mr. Smith's anxieties about trusting anyone with his history was, from the start, an important element in his analysis. He did not begin treatment by presenting his history in an organized or chronological way, but shared disconnected fragments of his past as his analysis proceeded. In this respect, a feature of this case was my experience of working in the dark. I knew very little about Mr. Smith's history in our earliest sessions: he appeared to be in his early 40s, boyish and blond. Only later did I learn that Mr. Smith was born in a foreign country and moved to Oxford with his parents and younger twin sisters when he was four years old, or that he was married to a hairdresser and worked regularly as an accountant. Mr. Smith referred occasionally to disagreements with clients or colleagues, but otherwise told me little about his current life. He was chronically anxious about not being given enough work, which he interpreted as a sign that he would be fired. In fact, during the course of his analysis his work life improved, and he became less anxious about the security of his position.

Consisting as it did of a barrage of fragmented memories, the first session with Mr. Smith left me with an impression of his transference to me as a sexually abusing lover, doctor, psychiatrist, or parent—someone not worthy of trusting with a complete thought, let alone an open emotional connection. Although Mr. Smith confirmed my observation that his fragmentation of sentences, long hostile looks at the beginning of sessions, and vacant or sullen periods of silence reflected defensive reaction to me as a seductive and persecuting person, he was never able to trust me enough to use the couch. For the purposes of this paper, I want to focus on Mr. Smith's transference, and on the way my reading of my counter-transference led to a deeper understanding of Mr. Smith's early life and his current state of mind.

## Honest doubt

Doubt, uncertainty about the truth, is inevitably present in all psychoanalyses. Patients arrive with doubts about their dreams, memories, fantasies, and real events; their past and their present; and their analysts, as played out in the transference. As analysts, we are trained to keep an open mind. We are also trained *to* doubt, to approach our patients and ourselves in every session with a non-judgemental open-mindedness, and to sustain a stance of uncertainty and not knowing, often for long periods of time. I refer to this doubt as *honest doubt*—a stance we maintain at a conscious level, the goal of which is to improve the quality of knowledge (Jacka 2011).

Of course, unconscious anxieties will always distort or partially block what we allow ourselves to know. In many cases, as a successful analysis progresses, these unconscious anxieties are more or less dealt with, while honest doubt is maintained. When anxieties persist, while I would not say that they alone create dishonesty, or sadistic doubt, they can contribute to what I am calling *inherent doubt*.

In my once-weekly psychoanalytic psychotherapeutic work with patients at the Portman Clinic, I have been struck by the depth and persistence of all three forms of doubt. In my more intensive private psychoanalysis of Mr. Smith—which took place five times a week over the course of three years—it was even more apparent. While working with Mr. Smith, I experienced feelings of doubt about what he told me that made it difficult for me to distinguish between real events and psychic events.

The nature of psychoanalytic knowing leaves me with the conviction that I can never be certain about the reality of Mr. Smith's experience; it is evident, then, that whatever understanding of Mr. Smith's psychic reality I present in this paper will, by definition, be shrouded in doubt.

## Inherent Doubt

### *The first phase of Mr. Smith's psychoanalysis*

During the first phase of Mr. Smith's analysis, his sessions were dominated by silence punctuated by fragments of sentences, expressions of his dissociated states of mind, which kept apart clusters of ideas and interrupted sequences of events (Akhtar 2009, p. 82). This made it difficult for me to follow what he was saying let alone make any sense of it. Mr. Smith came across to me as an empty, hollow, passively compliant man who would drift off and idly stare into space.

Researchers observing infants who react to trauma by dissociation have reported similar behaviour:

> ...in which the child disengages from stimuli in the external world and attends to an 'internal' world. The child's dissociation in the midst of terror involves numbing, avoidance, compliance, and restricted affect. Traumatized infants are observed to be staring off into space with a glazed look.
> 
> (Schore 2001, p. 211)

I wondered if Mr. Smith's behaviour was an unconscious survival strategy, triggered both by the revival of traumatic memories stimulated by the analytic process, and by fears associated with a transference to me as an intrusive, persecuting parent.

"During activation of a traumatic memory, the brain is 'having' its experience" (van der Kolk 1996, p. 234). Consequently, the abuse remains, as it was experienced, unorganized, unsymbolized and unspoken within the patient's psyche, beyond their control (Davies and

Frawley 1994, p. 97). Inherent doubt was in the nature of the traumatic experience. I think the difficulty that I had being attentive to Mr. Smith, distinguishing between fantasy and reality in what he said, making links between fragments of sentences, and remembering session material afterwards, was a consequence of the inherent doubt he communicated to me.

Mr. Smith recounted incidents of being abused by, the gardener and the family General Practitioner, and also by his father, his mother, and his uncle who I will refer to later. However, no corroborative evidence of these traumatic events emerged during the course of his analysis.

Mr. Smith's account of his childhood was dominated by a variety of actual or fantasied sexual experiences that served as substitutes for emotional warmth and love, and had become a way of organizing his internal world and controlling his relationships. In bits and pieces, Mr. Smith described his father as split between a 'shadowy' daytime dad and a bad nighttime dad. During the day he and his father occasionally shared hobbies; then, "during the night Dad put his penis into my backside while he was reading me a story. When I asked him what he was doing, he said, 'Nothing. Nothing happened'". It was, in Mr. Smith's words, "forbidden sex that hurt; that took place in private. That's what families are for".

Mr. Smith's mother was depressed and had made several suicide attempts. "She was only interested in me sexually. Otherwise she couldn't be bothered". He told me several times that his mum masturbated him when he was a boy and that, later, they had had intercourse. She made fun of the size of his penis. Unlike his father, who always denied that anything had happened, after an episode of abuse his mother would promise not to touch him again—but she always did. Each time, she made him promise to keep the incident their secret. Later she, too, would deny that anything had happened. Mr. Smith told me on several occasions that he hated his mother because she did not protect him from his father or from herself. He wanted to trust her, but felt repeatedly betrayed.

I was struck by Mr. Smith's lack of protest and the absence of any effort on his part to stop the abuse. In sessions he was outwardly compliant: coming on time, paying my invoices promptly, or agreeing with something I said and then changing the subject. I suspected that his anger was too dangerous to be expressed directly and would instead have been projected. (My suspicion was confirmed when this was enacted in the waiting room before a session, which I will discuss later.)

Mr. Smith's accounts of being anally penetrated by his father and having intercourse with his mother were delivered in a matter-of-fact manner. There were no reports of subjective feelings, only objective accounts of awful events. I began to carry, in my own thoughts and feelings, what I sensed was absent in Mr. Smith's account; I struggled to make links between fragments of sentences and to remember session material afterwards. I knew I was having difficulty functioning as an analyst, and at times I doubted that I could help Mr. Smith. I understood this as my experience of Mr. Smith's relating to me in a state of projective identification.

In Klein's (1946, 1955) original conceptualization of projective identification, she describes two archaic processes (projection and identification) that enhance communication between the infant and the mother and further the child's development. Bion (1962) extended Klein's view of the communicating function of the child's projective identification to include the mother's containing the infant's earliest communications, processing them into meaningful elements, and conveying these elements back to the infant. Projective identification is distinguished, on the one hand, by the wish to get rid of something that provokes pain, fear, or discomfort; and on the other hand, by identification—that is, the object's identification with the projected experience (Sodré 2012, pp. 134–135). As Sodré points out, massive projective identification of the self (in this case, Mr. Smith) into an object (myself, the analyst) can occur to the extent that the object "becomes" the self—in effect "carrying" the affects and mental states that are unbearable to the self (Ibid., p. 135).

I view these projective processes as largely unconscious for both parties. They may only be discovered by the analyst through the understanding of their derivatives, such as the analyst's own slips, changes in mood and attitude, and enactments. I struggled with my counter-transference enactments with Mr. Smith, both during sessions and afterwards. For instance, my practice is to write process notes after sessions, but after our sessions I could hardly remember the content or sequence of the material. My notes were sketchy. During sessions when I would become lost, confused, or angry about the way Mr. Smith was relating to me, I would withdraw emotionally. I would drift away, lose my focus on Mr. Smith, and doubt what he was telling me.

When a receptive analyst can experience a patient's projections of unbearable feelings—rather than defend against them—they can offer insights into the subject's mental state. In this way, projections become meaningful (though generally unconscious) communications to the object. My counter-transference, then, was an important medium for identifying Mr. Smith's projections. I thought of the doubt that I was experiencing at this time as *inherent doubt*, that is, as *an unconscious communication of the nature of abusive experiences* that had shattered Mr. Smith's orientation to reality and left a profound confusion about what was real and what was fantasy. I tried to contain and "read" Mr. Smith's projections as communications and interpret them as painful and disorienting aspects of his experience of being abused.

Following Heimann (1950), I view the counter-transference as an indispensable resource for understanding unconscious phenomena. Counter-transference enactments like slips of the tongue, or, in my case, difficulty remembering a session, represent leakage from the unconscious and provide an opportunity for the analyst to discover something he had not been conscious of before. My experience with Mr. Smith resembled Sandler's (1976) description of 'role responsiveness', whereby the patient evokes or provokes an unconscious role response in the analyst that actualizes an aspect of the transference: in this instance, a father who did not want to acknowledge his abusive behaviour. I came to see that in my reactions to Mr. Smith I had incarnated his parents' mental states of distraction and lack of engagement with him as a whole person.

I did not believe that role responsiveness accounted completely for my experience, and, at various times, I was stuck by Mr. Smith's more aggressive attack on linking (Bion 1959) that would occur whenever he felt afraid I would become intrusive, or when he was frightened about what he and I might discover together.

In working with patients who admit to, or are accused of, having abused children, I have found a pull in myself towards a binary judgemental view represented by such questions as: Is this patient's account true or false? Is this a report of a real event, or an imagined one? (By 'real event', I mean something that can be objectively perceived and consensually agreed upon [Akhtar 2009, 240]). In this case, the search for an answer to the binary questions pulled me away from Mr. Smith's psychic reality—that which was subjectively significant to him and included wishes, fears, fantasies and all mental activities (Ibid., p. 228). The lure of substantiality and the apparent knowability of concrete reality contributed to a preoccupation on my part with events from the past, and, I suspect, offered some relief from the tension represented by doubts about what was taking place in the session.

At the beginning of his analysis I wondered if Mr. Smith's account of his history of abuse was a manifestation of false memory syndrome, the condition in which a person's identity and interpersonal relationships are built around a memory of traumatic experience that is objectively false, but in which the person strongly believes (Mollon 1998).[4] Mr. Smith reported that memories of being abused began to emerge during the massage therapy that had preceded his analysis with me. Although he pressured his mother to admit that she had abused him, he was never interested in accusing either of his parents publicly or reporting them to the authorities, perhaps because of his own abuse of children, which he would not report until the second phase of his analysis. In order to identify Mr. Smith's psychic reality, I processed my doubts about the abuse he reported through a kind of affective attunement, that is, trying to sense what felt real and what felt fabricated. I listened for the persistence and consistency of material over time; I also interpreted from my countertransference and sense of the transference, and listened to his response for confirmation, increased openness, and exposure of more vulnerability. Effective interpretations were occasionally followed by a session of material that flowed without constant interruption.

During this first phase of Mr. Smith's analysis, which lasted about a year, I gradually came to believe that what he told me about being abused was not a product of a false memory syndrome, but based on real events, which may well have been elaborated later by fantasies. Mr. Smith's psychic reality appeared to be a confusing combination of real and imagined events, and this confusion itself became interesting to me as a key to his analysis.

### Incestuous sexual abuse and inherent doubt

I follow Chasseguet-Smirgel in assuming that the capacities to distinguish the difference between being a child and an adult, and to know whether one is a male or female, are fundamental to our orientation to reality (Chasseguet-Smirgel 1985, pp. 1–12). Paedophilia is distinguished from other perversions by virtue of the fact that the paedophile fundamentally attacks the sovereignty of generational difference. An inevitable consequence, then, of a child being sexually abused by someone from an older generation is doubt about what constitutes reality; sexual barriers are breached, and oedipal relationships are turned upside down. Incest fundamentally betrays the child's trust that the parent will recognize and protect the reality of generational difference. This betrayal shatters the "known" reflecting object, one of the building blocks upon which internal representations are established. The victim is left without a trusting orientation to the mind of the other within which to find a representation of itself; the mind of the other that has inflicted pain is now viewed as split between loving and hating parts. The victim is left in a state of confusion and doubt, and, in analysis, brings these contradictory parts into the transference, and, hence, the counter-transference.

In Mr. Smith's case, the doubt generated by his father's incestuous act was compounded by his father saying, "Nothing happened" after he abused him. By denying the abuse—that is, by rejecting the reality of the event—the parent betrays the child's trust that the parent will represent reality, by calling into question what the child "knows" happened. For Mr. Smith, the fact that his father lied to him and his mother told him to keep their sexual activity secret amounted to a breakdown in the communication of meaning (refigured as the incoherence of our first meeting): for the young Mr. Smith, when his own reality was denied or rejected by his parents, the known became the unthinkable.

During the first phase of the analysis, then, doubt functioned as a communication of abusive experiences and their consequences. I believe that Mr. Smith defended against this trauma by identifying with his parents, particularly with his father, and specifically with his father's denial. This left me in the transference as the confused and disoriented child plagued by doubts about my experience of Mr. Smith. Doubt was inherent in Mr. Smith's abusive experiences and in his memory of them; by generating doubt in me, he recreated a fundamental aspect of his experience of being abused.

Although Mr. Smith's experience of being abused was shrouded in doubt, it became clear that he did not doubt that he had been abused; he wanted me to believe his version of his childhood memories, and at various times I interpreted that he took my analytic stance—an openness to the multi-determined nature of internal and external realities—as "evidence" that I did not believe him.

Mr. Smith also confirmed my experience of other patients who had been sexually abused as children, namely the profound impact of unprocessed shame and disgust that accompanied their abusive experiences. The act of being sexually abused breaches what I refer to as the *shame shield* and leaves the child with no psychic place to hide.

> The protective function of shame as an external signal depends for its success upon the object perceiving the external manifestation of shame as a shield between self and object which the object recognizes as a signal of failure and respects enough to react sympathetically to the self.
>
> (Campbell 2008, p. 78)

When there is no sanctuary for retreat, relief is sought by projecting the abuse victim's confusion, passivity and disgust into others.

My interpretation that Mr. Smith was afraid the shame and doubt he felt about his abuse could not be shared with me had the effect of reducing his paranoid anxiety, increasing his trust, and opening up his memories of abusing boys. This ushered in the second phase of his analysis, which featured memories from Mr. Smith's adolescence and adulthood. Perhaps not surprisingly, Mr. Smith's material became more coherent. My note taking and my recall of sessions improved. Fragmentation and shame inhibited Mr. Smith's recall of experiences of being abused during the first phase of his analysis. During the second phase guilt and fears associated with a persecuting super-ego affected what Mr. Smith could tell me about his abuse of boys and determined the outcome of his analysis.

### *The second phase of Mr. Smith's psychoanalysis*

In the second year of his analysis, Mr. Smith banged into the back of another car while getting out of a parking space on his way to a session. He said, "It was the other driver's fault because he should not have parked so close". Much to his surprise, he had been seen and was charged with causing an accident and leaving the scene.

As the date of his court appearance approached, Mr. Smith asked me to write a letter on his behalf saying that he was disturbed about coming to a session and, therefore, not in a responsible frame of mind and should not be held accountable. Over subsequent sessions, I took up the 'accident' as a manifestation of his hitherto unacknowledged violent feeling towards me—represented by banging into the car—and his wish to disown them and drive away from me. I also interpreted that he wanted me to collude with his violence because he felt he was, in fact, my victim. I said, "I had disturbed you by 'parking too close' with my interpretations, and you reacted by attacking someone else 'who should not have parked so close'". Mr. Smith associated to memories of his experiences of being abused by his mother, who then reassured him that it was their secret. I interpreted his association to this memory as his feeling that he was being abused by me, and that we would not think about the abuse but would, rather, bury it as our "secret".

During the session following his court case, Mr. Smith told me he thought of the magistrates as abusers who were "getting away with it". He felt like a little boy who was going to be punished: a repetition of his earlier experiences. He then noticed that he had violent fantasies—"not memories"—of doing things to boys he had become friends with. I thought it significant that Mr. Smith drew my attention to the point that his violent fantasies were not memories. Although I did not say so, I felt he was using denial to cloak a memory in doubt. Instead, I took up Mr. Smith's fear of me as an abuser who was liable to hurt him, which aroused his violent feelings. I said, "But the problem is; I am too dangerous to attack and too corrupt, like the magistrates, to protect you. Your solution is to attack a boy when you think no one is looking".

After a long silence, Mr. Smith said he remembered pain while being buggered at bedtime before he was seven. He looked tortured. I verbalized how disturbing a memory of pain was and recalled that last week he had not mentioned the physical pain of penetration. I suggested that he was afraid to tell me about his pain because of his fear that I, like his father, would deny his abuse. Mr. Smith associated to watching a TV program about the war in Bosnia. "It showed an enraged wounded boy, and then I saw myself in pain". He broke a long silence by returning to abuse by his uncle, whom he had mentioned in passing in the first phase of the analysis,

> While I was being buggered by my uncle, I was told I was sexually excited, but actually I was in pain. I can't distinguish between pain and sex. What drives me sexually is linked with pain. There's more sexual violence with my wife Alice now. And I accidentally hit her a couple of times. I'm afraid she'll divorce me.

Although this was the only time in his analysis that Mr. Smith admitted he was violent towards his wife, I found this sequence of material believable because it resonated through my counter-transference as real. As was becoming typical in my sessions with Mr. Smith, my sense of what actually happened and what was imagined was based, finally, on the transference and counter-transference.

Gradually, during the second phase of his analysis, I became increasingly convinced that Mr. Smith's traumas arose from real events that were then elaborated and/or mediated later by childhood wishes to submit homosexually to his father and sexually seduce his mother. Arlow (1969) described characteristics of unconscious fantasies that pertain to Mr. Smith; particularly the way external events (being abused) can trigger unconscious fantasy, which in turn can influence the perception of external events (abusing boys).

Eventually, his account of his own sexual abuse was replaced by feelings of hate, wishes to castrate boys, and his envy of their happiness. Like his mother, Mr. Smith saw boys only as part-objects: "A boy is only a penis on legs", he said. His strategy was to make friends with boys, encourage their trust, give them a good time, make them happy, and then hurt them. Like his father, Mr. Smith's wish to hurt boys was enacted in his sexual abuse of them, which in turn was hidden behind a benign persona, a 'daytime self' he referred to as Roger—his real name (changed here for purposes of confidentiality)—which he considered to be his false self. "I became Roger, like a mask to hide behind, when I was ten". Roger, the false self, was modelled on the polite, deferential, dependent boy his parents needed him to be; and, above all, the one who was not abused and damaged by them.

Mr. Smith did not know who he was. Doubt infused his sense of self. While he told me he had no knowledge of abusing children as Roger, it was also clear that Roger provided an effective strategy for grooming and seducing children. It emerged in his analysis that the more real part of him—who, as he said, "wanted to exterminate children"—had no name, that it was an internal object he would not identify. He did not remember another self from that time until he undertook massage therapy two years before starting his analysis.

On returning after a weekend Mr. Smith reported being anxious around older women during a village fete and immediately starting to chat up a boy nearby. He said that he thought that his friendliness towards the boy was like his mother's seduction of him, and reluctantly admitted that he wanted to hurt the boy. I interpreted that the weekend break had aroused longings for me as well as rage at me (the same combination of emotions he felt for his mother). Throughout his analysis, any longing for a person he loved immediately increased his feeling of being vulnerable to a painful or disturbing seduction. This led to aggressive fantasies aimed at negating the now-dangerous object (Glasser 1979). I suggested that when he set out to seduce the boy, he was dealing with his anxiety about his mother's abuse by becoming her.

At that time, we were also able to identify a central ingredient in his abuse of boys, which was the creation of doubt about their judgement of him: doubt that he was the loving friend they thought he was. Bollas (1995) observed a similar pattern of behaviour in serial killers who lull their victims into a false sense of security and friendship before killing them. Although Mr. Smith never told me details of his abuse of boys, he was able to tell me several times that he derived sexual pleasure from the shock in the boys' faces when he shifted from being their best friend to hurting them. In this way, Mr. Smith turned his passive traumatic experience of being abused by his parents into an active one by abusing his victims. I expected Mr. Smith's abusive use of doubt to be enacted in the transference. I interpreted the uncertainty that I experienced with Mr. Smith as his evocation, in me, of his experiences of doubting that his parents were trustworthy, truthful and protective.

This session was a turning point in Mr. Smith's analysis. In the weeks following his recognition of his hatred of his mother, he noticed that boys did not sexually arouse him; in his analysis, the aim of his hatred and wish to hurt shifted from boys to his mother. He told me that he saw himself when he looked at a lonely, scared boy. This led initially to his giving his mother a tongue slashing and then threatening her with a knife in the kitchen.

As we worked on his hatred of his mother, Mr. Smith's longing for a safe father figure emerged in the transference, which in turn stimulated unconscious homosexual wishes and increased his resistance to analysis. His sense of feeling safe when I maintained analytic boundaries or understood him through an interpretation was often followed by the fantasy that I was seducing him in order to hurt him. As he let go of defences and began to allow himself to remember pain, his anxieties increased. Splitting and projection appeared to be less effective, and he became more anxious about his vulnerability to betrayal and an inability to control his behaviour.

During this period of the analysis, Mr. Smith arrived late for a session and I heard a crash in the waiting room before I went to collect him. Mr. Smith said that he had "accidentally" kicked over the magazine stand in the waiting room. As he walked into the consulting room, he smiled as usual, and handed me a cheque for the previous month's sessions. He said he was late because the trains were late. He said that he had been thinking about the fragmented nature of his memories. He announced that there was a time when he had stopped feeling; it was like he immunized himself against feelings, so that he had feelings on the surface, but no feelings underneath. Mr. Smith then recalled memories of hurting boys he didn't know, random pick-ups. He remembered hurting them and having no feelings for them. This sounded to me like a convergence of psychic reality and external reality; I also felt that what he was telling me was congruent with what I knew of him.

However, a sense of doubt pervaded my mind. I knew that he had just done something very unusual by knocking over the magazine stand, but I did not know enough to understand this action. I was aware that he had not referred to the incident again, which left me in the dark, but that was a familiar feeling with Mr. Smith. He said he thought I was feeling uncomfortable, uneasy. I remained silent and wondered if he picked up my sense of not understanding the 'accident'. I was not uncomfortable, but felt attentive.

After a silence Mr. Smith said, "I wonder if my perception of you is really true. Maybe you are not so benign as I thought, but actually are more dangerous to me". I said,

> I think you are anxious about what I might do to you, if I knew what you thought and did. I wonder if you came late and 'accidentally' knocked over the magazine stand in order to make me feel uncomfortable and anxious. To let me know what you could do to me.

Mr. Smith said that the problem is that he could not read my face, there was no reaction, and he was always waiting for me to respond.

I suggested that Mr. Smith referred to the incident as an "accident", as though he did not want me to think he intended anything by it, and then chose not to talk about it in the hope that the two of us would tacitly agree that nothing had happened—an experience familiar to him from his father's abuse. Mr. Smith agreed, adding that when he handed me his cheque he felt like he was paying me off so I wouldn't hurt him. I now felt that Mr. Smith was allowing contact between us. I said that he had reversed his fear that I might hurt him by hurting me first (knocking over my magazine stand). He recognized that the action actually obliterated his feeling of fear. I suggested that giving me a cheque was like paying me hush money to keep quiet—as if I was running a protection racket, threatening to expose him, and he resented having to buy my silence. Mr. Smith agreed and said that he felt this more strongly as he continued his analysis. I said that the more dependent he was becoming on me, the more he wanted me to be benign, a caretaker; but his expectation, based on his childhood experiences, was that I would become the opposite, an abuser interested only in exposing him and in treating him—as he treated the unnamed boys—without any feeling and with intent to harm. I added that these expectations raised profound doubts in his mind about me. After the session, Mr. Smith returned the magazine stand to its original position in the waiting room before he left.

Mr. Smith's anxiety about his violence increased. During sexual games his wife, Alice, pulled his shirt over his head, and he became wild and frightened about what he might do to her. He wondered if he was a murderer. This led him to associate to his mother's seductiveness, but he couldn't bear to think about her cruelty towards him. Meanwhile, incomplete and isolated images kept surfacing: the body of an anonymous boy in a woods at night; a ritual at the family doctor's in which he is naked and blood is poured over him, the blood of a bird that is buried. He recalls being afraid that the bird would rise out of the ground. The thought haunted him all weekend. These fragments were presented as though they had broken through into consciousness. Once again, his accounts of being abused and of abusing boys seemed to bring together psychic reality and external reality. He wondered, were they wishes or memories of events? Was he the victim or the perpetrator? Did someone else try to implicate him or blackmail him into secrecy? I was now unable to distinguish those fragments that I thought were memories from those that might be figments of Mr. Smith's imagination. This was a moment when I wondered if Mr. Smith's intention was to disturb me. I was not able to go beyond my counter-transference experience of doubt. I interpreted that Mr. Smith had projected his mental state of doubt into me because his thoughts frightened and confused him:

He recalled being told by his abusers on several occasions that if he said a word about what had happened, he would go to prison.

Although Mr. Smith felt shame about being abused, guilt was the predominant affect associated with what he had done to boys. Initially, he defended against this guilt by splitting and disavowal, that is, by both knowing and not knowing about his abuse. Later, he defended against an internally persecuting superego by projecting it onto representatives of law and order. Anxieties, which had been aroused by appearing before the magistrates for the traffic offence on the way to his session, emerged again. He had recently read about a father who had been convicted of sexually abusing his daughter years earlier on the basis of her recovered memory. I thought that he began doubting his memories, especially those in which he was the perpetrator, in order to mentally delete evidence that would arouse internal persecution from his superego; this was Mr. Smith's way of escaping its watchful eye while conveying to me his doubts that he could trust me.

My suspicions were confirmed when Mr. Smith told me that after reading about child sexual abuse and recovered memories he doubted all of his memories. I was knocked off balance. I thought that the internal persecuting superego had been projected into me and I was now the enemy. Doubt permeated my thoughts. I felt I had been seduced, led astray. I now felt like a victim of Mr. Smith's sadism. I told him I thought my experience resembled his when his father would say, "nothing happened" after anally penetrating him. I was acutely aware that he was afraid of going to prison and said that there was a protective function to his projection, that he wished to mentally disarm me so I could not report him to the authorities.

When Mr. Smith told me that a vicar had recently been murdered because he knew too much, I thought he was planning to terminate. I remembered that a vicar was the only other person he had ever confided in about his abuse of boys. I said that he clearly felt he had told me too much and would have to "terminate" me. I added that he also felt that he knew more than he could bear, especially about the cruel way his parents, whom he needed and trusted, had treated him, and that he wanted to terminate those thoughts from his mind.

Mr. Smith's termination was multi-determined: first, it functioned as a flight from remembering his parents' betrayal and the physical pain of his father's anal penetration. Second, it represented an attempt to stop thinking about memories of abusing children and wondering if he was a murderer. Third, it was an escape from his corrupt 'magistrate' analyst who he feared would send him to prison. At this point he also told me, for the first time, that his "breakdown" (referred to without elaboration) occurred after a boy whom he had abused later committed suicide when he was an adolescent. I thought that feelings of guilt and anxiety over the boy's suicide were a major factor in Mr. Smith's pursuit of an analysis. I wondered aloud if this was the thought behind the question, could he do something without knowing it? But he avoided all my references to his remarks and my interpretations. I think he was terrified of breaking down, under pressure from his superego, if he continued to think about himself—especially his abusive self. In spite of my interpretative work on his shame and guilt, and on the projection of his persecuting superego and doubts about himself onto me, Mr. Smith was not able to take back his projections. His doubts about my intentions increased. He could only deal with his doubts about me by terminating me, his analytic confessor.

There was an inexorability about Mr. Smith's termination, which I had experienced with other abused perpetrators of child sexual abuse once they moved beyond an image of themselves as "befriending" children, to one in which they deceived and inflicted pain on young persons.

Although I felt that Mr. Smith's decision to terminate was premature, he believed that he had benefited from analysis. Mr. Smith's lack of sexual interest in boys persisted. However, I thought the libidinization of his relationships with boys was reactive to primitive anxieties about being taken over by his mother and was in danger of being revived if he felt threatened by her. He had stopped contact with children in recognition that he could never trust himself to not abuse them. He felt less revengeful towards his mother and accepted that he could never persuade her to confirm his memories of her abuse. He noticed a decline in self-defeating behaviour at work. Although violent fantasies persisted, he stopped hitting his wife.

In his last session, after three years of analysis, Mr. Smith said with equanimity and directness that he wondered if I felt deceived, misled? He seemed unusually self-assured this this point, which aroused my suspicions. As he got up to leave my consulting room for the last time, he said, "The fragments of memories were only feelings, not actions. Nothing happened. I made it up. I only imagined things to try to explain what I was feeling. Child abuse is only a label for unacceptable feelings". This came at me from out of the blue. I felt as though I had been kicked in the head. I was shocked and had no time to respond—once again, I was destabilized by doubt. I would come to understand this experience as a repetition in my counter-transference of the patient's breakdown in his orientation to reality during abuse.

## Sadistic use of doubt

### Memory, trauma and doubt

Although Mr. Smith's early traumatic memories may not have been fully available to consciousness or remembered unequivocally, they were represented in his associations to physical sensations stimulated by the massage therapy, and in his enactments in the transference. The experience of being the object of denial contributed to an expectation that external or internal objects would not believe what he said. Consequently, Mr. Smith was filled with doubt about what happened to him, about his identity and what he did. It was this expectation that Mr. Smith re-created with me during his analysis. My struggle with doubt left me feeling abused in the transference and became an important piece of evidence about Mr. Smith's experience of being abused and of abusing.

Freud conceptualized trauma as a break in a protective shield, flooding the ego "with large amounts of stimulus" that cannot be discharged. Freud maintained that these bodily sensations transform themselves into unpleasure and thereby become emotional experiences (1910a, p. 14) that animate our inner world of internal objects, fantasies and affects (which can be observed in psychoanalysis). In Mr. Smith's case, the trauma of real events had an immediate impact, rather than emerging retrospectively (*après coup*).

How do we reconstitute ourselves after a trauma? Freud (1926, pp. 130ff) viewed the external trauma as unconsciously condensed with the primary object that failed to protect the subject—hence, Mr. Smith's rage at his mother for not protecting him from his father or her. In my experience, post-traumatic restructuring of the ego is often determined by the internalization of the person who was responsible for the trauma, that is, an unconscious identification with the aggressor (A. Freud 1936, pp. 109–121), which leads to behaviour that reverses the experience of being the victim by becoming a perpetrator. However, as appeared to be the case for Mr. Smith, sometimes the trauma has to be revived again and again, with the original roles reversed, because it is never permanently mastered.

## Paedophilia, reality and safety

The experience of being the object of denial fundamentally challenges one's reliance upon internal perception of experience and one's sense of self. The object of denial must choose between what he or she 'knows' as reality and a contradictory and false reality represented by his or her objects. The survival of the self is at stake, and the choice is between reality, neurosis, psychosis or perversion. Mr. Smith did not defend what he knew to be true and ragefully attack his abusers, nor did he withdraw from reality and become psychotic. Instead, he preserved an orientation to reality, outside his abusive encounters, by libidinizing the early traumatic experiences (Glover 1932, pp. 228–230) and developing a paedophilic perversion (Glasser 1990, p. 739). In this respect, Mr. Smith's perversion served a self-preservative function. Mr. Smith reversed his experience of pain, confusion and doubt by projecting it into children when, in identification with the abuser, he molested them.

When Ferenczi (1930/1955) maintained that "it seems likely that a psychotic splitting off of a part of the personality occurs under the influence of shock" (p. 121), he was referring to the splitting of the ego as a consequence of childhood rape. Today, the link between childhood sexual abuse and dissociative states is well documented (Davies and Frawley 1994; Mollon 1998). As we can see in Mr. Smith's case, splitting reinforced not knowing. By becoming a false "daytime self" he referred to as "Roger", Mr. Smith claimed that he had no memory of being abused or of abusing. The outcome of Mr. Smith's new identity was similar to the hysterics described by Brenman (1985), who "change identities in order to destroy the intuitive knowledge of what is real and true" (p. 427). Socarides (1959) describes a similar dynamic in a paedophile patient who moved from ordinary relating to sexually abusing children when he was invaded by anxiety.

By generating doubt in me, Mr. Smith recreated in me a fundamental aspect of his experience of being abused. Mr. Smith employed projective identification to abuse young boys; it was through the medium of my counter-transference that I experienced what

Mr. Smith projected into the children he abused. The projection of doubt was fundamental to the sadistic gratification Mr. Smith derived from abusing boys. Doubt functioned both as a defence and as an expression of sadism.

Mr. Smith's reliance upon dissociation contributed to my doubt about what he told me. By dissociating, he cut links between memories of being abused and the emotional impact of those experiences, between memories of abusing children and the guilt and shame he felt about his behaviour. De Masi (2007) noted how his paedophile patient, Michael, fiercely defended his view that absolute well-being could be obtained from the world of 'boy-ness' and pressured his analyst to confirm this delusional construction (p. 161); De Masi understood this behaviour as a defence against being identified with an absent and confusing parent, a dangerous source of madness. This anxiety motivated De Masi's patient's participation in his analysis. But unlike Michael, Mr. Smith was not consciously anxious about becoming colonized and engulfed by the world of paedophilia. In Mr. Smith's case, there was also less idealization of his nurturing relationships with boys. Mr. Smith reconstituted himself following the trauma of his abuse and his father's denial of reality by identifying with the lying, abusive behaviour of his father, which was eroticized and enacted in paedophilic behaviour. My recognition and understanding of this identification as a defence against being overwhelmed by traumatic anxieties threatened to expose Mr. Smith's unbearable guilt and shame.

I have found from my experience of treating different types of perversions that paedophilia often underpins other perversions. Early self-object differentiation, before the recognition and enforcement of an incest barrier, leads to a sense of the nurturing Breast and protecting Other as having qualities and capacities that the infant does not possess. Trauma may arise from pain inflicted by parental intrusion or deprivation, and lead to a child's identification with a parent who hurts or abuses weak, dependent objects. When the aggression behind that identification is erotized—that is, when the aggression is converted into sadism—the foundations are laid for a paedophilic sexual orientation. The abolition of self-object differentiation is reinforced by the paedophile's primitive narcissism (Fenichel 1945; Glasser 1987, 1992; Kernberg 1992; Schinaia 2010). However, the adult's often deeply unconscious identification with the parent as aggressor, or the shame that is generated by any awareness of sexual attraction to children, motivates repression, denial and dissociation.

One aspect of Mr. Smith's experience of being abused by his parents was the belief that they betrayed his fundamental trust that his parents would protect him. Similarly, Mr. Smith's doubt that I would protect the confidential nature of our relationship contributed to his premature termination.

In the "Three Essays on Childhood Sexuality" (1905) Freud maintained that sadism, the libidinization of aggression, was "the most common and the most significant of all the perversions..." (p. 157). With his last remark that "Nothing happened", Mr. Smith was warning me that if I, as a projection of a corrupt, persecuting superego, reported him to the authorities, he would maintain that the source of what he told me was not experience but his imagination. However, at a deeper level, Mr. Smith was trying to project into me the destabilizing confusion and doubt he had experienced when his father denied his abuse—and, by way of that instigation of doubt, to escape his own guilt, just as his father had done.

I felt shock and helplessness at the end of the last session. My affective response conveyed the sadistic impact of Mr. Smith's last remarks. Later, as I reflected on the look in Mr. Smith's face as he left the consulting room, I was reminded of Meltzer's observation that "signs of the collapse of hope in the analyst are greeted with triumph..." (p. 138) by the perverse patient, and wondered if this was another of Mr. Smith's aims.

Unlike honest doubt that exists within us or between analyst and patient in order to deepen and expand knowledge, the doubt I felt at the end of Mr. Smith's last session was a response to a betrayal of trust, denial, sadistic manipulation of communication, and profound disorientation. I believe that Mr. Smith sadistically created doubt in order to attack unbearable knowledge.

Based on my experience of Mr. Smith, I believe that his recantation was a lie—in accordance with the dictionary definition: "an untrue or deceptive statement *deliberately* used to mislead" (Collins 1994, p. 652, my italics). I have emphasized the conscious intent behind a lie in order to distinguish it from dissociation, denial, unconscious disavowal and repression, which may occur with or without an intention to mislead either self or object.

I consider lying to be a sadistic act when conscious or unconscious libidinal gratification is derived from the deception of the other. In order to lie, the subject needs to know the difference between good and bad, right and wrong; lying involves an internal relationship with the subject's superego. (A lie may be motivated by an attempt to escape or triumph over an unattainable ego ideal or a punitive super-ego.) While we may lie to ourselves in states of splitting, we also lie to others. Bion (1970) reminds us that a lie functions to deny an unacceptable truth. But, in order for a lie to fulfil its function, it needs an audience—a thinker who believes the lie. It is the thinker who validates the lie and, thereby, confirms its rejection of the unacceptable truth, but at the price of a parasitic relationship between the host (the thinker who believes the lie) and the lie, which creates doubt that undermines the host's orientation to reality.

My understanding of Mr. Smith's lying confirms the findings from several psychoanalytic case studies of pathological liars. Bollas (1987) found that lying supported his patient's false self, much as Mr. Smith's false self Roger was, itself, a lie. The habitual lying of O'Shaughnessy's (1990) patient was based on an identification with a lying object, as Mr. Smith's was based on an identification with his lying father. Lemma (2005) noted the sadistic character of her patient's lying, which I also experienced with Mr. Smith. Feldman (2009), like O'Shaughnessy and Lemma, was struck by the perverse gratification derived from creating doubt in the analyst's mind, similar to that which dominated the end of Mr. Smith's analysis.

I think that Mr. Smith was lying when he said, "Nothing happened". His lie aimed to destroy my belief in what he had confessed to me about his abuse of children. His lie was an attempt to destabilize the object of his projected superego that, in his mind, would report him to the authorities. I also think Mr. Smith hoped that by creating doubt in my mind he could re-establish control over me when I appeared to be out of his control—that is, to have a separate and independent mind. However, there is more to it than this. In retrospect, I think that Mr. Smith's calmness and self-confidence at the end of the last session reflected his belief in the lie. Mr. Smith did not appear to be in any doubt. In order to escape his persecuting guilt, he convinced himself that he had not abused boys, but only imagined it.

## Confidentiality

Doubt permeated my sessions with Mr. Smith. On one occasion in the early phase of his analysis Mr. Smith hinted that he might have touched a boy's genitals. When I took up this 'hint' he immediately denied that he had done anything. When I said that he might have wanted to alert me to the possibility that he might act on an impulse, he said that I was wrong. I then suggested that he was creating doubt in my mind about whether he had abused a boy or not. He did not say anything, but I detected a slight smile.

The reader may think that the analyst has a duty to report a patient he or she even suspects may be abusing children. I don't hold this view and did not report Mr. Smith to the authorities. Three issues played a part in my decision: (1) the role of confidentiality in psychoanalytic treatment, (2) the viability of the psychoanalytic treatment of a paedophile, and (3) the nature of evidence in psychoanalysis.

The first issue is confidentiality. I am a Fellow of the British Psychoanalytical Society (BPAS), which is a member of the British Psychoanalytic Council (BPC) and subscribes to the BPC's detailed Statement of Confidentiality. That statement confirms that psychoanalysis

> …can only occur in a situation in which the patient trusts there to be a high degree of neutrality and confidentiality; any breach of confidentiality would be acutely damaging to the essential relationship between the patient and the…[psychoanalyst]… and a violation of the patient's innermost thoughts, feeling, fantasies and dreams.
>
> (www.psychoanalysis.org.uk 2005)

This puts the maintenance of privacy and confidentiality at the centre of the psychoanalytic relationship. Needless to say, the privileged relationship of the psychoanalyst and the paedophile patient is a controversial subject, made more complex by government and professional regulations to report offenders. For a thorough discussion of these dynamics, which is beyond the scope of this paper, I recommend *The New Informants* by Bollas and Sundelson (1995); for a comparative study of confidentiality in psychoanalysis across seven countries, I recommend Comparative *Confidentiality in Psychoanalysis* (Garvey and Layton 2004).

When working with paedophiles who are a potential threat to children, the clinician is often drawn into a wish to protect potential victims. My frequent anxiety that Mr. Smith might be a danger to a child existed in an uneasy tension with my wish to help him analytically. Although the BPC's Ethical Code permits consideration of breach of confidentiality, the analyst is never obliged to do so. Garvey and Layton (2004) suggest that "disclosure demanded by law but in conflict with the Code would not be in the interests of the patient; part of the therapeutic process is to allow such tendencies to emerge in order that they can become more manageable" (p. 22). Psychoanalysts believe that the way to help those individuals, who have dealt with unconscious conflicts by pathological means, such as by abusing children, is by facilitating a free associative process in which the unconscious becomes conscious. Patients like Mr. Smith, who feel shame and guilt about what they have done, or whose behaviour breaks the law or could be construed to do so, are highly unlikely to trust an analyst with their worst secrets without the reassurance of confidentiality. Still, I often felt torn between my clinical commitment to my paedophile patient and personal, moral, legal and ethical concerns. There is not an easy solution to these tensions.

The second issue is the relationship of confidentiality to the viability of the analysis. Interestingly, I have never had a paedophile say that he was abusing a child while he was in treatment with me. Analysis cannot always prevent acting out. However, an analyst may be able to distinguish between the patient's efforts to confuse the analyst with doubts about current abusing behaviour, from anxieties about a patient's uncontrollable impulses to abuse children—for instance, before a holiday break in treatment. While both need to be taken up in terms of the transference, the latter may also need to be addressed in terms of resistance to seeking outside containment and support.

It is important to assess the threat a particular paedophile poses to a child while in analysis, and to do so with trusted and knowledgeable colleagues. This should be done during the initial assessment and may be required to be repeated during treatment. It is beyond the scope of this paper to discuss the criteria for the assessment of danger and suitability for treatment; however, I think one component of that assessment should include the viability of treatment. This would involve consideration of the analyst's commitment and ability to work analytically with the paedophile, as well as the patient's motivation and capacity to change or control his or her abusive behaviour, to reflect on the anxieties that trigger the impulse to abuse, and to experience guilt and shame. When the transference, and with it the treatment, becomes an overwhelming source of perverse gratification in the session—and, as a consequence, impermeable to interpretation—the analysis is no longer viable and should be brought to an end. However, if the analysis is viable, I would consider it in the patient's interest to protect confidentiality because, in an imperfect world, I believe that a psychoanalysis of a paedophile will increase our understanding of this kind of perpetrator and, most importantly, can help the patient control his offending behaviour and thereby protect current and future generations of children.

The third issue is one of evidence. What would I use as evidence of abuse from a psychoanalytic session? I hope it is clear in the clinical illustration above that what Mr. Smith told me was influenced by the transference, and, as such, was not a reliable medium for identifying external reality. We can come to understand the patient's psychic reality, but knowing about the patient's external reality is more problematic. My work with Mr. Smith proceeded in a chronic tension between trust and suspicion, responsibility for my patient and worry about children, awareness of my patient as a perpetrator and as a victim. The danger would be in abandoning that tension and adopting a dogmatic position, or becoming a forensic investigator, which undermines the psychoanalytic task.

My decision to write a paper about my work with Mr. Smith was not taken lightly. I treated paedophiles in once-weekly psychoanalytic psychotherapy during my 30 years at the Portman Clinic in London. I believe that if we are to help paedophile patients we need to learn more about their psychopathology, how to assess their suitability for psychodynamic work, and discover how to resolve problems encountered in their treatment.

It is common for paedophiles to fear being reported by their therapist to the authorities. Therefore, any decision to publish clinical material from my work with Mr. Smith needed to be considered carefully and on its own terms, which I did with the help of trusted colleagues. I also found Bollas and Sundelson's criteria for safeguarding the patient useful (1995, p. 189). In Mr. Smith's case, it was my judgement that it was not in his best interests to ask his permission to publish because it would be needlessly distressing for him to read this paper. Mr. Smith was not in the profession, did not have friends in the profession or in therapy, was not interested in psychoanalytic writing, and in all likelihood would not come across this paper; I also waited many years before publishing this account.

Mr. Smith's fear of being sent to prison made it imperative that his history and external factors be disguised to the extent that he could not be identified by anyone other than myself. To this end, I have heavily disguised his identity and history. I have tried to provide enough detail from sessions to give the reader an opportunity to determine whether my clinical 'evidence' supports my conclusions or not. As a consequence, if Mr. Smith were to read about a session in this paper, it is likely that he would recognize himself. However, the reader will not be able to identify Mr. Smith. As Bollas and Sundelson point out:

> …psychoanalytic writing does not result in dire consequence to the patient or to anyone else. It falls within the domain of what we might call benign revelation. It is a disclosure aimed to advance the understanding of psychoanalysis, revealing something of what takes place. The reader will learn something about a patient's problems and psychoanalytical treatment, but will not learn who the patient is.
>
> (Ibid., p. 187)

I can only speculate about what Mr. Smith's reaction might be if he were somehow to discover this account. He might think that I have abused him as he abused young boys by betraying their trust. Or, he might feel grateful that I (someone else besides himself) acknowledged his abuse by his mother and father, something his father was never able to do. These are, of course, only two possibilities among many.

## Conclusion

I have distinguished between honest doubt, which is an essential part of an analytic orientation with the aim of improving the quality of knowledge; inherent doubt, the communication of a confusing, frightening, and/or fragmented experience; and sadistic doubt, motivated by an intention to deceive. During the second phase of Mr. Smith's analysis, as fragments of his abusing behaviour emerged, it became clear that creating doubt was an integral part of the sadistic gratification he derived from sexually abusing boys, which he repeated with me. The creation of doubt was also his last line of defence against an increasingly punitive superego. I think that Mr. Smith felt guilty about his abuse of children, which is why he sought psychoanalysis to find out if he "could do something without knowing it". Doubt functioned to undermine Mr. Smith's guilt. When I was no longer someone who doubted that he had abused children, I became (in his mind) someone who would expose him to the authorities. Mr. Smith tried to re-establish doubt in my mind with the lie that "Nothing happened". Mr. Smith also wanted to deceive himself that he did not abuse boys in order to escape an internally corrupt and persecuting superego.

## Notes

1 This paper first appeared *Int. J. Psycho-Anal.*, 95(3): 441–463.
2 Following Akhtar 2009, I have used the term 'dissociation' to refer to a process of keeping apart disturbing mental processes, and distinguish it from 'splitting', which affects structures, as in 'splitting of the ego' (p. 82).
3 The Portman Clinic is a National Health Service out-patient facility in London that offers psychoanalytic assessment and psychotherapy for violent or delinquent patients, and those suffering from a perversion.
4 It is beyond the scope of this paper to represent the extensive body of literature that discusses the differences between false memory syndrome and recovered memory, that is, memories of traumatic experiences that emerge before and/or during therapy. However, *Childhood Trauma Remembered* (International Society for Traumatic Stress Studies, 1998) offers a balanced view of the controversies. (See also Davies and Frawley 1994; Mollon 1998.)

## References

Akhtar. S. (2009). *Comprehensive Dictionary of Psychoanalysis*. London: Karnac Books.
Arlow, J. (1969). Unconscious fantasy and disturbances of mental experience. *Psychoanal. Q.*, 38: 28–51.
Bion, W. R. (1959). Attacks on linking. *Int. J. Psychonal.*, 40: 308–315.
Bion, W. R. (1962). *Learning from Experience*. London: Heinemann.
Bion, W. R. (1970). *Attention and Interpretation*. London: Tavistock Publications, pp. 97–105.
Bollas, C. (1987). The liar. In *The Shadow of the Object: Psychoanalysis of the Unthought Known*. London: Free Association Books, pp. 173–188.
Bollas, C. (1995). *Cracking Up*. London: Routledge, pp. 180–220.
Bollas, C. and Sundelson, D. (1995). *The New Informants*. London: Karnac Books.
Brenman, E. (1985). Hysteria. *Int. J. Psychoanal.*, 66: 423–432.

Campbell, D. (2008). The shame shield in child sexual abuse. In *Shame and Sexuality*, eds. C. Pajaczkowska and I. Ward. London: Routledge, pp. 75–91.

Chasseguet-Smirgel, J. (1985). *Creativity and Perversion*. London: Free Association Books.

*Collins Shorter English Dictionary* (1994). Glasgow: A Ted Smart Publication.

Davies, J. M. and Frawley, M. G. (1994). *Treating the Adult Survivor of Childhood Sexual Abuse*. New York: Basic Books.

De Masi, F. (2007). The paedophile and his inner world. *Int. J. Psychoanal.*, 88: 147–165.

Feldman, M. (2009). *Doubt, Conviction and the Analytic Process*. Hove: Routledge.

Fenichel, O. (1945). *The Psychoanalytic Theory of Neurosis*. New York: Brunner,

Ferenczi, S. (1930/1955). The principles of relaxation and neocatharsis. In *Final Contribution to the Problems and Methods of Psychoanalysis*, ed. M. Balint. London: Hogarth Press, pp. 108–125.

Freud, A. (1936,1976). The ego and the mechanisms of defence. Hogarth Press and The Institute of Psycho-Analysis

Freud, S. (1896a). Further remarks on the neuro-psychoses of defence. *S.E.*, 3: 157–188.

Freud, S. (1896b). The aetiology of hysteria. *S.E.*, 3: 187–222.

Freud, S. (1905). Three essays on the theory of sexuality. *S.E.*, 7: 125–247.

Freud S. (1910) Five Lectures on psycho-analysis SE 11 9-20

Freud, S. (1916–17). Introductory lectures on psycho-analysis. *S.E.*, 15–16.

Freud, S. (1926). Inhibitions, symptoms and anxiety. *S.E.*, 20: 75–174.

Freud, S. (1940). Splitting of the ego in the process of defence. *S.E.*, 23: 275–278.

Garvey, P. and Layton, A. (2004). *Comparative Confidentiality in Psychoanalysis*. International Psychoanalytical Association and The British Institute of International and Comparative Law: London.

Glasser, M. (1979). Some aspects of the role of aggression in perversions. In *Sexual Deviations*. 2nd edition, ed. I. Rosen. Oxford: Oxford University Press, pp. 278–305.

Glasser, M. (1987). Psychodynamic aspects of paedophilia. *Psychoanal. Psychother.*, 3: 121–135.

Glasser, M. (1990). Paedophilia. In *Principles and Practice of Forensic Psychiatry*, eds. R. Bluglass and P. Bowden. Edinburgh: Churchill Livingstone, pp. 739–748.

Glasser, M. (1992). Problems in the psychoanalysis of certain narcissistic disorders. *Int. J. Psychoanal.*, 73: 493–503.

Glover, E. (1932). The relation of perversion-formation to the development of reality sense. In *The Early Development of the Mind*. London: Imago, 1956, pp. 216–234.

Heimann, P. (1950). On Countertransference. *Int. J. Psychoanal.*, 31: 81–84.

International Society for Traumatic Stress Studies (1998). *Childhood Trauma Remembered*.

Jacka, K. (2011). Personal communication.

Kernberg O. F. (1992) Psychopathis, paranoid and depressive transferences. *Int. J. Psychoanal.*, 73; 13-28

Klein, M. (1946). Notes on some schizoid mechanisms. *Int. J. Psychoanal.*, 27: 99–110.

Klein, M. (1955). On identification. In *Writings*, ed. M. Klein, Vol. 3. London: Hogarth Press, 1975, pp. 141–175.

Lemma, A. (2005). The many faces of lying. *Int. J. Psychoanal.*, 86: 737–753.

Mollon, P. (1998). *Remembering Trauma*. Chichester: John Wiley & Sons.

O'Shaughnessy, E. (1990). Can a liar be psychoanalysed? *Int. J. Psychoanal.*, 71: 187–204.

Sandler, J. (1976). Countertransference and role responsiveness. *Int. Rev. Psychoanal.*, 3: 43–47.

Schinaia, C. (2010). *On Paedophilia*. London: Karnac Books.

Schore, A. N. (2001). The effects of early relational trauma on right brain development, affect regulation and infant mental health. *Infant Ment. Health J.*, 22: 210–269.

Socarides, C. W. (1959). Meaning and content of a pedophilia perversion. *J. Am. Psychoanal. Assoc.*, 7: 84–94.

Sodré, I. (2012) Who's who? Notes on pathological identifications. In *Projective Identification: The Fate of a Concept*, eds. E. Spillius and E. O'Shaughnessy. London: Routledge, pp. 132–146. See also Sodré. I. (2004). Who's who? Notes on pathological identification. In *In Pursuit of Psychic Change: The Betty Joseph Workshop*, eds. E. Haragreaves and A. Varchevker. London: Brunner-Routledge, pp. 53–68.

Statement on Confidentiality. (2005). www.psychoanalysis.org.uk (Members only section).

Van der Kolk, B. A. (1996). The body keeps the score: approaches to the psychobiology of post-traumatic stress disorder. In *Traumatic Stress*, eds. B. A. van der Kolk, A. C. McFarlane and L Weisaeth. New York: Guilford, pp. 214–240.

# 13

# "I'M LIKE A SHATTERED WINDSCREEN"

Struggles with sadism and the self

Marianne Parsons

### Introduction

For many concepts, such as aggression, sexuality and narcissism, there is a continuum between health and pathology, and the question of balance. It may be similar for sense and sensuality. Making too much sense of things may preclude the healthy potential for doubt and the touch of nonsense vital for creativity, curiosity and play; too little sense brings confusion and madness. Too much sensuality may be unhealthy if it defensively precludes the realistic acceptance of ordinary life and relationships; too little makes life and loving grey and joyless.

I found relatively few references to sensuality in the early literature. In 1912 and 1916 Freud equated sensuality with passionate genital sexuality, but more recently sensuality has been considered in its sensory and not necessarily sexual aspects in terms of the development of attachment love and of the self in the intimate interactions between mother and baby. Gaddini (1987) suggests that "much of what was for Freud the early expression of sexuality may be referred to, now, in terms of sensuality; namely sensual experience". Her emphasis on the importance of continuity and sense-of-being, based on interactions with the mother, echoes ideas by Balint (1952), Winnicott (1945, 1963a), and Stern (1985) on the development of the self. Lichtenberg (2008) suggests that sensuality originates from the sharing of pleasant bodily and aesthetically arousing (selfobject) experiences that vitalize or soothe as needs for each arise... It lies ... in activities that promote a cohesive sense of self (which) become a consistent pattern involved in attachment.

(p. 7)

The patient I will present lacked ordinary caring maternal sensuality and secure attachment in her early years and experienced instead sometimes intrusive, violent, excited sensuality at the hands of her father. She was unable to develop a coherent sense of self and her ego development was compromised, leaving her unable to make sense of her feelings.

Lichtenberg (2008) suggests that sensual expression may be compromised in the perversions. This concurs with my own work with perverse patients, whose core complex anxieties of feeling both abandoned and intruded upon (Glasser 1996, 1998) invariably propel them away from mutual sensuality and into sado-masochistic relationships with rigidly prescribed sexual agendas precluding emotional intimacy. Although my patient didn't have an established perversion, she too longed for but feared intimacy, and defensively used sado-masochistic ways of relating to try to hold onto her objects at a safe distance. Her self-destructive use of her body and of sexuality to defend against annihilation anxiety constituted a kind of pseudo-sensuality.

## Lisa

I will present some aspects of the six years of analysis of a late adolescent girl to focus on the distortions in her development, which led to severe conflicts about intimacy and consequent problems with sensuality, sadism and the self. In her early years Lisa had great difficulty internalizing safe and pleasurable sensory experiences that normally promote secure attachment, a cohesive sense of self (Kohut 1977; Tolpin 1978) and the capacity for self-regulation (Greenspan 1985). Instead, she experienced inconsistent care, which ranged from emotional and sensory neglect from her mother to aggressive and sexualized overstimulation by her father. As a result, she was often overwhelmed by anxiety, confusion and distress, and defensively developed a rigid but unreal sense of identity that was constantly undermined by the threat of fragmentation. The developmental process of adolescence, with its disturbed narcissism, strains on the ego, and what Balint called its "powerful sensual stream" (Balint 1952), heightened her frantic pseudo-sensual stimulation (Blos 1966). I hope to show how the analytic relationship and work on her defences gradually enabled Lisa to develop a more stable sense of herself and her body, to bind aggression with some loving feelings (towards herself and others) and to relate differently both in her internal world and in actual relationships, thus paving the way for a potential to integrate sensuality with sexuality.

Two things she said during the analysis are particularly significant. First, her poignant cry, "I don't know what I feel". Second, when she blurted out in despair,

> I think of myself as a shattered windscreen. I suppose analysis is to find all the tiny pieces of glass and put them back together, but maybe I was born in pieces. Perhaps there just aren't enough bits to make a whole and it's impossible... At the very least, it could take years and years.

This graphic metaphor for Lisa's sense of disintegration suggested what lay behind her sado-masochistic and demanding modes of relating: to quote Sharpe, a "massive infantile rage and fear...associated with the phantasy of an immense thing inside in countless pieces" (Sharpe 1935, p. 146). Lisa's fragmented self-image contrasts with the characteristics of a healthy sensual self - warm, soft, flexible, and lively.

## Lisa's background

There is an unusual amount of detail about Lisa's family background and development: material from her first diagnostic assessment at the Anna Freud Centre at age 8, her ensuing 2 years of 5 times weekly analysis and from the parent work meetings at that time, as well as from her second assessment at the age of 19 and her 6 years of 5 times weekly analysis with me.

Lisa was born in America, the only child of parents whose marriage was constantly fraught with tension. Her highly anxious mother was so overwhelmed and nervous that she left most of the feeding and caring for the baby to her husband, who became extremely resentful. Mother began to disappear from home at periodic intervals, leaving father to cope with a bewildered child. Lisa's sensory experiences were thus probably very confusing, and she largely missed out on the maternal mirroring gaze of delight, calm soothing vocalizations and warm touch of skin-on-skin. All this will have affected her sense of safety, being 'held', going-on-being, and containment (Winnicott 1960).

Lisa was ferried to many different child-minders, and mother spoke guiltily of throwing sweets into the back of the car to her screaming child. At Nursery at age three Lisa attached herself exclusively to another little girl but, when this friend left, she reacted by taking naps until she was spending four hours of the school day asleep.

The family moved to London when Lisa was five. A year later they were involved in a car crash—father was driving when a lorry hit them. Both parents and the paternal grandfather were hospitalized, and only Lisa escaped unharmed. Two weeks later, the grandfather died and Lisa's father "fell apart", feeling guilty about his father's death.

Lisa's parents treated her inconsistently: they gave in to her demands to avoid confrontations, but sometimes neglected her, leaving her to "baby-sit" herself. Father was indulgent and sexually seductive – they shared a bath until she was seven when she began prodding his genitals, and he allowed her to kiss him passionately on the mouth until she was eight. They had a mutually teasing relationship and he often reacted violently to Lisa's sleeping difficulties, beating her "until she was in hysterics". Lisa had two years of analysis in latency because of her defiant and aggressive behaviour. The transference was characterized by demanding and exciting sado-masochistic provocations, and Lisa attempted to scare and control her analyst, to whom she became very attached. She fled from recognition of painful affects and resorted defensively to masturbatory games. Separations proved difficult, and towards the end of treatment, which was terminated prematurely by father's decision that the family should return to America for a year, Lisa invented an imaginary friend.

After a year in America, the family came back to London and father returned to teach at the school that Lisa also attended throughout her education. In Lisa's early teens, her mother had a breakdown and started non-intensive therapy with an analyst connected with the clinic. Mother's therapy continued throughout the course of Lisa's second analysis.

At 16 mother referred Lisa again because of extreme anxieties, particularly about her father dying, but Lisa refused to attend. As father had become increasingly careless about his diabetic regime, Lisa's fears had some basis in reality.

## Referral in late adolescence

At 18 Lisa had a depressive adolescent breakdown at college in America (Laufer 1984). She was utterly miserable, made few friends and her relationship with a boyfriend, Steve, rapidly deteriorated into sado-masochistic fights. Lisa longed for Steve's exclusive attention but constantly provoked him to mistreat and reject her—a repetition of her relationship with father. Feeling isolated and convinced that she had to do everything perfectly, she retreated into smoking marijuana and getting drunk. She felt depressed and suicidal and became obsessed with compulsive ruminations, such as "Why is the telephone the shape it is?" In a panic, as if nothing made sense to her, she rushed home to her parents in England.

At referral she felt depressed and unreal and tried to fill herself with alcohol, marijuana, food and sex, she was provocative and nasty to people, but desperately searched for someone perfect to merge with so that she might feel soothed, safe and loved. Yet these pseudo-sensual experiences brought no true comfort or pleasure.

When Lisa's assessment was discussed, I attended the Diagnostic Profile meeting at the Anna Freud Centre as usual and read the pre-circulated material about her referral in latency. At this point I had no idea that I would be working with her in analysis. On reading this material I learned of two issues in Lisa's background about which she had no conscious awareness when she entered her second analysis. The first of these "secrets" concerned the extent of the sado-masochistic relationship between Lisa and her father in early childhood, much of which had been repressed. The second secret was about mother's first baby born before the marriage and given up for adoption. I often wondered how my knowledge of these "secrets" might affect the analysis and if they would ever come to light during treatment. In fact, they did eventually come into the analysis, and I will refer to them later.

## The analysis

In the early years of our work, the transference and countertransference reflected Lisa's childhood sado-masochistic relationship with her father. She was provocative, dismissive and very difficult to engage, and I struggled with feeling helpless, exasperated and held in contempt. These feelings engendered others of irritation, impatience and boredom—unpleasant sensual experiences that I struggled to tolerate. At the most difficult moments, thinking of Lisa as an omnipotent but panicky toddler in a tantrum sometimes helped me to regain empathy with the frightened, uncontained little child within; and my awareness of her need for sado-masochism as a defence influenced not only the content but also the affective tone of what I said to her.

Seeming more like an excitable girl than a 19 year old, she brought soft drinks to the room, giggled and made loud yawns, sighs and stretches, as if to say, "See what a good little girl I am to come here when I'm *so* tired!" Her child-like distorted sensuality evoked my irritation, but also gave a useful clue to her likely need to regress in order to re-create a situation in which she might not only relive past experiences but also rework them to make sense of herself in a more benign way. My negative feelings about Lisa were offset by appreciation of her creative gift for describing her experiences in expressive visual images.

## Beginning to make sense of her defences against underlying emptiness and confusion

In her first hour, Lisa said she felt neither depressed nor happy but the last 19 years had been "a scrambled mess". She made it clear I was to be firm with her and not let her mess up the analysis, but she also expected us to get into fights. Although she wanted me to be a "human being", her most significant perception of me was as a robotic and unempathic object, based on her perception of her mother as distant and uncaring and on her projected view of herself as a "nothing".

She felt she belonged nowhere but her "destiny" was to live in America, and during the first three years of analysis she repeatedly planned to return. I tried to make sense of this in terms of her longing for an 'ideal' union with Steve and her first analyst who lived in America, and as her wish to escape from analysis because she feared becoming attached to me and therefore vulnerable to separation and loss. Lisa resisted such transference interpretations and tried hard to battle with me over changing session times, didn't turn up or arrived very late. She blocked her affects and tried to fill herself by gorging on food, alcohol, cigarettes and marijuana. Interpretations about such defences against her underlying emptiness enabled her gradually to express some neediness and fragility. She saw her wish to return to America as a search for the lost magic of childhood, but also described lonely hours immersed in a fantasy world with Barbie dolls. Her sad comment, "but the Barbies didn't even know I existed", indicated her fragile sense of self and experience of a detached mother. When I noted the terror of feeling utterly empty inside and how the wish to need no one defended against anxiety over loss, Lisa blurted out desperately, "I don't get attached to *anybody*! I detach myself beforehand so that I won't. What am I *here* for? What am I supposed to *do* with my life? I feel lost".

Shortly before the first break, Lisa brought childhood memories and nightmares about loss and confusion, including a memory of riding her tricycle downstairs, knowing she would hurt herself. She said, "I thought I'd break into little pieces, but I made myself do it anyway, probably to get attention". Such desperate self-destructiveness revealed her sense of falling apart and longing to be 'held'. She said her mother never talked to her or noticed how she felt. Recently, mother had talked incessantly and Lisa began to panic, terrified that she didn't know her mother and that mother didn't know her. She quickly changed the subject, saying she hated fighting with her father because then they aren't friends, but she didn't care what mother felt, so rowing with *her* was fine. Such resistances happened often, revealing her defensive flight to distorted violent sensual experience. Fighting offered a sense of self with another, however disturbed, whereas disconnectedness brought only terrifying confusion and fragmentation.

After the break, Lisa described her panic after hurried, unsatisfactory sex with Steve. Her frustrated longing for tender closeness with him aroused the same confused disconnectedness experienced during her anxiety attacks with mother. It was as if, through sexuality, she sought the sensuality of secure attachment. She said desperately, "If I feel depressed, I have to fight. Fighting and provoking are my best talents. I'm not good at anything else"; then added triumphantly, "I torment people when they reach the danger zone of showing they like me - then I know they'll *really* be hurt".

Lisa became increasingly provocative towards me and I suggested she needed to see if I liked her enough to stick with her even if she was sometimes bolshy. I also said that she might want to get an angry reaction from me and engage me in an exciting battle to escape feeling depressed and empty and to keep control over the analysis for fear of being helplessly dependent on me. Lisa then confessed she had acted crazy with her first analyst to get her agitated. She said, "Nobody has been able to understand my tricks and tell me 'You're lying' when I play these games. I'm looking for someone who can see through it and not be duped". When I suggested that she hoped I'd be able to see the real her, she said, "My parents get wound up when I say 'I don't care. I'll kill myself'. They don't realize I'm tricking them to get a reaction".

Lisa began to fear what she might discover about herself, comparing her dilemma about analysis to having a "thorn in the flesh". Should she leave it in, or dig it out knowing it would hurt? She announced, "Analysis is pointless anyway - I'm too crazy. Even a hundred Sigmund Freuds would never figure *me* out". I took up her terror that she was irreparably damaged and mad, and her disappointment in having an ordinary analyst, not 'the best': if she couldn't be perfect, she felt worthless; and if I wasn't Freud, I was useless. I decided not to address her omnipotence or contempt of me at this stage, sensing she would perceive this as a retaliatory attack and incorporate it into her urge to provoke a battle between us, thus fuelling the sado-masochistic transference. By acknowledging her sense of being deprived of "the best", I hoped she'd recognize that I saw the needy "child" in her, not just the vindictive one.

She gleefully called herself a "spoilt brat" and "prize bitch", then described two conflicting parts of herself: the "willful child" and the "conscience". As her "conscience" could set no limits, even though she knew this would help, she thought she should kick her "willful child". Addressing this internal sado-masochism, I said it was sad that she could only think of attacking the child part of herself instead of trying to understand and help it gently, and maybe she lacked a sufficiently strong part of herself to mediate between the "child" and her punitive "conscience".

Perhaps feeling more gently "seen" enabled her then to speak of many physical aches, pains and bodily anxieties. She felt fat and ugly, and imagined her body didn't belong to her and that her face in the mirror wasn't real. Struggling with embarrassment, she divulged how she got into an obsessional frenzy tearing out hairs from all parts of her body. This identification with the aggressor (Freud, A. 1937), linked to her battles with father, seemed to provide sado-masochistic gratification and relief from unconscious guilt by punishing herself, but at this point I addressed her self-attacks in relation to her disgust with her body and her feeling that she wasn't worth caring about. She responded, "But I can't look after myself! I don't wash, clean my teeth or eat properly". When I suggested she wished I'd take care of her, she denied this at first, then hinted at her wish to be special to me and see me at weekends.

## The struggle to make sense of her sensual longing

Lisa began to complain of mother's intrusiveness and secretiveness. Defensively, she claimed she had never wanted mother's love, only father's, and described secretly throwing away the packed lunches that mother provided. She was increasingly provocative towards me and threatened again to leave analysis, then became depressed and feared "building up to do something drastic". She recognized that she behaved nastily to people and said, "I *do* long for someone to feel close to, but if someone is nice I always spoil it. Fighting is the only way I know of relating to people and finding out if they care or not". She could now listen carefully to my thought that her talk of leaving analysis was to test if I cared about her.

She said,

> Often I don't know what I feel. I can't even tell if I'm hungry or not…. I think I know all about myself, but I don't know why I feel so angry. Maybe I'm scared about feeling angry and not knowing why.

She brought many confused frightening memories, including a drama course with mother where Lisa was dragged in to act the child roles. A horrible man stared menacingly at her, but when she ran to mother for protection, mother sent her away without explaining if they were acting a scene or not. These memories, together with a nightmare about father sexually abusing her, indicated Lisa's sense of having been unprotected by mother from the frightening, but also exciting sensual interactions with father. Her destructive wishes and all-consuming hatred now took centre stage. She murderously envied everyone for having a better time and erupted in narcissistic rage whenever she felt slighted or ignored (Joffe and Sandler 1967; Kohut 1972).

Lisa's pre-oedipal longings and angry disappointment with mother became increasingly implicit. I addressed her sense of feeling deprived and unwanted, her angry avoidance of taking responsibility for herself, and her search for an exclusive object to fill up an inner emptiness. She insisted that she'd never want to become a mother because she'd either ignore her child and not feed it, or become physically abusive. She felt she hadn't been taught to work for things she wanted and complained poignantly, "*Other* mothers don't spoil their kids as if they don't care". When I suggested she felt I didn't care about her, she brought a nightmare: terrified by the screams of people being crushed under a collapsing building, she desperately called mother to ask what was happening, but mother ignored her. I noted the terror of being ignored and lost, and her fear that without someone to cling to she might collapse, like the building in the dream. She replied, "You know, I hoard everything, even old cinema tickets and sweet wrappers". It was as if she could only believe that she existed with such tangible evidence of her past.

Lisa's ideas for an art project entitled "The Unbearable Message" vividly expressed how she felt stuck and excluded from joyous sensuality, but also showed an emerging capacity to play with ideas. In one image she stood behind a group of people looking at something bright and wonderful that she couldn't see or reach. In another she was stuck in a deep hole trying to climb a ladder leading up to a tiny door; but the ladder kept melting, causing her to fall, so she had to attempt the impossible climb over and over again. I suggested she felt she was not intact, like the ladder, and she thought she *should* be independent but was emotionally unready and first had to build secure intervening steps. After an uncharacteristically still silence, full of tension, she said,

> It's right really. I wish I wanted to be separate from my parents, like other people, but I'd really like to live with them forever. But what will happen when they die? I wish I was a baby or a cat that didn't have to do anything and is just looked after…I *can't* look after myself. If mum didn't feed me, I'd probably die.

Just before the next break, her maternal grandfather died, and Lisa said that he'd "beaten" mother as a child. When I linked mother's upsetting ambivalence about his death to Lisa's fears about her own father, she voiced a worry about his health for the first time. Later that session she described her humiliation when "beaten" at cards and said, "Being beaten, physically and emotionally, both involve being hurt and defeated". She suddenly announced that she had just realized that she usually let things drift and might end up with nothing if she didn't make an effort. When I wondered if this also related to the analysis, she said,

> Yes. I've been waiting for something to happen and just wasting time. I realize it's up to me to make changes and I can't expect you to do that for me. I used to think of analysis as always being there, but now I know I have to work at it.

This insight seemed to arise from some recognition of the need for self-responsibility and preconscious awareness of ambivalence towards both parents—potential sympathy with her bereaved mother and latent anger towards her idealized father.

This proved a turning point though it took many months before Lisa could make use of the insight. After I had to cancel four sessions, I took up her anger at being deprived by me and she complained that I was like a machine that gave her no feedback. When I noted how lonely she must be coming to analysis every day feeling not understood and deprived, she brought her "shattered windscreen" metaphor, quoted earlier. She expressed some curiosity about me for the first time, but then, as if to protect herself from recognizing her neediness in the transference, quickly found another boyfriend, James.

## The search for identity and a sensual self

She described different parts of herself taking over the "real Lisa" hidden inside. The "real Lisa" wanted to be nice to James but felt nothing, only boredom, whereas more powerful parts of her were intent on the excitement of spoiling everything. For the first time she cried hard in a session. Though more in touch with her affects and her fear of being unable to stop spoiling her relationships, her sense of self was still very fragile. Threatened by a separation from James, she defensively provoked battles with her parents. Father hit her, and she spoke for the first time of this happening in childhood and curling into a ball to ward off his blows.

Lisa had begun to show more of a wish to be responsible for herself, so I wondered about her making a contribution to the analytic fee. She refused furiously and acted out by stealing from the till at her evening bar job. I interpreted her anger that *I* was stealing from *her* by suggesting she might pay towards analysis, linking her stealing to the way a miserable child gorges on sweets to feel better but only succeeds in gaining temporary relief. Lisa exclaimed, "*I* do that! I can never get enough. Even if James tells me he loves me a hundred times and then says something unfriendly, all the love is wiped out".

In the fourth year she began to take analysis seriously. Her increasing wish to develop inner resources and a slowly changing view of her parents and herself paved the way for both internal and external changes, but her longing for a merged relationship remained paramount. When James left her, Lisa was in despair that she had lost "Mr. Right". We worked on her need for a boyfriend to make her feel whole, and she decided against another relationship until she could trust herself to relate without merging or battling. She wanted to make changes in her life but was unsure if she could stick at anything. I reminded her that she had struggled for three years with her wish to leave analysis but *had* stuck at it. Lisa decided she was now more of a good than bad person and saw herself as a ball of clay, which she hoped to mould into a "shape" that both she and others would like (Sandler et al. 1963). Perhaps this shift in self-representation from the sharp, unyielding "shattered windscreen" image indicated a first step towards a potentially healthier sensual self.

Lisa planned moves towards independence – from taking more responsibility, to living independently of her parents, to feeling ready to end analysis. We worked more on the internal sado-masochistic tension involving her punitive superego and difficulty in developing a mediating 'third party' internally (i.e. benign superego and ego functions), and linked this to Lisa's battles with father and mother's emotional unavailability and inability to protect her. Lisa began to see me as this 'third party' and her growing capacity to internalize a mediating function fostered psychic change (Loewald 1960, 1962).

After months of avoiding men, she met Tim and let their relationship develop slowly. She also began to develop a capacity for concern (Winnicott 1963b). Previously having delighted in hurting people, she now recognized the pain she inflicted and how her nastiness made her lose friends. She still felt enormous hatred and anger, but concern for the object and a growing capacity to tolerate guilt gradually enabled her to contain her aggression more and to treat herself and others with some patience and respect. She also recognized her anger towards me (previously denied), which aroused her fear of destroying me and of provoking me to reject her.

## Developing more sense and potential for healthy sensuality

Near the end of the fourth year of analysis, the first of the family secrets came to light, namely the extent of the seductive and battling father-daughter relationship. Lisa described a strange sound at night and associated to confusing childhood feelings, but thought she would never be able to recall them. When I suggested that shadowy memories might come to light through dreams, feelings or sensations, Lisa was quiet for a long time, then remembered a visualized sensation, when she went to sleep, of a long thin piece of wire. When she reached out to touch it, it seemed hugely powerful and got thicker and bigger. She giggled, "It's as if I'm talking about a penis".

She phoned later that day in tears to ask if I could offer an extra hour, having panicked after the session that father might have sexually abused her as a child. Although terrified, she was able to tell him this. In great distress, he said he hadn't sexually abused her, but they had shared a bath and he'd beaten her at night when angry with his wife for leaving him to look after her. He spoke of the marital problems, his heavy drinking and unhappy childhood, and told her more about the car accident when she was six. Using this material, we worked on her anxiety about death wishes, loss and fragmentation, linking this to her fear of losing me, and she was able to express some empathy and forgiveness towards both parents.

A year later Lisa began to think about facing separation from me and ending analysis. We set a date one year ahead. She had moved into a house-share, taken over her parents' financial contributions towards analysis, given up smoking and heavy drinking, and had friends and a steady job. With Tim, sado-masochistic battles and enactment of merging fantasies were scarcely evident. Two months before termination, Lisa's mother found the courage to tell her that before meeting father she'd had a previous child, a girl, whom she'd given up for adoption. - the second family secret. This news came as a huge shock and was extremely upsetting, but it made sense of some of Lisa's confusing and angry feelings, especially that mother had a sort of "slide" in her eye that prevented her from 'seeing' Lisa as herself. Lisa now perceived this "slide" as mother's grief and guilt about the lost baby, and expressed compassion for her.

Lisa had never been able to enjoy reading, thinking she would look a fool if asked her opinions, and obsessionally looked up every unknown word. We worked on this but I felt we'd never really analysed it. To my surprise she announced near the end of analysis that she now enjoyed reading. The fact that she also derived more pleasure from painting, dancing and playing the piano and guitar indicated that analysis had fostered her increased capacity for sensory pleasure, sublimation, creativity and play.

At the beginning, Lisa couldn't tolerate sharing or giving, and hated being given anything as she felt obliged to reciprocate. She wanted to give me a goodbye present but felt nothing would be enough, then remembered how an impoverished friend gave her one of his books and was touched that the gift had personal meaning to him. In her final hour she brought flowers and chocolates and an envelope, which she wanted me to open later as it contained "the most important gift". Inside was a woven bracelet she had made and the words, "It's hard to say goodbye and it's frightening to let go of something which once held me up, but I don't feel afraid of my future". I was deeply touched. It indicated that she could perceive herself and the object (her analyst) as "good-enough", and that we could both feel pleased about her progress even though everything wasn't perfect and she'd need to continue working on herself.

## Conclusion

The course of the second analysis followed the prediction made by Anna Freud during Lisa's assessment in latency. Anna Freud had thought that after initial attempts to ward off painful feelings and memories, the analysis could go deeper: to the sado-masochistic relationship with father, and then perhaps to her deep dissatisfaction over lack of mothering.

In considering the topic of sensuality I remembered a scene from the 1963 film *Tom Jones* vividly portraying sensuality as a deliciously intimate aspect of sexuality. Tom Jones and his lover-to-be delight in a wildly abandoned orgy with food—they fondle, smell, lick, bite and taste it, all the while devouring each other with their gaze. Their sensory savouring of the food acts like foreplay and expresses their sensual desire to savour each other's bodies sexually. This integration of sensuality with adult sexuality implies enjoyment of intimacy and mutuality, self-confidence and pleasure in one's body, a capacity to bind aggression with libido, and a balanced unpersecuting superego—all lacking in my patient. Sadly, it seems Lisa's mother wasn't able to respond to her baby with delighted sensual 'gobbling up', smelling, cuddling, kissing and cooing, and instead absented herself both physically and emotionally. And with father Lisa's sensual experiences were often intrusive, violent and overstimulating.

Sensuality derived from good early attachment experiences can be experienced throughout development, for example in relation to the arts, physical activity and nature, where there is a sense of being-at-one, immersed in the sensory experience. Here, sensuality is not connected with actual sexual intimacy. For the integration of sensuality with adult sexuality, the central issue may be the developmental capacity for *intimacy* and concern for another. Sexuality *without* healthy sensuality—where there is dread of intimacy and an abundance of unbound aggression—is one of the hallmarks of the perversions.

Although Lisa didn't have an established perversion, she did rely on sado-masochism as a defence. The intrusively violent sensory experiences with her father and the lack of sensually attuned care from her mother contributed to her need to engage her objects sado-masochistically at a safe distance and within her control to protect her from terrors of abandonment, engulfment and fragmentation. As we both struggled to make sense of her internal world, the analytic relationship slowly enabled her to begin to recognize and rework some of her developmental distortions and defences regarding attachment, intimacy, affects, sadism and her fragmented sense of self. With more realistic perceptions of others and the change in self-image from "shattered windscreen" to mouldable "ball of clay", Lisa began to move away from destructive, excited pseudo-sensuality towards more healthy sensuality, expressed through her painting, dancing and music. Perhaps this would enable her in time to make her first tentative steps towards integrating sensuality with sexuality.

To conclude, Lisa's gift of the woven bracelet may offer a metaphor for the analytic work in relation to the theme of sensuality. I needed to gather the threads of my sensual experiences with Lisa and hers with me, and together we tried to make sense of the different strands of her past and current feelings, experiences, ways of relating and fragmented sense of self. This facilitated the emergence of new strands of ego and superego development and of self-and object-representations. In a follow-up session, Lisa suddenly noticed her "favourite" picture above my chair, Picasso's 'Harlequin'. She hadn't consciously noticed it there before, but said she had deliberately used the Harlequin colours for my bracelet. Perhaps she'd internalized the sensuality of the 'colours' in our relationship and the sense of being 'seen' by me to begin to weave a more cohesive picture that made some sense of her life and enabled the emergence of a self that felt more vivid and real.

## References

Balint, M. (1952). *Primary Love and Psycho-Analytic Technique.* London: Tavistock.

Blos, P. (1966). The concept of acting-out in the adolescent process. In *The Adolescent Passage.* New York: Int. Univ Press, 1979, pp. 254–277.

Blos, P. (1967). The second individuation process of adolescence. *Psychoanal. St. Child*, 22: 162–186.

Freud, A. (1937). *The Ego and the Mechanisms of Defence.* London: Hogarth.

Freud, S. (1912). On the universal tendency to debasement in the sphere of love. *S.E.*, 11: 177–190.

Freud, S. (1916). Introductory lectures on psycho-analysis: lecture X: symbolism in dreams. *S.E.*, 15: 149–169.

Gaddini, R. (1987). Early care and the roots of internalization. *Int. Rev. Psycho-Anal.*, 14: 321–333

Glasser, M. (1996). Aggression and sadism in the perversions. In *Sexual Deviation*, 3rd edition, ed. I. Rosen. Oxford: Oxford University Press. pp. 278–305.

Glasser, M. (1998). On violence: a preliminary communication. *Int. J. Psycho-Anal.*, 79: 887–902.

Greenspan, S. and Thorndike Greenspan, N. (1985). *First Feelings.* Harmondsworth: Penguin Books.

Joffe, W. and Sandler, J. (1967). On disorders of narcissism. In *From Safety to Superego*, ed. Joseph Sandler. London: Karnac Books, 1987, pp. 180–190.

Kohut, H. (1972). Thoughts on narcissism and narcissistic rage. *Psychoanal. St. Child*, 27: 360–400.

Kohut, H. (1977). *Restoration of the Self.* Madison, CT: Int. Univ. Press Ltd.

Laufer, M. and Laufer M. E. (1984). *Adolescence and Developmental Breakdown.* New Haven, CT: Yale Univ. Press.

Lichtenberg, J. D. (2008). *Sensuality and Sexuality across the Divide of Shame.* New York: The Analytic Press.

Loewald, H. W. (1960). On the therapeutic action of psychoanalysis. In *Papers on Psychoanalysis*. New Haven, CT: Yale Univ. Press, 1980, pp. 221–256.

Loewald, H. W. (1962). Internalization, separation, mourning, and the superego. In *Papers on Psychoanalysis*. New Haven, CT: Yale Univ. Press, 1980, pp. 257–276.

Loewald, H. W. (1970). Psychoanalytic theory and the psychoanalytic process. In *Papers on Psychoanalysis*. New Haven, CT: Yale Univ. Press, 1980, pp. 277–301.

Sandler, J., Holder, A. and Meers, D. (1963). The ego ideal and the ideal self. *Psychoanal. St. Child*, 18: 129–158.

Sharpe, E. (1935). Similar and divergent unconscious determinants underlying the sublimations of pure art and pure science. In *Collected Papers on Psycho-Analysis*. Marjorie Brierley, ed. London: Hogarth Press, 1950. pp. 137–154.

Stern, D. N. (1985). *The Interpersonal World of the Human Infant*. New York: Basic Books.

Tolpin, M. (1978). Self-objects and oedipal objects. *Psychoanal. St. Child*, 33: 167–184.

Winnicott, D. W. (1936). Appetite and emotional disorder. In *Through Paediatrics to Psycho-Analysis*. London: Hogarth Press, 1958, pp. 33–51.

Winnicott, D. W. (1945). Primitive emotional development. In *Through Paediatrics to Psycho-Analysis*. London: Hogarth Press, 1958, pp. 145–156.

Winnicott, D. W. (1960). The theory of the parent-infant relationship. In *The Maturational Processes and the Facilitating Environment*. London: Hogarth Press, 1965, pp. 37–55.

Winnicott, D. W. (1963a). From dependence towards independence in the development of the individual. In *The Maturational Processes and the Facilitating Environment*. London: Hogarth Press, 1965, pp. 83–92.

Winnicott, D. W. (1963b). The development of the capacity for concern. In *The Maturational Processes and the Facilitating Environment*. London: Hogarth Press, 1965, pp. 73–82.

# 14

# THE PATIENT'S DISCOVERY OF THE PSYCHOANALYST AS A NEW OBJECT[1]

Ronald Baker

### Introduction

This paper explores the relationship between the analyst as transference object and the analyst as new object, and their mutual roles in therapeutic, i.e. structural, change. It is influenced by my interest in studying the importance of the role of the psychoanalyst as a new object, whilst not relegating the importance of the patient's relationship to the psychoanalyst as a transference object. In adult analysis, both are essential, and both must be subject to analysis and interpretation in depth, whilst alone neither can be decisive so far as the therapeutic action of psychoanalysis is concerned.

### Brief overview

Numerous authors (Alexander 1950; Balint 1968; Ferenczi 1928; Kohut 1971, 1977; Winnicott 1965) have stressed the importance of non-interpretive elements that support the psycho-analytic process, not least Freud, who in a letter to Jung, in 1906, states, 'Essentially, one might say, the cure is effected by love' (1974, pp. 8–9).

These non-interpretive elements include: the setting, the frame, the space; benevolent neutrality, including silence, tolerance, reliability, empathy, consistency; holding, including the provision of boundaries that protect the analytic space and encompass concepts such as the survival and use of the object; and regression—facilitating and tolerating it without resorting to interpretation (Balint 1968), and through avoiding premature interpretation and impingements (Winnicott 1958, 1965).

Some analysts believe that in cases of developmental arrest and structural deficit, amelioration of infantile trauma comes about through provision of a new object relationship, a self-object or a safe space, the implication being that in such cases factors other than or in addition to interpretation are responsible for change (Treurniet 1991).

Let me emphasise, however, that the central and important role of transference and its interpretation is not at issue in this paper. For a large majority of psychoanalysts, myself included, it is the cornerstone of psychoanalytic technique.

Although Freud (1912a) advised that all conflicts should be fought out in the transference, so that unresolved problems rooted in early relationships could be tackled in the present, he regarded 'rapport', i.e. the non-sexual, positive or 'unobjectionable transference', as 'the vehicle of success in psychoanalysis', a position which in various guises continues to attract adherents (Greenacre 1954; Greenson 1967; Kohut 1971; Modell 1990; Stone 1961; Zetzel 1958). For instance, he wrote,

> what turns the scale in his struggle is not... intellectual insight... but simply and solely his relation to the doctor... In the absence of such a transference, or if it is a negative one, the patient would never even give a hearing to the doctor and his arguments.
> (1916–17, p. 445)

For Freud (1912b), it is the analyst's non-intrusive, non-gratifying, neutral behaviour that makes the patient's transference reactions capable of being demonstrable to him. He also stressed (1913) that a cold or unresponsive analyst would negatively affect the rapport, yet to be too warm or too aloof would be to deny the patient the crucial but delicately balanced mixture of the analyst's humanity, empathy, and dispassionate understanding.

Greenacre (1954) viewed the matrix of the transference relationship in terms of early mother-infant union and advised against its contamination by premature or indiscriminate interpretation. Winnicott (1958) emphasised that modifications in technique are required where patients have not experienced adequate or good- enough mothering in their early months, implying that it is only when a patient has the capacity to develop a transference neurosis that we can depend essentially on interpretive work. Both authors stress the importance of safe and trusting psychoanalytic provision but agree that a high-quality relationship alone will not lead to therapeutic change or insight.

The concepts of treatment alliance, non-neurotic and real relationship with the analyst (Greenson 1967; Greenson and Wexler 1970), suggest that it should be possible for an analyst to show compassion, spontaneity and concern without it becoming a transference gratification.

Kleinian literature holds that only transference interpretations are mutative and that interpretation of the unconscious meaning of transference phenomena is at the crux of the therapeutic process. The relationship with the analyst is seen as being one almost entirely of unconscious fantasy; thus, concepts such as treatment alliance, real and non-neurotic relationship, empathy, etc. receive less attention.

Psychoanalysts continue to describe two distinct pathologies: one rooted in conflict, the other characterised by developmental arrest (Cooper 1992; Fonagy and Moran 1991; Pine 1992). Many believe that the treatment model of interpretation and insight applies mainly to conflict states, whereas non-interpretive and relationship factors are more important where there is structural deficit. This paper is a contribution to that debate.

## The therapeutic action of psychoanalysis

In order to develop my argument and establish a basis for discussion, I shall begin by abstracting some of the abundant literature on this subject, particularly the work of Strachey and Loewald, both of whom have contributed seminal papers.

Strachey (1934) builds on his notion that neurosis consists of the following vicious circle: infantile aggression produces hostile introjects and in turn a harsh superego; these introjects are projected on to the external object, which is then experienced as dangerous and frightening. In self-defence this elicits more aggressive impulses towards the object, leading to yet more destructive introjects.

The circle is broken through modification of the superego. A benign circle with a milder superego is set up, thus making the patient less frightened of it. The person's ego will now have a relatively undistorted relationship with reality.

Strachey's understanding of the therapeutic shift is that the patient transfers the bulk of his id impulses on to the analyst, who, because of his neutrality, enables the patient's introjected imago of him to be separated off from the rest of the patient's superego. The analyst thereby becomes an "auxiliary" superego, whose advice to the ego is consistently based on real and contemporary considerations. This having been achieved, the analyst can now give mutative interpretations to break the circle of hostile introjects and projections. In this way, id impulses towards the analyst are made conscious, with the patient becoming increasingly aware that the hostile id impulses are directed towards archaic fantasy objects and not at a real object, as represented by the analyst.

In Strachey's schema, only transference interpretations are mutative. They must be exact, work in small increments and represent small doses of reality; this, in time, modifies the ego. Strachey saw extra-transference interpretations as essential lines of advance, which pave the way for mutative interpretations and progress to be made: "A cake cannot be made of nothing but currants" (1934, p. 158).

Strachey's starting-points are the power of transference and the importance of interpretation; therefore, the interpretation of the distortion or delusion that is inseparable from an understanding of transference is conscientiously pursued and central to his thesis.

This model is a closed system based on Freudian instinct and conflict theory, supplemented by the Kleinian object-relations theory of that time. The analyst is a benign interpreter of reality using the 'mirror' metaphor, and internalised as a temporary new object who helps to make the unconscious conscious. The analyst as new object is a therapeutic factor, 'the patient shall introject him [the analyst] not as one more archaic imago added to the rest of the primitive superego, but as the nucleus of a separate and *new* superego' (1937, p. 144, my italics).

Loewald's (1960) model is the parent-child relationship, with the parent in an empathic relationship with the child's particular stage of development and future. This vision of the future is informed by the parent's own experience and knowledge and is ideally a more articulate and integrated version of the core of being that the child presents to the parent. The parent mediates what he sees and knows so that the child, in identification with it, can grow. By internalising aspects of the parent, the child internalises the parent's image of him—an image mediated to the child in the manifold ways in which he is handled, bodily and emotionally. Ideally, the analyst should approximate this parental empathic role in his relationship with the patient. Loewald and Strachey agree (but for different reasons) that the process of normal development is resumed in analysis with the analyst in the role of better parent.

For Loewald, mental life begins with interactions not instincts. Interaction is central, and analysis is an interactive process. Object relations is based on the integration of an interaction with the object, not simply internalisation of the object itself. The empathic milieu of the child during development, and of the patient during analysis, is vital for healthy psychic development (Cooper 1988). Thus, Loewald, together with pioneers such as Balint (1968), Bowlby (1969, 1973, 1980), Fairbairn (1958), Kohut (1971) and Winnicott (1958, 1965) anticipated work that is being scientifically delineated today by Stern (1985) and others.

Like an adequately empathic mother, the analyst is a participant in an adaptive and co-operative unit. To achieve structural change the analyst 'requires an objectivity and neutrality the essence of which is love and respect for the individual and for individual development' (Loewald 1960, p. 20), including the parent-child relationship. The "mirror" metaphor is thus rejected, as is the classical view that the psychic apparatus is a closed system.

The language of human interaction at its best is the base-line in good analysis, i.e. empathic understanding and communication, together with an uncovering and guidance, which leads to a new synthesis (Cooper 1988). This resembles Winnicott's holding environment. The patient uses the analyst for self-regulatory functioning and in facilitating this the analyst's role is that of new object rather than transference object. Loewald explains:

The transference neurosis… is set in motion not simply by the technical skill of the analyst, but by the fact that the analyst makes himself available for the development of a new 'object-relationship' between the patient and the analyst. *The patient tends to make this potentially new object-relationship into an old one.*
(Loewald 1960, p. 17, my italics)

The analyst's objective interpretation of transference distortions is central to his emergence as a new object. Increasingly, he becomes not only potentially but actually available as a new object, by eliminating, step by step, the impediments represented by these transferences. There is no manipulative moulding or imposing on the patient to comply with the analyst's concept of what he should become. In this way, ego development, arrested or distorted, can be resumed in analysis. Through interpretation of transference and resistance, the repressed unconscious is recognised and revived, memories are recovered, and reconstructions made.

Alexander (1950) held that the crucial therapeutic factor is that the analyst's reactions differ from those of the parents. For example, if intimidating parents have encouraged dependence and caused inhibitions, the therapist's role is to present himself in the opposite way, which in his view had a corrective therapeutic effect. Alexander and his followers advocate regulation, control and manipulation of the transference. Role-playing by the therapist is approved of and encouraged.

The debates of the 1950s concluded that this was not analysis but analytically oriented psychotherapy (Gill 1954; Rangell 1954). The "true" analytically corrective experience was seen to arise in the context of technical neutrality combined with "physicianly concern" (Stone 1961).

Eissler (1953) defined the base-line for mainstream psychoanalysis as the resolution of conflict through interpretation and working through, leading to insight and change (see also Zetzel 1956). All deviations are regarded as "parameters", which must be analytically resolved before termination, by interpretation and working through.

Fairbairn (1958), proposing that disabilities are rooted in unsatisfying or unsatisfactory early object relationships, states: "the actual relationship existing between... patient and... analyst... must be regarded as in itself constituting a therapeutic factor of prime importance" (later he says, "the really decisive factor" [p. 379]), as a means of

> correcting the distorted relationships which prevail in inner reality... [This] provides the patient... with an opportunity, denied to him in childhood, to undergo a process of emotional development in the setting of an actual relationship with a reliable and beneficial parental figure.
>
> (1958, p. 377)

Today, many analysts agree that corrective experiences are at least "a factor" in therapeutic change; for example, Hanna Segal writes: "it is a general psychoanalytical tenet, that psychoanalysis is a corrective emotional experience and that purely intellectual insight produces no changes" (1990, p. 409). But, she continues, in sharp contrast to Alexander:

> The real corrective experience would be in reliving in the transference of how such an object was formed and gradually discovering what were the real attitudes... and what was due to the child's projections... what was denied and where was the other aspect projected? etc.
>
> (p. 411)

For Segal, only through transference analysis and reconstruction can such an object be modified.

Kohut, with his emphasis on parental empathic failures and the need for the analyst to correct these within the narcissistic transference by empathic attunement and immersion, was initially aware that some of his ideas might be regarded as close to those of Alexander. He therefore warned of the danger of wish gratification and distanced himself from "that abrogation of the analytic work implied in... a corrective emotional experience" (1971, p. 292). Later, (Kohut 1984; Wolf 1983) empathy emerged more clearly as a replacement for interpretive work rather than a prerequisite, and empathic failure became the focus of blame for therapeutic failure. Many analysts, including Loewald, criticised this development. Tolpin (1983), however, continued to stress that it is not possible to cure structural deficits by designing (as did Alexander) a corrective experience aimed at counteracting parental distance, unavailability, coldness, etc. Such defects can only be cured and corrected by interpreting and working through a self-object transference, including reconstructions.

Those analysts who see the corrective experience as but one of a number of therapeutic factors, offer explanations that incorporate it into their theoretical orientation, but emphasise the centrality of transference analysis, so sharing what might be loosely regarded as common ground. This is the case whether the analyst is classical (Eissler 1953), Kleinian (Segal 1990), Kohutian (Tolpin 1983), or Independent (Winnicott 1958, 1965).

Recently, Blum returned to this issue from the important vantage-point of the central role of insight as an agent of psychic change: "*all appropriate interpretation* involves a corrective analytic experience, as does the analytic alliance and the continued analytic experience of acceptance, interest, and empathy—of understanding and being understood" (1992, p. 259, my italics).

## Clinical vignette

C, an architect aged 28 and married, sought help because she saw herself as unlovable and unable to hold the interest of her husband. In many ways she was not unusual, but she had been traumatised as a child through separations due to her mother being hospitalised for severe and recurring physical illnesses. She experienced these as rejections, despite being well cared for by her father and nanny at these times. However, the mother's return from hospital and the parental reunion compounded her feelings of loss. Indeed, the reunion made her feel even further excluded and she showed her unhappiness by whining miserably for long periods. In particular, she recalled her mother's irritated and unsympathetic response to these feelings of exclusion and her complaint and criticism that she was a "moaner".

When she began her analysis she had been married for a year. She described Tom in idealised terms, "the most wonderful man", "my best ever relationship", and so on. However, severe marital difficulties soon became evident. Before the marriage, they had only occasionally had sexual relations. Afterwards, Tom continued an earlier attachment to another woman, which he was always promising to sever but never did so. He was impotent, except very occasionally, and would not share her bed, nor would he share a social life with her.

When I first pointed out how little joy her marriage brought, she attacked me fiercely. She accused me, in a paranoid way, of trying to break up the marriage, stressed how good Tom was, how hard he was trying, how loving and considerate he was. She made absurd allowances for him, not least that it was she who was unlovable. Over several months she unleashed a reaction of ever-increasing hostility towards me. She attacked my competence with derision, compared me unfavourably with Tom, scorned my efforts to help her get in touch with ambivalent feelings towards him and denigrated my appearance and office. She especially devalued interpretations aimed at showing her how she split the transference. She seemed to set me up to comment on the unhappiness of that liaison, only to demolish me if I did so. This was an exceedingly testing, frustrating and irritating experience, which, of course, had countertransference implications.

After some years, Tom abandoned her. However, the negative reaction persisted, despite a new capacity to gauge that I had been helpful to her. An important characteristic of this was the tenaciousness of its expression in the transference, the clinging to and not letting go of it being especially striking. In the countertransference it felt as if the "moan" would never end, with the analyst struggling to survive the misery and attacks, feeling fed up and inwardly empathising with a mother unable to be free of a moaning child.

In such clinical situations there is always the danger of countertransference acting out. Although it is apparent that a rejection is being invited, and in fact the patient is insisting that the analyst becomes and indeed is a transference object, i.e. a replica by role in the here-and-now of the "rejecting" parent of the past (see Sandler 1976), the truth is that this is precisely what the patient dreads, since that trauma would be a clear repetition of the one that caused the original damage.

For this reason, the negative reaction is best regarded as a *communication* in the transference (King 1978), the analyst's feelings of rejection, uselessness and impotence coinciding with those of the helpless infant, and should be interpreted as such. Hence, an interpretation by the analyst that what she is doing to him in the relationship is the only way at her disposal to convey what it was like for her to feel rejected, useless and impotent. This is both more pertinent and superior to interpreting her behaviour as attacks on the analyst and the work at this stage of the treatment (and I hasten to accept that there is such an attack). Even more important is the analyst's capacity to tolerate and survive such attacks, and so obviate the impasse that would ensue were he to endorse himself as a transference object through adopting the role required of him by the patient.

In the past year C has realised that I will not provide this escape and has said, "I don't like you, but that's not the worst thing, what is unbearable is that you do not mind". Her tolerance of my limitations has also grown. For instance, she has been able to say,

> Every child wants to have a perfect parent, but you have helped me by letting me see you cope with not knowing from time to time, through being open about it. I can cope better with this now, so maybe I am more mature. I can see you now as a different mother, a new mother, a mother who doesn't need to criticise, moan, control, be miserable, withdrawn, tired, complain, not admit her mistakes and so on.

Handling such problems is not easy and countertransference acting out is sometimes inevitable, even in the most experienced hands. Some mothers too will fail to meet a particular baby's expectations, since for some babies the ordinary devoted mother is just not good-enough (Winnicott 1965).

In C's case, that which she felt to be unlovable in her had to be survived by the analyst before she could begin to mourn the loss of the mother she never had, allow herself to feel hope, begin to resolve her image of the analyst as a transference object, and finally negotiate the painful risk of discovering a new object in him.

Many patients find themselves tied to unhappy relationships for which they blame themselves. In their treatments they attack their analysts, and in response the analyst may confirm their worst fears, namely that they are to blame. Sometimes when this happens the analyst has become a transference object, i.e. like C's mother, who tells her that she is a moaner. This can result in treatment failure or impasse.

## Discussion

What exactly is meant by the term new object? In some ways it is easier to define what it is not, than what it is. For instance, it is not a transference object; it is not a corrective emotional experience; it is not an "empathic" self-psychologist. Nor is it an "alliance" or "real relationship" that reflects a conscious working together and collaboration of patient and analyst, including what some workers might regard as provision of gratifications through the analyst making "human" comments, e.g. when there is an illness or death, etc. (Fenichel 1941; Greenson 1967; Stone 1961; Zetzel 1956).

The more complex question is whether the new object is a repetition of early fantasies or experiences of good mothering, which are later overtaken by failures, optimal or otherwise. In that case the new object would itself be a transference. In particular, that transference must be distinguished from the analyst as idealised transference object. A defensive idealisation should be subject to detailed transference analysis and resolution if therapeutic change is to ensue.

The analyst as new object in Loewald's schema has certain similarities with Bollas's notion of the transformational object,

> that is to say, [it] is the trace of the mother's and father's facilitative handling of the infant self. The other is known and needed not

as an object but as a process that perceives, facilitates, remembers, anticipates and gratifies the analysand's personal needs.

(1987, p. 247)

The transference implications are thus clear. Treurniet writes in a similar vein:

> the patient allows the analyst to participate in his internal dialogue... as an expression of his need to use him, the analyst... as the live container of infancy and childhood, as a new, solid, object that will "transform" him.
>
> (1991, p. 13)

For Loewald, the analysis of the transference is crucial because he sees the patient as defensively transference object-seeking. Indeed, the emergence of the analyst as a new object is only possible when the transference is deeply analysed. For Bollas the emphasis is more on the patient seeking the transformational object, or more correctly, its shadow. For both, it is a late development in the treatment. The new object described here is thus a distinct concept, and not an "ambiguous concept" as suggested by Blum (1992, p. 264).

Turning to more general issues: frustration is inevitable and necessary in every well-conducted analysis; not as a contrived element but simply as part of the limitations in the method, e.g. breaks, errors, unavoidable intrusions, etc. It is these frustrations together with the compelling power of the repetition-compulsion that tilt the balance towards the patient experiencing the analyst as a transference object.

Theoretically, the provision of a perfect setting would of itself not be conducive to structural change. Psychoanalysts know that for some patients it is the frustrations inherent in the analytic situation that bring them in touch with feelings that centre on the person of the analyst and fantasies connected with those feelings. Because of the intensity and discomfort of such feelings and fantasies these patients prefer to isolate their analyst from real life, insisting that he exists only in his consulting room. This is especially evident in patients who react with anxiety to the analyst's affective presence, a communication which always calls for careful analytic scrutiny.

For many patients, it is safer to see their analyst as a transference object in a closed system. Some analysts, for countertransference or other reasons, wear this mantle of transference object and in so doing compound an already defensive situation by further transference interpretation, which is often all too readily accepted by the patient. It suits many patients that the analyst is a transference object, so as not to experience him as a new object. Over-emphasis on "here-and-now" interpretation can reinforce the image of psychoanalyst as transference object. In such a situation, an inauthentic analytic experience may be created with both patient and analyst deluded into thinking that they are working effectively. This raises the question of whether the "old" technique of the genetic transference interpretation should be invoked earlier in modern treatments, to obviate this possibility.

Working only in the transference may move the treatment in a direction which precludes the patient seeing the analyst as a *new object*. Winnicott was sensitively aware of this when, in his 1968 paper, he criticised himself for interfering too much. When this occurs, there is little possibility that the patient can make the move in the later stages of analysis from experiencing the analyst as only a transference object to experiencing him as a new object. That move is essential if true transference resolution and growth is to take place.

I would suggest that it is vital that this transference "resistance" becomes the focus of analysis. When successfully analysed, it will be apparent to both patient and analyst that it is the analyst as a *new object* against whom the patient is most defended. This may explain the wish to remain ill and, unfortunately, the analyst who is obsessed with transference interpretation may be in unconscious collusion with this.

The more ill or damaged the patient, the less able he will be to experience the analyst as a new object. In these cases, the analyst's survival is crucial: he may be the first such survivor in the patient's life; this is what is therapeutic. But it is therapeutic because *the survival is itself an implicit transference interpretation.* Eagle (1984) argues against a radical distinction being drawn between the interpretive, insight-facilitating function of the analyst, and relationship factors, such as his provision of "holding", empathic mirroring, etc. The "safety" resulting from non-impingement and benevolent neutrality is seen as promoting insight and awareness, as well as reducing anxiety and ameliorating symptoms, by facilitating regression and allowing the emergence of warded-off unconscious contents. Above all, safety, like survival, "can itself be seen as an implicit interpretation to the effect that the patient is not in the original traumatic situation" (p. 105), i.e. the analyst is different from transference figures of the past and is indeed a new object. Furthermore, I would suggest that *an implicit, as distinct from verbalised, transference interpretation can also be potently mutative.*

Recently, Rosenfeld investigated the therapeutic action of psychoanalysis, not as Strachey or Loewald did before him, but from the perspective of "those factors which may be responsible for treatment failures or impasse" (1987, p. 265). His findings emerged in the context of his devotion to the centrality of transference analysis, the crucial role of projective identification, and the special presence of destructive narcissism in the psychoses and borderline states.

He drew attention, however, to various ways in which analysts' limitations contribute to failures and impasses. For instance, he warned that the too-frequent or automatic interpretation of envy could lead to impasse and suggested that the patient's sense of being helped "to bear the pain, discomfort and shame that envy causes" (p. 266) was more pertinent in restoring the patient's capacity to love. He advised against interpretation of separation reactions based on the general theory of psychopathology rather than on the clinical evidence. Regarding idealisation, he suggested, as did Kohut (1971), that the analyst should not break this down too rapidly, by interpretation, because it destroys the benign, trusting and safe atmosphere that the patient is trying to create. Thus, he became dubious of the attitude of detachment and, whilst not advocating personal involvement, he suggested that it was essential for the analyst to convey to the patient his acceptance of him and his understanding of the material through empathic as well as interpretive means (see Stewart 1990). Some of these recommendations would seem to focus on the pitfall of the analyst becoming a transference object, which, if not recognised by him, would evoke an impasse.

An example of this would be an analyst who could only interpret a patient's criticism of him as an attack. If this was because the analyst could not see himself as having approximated a parent who could not admit his mistakes, then he would surely be stuck in the position of a transference object and at risk of contributing to an impasse. The analyst's role is, of course, to analyse the transference, not to communicate his empathic failure to the patient, but he does need to be in empathic touch with the patient's unconscious in order to succeed effectively in doing this.

Although Rosenfeld's later contributions have not had the same impact as his earlier, unquestionably influential, ones, his increasing conviction that many patients had been traumatised in their earlier years, and that these environmental traumas led them to recreate the traumatising object in the transference, cannot be disregarded.

In some of his examples, Rosenfeld sees the analyst as having played a crucial part in not recognising himself as representing the original traumatising object in the transference. In his view, the impasse might not have occurred if the analyst had had the understanding and empathy to have prevented this, and it is apparent that he had come to feel that transference interpretation was enabled when coupled with high empathic resonance.

No doubt Rosenfeld, Loewald, Winnicott and others would have struggled in controversy with each other about the theory of technique in general, but there does seem to be some coming together in the area of the therapeutic action of psychoanalysis and the role of the psychoanalyst as a new object—a matter clearly worthy of further debate.

The problem and danger that all analysts must be aware of is the acting out of a *positive* countertransference. This is a subject much neglected in the literature and which is frequently unrecognised as a major cause of impasse, transference cure, and second analyses. It is most likely to occur when the boundary between an analyst's empathy and his dispassionate understanding is blurred. Therefore, it is incumbent on him to monitor his countertransference carefully and not provide gratifications. Psychoanalysts are therefore rightly concerned that overemphasis on idealisation, together with a reluctance to be experienced as a bad object, could lead to the negative transference being neglected and unanalysed.

Patients consistently invite their analysts to abandon neutrality and enact a supportive or destructive role from a past relationship (Sandler 1976; Segal 1990). This is a posture to be resisted and one which reflects the least helpful and probably most damaging form of provision. When acted out, the analyst has become a transference object; it has nothing whatsoever to do with the analyst as a new object.

Ideally, a psychoanalyst should have a relaxed, stable, and undriven awareness of what a corrective *analytic* experience is. Within his free-floating attention such a concept may well be an excellent and creative therapeutic tool that could help the analyst to know what not to do, i.e. to be aware of the type of interventions that could damage a vulnerable patient's self-esteem, confidence, optimism, etc. The patient would then be protected against the poorly judged or badly timed interpretation, the too-clever interpretation or the correct interpretation given too early or without empathy, which, as we all know, can be deeply traumatising. This is the very opposite of active technique and is quite different to the provision of a corrective emotional experience, but it is a reflection of empathic listening.

The fact is that over a period of time the analyst's silent communication of his understanding of the patient's vulnerability has a cumulative effect and it is on this which rests the possibility that, when correct transference interpretations and reconstructions are eventually given, the patient will have enough of a relationship with the analyst as a new object to be able to work analytically and transferentially with him.

My formulations allow for the notion that transference interpretations are mutative; however, if an analysis consists *only* of transference interpretations, an anti-therapeutic result may ensue, i.e. nothing but resistance, or worse still collusion through submission. With the patient's discovery of the analyst as a new object, a new phase of growth and development may begin, especially the potential for improved external relationships. For some patients, it is the advent of this major step forward that can pave the way for them to consider termination of analysis. It follows that the patient or analyst who cannot allow the analyst to be other than a transference object, cannot permit this essentially therapeutic resolution.

## Summary

Two groups of contributions are reviewed and integrated: those pertaining to non-interpretive elements that support the psychoanalytic process and some seminal papers on the therapeutic action of psychoanalysis.

The notions of the psychoanalyst as a transference object and new object are conceptualised and differentiated. It is shown that the corrective analytic experience is related to the objective interpretation of transference distortions, this being the essential step in the process whereby the analyst emerges as a new object. This is contrasted with the discredited corrective emotional experience.

Finally, it is suggested that in cases of structural deficit or developmental arrest, unverbalised features, such as the analyst's survival, the atmosphere of safety and tolerance, etc. are themselves implicit transference interpretations and that they are mutative.

## Note

1  This paper first appeared *Int. J. Psycho-Anal.*, 74: 1223–1233.

## References

Alexander, F. (1950). Analysis of the therapeutic factors in psychoanalytic treatment. *Psychoanal. Q.*, 19: 482–500.

Balint, M. (1968). *The Basic Fault*. London: Tavistock.

Blum, H. P. (1992). Psychic change: the analytic relationship(s) and agents of change. *Int. J. Psychoanal.*, 73: 255–264.

Bollas, C. (1987). *The Shadow of the Object: Psychoanalysis of the Unthought Known*. London: Free Association Books.

Bowlby, J. (1969). *Attachment and Loss*, Vol. 1. New York: Basic Books.

Bowlby, J. (1973). *Attachment and Loss*, Vol. 2. New York: Basic Books.

Bowlby, J. (1980). *Attachment and Loss*, Vol. 3. New York: Basic Books.

Cooper, A. M. (1988). Our changing views of the therapeutic action in psychoanalysis: comparing Strachey and Loewald. *Psychoanal. Q.*, 57: 15–27.

Cooper, A. M. (1992). Psychic change: developments in the theory of psychoanalytic techniques. *Int. J. Psychoanal.*, 73: 245–250.

Eagle, M. N. (1984). *Recent Developments in Psychoanalysis: A Critical Evaluation*. Cambridge, MA: Harvard Univ. Press.

Eeissler, K. (1953). The effect of the structure of the ego on psychoanalytic technique. *J. Am. Psychoanal. Assoc.*, 1: 104–143.

Fairbairn, W. R. D. (1958). On the nature and aims of psycho-analytical treatment. *Int. J. Psychoanal.*, 39: 374–385.

Fenichel, O. (1941). *Problems of Psychoanalytic Technique*. Albany, NY: Psychoanal. Q. inc.

Ferenczi, S. (1928). The elasticity of psychoanalytic technique. In *Final Contributions to the Problems and Methods of Psychoanalysis*, ed. M. Balint. New York: Basic Books, 1955, pp. 87–101.

Fonagy, P. and Moran, G. S. (1991). Understanding psychic change in child psychoanalysis. *Int. J. Psychoanal.*, 72: 15–22.

Freud, S. (1912a). Postscript to a case of paranoia. *S.E.*, 12: 80–82.

Freud, S. (1912b). The dynamics of transference. *S.E.*, 12: 97–108.

Freud, S. (1913). On beginning the treatment. *S.E.*, 12: 121–144.

Freud, S. (1916–17). Introductory lectures on psycho-analysis. *S.E.*, 15–16.
Freud, S. and Jung, C. G. (1974). *The Freud/Jung Letters*, ed. W. McGuire, trans. R. Manheim and R. Hull. Princeton, NJ: Princeton Univ. Press.
Gill, M. (1954). Psychoanalysis and exploratory psychotherapy. *J. Am. Psychoanal. Assoc.*, 2: 771–797.
Greenacre, P. (1954).The role of transference. *J. Am. Psychoanal. Assoc.*, 2: 671–684.
Greenson, R. R. (1967). *The Technique and Practice of Psychoanalysis*. London: Hogarth Press.
Greenson, R. R. and Wexler, M. (1970). Discussion of "The non-transference relationship in the psychoanalytic situation". *Int. J. Psychoanal.*, 51: 143–150.
King, P. (1978). Affective response of the analyst to the patient's communications. *Int. J. Psychoanal.*, 59: 329–334.
Kohut, H. (1971). *The Analysis of the Self*. London: Hogarth Press.
Kohut, H. (1977). *The Restoration of the Self*. New York: Int. Univ. Press.
Kohut, H. (1984). *How Does Analysis Cure*. Chicago, IL: Univ. Chicago Press.
Loewald, H. (1960). On the therapeutic action of psychoanalysis. *Int. J. Psychoanal.*, 41: 16–33.
Modell, A. (1990). *Other Times, Other Realities: Towards a Theory of Psychoanalytic Treatment*. Cambridge, MA: Harvard Univ. Press.
Pine, F. (1992). From technique to a theory of psychic change. *Int. J. Psychoanal.*, 73: 251–254.
Rangell, L. (1954). Similarities and differences between psychoanalysis and dynamic psychotherapy. *J. Am. Psychoanal. Assoc.*, 2: 734–744.
Rosenfeld, H. (1987). *Impasse and Interpretation*. London and New York: Tavistock.
Sandler, J. (1976). Countertransference and role responsiveness. *Int. J. Psychoanal.*, 3: 43–47.
Segal, H. (1990). Some comments on the Alexander technique. *Psychoanal. Inq.*, 10: 409–414.
Stern, D. (1985). *The Interpersonal World of the Infant*. New York: Basic Books.
Stewart, H. (1990). Interpretation and other agents for psychic change. *Int. J. Psychoanal.*, 17: 61–70.
Stone, L. (1961). *The Psychoanalytic Situation*. New York: Int. Univ. Press.
Strachey, J. (1934). The nature of the therapeutic action of psychoanalysis. *Int. J. Psychoanal.*, 15: 127–159.
Strachey, J. (1937). Symposium on the theory of the therapeutic results of psycho-analysis. *Int. J. Psychoanal.*, 18: 139–145.
Tolpin, M. (1983). Corrective emotional experience: a self psychological re-evaluation. In *The Future of Psychoanalysis*, ed. A. Goldberg. New York: Int. Univ. Press, pp. 363–380.

Treurniet, N. (1991). Support of the analytical process and structural change. Private Publication.

Winnicott, D. W. (1958). *Through Paediatrics to Psycho-Analysis.* Ed M. Masud R. Khan London: Hogarth Press.

Winnicott, D. W. (1965). *The Maturational Processes and the Facilitating Environment.* London: Hogarth Press.

Winnicott, D. W. (1968). The use of an object and relating through identifications. In *Playing and Reality.* London: Tavistock, 1971, pp. 86–94.

Wolf, E. S. (1983). Empathy and countertransference. In *The Future of Psychoanalysis,* ed. A. Goldberg. New York: Int. Univ. Press, pp. 309–326.

Zetzel, E. R. (1956). The concept of transference. In *The Capacity for Emotional Growth.* London: Hogarth Press, 1970, pp. 168–181.

Zetzel, E. R. (1958). Therapeutic alliance in the analysis of hysteria. In *The Capacity for Emotional Growth.* London: Hogarth Press, 1970, pp. 182–196.

# 15

# THE DREAM SPACE, THE ANALYTIC SITUATION AND THE EATING DISORDER
Clinging to the concrete[1]

## Sara Flanders

Patients frequently bring to the analytic situation objections to the boundaries and limitations of that space, their argument with the fundamentally symbolic nature of the psychoanalytic situation. The argument is particularly intense in those patients who come to the analytic situation still "clinging to the concrete", still holding on firmly to the belief in magical, omnipotent solutions, without which anxiety leads too readily to an experience of helplessness (Freud 1926). Their struggle with the analytic space, and the confusion provoked by its demand on symbolic capacities, will find expression in their idiosyncratic use of the dream. Within that context, Masud Khan, in particular, has drawn attention to the similarities between the dreamer's capacity to have a "useful" or "good dream", one capable of processing symbolically the ego's *awakened* (Lewin 1955) wishes and fears, and Ernst Kris's classical conceptualization of the "good analytic hour". He reminds us of the many emotional achievements implicit in these capacities. Both the "good dream" and the "good analytic hour", for example, require a trust in a benign regression, an ability to suspend involvement with external reality, a capacity for symbolic satisfaction, all complex developments born out of the object relationships which are their foundation (Khan 1962).

Later, Khan went on to link the capacity to use a dream creatively within the psychoanalytic situation to Winnicott's conceptualization of play, relating the "dream space" to "transitional space", the field of play in which the child and then the adult learns to express and explore, symbolically, his wishes and fears. Winnicott's exploration of the child's complex developmental achievement in acquiring symbolic capacity, informs our understanding and recognition of its failure, or breakdown, within the facilitating, but also demanding, environment of the psychoanalytic situation (Winnicott 1971).

I will use the unfolding analysis of a young woman with an eating disorder to illustrate the profound anxieties awakened by the demands of the analytic situation, both its boundaries and its intimacy, and disclose those tensions illustrated in significant dreams. I will show the relationship between her eating disorder and her difficulty in making use of the analytic situation, her clinging to the concrete in preference to the more problematic metabolization of complex and confusing emotions, and then show this tension disclosed in some of her dreams, as they appeared at significant moments. The opposite emotional catastrophes of invasion and abandonment, awakened by the power of the transference and linked to the analytic activities of interpretation within a context of a firm psychoanalytic boundary, provoke explosive anxieties and frustrations which compel the patient to use an eating disorder: her omnipotent defence. It is her triumphant way of controlling and combating the effects of the psychoanalytic understanding she both seeks and dreads. The movement in this analysis, for many years, will be constantly back and forth, between the good work of dream, symbolic work, thinking, emotional growth, and its negation, often made real in the concrete undoing of the eating binge. The binge, I understand as a product of the temporary breakdown of the symbolic capacities, the loss of safety in the symbolic activity, which becomes a bad experience, one that needs to be defended against, triumphed over, and attacked. My understanding of the breakdown of the symbolic process, depends on Bion's conceptualization of containment and its failures, and Hanna Segal's elaboration of these failures as they are specifically disclosed in the patient's relationship to dreaming, particularly her understanding of symbolic equation. Using Bion's notion of the contact barrier (Bion 1962), conceptualized, like Lewin's dream screen and Winnicott's transitional space, as an internalization and development of maternal care and handling, Segal describes the failure of that capacity in the mind to bind symbolically the information coming from outside and inside. The failure eventuates in a foreclosure of the mind, and in concrete manifestations, such as the symptomatology of the patient, Ms X.

Ms X was referred for treatment in her late twenties, having been encouraged by her boyfriend to get psychotherapeutic help. She had recently moved into his small flat, and they were not having a happy time. She could feel the danger of repeating a sadomasochistic, eventually violent sexual relationship of the past, and she feared that her present partner, himself in intensive psychotherapy for a number of years following a serious breakdown, would finish with her if the relationship took this turn. She acknowledged, though not quite directly, that she did not know how to have pleasure that did not bring violent anxieties along with it. I did not know at this initial meeting that she had already begun to gain the weight she had lost after she had finally extricated herself from the relationship that had become so mutually abusive, though she observed at our first meeting that all the women in the family, her mother, and her spinster sister, eleven years her senior, had a problem with food. As an adolescent, this intelligent and pretty young woman had kept her weight low enough not to have regular periods, disclosing the determined control of which she was capable, the concrete solutions on which she was reliant, and the degree of anxiety about becoming an adult and sexual woman which marked her adolescence. She wanted help with this anxiety, which was now disturbing her with fresh intensity. She had long ago consciously rejected her sister's solution—the sister who had announced to her at an impressionable age, when the elder was seventeen and the patient six, that she would never have a boyfriend, she would never be kissed. The sister has remained true to her word, carving for herself a very successful professional career, establishing an emotional equilibrium at the expense of a sexual life. The extremity of her sister's situation represents a disturbing conundrum for Ms X, who perceives her as the "good" daughter in the eyes of her parents, a place she would like to occupy, even though she rejects the conditions, as she perceives them, and regards her sister's renunciation as a profound and painful price to pay for parental approval and emotional stability. When she came into treatment, in her late twenties, Ms X described herself as still bound to her own mother, who claimed to know everything about her, to be just like her, and who demonstrated her closeness to her well into her adolescence, for example, by meeting her every day without fail on her way home from school, until the patient went off to university. Once there Ms X stopped being anorexic and, after her first sexual relationship, discovered in bingeing a more active method of displacing and controlling anxiety. Unlike her sister, she had claimed a sexual life, and she had concurrently moved from anorexic defences to bingeing, though never to vomiting. Moreover, Ms X felt aware that the "special" relationship she had in relation to her mother partly facilitated her entering sexual life. Her mother, in affectionately calling her "horrible"—often presented by the patient as contrary to the "good" big sister—proffered a protective shield, which in some measure saved her youngest daughter's right to pleasure, while linking it in her mind with a rather caricatured image of badness that haunted and delimited her determined pursuit of happiness.

The complexity of this "badness", which includes features of destructive narcissism (Rosenfeld 1971) as well as the salvation of her sexual life, even the salvation of life itself, has been one of the very difficult knots in her psyche to untie, and her ferocious loyalty to the confusion bound up with "badness", one of the underlying difficulties in helping her to develop. At the time of referral, she was driving her partner crazy, unable to bear his turning his attention away from her, experiencing the most ordinary separation as abandonment and simultaneous confirmation of the "badness" which, according to the mother/daughter mythology, only her mother, not her father, and probably no man could enduringly love.

To add to the paradox, her "badness" was associated with the actual fact of maturation, not only the bad periods, which she kept at bay in adolescence, but the maturing out of infancy which she associated with being dropped from her father's affections. Her memory has never wavered from a conviction that he radically lost interest in his beautiful baby daughter when she reached the age of six or seven, roughly the time at which her mother and she became inseparably bound up, also the time at which her own mother's aged and ill mother, who lived in the home, died. A cloud of deadly depression hangs over the bond with her mother, while an equation of separation and death is often implicit in the anxiety she has brought to treatment. From the very beginning, she articulated the feeling that embarking on psychotherapy was a betrayal of her bond with her mother; she was convinced she was really hurting her, and she voiced early on the adolescent conviction that if she were really to own her separation from her mother, she would kill her mother. Gaining weight saved her from feeling she had got away: they were both overweight; the same. The concrete solution obviated the need for mental work. It constituted a triumph over the conditions of reality, over the losses which are the crucial building blocks of emotional growth and the symbolic functioning, which is its complement and compensation. It also enacted a masochistic reproach to both the hard-working analyst and the hard-working patient.

## The analytic boundaries, the eating disorder, and the dream

In the beginning, the analytical boundaries which Ms X experienced as cruel in the extreme, became a central and dominant preoccupation. Like many patients who have had acute difficulties in owning their own separateness, she complained of feeling totally devastated by the end of the session, describing a radical temperature drop, for example, on leaving the consulting room. In the beginning, the hell of exclusion was mitigated by a vacancy becoming available, then another. My ability to increase the frequency of her sessions—initially she came twice a week—proved useful, inasmuch as she needed full analysis, but this also delayed the full crisis of an encounter with actual limits, and fitted in too neatly with demand for concrete gratification; a session instead of a cake.

Ms X brought her first dream after coming four times per week for three weeks, that is, after entering analysis, and then being able to have consecutive sessions. The value of continuity has long been a cornerstone in support of psychoanalysis. It is an aspect of the safety of the psychoanalytic session for the patient, who is not left too long with potentially unbearable anxiety. For the analytic study of the patient's mental processes, continuity provides a laboratory best able to disclose the unconscious processes, the mental metabolization of the day before, the day's residue, which includes the psychoanalytic hour. A session supported by preceding and succeeding sessions provides a window most likely to disclose, often through the dream of the night before, the patient's own experience of the "awakening" of the analysis (Khan 1962; Lewin 1955).

In the chaos of controlling her anxiety in the first ten months of treatment, Ms X had gained two stone, a fact I failed to register until the patient came to a session upset by a confrontational GP who told her to lose ten kilos or she would not renew her birth control pill prescription. This encounter with the GP preceded the first dream. On the day before the dream, she had dieted, but before bed she ate a bowl of cereal and a tin of beans, her sleeping draught, her baby-like method of quieting the anxiety and rage associated with the GP's intrusion, and my recurrent abandonment. Her dream:

*She came to a session, but arrived at a different house. There is a large garden and about fifty people milling around. These are my patients. She cannot have a Monday session. She knocks on windows with a rock, angry and upset. There is an older man and a younger woman who want to help her. They seem to be extensions of my power and me.*

She was able to think about the dream, and quickly agreed that the overt anger, the knocking with a rock, found expression in the dream, as it does not in her sessions. She associated to the older man and younger woman, her female GP and her boyfriend, perhaps also his analyst. Grievances about deprivation continued the theme of "cannot haves": her boyfriend had asked her to move out of his flat, her boyfriend had more sessions than she did, he didn't have to leave work, his therapist told him he was "the best" when he applied for a job, I would never do as much, her boyfriend even had sessions on the telephone. Threaded through the litany of complaints was recognition of an achievement over the past months. In her new flat she could sometimes bear, though certainly not enjoy, being in a separate room from her boyfriend. She no longer compulsively involved herself in the constant touching which she thinks drove her partner crazy when they lived together in his smaller flat. In some way, she was being helped to stay in the sexual relationship, to turn some of her anxiety to the hated depriving analyst, rather than torturing the boyfriend for being other and therefore outside her control. Against the rather grim observation of the bleakly bearable separateness came an ambiguous association to her mother, superior and dangerous, who "knows everything", probably even the fact of her being in therapy, even though she had not told her anything of it. I took her mother's superiority to mean the mother who, a priori, knows everything, not like the analyst, with whom she needed to work. Fundamentally, this was an interpretation aimed at her disappointment in not having the narcissistic support of an alliance with an omnipotent analyst, the loss she struggled with bitterly. The interpretation aimed to meet the opposite dread, the fear of the all-knowing analyst, a dread which would materialize more intensely in the future. She surprised me with an unexpected link to toilet training, one associatively relevant to the troubled state she found herself in: She said that she'd been told she was toilet trained before the age of one, and added, with a cryptic mixture of dismay and pride, before the "age of awareness". I understood her to be describing compliance, the dangers of being a patient having to fit in with whatever sessions I deigned to offer, without understanding the process of which she is told she has the need, for which she feels need, but in which she is not an equal partner. In connection to the toilet training, I said that she did not expect her needs to be attended to, nor to experience herself held, a word I knew was full of ambiguous possibilities, which I hoped would link with the deep anxieties of both abandonment and intrusion to which she was alluding in her various associations. She responded that, if as an infant she was held much, she thought it was by her father. I noted that her father was the one whom she described as setting limits, the limits she associated with me, the finality of the ending of the sessions, like a cliff, an unbearable boundary, one which left her feeling bad.

At the time I understood this dream to mark a level of increased interest in and concern with an inner world even as the preoccupation remained so focused on my hated boundaries and me. Having conceived the limits of concrete gratification from me, although she had not quite at this time achieved the limit, which is coming five times per week, she had begun to realize, in a very conflicted way, the actual limits as well as the symbolic possibilities of the psychoanalytic situation. She had begun the work, which would carry on for most of this analysis. The experience of a boundary within a context, which promises and indeed delivers an experience of continuity, contributes to the development of the symbolic capacities attributed to what Bion calls the "contact barrier" or, in another, more embodied conceptualization, the ego skin of Anzieu (1989), as well as the dream screen of Lewin (1955). The contact barrier, conceived by Bion, is built up out of the transformation of inchoate infantile experience through the work of maternal containment. It contributes to the differentiation of conscious and unconscious thought, to the establishment and maintenance of Khan's "dream space" (1974). Ms X's rage has found a dwelling place, in the dream, where it is bound; (de Monchaux 1978; Pontalis 1974) and in keeping with a rigidity which will shift very slowly, where it remains. This patient never raised her voice in my presence, never threatened my pane of glass, and she remained careful and modulated in the sessions. It would be a very long time before the anger found direct expression in a session. Her own concrete contribution to producing a good enough sleep to produce her dream of bearable deprivation, which had been one bowl of cereal and one tin of beans, marks the limits of her faith in the symbolic, or her tolerance of needing or valuing my understanding, or her belief in my tolerating a rage which she thinks no one can bear.

The food, unlike my understanding or concern, is finally under her control, in her possession, concretely in her grasp, in her mouth, in her stomach and does not retaliate or punish, until it confirms her shittiness masochistically. Much later, when she is in touch with her fury at her mother for preferring sleeping babies, for having given birth to her under general anaesthetic, for having been ill during her first months, she will clarify the great dread of her own emotional life which is awakened in the analytic situation, provoked by the analytic limitations and controlled by the displacement onto food. In this dream she has been able to acknowledge the rage at feeling thwarted by my not being 100 per cent available. At this time, this painful realization reflected the dominating and humiliating pain of her life, as her boyfriend had asked her, in the interests of preserving their relationship, to move out of his tiny flat. Her great difficulty in tolerating the fact of their separateness, her great difficulty in coming together and then separating, dominated her intimate relations, and had done so since she actually embarked on the intimate relations she was determined to have when she left home as an adolescent. This had been the crux of her young adulthood, and the motivation for the bingeing, which had replaced the anorexic defence when she entered sexual life.

## The dream space invaded

The tension in the analysis eventually shifted away from the attack on my limits, my separateness, yielding to a more paranoid anxiety about my intrusion, an anxiety already disclosed in the associations to the first dream. These anxieties too had been controlled by the anorexic defence in adolescence, and were now expressed in the defiant relationship to food, an expression of omnipotence in relation to an object stripped of its capacity to feel or to think. Inasmuch as I had made inroads into her mental life, as manifested by the dream, I became the dangerous internal invader. To the extent that the analysis came between her and her conviction of being the same as and bound to her mother, it awakened her immense anxiety and guilt about separating from her mother. This anxiety became manifest in pressurized torment that she would have to have a hysterectomy, as her mother had in the second year of Ms X's analysis. (Ms X, who consciously hated her mother's relation to physical medicine, perceived by Ms X as hypochondriacal, nevertheless had, in late adolescence, the same surgical procedure shortly after her mother, in an unconscious identification which confirmed for Ms X her mother's potent and witch like magic, rather than the power of her unconscious identification.) Shortly after her mother's hysterectomy, she herself became racked with a pain that both she and I believed to be entirely psychological until it began to have an insistence that signified a real danger. Finally, it would be diagnosed as the product of an infected appendix that did indeed threaten her ovaries, requiring surgery. The necessity of the operation displaced her paranoid hatred of the intrusive aspect of the analysis onto the real intrusions of medical practice. Boundaries were again a dominant issue, both of the body, and of the mind. The intrusions by interpretation into the inner world and its precarious equilibrium were made concrete in the actual intrusions by doctors, who eventually cut into her body, and took out the infected part.

A series of dreams from the next period of her analysis marks the process of the analytical evolution, more clearly focused on the problematic anxiety of her analyst getting inside her rather than keeping her on the outside. This series bears witness, I think, to her struggle to trust in the analytic situation, and to a corresponding access to a dream space. In particular her argument is with the confusion she associated with complex emotions, the recognition of which is the business of the analytic process. She brought these three dreams in a sequence, some weeks after she had come back to analysis following the appendectomy, which had terrified her.

Her first dream:
*She and her boyfriend are at the beach, at the water's edge. There is a black ship at sea, and off it floats a little white boat. There is a battle between those in the sea and those in the boat. [The battle was obscure to*

*me, even when I asked her about it.] She and he go to the beach house, which is bleak inside. It looks as if the outline of a head is under the sheets on a bed. She takes her boyfriend away to a hotel, which is lit up and full of people.*

She associates the bleak beach house with his family, which she thinks of as sterile and depriving and the warm hotel with herself and her family, which is also "bad". This badness is also associated with the bigger black boat.

Her second dream:

*She dreams of being bathed, soothed but not interfered with, clean, no longer dirty.*

Her third dream:

*She dreams she is washing her hair. There are big bugs falling out of it. There is a very concrete feeling to this last dream; I can almost hear the bugs making contact with the floor as she speaks.*

This interesting series of dreams was paradoxically presented as the patient complained of an emotional state of feeling isolated, untouchable, unreachable, a state that on this day upset her; it was not presented as desirable, safely out of reach. The dreams convey some good spaces: particularly the bath, more problematically the hotel: and some clearly frightening objects: the bugs, the head under the sheets. Ms X was unusually generous in her associations, although there were some significant blanks, notably the nature of the fight or battle, which was very obscure, and the head under the sheets remained a mystery, containing a powerful atmosphere of dread. Material from previous sessions, previous interpretations of mine relating to a black and white view of the world, had entered into the first dream, including the problematic ambiguity of her "badness". The black boat was associated with her "bad" family, but so was the hotel, which seemed to promise warmth, pleasure, and welcome. Leading her boyfriend to the hotel, a container of something lively, implied access to something good which she could also give, something inside her which she could use. She acknowledged this movement in the dream, which at this point marked some small change in her feelings about herself. There is, therefore, in this first dream, an unravelling of some hardened convictions; they include a belief that her own parents were too dangerously destructive to be encountered, even psychologically encountered, for fear of a psychic collapse, a loss of the rigid and paranoid structures which sustained her capacity to be separate, to have a sexual relationship. She was frightened of a physical and emotional contamination of dire consequence.

In relation to the second dream, we had observed the feeling of harmonious contact, the feeling held, soothed, warmed though not touched, in a bath which also, she noted, meant she was no longer dirty. Being bathed is one way of soothing the body and physically restoring an equilibrium that is almost as close as possible to the intrauterine, narcissistic state to which Freud (1916) suggested we try to return at night, in our sleep. Being bathed is the image Didier Anzieu returns to frequently when he writes of the repair or restoration of the body ego, the ego skin, a repair which he conceived the ego returning to nightly in dreams (Anzieu 1989). In this dream, Ms X clearly brings in the anguished problematic of bad feelings confused with dirt, complexity confused with contamination, and the body as container and field on which this confusion is enacted. As may be expected of anyone with an eating disorder, Ms X struggled with great torment in relation to a body she tried hard not to hate, but which she associated with her convictions of her father's rejection of her and her mother's self-loathing.

So far, I felt that she had let me get alongside her to think about her dreams in a creative way, and she herself was involved in thinking and associating in a way that seemed to belie the isolated state of mind of which she complained. However, when I hazarded a view regarding the bugs in the third dream, she pushed me away quite vehemently.

> I said to her, late in what seemed to be the "good analytic hour" fostered by the bringing of "good dreams" for analytic work, that along with a willingness to explore, she was actually feeling like she wanted to be rid of the thoughts which made her seem bad, or even at risk of being mad, that she was disturbed by bringing her thoughts more openly to the session. She said to me very firmly "no", less it seemed to me to the content of what I was saying, but more to my intrusiveness, myself experienced as a disorganizing function (Williams 1997). There was no elaboration on this "no", it was pushed up as a protective shield. I felt myself intruder, even potential abuser, and I felt aware of the sensitive reality of her head being the part of her so close to me in reality in the consulting room.

At the time, I was deeply impressed by the combination of unprecedented cooperation in thinking about the first and second dream, and unprecedented conflict with me, in the outspoken "no entry" defence (Williams 1997) so firmly erected against me, when I interpreted the concreteness of the final dream. I posited to myself that if she could disclose such a dream to me, and yet also say no to my interpretation as it impinged on her intrusively, perhaps she would be able to allow greater contact with her inner world, her rigidly controlled inner objects and would likewise be more available to what I had to say. I thought she might not feel so endangered of helplessly submitting to either the dangerous internal objects, or me as their representative, and in this submission, lose the prospect of a separate and sexual identity—one of the terrors of her emotional life. I thought, in this session, of Spitz's study of the developmental function of negation (Spitz 1957), the acquisition of the toddler, and related it to her history, as I conceived it, of a toddler much projected into by the family, particularly the mother, father, and pubertal sister. Such thinking on my part was seeking the developmental positives in what was without doubt a sample of concrete thinking, an expulsive process (Segal 1980), a radical undoing of integration or working through. Washing big bugs out of her hair is her way of keeping to an unambiguous, concrete understanding of good and bad, turning complex and frightening feelings and thoughts to small things which can be omnipotently controlled, washed out. There is a foreclosure in her "bugs", and a negation of the evolution, the change or development through understanding with which I continued to bug her.

It is notable that these dreams and this open "no" to me, which I, as analyst, thought marked a capacity to reinforce a boundary, therefore a potential to more safely suspend her boundaries, potentially facilitating the "regression in the service of the ego" which marks the "good analytic hour" (Kris 1952, 1956) left her feeling something so miserably different: isolated, exposed, vulnerable, perhaps skinless. I saw, particularly in her first dream and most importantly, in her associations to it, a capacity to use her experience of feeling loved in a good way. She was able to acknowledge that she had, for example, been raised in an atmosphere of concern and warmth, however much that atmosphere was marked by her fathers rigid obsessionality and her mother's hypochondriacal possessiveness, a context of great anxiety, and much symptomatic structuring of powerful dreads. But

Ms X did not share in my optimistic understanding of her capacity to hold inside of herself these more complex and I think more realistic conceptualizations. That session was followed by abject terror of change, a sense that analysis was too difficult; she could not pursue it without becoming hopelessly contaminated and confused. Her deep ambivalence about the analytic process, a process which has found its way into her dreams, here ended on a strongly repudiating note, the denigrated and concretized image of the bad thoughts analysis is experienced as putting into her.

## The struggle continues

This analysis nonetheless continued. Ms X was committed to her emotional growth despite the overwhelming anxiety which accompanied it. Slowly, she was able to develop a more complex and sustainable relation to the inner objects she nonetheless continued to dread. When an experience of contamination, or the bleakness of emotional impoverishment, or an intolerable rage overwhelmed her, she would binge. (This bingeing never resulted in vomiting, nor did Ms X ever, since entering treatment, abuse or even use any potentially destructive or "bad" substances, except insofar as chocolate or crisps could be described as bad.) The bingeing became confined to weekends, almost ritualized around the time that her boyfriend would have a weekend session with his therapist, something I did not offer. This compulsive and driven eating was almost always associated with a reproach for my absence, my not being present for her in the hour of the weekend when she needed me to help her contain the envy and humiliation of not getting what her boyfriend got, in short, my making her feel bad.

For a number of years the psychic movement in and, significantly, between sessions moved along the lines made clear in the sequence of dreams reported: understanding would be followed by a radical undoing of the integration experienced by Ms X as dangerous, exposing, and contaminating. Her somewhat triumphant negation of psychoanalytic work would be accompanied by an almost palpable masochism, which was often visibly apparent in an abject appearance, her clothing ragged and self-denigrating rather than bohemian chic, a certain sign that a binge had taken place. Sometimes the dangerous understanding was lost to the mind and sent into her body, which would develop some remarkable and real, psychosomatic, but not hypochondriacal, physical symptom. All of Ms X's physical symptoms carried historical and symbolic significance; all, she could acknowledge, contained meaning which the analysis could elaborate; most also carried insistent physical impact which required the medical intervention Ms X deplored and dreaded. Just as I was kept at a distance and controlled by the eating disorder, so I, or we, failed in words to contain the violent antagonisms which erupted in the body. The violent eruption of physical symptoms, the most serious being the appendicitis which preceded the previous set of dreams, delineated the boundary of my potency, the limits of analytic insight. Ms X produced dreams, intermittently, but the associations to those dreams were often minimal, cryptic, keeping me out. I believe there is a correspondence here between the dream space and Ms X's experience of her bodily boundaries; the shallow or truncated symbolical elaboration of the body is reflected in the need to keep me out of the dream space, as was illustrated in the response to my interpretation of the last dream in the sequence previously discussed.

The extent to which the psychoanalytic situation was not in Ms X's control was made more real when, in the fourth year of the analysis, I moved consulting rooms, something which she resented bitterly, although it marked a significant turning point in the analysis. This proof that I was not in her control, shook what safe foundations we had managed to establish, and the extremely punishing sessions which surrounded this dreaded event are testament to the extreme anxiety with which Ms X struggled. It no doubt also discloses the extent to which the anxiety driven need to feel in control had become identified with the unchanging parameters of the psychoanalytic situation. At the news that I would be working from a new consulting room, she experienced herself torn away from those parameters, ripped from the boundaries which had become merged with her own, the imaginary baby ripped from the body of the mother/analyst. Day in and day out prior to this move Ms X came to her sessions with a grim furious grievance, and a conviction that this change, which I had arrived at without consulting her, constituted a profound and damaging betrayal which put all her trust in jeopardy, and awakened the hatred which made her feel mad and bad.

# Dream space, analytic situation, eating disorder

The actual fact of the move was, when accomplished, most creative for Ms X. To her amazement, her analysis continued and she was able to accommodate the change. There was, therefore, a continuity of a process which she came to recognize as a symbolic process, and a simultaneous strengthening of the living relationship with me. The room changed, the procedure continued, a structure held, I remained the same, the space for thinking, the symbolic space, survived her attacks. In her relief at the continuation of the analysis, she herself initiated questions provoked by her own conscious awakening to an emotional appreciation of the difference between her phantasy and reality and the symbolic space in which the two are mediated. Having survived this move, which she had tenaciously fought as a symbolic equation (Segal 1980) of parental abandonment (both a maternal abandonment and most, consciously, a repetition of her father's withdrawal from her as she moved from infancy into childhood), she woke up, as it were to find that it *represented* such an abandonment, but it was not a raw repetition. This was a mutative moment in in her analysis, though not before I experienced myself as her executioner. The battle she fought with me was, for her, a life and death battle, the anxiety at the heart of it a struggle for survival. And her relief, to discover that the terms of the struggle were a delusion, was not unqualified. Reflecting on the painful learning from experience, she articulated, to my surprise, that there is a loss of control when the separation of symbol and symbolized is acknowledged, and it seemed too much to lose.

There was, nonetheless, on an unconscious level, a release from some of the burdens which omnipotence weighed on her. She was able to grieve for some real sadness that she could experience and momentarily acknowledge as beyond her control, beyond also the omnipotent control she had associated with the idealized parents of her childhood. She grieved for a real damaged baby, born recently in her extended family, a beautiful boy who would never develop, and she grieved again for the cousin who had briefly graced her adolescence and then been killed in an accident. She had suddenly a very strong realization of the extent to which she had been in conflict with her development, trying to remain her mother's and her father's permanent baby and still not pay the price paid by her celibate sister, of never entering the world of adult sexuality. This awareness of a battle against change, against development, fundamentally against the reality of the body's time-bound and changing existence, is a familiar theme amongst eating disordered patients, and the argument is with the reality of development, the losses it entails, the demands of internalization, and the changing relationship to the parents of childhood. The determinedly held illusion of control struck her forcibly: she could not believe, she said, again to my surprise, how powerfully she had attacked the truth. The full tragedy of a permanently damaged development confronted her attention, and I did not have to work hard to enlarge her realization of the damage she could do to her own development, through her terror of the inevitable changes which are the result of living in time.

She betrayed a feeling of frustration, a wish for more from me, rather than simply suffering my interpretations.

> She came to a session feeling, she said, curiously, hungry, in which it was my understanding that she was asking for more from me, she was hungry for food for thought. She brought a dream which I believe discloses an increase in a willingness to trust in the analytic situation and process, which was supported by the survival of her analytic sessions.
> 
> *She is swimming. She is leading a group in choppy, turbulent water. They are going out, further, into the ocean, yet when she puts her feet down, she can touch.*

Though the dream has the quality again of the magical baby she still aspired to be, it also has bottom, a basis, which I interpreted as the firm boundaries of the analytic situation she had come to believe in. The anxiety about abandonment, or annihilation, the infinity of terrors which plague her are bound by the fact that she can "touch". She has acquired a more reliable dream space, as well as a more reliable transitional or framed space in the psychoanalytic consulting room with me. This dream has resonance with the true history of her swimming, an activity which she has enjoyed since she learned to swim in the pool built in the garden of her childhood home by her father, when she was approaching puberty. It was a pool in which she could touch the bottom, a pool in which she taught herself to swim. In and around this pool, where she often swam and sunbathed alone, she had been befriended by a relative regarded as the golden youth of the extended family, and his choosing her to be his friend marked a precious turning point as well as a painfully lost period of her life; this beloved and gratefully appreciated youth (already referred to in this paper, and a recurrent figure in her analytic narrative) was tragically killed in an accident a few years after he befriended Ms X. This loss represented a punishing trauma to Ms X, and the bleakness of her adolescence owes something to her unbearable anxiety and guilt about this boy's death. However, her father's provision of a place of warmth, protection, pleasure, remained in her mind a benign and generative, if largely latent patriarchal provision, and at this point in her analysis, it gained some weight in her psychic structure.

This analysis continues. The omnipotent and panic driven baby inside Ms X is not in total control and she has been able to use creatively much of what she has allowed herself to learn. In the months following this dream, she taught her boyfriend to swim. She would, in one year's time, become pregnant with her first child, sell her flat, and move in with her boyfriend. All of this would sorely tax her capacity to think, to bear the ambivalence she found so confusing, and the guilt which accompanied so much of her joy. There would be much greater demand on her to integrate feeling, and corresponding recourse to her concrete defence, but except in the most paranoid phases of pregnancy, she retained a capacity to dream, and to think about her dreams.

## Note

1 This paper first appeared in *Dreaming and Thinking*, ed. R.J. Perelberg, London: Routledge.

## References

Anzieu, D. (1989). *The Skin Ego*. New Haven, CT and London: Yale University Press.
Bion, W. (1962). *Learning from Experience*. London: Heinemann
Freud, S. (1916). Introductory lectures on psychoanalysis. *S.E.*, 15. 149–169.
Freud, S. (1926). Inhibitions, symptoms and anxiety. *S.E.*, 20: 75–176.
Green, A. (1998). The primordial mind and the work of the negative. *Int. J. Psycho-Anal.*, 79: 649–665.
Khan, M. R. (1962). Dream psychology and the evolution of the psychoanalytic situation. *Int. J. Psycho-Anal.*, 43: 21–31
Khan, M. R. (1974). The use and abuse of dream in psychic experience. In *The Privacy of the Self*. London: Hogarth Press, pp. 306–315.

Kris, E. (1952). *Psychoanalytic Explorations in Art*. New York: International Universities Press.

Kris, E. (1956). On some vicissitudes of insight in psychoanalysis. *Int. J. Psycho-Anal.*, 37: 445–455.

Lewin, B. (1955). Dream psychology and the analytic situation. *Psychoanal. Q.*, 25: 169–199.

de Monchaux, C. (1978). Dreaming and the organizing function of the ego. *Int. J. Psycho-Anal.*, 59: 443–453.

Pontalis, J.-B. (1974). The dream as an object. *Int. R. Psycho-Anal.*, 1: 125–133.

Rosenfeld, H. (1971). A clinical approach to the psychoanalytical theory of the life and death instincts. *Int. J. Psycho-Anal.*, 52: 169–178.

Segal, H. (1980). The function of dreams. In *The Work of Hannah Segal*. London: Free Association Books, pp. 89–97.

Spitz, R. (1957). *No and Yes: On The Genesis of Human Communication*. New York: International Universities Press.

Williams, G. (1997). Reflections on some dynamics of eating disorders: "no entry" defences and foreign bodies. *Int. J. Psycho-Anal.*, 78: 927–941.

Winnicott D. W. W. (1971) Transitional Objects and Transitional Phenomena. In *Playing and Reality*. Routledge London and New York, pp. 1–25.

# 16

# THE FATE OF THE DREAM IN CONTEMPORARY PSYCHOANALYSIS[1]

## Susan Loden

This paper will explore how the contemporary preoccupation with the analytic relationship and with transference/countertransference phenomena has resulted in the diminution of both the study and practice of in-depth dream interpretation, to the detriment not only of our understanding of the full complexity of the mind but also of the patient's opportunity to acquire and integrate insight from an especially fertile resource. A dream is by definition an intrapsychic event; in analysis it is of course also a communication. In some analytic schools there is an insistent and I would say dogmatic belief about the nature of this communication—that is, a patient producing a dream in an analytic session necessarily conveys something to the analyst about the analytic relationship, either by way of the dream's symbolic content or in consequence of the more immediate use the patient has made of the dream within the session.

However, analytic listening tuned to any particular wavelength abrogates Freud's most fundamental psychoanalytic principle. Listening *for* transference or making any a priori assumption about what a dream must mean by way of countertransference is putting the cart before the horse and effectively imposing a theoretical pre-conception on the patient. I believe this trend creates serious clinical problems. An exclusive focus on a single facet of experience, the analytic relationship - often called the transference but without reference to the past - is not respectful of the patient's own thought connections and does not promote the patient's development of a capacity for self-inquiry.

In the literature on borderline patients, an argument is commonly made (Kernberg et al. 1989) that interpretations outside the here-and-now are better avoided, and that these patients cannot use interpretation of the unconscious content of their dreams as they lack the developmental capacity to do so. I am arguing for a reversal of that assumption: I maintain that we should start first with an attempt to use the classical model that has so many advantages, and that only if that fails should we move to a less ambitious programme. An exploratory stance towards the dream associations provides a special opportunity for collaborative effort between patient and analyst; it can, I believe, lead to an improved reality sense, including re-evaluative reconstruction of the past, even in borderline patients, without by any means neglecting affective realities.

## Ego capacities and dreaming: implications for technique

For Freud (1900), the phenomenon of dreams was important not only as a "royal road to a knowledge of the unconscious activities of the mind", but also as a path to understanding "the normal structure of our mental instrument" (p. 607), the functional organization of the mind. But is the dream simply a fascinating intrapsychic phenomenon, of no more or less use in psychoanalysis than any other compromise formation? In the *Outline* (1940), Freud put it succinctly, writing that the dream is a kind of normal psychosis, which can be interpreted with the patient's help, as a demonstration to him of his potential for becoming master in his own house. The dream is a regression to "older psychical structures", to earlier developmental stages (1900, p. 699). However, the patient's current life, including transference conflicts and inadmissible thoughts about the analytic relationship, will often be represented in the resonant web of associations evoked by a dream. It can be demonstrated to the dreamer that wishes deriving from childhood instinctual wishes or from an attempt to solve a current conflict are currently active, but unavailable to the ego for evaluating the possibility of making changes in the external world.

However, Freud's lengthy exposition on solving the puzzle of his own dreams in *The Interpretation of Dreams* was aimed at understanding the workings of the primary process and compromise formations, not at promoting a clinical method. As early as 1911, on the basis of his own clinical experience, Freud introduced the idea that dream telling in the session could be used as a resistance to the analysis. Later, he repeated that the patient's accessibility to dream interpretation is dependent on "high or low pressure of resistance" (1923, p. 110), noting that a patient in a difficult analysis in a high state of resistance cannot make use of dream interpretation, as there is little chance of collaborating with the dreamer. In such cases, ordinary defence analysis should precede dream interpretation.

Following the development of Freud's "ego psychology" (1923), many of the clinically oriented papers on dreams took as their subject the enlargement or strengthening of ego boundaries through the analysand's assimilation of knowledge of the unconscious mind (Federn 1934; Sharpe 1937). Analysts working with the structural theory recognized that the dream itself can serve a useful temporary defensive function. The ego's defences are lowered not only within the dream, but also in relation to telling it, as the dreamer finds it possible to maintain the temporary fiction that the dream is not entirely his or her responsibility. The dream appears to the sleeper and to the later dream narrator as something that has come to him or her from the outside, as a realistic perception (Federn 1934). In fact, the sense of reality of the dream scene is a basic unconscious wish. The impression of a mysterious visitation from outside is compelling enough in itself, but it aids the analyst in a particular way. The dream is, intriguingly, both personal and impersonal, and can be contemplated at a safe distance by the analysand until defences are lowered in relation to the instinctual content.

In classical Freudian thinking this dream *content* remains a valuable source of insight into a patient's developmental history and mental dynamics—"what is hidden, how it is hidden, and why it is hidden" (Greenson 1970). The *process* of the associative method of dream analysis helps to promote a benign "dissociation" in the ego (described by Sterba in his classic 1934 paper) which occurs when an alliance is formed with the analyst's ego that helps the patient to recognize his or her own experiencing ego and dissociate it from instinctual and repressive forces active within it. In this way a capacity for self-reflection is developed; many would still agree that this should be a primary aim of analysis, along with the growth of autonomy accomplished by strengthening the ego's observational abilities. The growth of a capacity for self-exploration is predicated on an analytic experience in which the analyst is not felt to be omniscient in regard to the content of the analysand's mind, and in which the analyst does not "claim" the analysand's dream thoughts. The analyst who interprets all communications including dreams with a focus entirely on the analyst and analytic process implies to the patient that he has deflected thoughts elsewhere which properly belong to the analyst. I think this can actually strengthen the patient's defences against becoming aware of the crucial past (Arlow 1993). Classical psychoanalysts have always been aware that it is important first to determine whether a patient is bringing a dream to the session to serve resistance, in which case it is counterproductive to interpret content (Waelder 1987). Freud's essential point is that the dream is a special, if not unique opportunity to find out something *new* about the patient and to demonstrate to him how this one new bit of revealed history and unconscious thinking fits into his current conflicts.

This formulation is cogently explained by Morton Reiser (1997) in a paper in which he expands on ideas taught by Otto Isakower: the dream resonates in two directions; its nodal or organizing points have reference to current conflicts and to old, affectively related conflicts. By matching past and present experience, the patient is given another chance to master the original conflict. To lose this opportunity to demonstrate to the patient that his present reactions are repetitions of the past is to lose a very powerful analytic tool. The patient, after all, wishes to disavow the importance of his own history and his own skewed perceptions of the present.

Current orthodoxy, however, is to interpret dreams in terms of their reference to the transference, and most particularly to the "here and now" transference, which is deemed to be charged with affect and to be therapeutically alive and experience-near, and also to replicate early and therefore formative models of experience (Fonagy 1999). There is an assumption that not only is the patient's past history unverifiable, but also that talking about it is clinically distant, secondary, and incapable of bringing about psychic change. Consequently, less attention is paid to the exploration of the formal elements of the dream, to the process of "cutting the dream into pieces" in order to lower resistance to the whole, as suggested by Freud (1900, p. 103). In contemporary theory the complexity of this work is regarded as distracting the analytic pair from the main purpose of their encounter, which is to acquaint the patient with his current ways of relating. Analysts who understand their patients' dreams in terms of unconscious reference to the transference may attend even more exclusively to the dream's function and meaning within the session.

Joseph (1985), for example, believes the dream reveals its meaning only by being lived out *in the session* in the transference. The dream is thus not treated as a regression, nor is there a distinction between primary and secondary process thinking. This trend seems to have gained more general acceptance. Tuckett (2000) fundamentally concurs with Joseph that we should base our understanding not on dream content but on both the telling of the dream and the role taken by the analyst in interpreting the dream. The analyst's attempts to understand the dream material is seen in terms of countertransference enactment or role responsiveness (Sandler 1976) under pressure from the patient's unconscious need for a certain kind of object relation.

The product in the current trend of interpretation is always the patient's relation to the analyst and the analytic process, whether at an interpersonal or intrapsychic level. This is evident in the writings of O'Shaughnessy (1983, 1992), and it rests on an assumption that the only unconsciously highly cathected representations are those of the analytic relationship or displacements from it. This theory of a fixed reference, whatever its clinical merits, really does not account for the dream's complex mode of construction.

According to Freudian theory, the dynamically unconscious material is expressed quite obscurely in the manifest dream, through chains of substitution. Thus there is a great challenge to the analyst's capacity to listen, to remember other words from other sessions, and to be alert to possible reversals, obfuscations by the patient in recounting the dream (a sign that the censorship is still active), or displacements of affect from one element to another. The analyst is in the difficult position of not knowing in advance to what the patient's production might refer.

The dream interpreter is very likely to stress the wrong element in the dream if his or her assumption is that all manifest elements have equal symbolic weight. It was *Freud* who did not regard the dream simply as a text to be decoded but rather as indecipherable without the associations that would insert the missing grammatical links, the negations, conjunctions and so forth. The to and fro of the collaborative effort between patient and analyst to find the dream's multiple meanings promotes the patient's freedom at the same time that it promotes efforts towards verbalization (and the establishment of secondary-process thinking) over unconscious enactment dominated by the repetition compulsion.

## Widely diverging trends in interpretation in contemporary technique

Fonagy (1999), questioning the role of memory in the therapeutic process, states that the modern emphasis on the analytic relationship as the "motor" of therapeutic action has *succeeded in eliminating* an emphasis on the recovery of childhood experience. He believes that current memory studies show that patients cannot possibly remember why they behave as they do, because models of how they behave exist non-consciously as procedures of internalized object relationships (whereby the patient lives out the attachment patterns of infancy). Fonagy further believes that the only way we can know what "really" goes on in a patient's mind is through countertransference. The patient, in other words, is an exceedingly unreliable witness; we can only reliably be sure of our own feelings. Fonagy charges classical psychoanalysis with incorrectness and superficiality in focussing on "recovery" of memory, while the newer model focuses on making conscious an implicit or procedural memory system. "Implicit" memory is defined as pertaining to early mother/infant patterns of interaction. Traditionally defences have been conceived of as implicit unconscious adaptive mechanisms and, as such, a central focus of analytic technique, which includes taking account of the patient's entire developmental history. The redefinition of the analytic task based largely on attachment theory leads once again to here-and-now analysis and ineluctably to the model of interpersonal or relationship therapy.

The emphasis in these contemporary psychoanalytic movements is to get to pre-verbal affective states. It is not surprising that in this "total transference" approach, with the analyst's positive avoidance of reconstruction and genetic transference interpretations, the complex architecture of the dream's structure, deriving as it does from the interplay of more than one mental system and from the patient's conscious and unconscious representations of his entire history, is given short shrift. It is perhaps more surprising that the dream is still given so much prominence in clinical reports; *but I believe the dream is now often brought forward as a proof of the analyst's correct understanding of the patient's wish for or fear of a certain kind of object relation.*

Classical psychoanalysts (Couch 1995; Freud, A. 1976; Yorke 2001) have long advocated a balanced focus on transference and resistance, past and present in technique, and have argued that the kind of analysis rooted in a purely here and now approach would foster isolation from life and promote an analytic *folie à deux*. One result of this emphasis on a preoedipal object relations model is that a keystone of Freud's dream theory—the idea that repressed infantile instinctual wishes are the strongest force motivating the construction of dreams - has tacitly been removed. Sexuality itself is underemphasized and often left unexplored; aggressive and destructive impulses seemingly get more attention.

There are many examples in the literature of the development whereby this allegorical method of exposition is combined with interpretation based on projection, containment, and what O'Shaughnessy (1992) calls "accepted interactional clinical thinking". I cannot help but feel that interpretations based on this model may be heard by a patient as persecutory and judgemental, and as confirming an experience of his object as essentially concerned more with his own fate and the position into which he is put than the patient's reality. It seems to me that the analytic stance is not essentially exploratory, and is possessed of a value system to which the patient must accommodate or with which the patient must comply. Reiser (1997) recalls Otto Isakower saying that using a dream to restate or reinforce an earlier interpretation, rather than arriving at some new historical information, was "using the dream like a sack of potatoes, hitting the patient over the head with it to drive home a point" (p. 893). If we move away from the principle of helping the patient's ego master those parts of his mind which have heretofore remained unconscious, as well as from the principle of moving from surface to depth, we are, as André Green (2001) also puts it, using premature "deep" interpretations as weapons and potentially repeating traumatic earlier relationships, only reinforcing the patient's defences.

But can patients apparently incapable of collaborating with the analyst in the analysis be helped by the classical dream method? Masud Khan wrote a series of papers (1962, 1972, 1976) on dreams and ego capacities which were influential in changing the way analysts approached dream interpretation with borderline patients. His views evidently began to influence dream interpretation generally, as more and more patients were deemed to be narcissistic. Khan (1972) coined the term *dream space*, influenced by Winnicott's concept of *transitional space*, to denote a structure or capacity in the mind that evolves in the course of psychic development.

In a Dialogue on "The Changing Use of Dreams in Psychoanalytic Practice" at an IPA Congress in 1975 (reported by Curtis and Sachs 1976), Khan and Harold Blum exchanged views illustrative of the major division in psychoanalysis since Freud. Khan (1976) asserted that the patient who is unable to "make dreams" and share them is unable to play in the analytic "space". "Space" in this context connotes a here-and-now experience. Khan took a "romantic" view that the dream experience actualizes the self and that such actualization occurs through pure primary process (Curtis and Sachs 1976; Khan 1976). Narration destroys the emotional experience; in other words, something gets lost in the translation from visual to verbal. Blum (1976) agreed that the dream is a different psychic state that is especially illustrative of personality organization, and that the capacity to recall and report dreams is an ego achievement. He recognized that the dreams of borderline patients may be reported with magical assumptions, might be narcissistic displays or representative of primitive preoedipal transferences. However, this data is analytically useful, as archaic ego states and traumata may become accessible through dreams, which amplify other analytic observations. But in the Freudian view, the dream experience is not sufficient to resolve conflict or to "actualize the self". It needs verbal, secondary-process interpretation, and this does not preclude affective experience.

If the capacity to dream is a developmental acquisition, then dream interpretation with patients who have severe developmental deficits will require modification according to the patient's level of functioning. There is widespread recognition that the dreams of such patients are often very primitive, with little secondary elaboration, and that they often do not have a disguising function (Fonagy 2000). A large question thus arises, as to whether the classical method in which the dream, regarded as an intrapsychic event, brought to the analysis by the patient for help from the analyst in understanding its unconscious determinants, has any real therapeutic value in the treatment of borderline patients.

## Case illustration: using unmodified classical technique with a borderline patient

Patients with borderline character pathology have difficulty tolerating anxiety and are prone to rage states, poor impulse control and self-damaging behaviour. Ego functions are generally impaired, including reality testing and reliably functioning defences (Yorke et al. 1989); these developmental deficiencies (Freud, A. 1965) probably arise from very early injuries to the infantile self. These injuries result in a dramatically impaired capacity for stable attachment to objects, posing a fundamental problem for the development of a therapeutic alliance and for the reality testing that permits integration of insight in analysis. Borderline patients often have an excessively punitive superego, an ego deformed by and in awe of this tyrannical superego, and a tendency to externalize the superego within the analytic relationship.

These problems have led many analysts to discard the psychoanalytic techniques that rely on a collaborative attitude on the part of the patient. There is some concordance in the literature, beginning with the "Widening Scope of Indications for Psychoanalysis" Symposium published in *JAPA* in 1954 (Stone 1954), to the effect that borderline patients, lacking a capacity for insight and introspection, need important modifications in therapeutic technique (Fonagy 1991; Grotstein 1984; Kernberg et al. 1989). Dream analysis should initially be limited to linking meaning to dominant themes in the transference, although at later stages the patient can be encouraged to associate to manifest content. "In very advanced treatment stages, standard dream interpretation along psychoanalytic lines may become feasible" (Kernberg et al. 1989, p. 134). By contrast, I would like to discuss a borderline case in which the converse was true. Analysis of the patient's dreams along the lines suggested by Freud was the very means by which a capacity for collaboration and eventually for self-inquiry was developed, for reasons which I hope to illustrate.

My patient was a woman in her early fifties who had had a long history of involvement with psychiatrists, the mental health services, and antidepressant medication. She had also had group therapy, individual psychotherapy with an analyst for many years, and admission for 18 months to an in-patient therapeutic community after a serious suicide attempt in her early forties. She was an intelligent woman who had apparently had a very repressive childhood. After university she entered a religious order, which she was forced to leave after a few years on account of personality clashes with her community. She next worked in the civil service but was socially isolated and became increasingly dependent on alcohol. She found her analytic therapy supportive for many years, but a failed attempt at a sexual relationship led to a near-fatal overdose and hospitalization. After she left the therapeutic in-patient hospital she formed a relationship with, and married, a decent man of lower educational and social status. She was referred to me by her former consultant at the hospital, to whom she had turned because she feared that she would be "too much" for her new husband and that he would leave her. One of the demands she made was to awaken him repeatedly in the night for help when she had nightmares. It appeared that she had an ability to defeat the good intentions of anyone who might try to help her.

I was struck in no uncertain terms by the remorseless cruelty of her super-ego, which she projected onto me from the beginning; whatever I said was taken as a taunt or demonstration of how pathetic, useless, "attention-seeking", and needy she was. She would then turn the same criticisms on herself, or seek to convince me that what I could offer was of no use to her. When not attacking one or the other of us, she would intellectualize, losing any connection between feeling and thinking. There was a bizarre quality to this dissociation when, some of the time, she would suddenly ask what we were doing here, saying that she had forgotten why she had come. She wore a thin chain around her neck, which I imagined had once been threaded through a silver cross, and this she twisted with one finger as she spoke until it raised angry red lines in her neck. On occasion (outside the sessions) she scratched the insides of her thighs until they bled.

Hanna Segal (1986) describes being with a borderline patient whose sessions took on the form of an extraordinary automatic progression into a row, in which the analyst's response was irrelevant. She describes feeling like the puppet in someone else's nightmare, unable to do anything but play the allotted role of persecutor. I had essentially the same experience with my patient of being manoeuvred, sometimes with incredible ingenuity, into being her tormentor. While I recognized that my patient found it a relief to externalize her violent, archaic superego in this way, the entrenched, monotonous character of the transference, which clearly went back over decades with a number of analysts and therapists, made me feel it was worth experimenting with other approaches to see if we could gain any new ground. If we take seriously the power of the repetition compulsion in mental life and object relations, we must understand that clearly it is inimical to new experience, with the analyst as a new and different object (Baker 1993) that the patient is most defended against. I think that too much insistence on here-and-now transference interpretation with this patient would have resulted in a fruitless impasse in which I would have remained the original traumatizing, hated and envied object.

Paradoxically, the patient was herself fixed on focussing exclusively on the present relationship with me. I was interested to learn from her that she did not regard talking about her past, or even her life outside the therapeutic hour, as "allowed" or even relevant. She became rather indignant when I interrupted her flow of hostile accusations against us both to ask her about her childhood experiences. Mt patient seemed to think this was against the rules of the encounter, and I realized that over the years she had learned what was expected from her, and now used it in the service of the repetition compulsion. This is an example of Arlow's (1993) conception of the defensive use of a transference focus, as a warding-off by patients so as to avoid fully exploring the deeper feelings in their original life situations.

She denied that her past experience could have any bearing on her present problems; in her view, her present problems stemmed from some kind of inherent flaw, like original sin. Her early description of her parents was bland: her mother had a "warm personality and made friends easily" but "thought she [the patient] was pathetic and did not like her" - which assessment the patient felt she surely deserved. She did not seem to expect any gain from therapy other than as an outlet for her pent-up frustration and aggression; to the extent that she was better able to contain her anger with her husband and work colleagues, it was a useful outlet. We could remain endlessly in that impasse from my perspective if I could not find some way to begin to help the patient make links between her different experiences. Above all, it seemed important to work with her in a way that would reduce her belief in the powerful omniscience of the analyst.

## Primitive content of dreams in the first phase

I did not expect to be able to work much on dreams with this patient, as she initially brought only impoverished reports of her nightmares. However, I learned by following her lead closely that the telling of dreams could provide a kind of breathing space where she could begin to feel more genuinely in control of her own dreadful feelings, and less need to control me. I found that it was useful specifically to pay attention to her dreams as a phenomenon *separate* from the immediate transference, to encourage her to associate to her dreams, allowing them a privileged space for mutual exploration—that is, to treat her as though she were capable of an alliance for the purpose of looking at dreams. Talking about dreams became a kind of haven of safety where her anxiety was diminished enough to allow her to think.

This situation took time to develop, and certainly evolved as the patient acquired more trust in the analytic relationship. When, during the first two years, she would occasionally report a dream, it had a monotonous, stereotyped quality: "I dreamed I was being chased by a big animal, a kind of dog or wolf. "I was terrified and I woke up screaming". She stated flatly that such dreams had no meaning. I suggested to her that although she could think of nothing in connection with her dreams, I thought that one day we might be able to make more sense of them. It transpired that she had been having this particular dream for as long as she could remember, since childhood. Sometimes she felt unable to move as the animal attacked; sometimes she just woke up. At other times her husband awakened her as she became restless in her sleep. While there was some symbolic transformation of anxiety-producing content in the dream (into the animal), she was unable or unwilling to associate to it. The intrapsychic state of the dream seemed to be one of superego merged with id (the biting animal), with a failure of the defensive functions of the ego and of the disguising functions of the dream censor. At least her tendency to seek reassurance from her husband showed some self-preservative trend.

Another hypothesis is that a repetitive anxiety dream experienced throughout a patient's life is not a phenomenon arising from intersystemic conflict, that it does not relate to a wish that was once a source of pleasure (Freeman 1998). The dreams in question here would be more like the dreams of traumatic neurosis, wherein the pleasure principle is rendered inoperative by the compulsion to repeat (Freud 1920). These dreams have primarily a binding function, against the ingress of too much stimuli. I had a working hypothesis that my patient's dream might be a sign of early traumatic experience. Her addiction to negative therapeutic reactions supported this idea.[2] I wondered if she had been abused, and if the dog was representative of a real attacker. When asked about childhood experiences that had frightened her, she said that she had never been physically punished by her parents, but that she knew that she had to be very still when her father was around. He was a "Victorian" father who "hated children who made a noise" who became very angry if he was disturbed. She had been quite frightened of him. I suggested that her paralysis in the dream might be linked to her stillness when around her father, but she did not find the suggestion convincing.

At first, I thought there was little I could do with these nightmares beyond linking them to anger and fear, which I also took up as possible feelings towards me that she had to struggle with at night. But I continued to ask if she had any other thoughts about her dreams, if there were any memories aroused by them, if something had happened during the day she could connect to the dream, and so on, *in an effort to bolster the idea that there might be an adult perceiving part of her separate from the primitive dream feelings*. Essentially, this was an ego-strengthening technique. If words could begin to attach to previously unverbalized images, we might work together to begin to establish more secondary process thinking. Discussion of the dreams in this phase, however, inevitably became part of a dialogue in which I was perceived as telling her she was silly, attention seeking, and trivial.

## A shift in the patient's intrapsychic ego experience

After two years or so, either because she realized that I was interested in dreams, and wished to please me, or because she felt less "ridiculous" about producing apparently random material, or because of some other essential movement in the transference, the patient began to report variations in her nightmare. I think it is worth interpolating here, that had I begun to pick apart her motivation in producing an elaborated dream in the session by, for example, relating it to my interest in dreams, the whole topic would have been shut down. However, I encouraged her to continue with thinking about her dreams, and one day she told me, with a slight smile as if at the absurdity of the notion, that the savage dog in her dream had been half asleep, and she realized she had to teach it something - to do sums, or to count. If she pushed the dog too hard in this task, it would waken and get angry, but if she failed to give it enough to do, it would also turn on her. I took this as marking an important shift in her intrapsychic ego experience in regard to the events in the dream.

Harold Stewart (1973) outlines such a shift in the analysis of a borderline patient. Stewart believes the manifest content of the dream reveals to what extent the dreamer's ego is or is not restricted to one single type of experience. I wish first to consider the manifest content of my patient's dream here, before looking to the underlying meaning, because the form of the manifest content bears witness to improvement in the verbalizing and symbolizing functions of her ego sufficient to permit the elaboration along with interest in communicating it in the session.

In her new variation of her dream, she began to take an active role, with apprehension, but without having to wake up. Although it would have been possible to take up the manifest content in terms of tasks imposed upon her in the session, I stuck with the idea of asking her for associations to dogs and counting or sums, absurd though that might seem. Against my expectations, she did have associations, which had to do with her having taught arithmetic to primary school children when she left university; the job had frightened and appalled her as she felt she had no control over her pupils. The patient also made a tentative reference to the fact that her previous therapist had had a cat, and that I had a dog, "though I don't see what that has to do with anything". She was experimenting with the idea of association. I showed my interest in these thoughts and wondered if we could make sense of them in terms of how frightened she had felt in her dream, and how hard she felt she had to work to control her feelings all the time, just as she had been frightened of not being able to control the unruly children in her class.

Perhaps her fear came from her struggle to control herself when she was a child. She remembered how scornful her mother was if she failed to do housework quickly or deftly enough—if she ironed a collar clumsily, or made a muddle of the cooking. While needing her to help with the younger children, her mother made it clear that she was hopeless at the task. Her mother's method of control was not physical punishment but verbal shaming; she had a "sharp tongue". The little girl was not permitted to express "negative emotions" like anger, and the rule was constantly reinforced by her religious education. In this imperative too she often failed, and she remembered a pubertal fantasy of having "a little animal or child all of her own she could keep near her and torture and strangle". I think it was extremely important that she felt she had some success with the task now at hand, which was to associate to her dream. It was clearly a relief to her that I could not

## The fate of the dream in contemporary psychoanalysis

instantly "see through" the disguises of the dream, that it required her active participation to make sense of it.

The next session, predictably, opened with the usual scenario that I had been laughing at the triviality of her dream, that I could not possibly be interested in anyone as pathetic as she. Now that we had memories of her mother's sharp tongue ready to hand, I could connect her scornful remarks about her own attempts to talk about her dream to the way her mother would have made her feel. The patient became interested in the notion of these connections. I sensed that a small space had opened up, within which she might begin to feel freer of the repetition of suffering and punishment. In the next phase of the therapy she began to bring dreams to almost every session. Many were nightmares in which she was trapped and had to escape, but often the anxiety was contained within the dream.

Although the function of telling dreams may have been to distance the immediacy of her transference feelings, I think that the threatened ego of the patient *needed* the asylum offered by dream telling, since by the time she told her dreams, they had already been experienced, *away* from the therapist. In the act of telling the dream the patient can regain a sense of mastery by saying "*I had* a dream". Thus, telling a dream can keep anxiety in the session within bounds, and the resistance itself temporarily serves a useful function.

I also believe the idea that she had anything of interest to offer was immensely useful in beginning to repair her shattered self-esteem and to diminish the degree of her envy. Far from regarding this as a seduction, I think this new found ability to evoke interest in her object without resorting to blind attacks paved the way for the establishment of a therapeutic alliance, and ultimately for the discovery of a new object.

### Dreams illustrative of a structural change

Here I will report a typical dream from this period and next one from the termination phase, to illustrate what I believe to be a substantive shift in the patient's psychic structure. At the beginning of the second phase, the patient brought prolific dreams with more elaborate content: *I had a nightmare last night. I was in our garden, but it was much bigger. The ground was covered with dirty white—probably snow. I was digging a hole, a pit. At the far end of the garden was an ice wall or fence. In it was a person-shaped hole, like the man on a gentleman's lavatory sign. There was a sense of danger that something might get through the hole—then a big dog appeared, an Alsatian, leaping over the fence. I was in the pit—looked up—and saw that there was a person with him. My husband woke me up by putting his hand on me.*

The patient asked me in a frightened voice: "Why would I have a hole in my garden?" I replied: "Didn't you dig a pond there last summer with your husband?" She asked for an association and I gave it! I think this came from my own associating to the material as if I were the patient, in an auxiliary ego role. I could demonstrate to her a bridge between various kinds of psychic representations (Greenson 1970). Had my association been meaningless, I think no harm would have been done. As it was, it worked. Surprised, she laughed, and said, "Yes, of course. We dug it last summer: we liked watching the tadpoles—and planned to have fish this year. But in the dream it was all frozen over, icy and barren". She then said she had been angry with her husband about a failure to put up some shelves the night before. The word "barren", which related to her sadness about never having borne a child, along with the "person shaped hole", made it possible for me to make explicit links to her body and sexuality. I asked if she had sexual thoughts or wishes she did not like to acknowledge. She said that she had been feeling sexually frustrated lately, but that she didn't want to bother her husband about it. Later in the session she remembered the feeling of having been "frozen" in position as a child when she would wet the bed, afraid to move or let anyone know what had happened. She would lie awake all night, getting colder and colder, but unable to call out, which experience was once again linked to fear of being shamed. I wondered again to her if this could be one of the reasons for the stillness or paralysis in her nightmares. She then recalled being deeply affected by the story of the little mermaid, who had to endure thousands of years as a mist or cloud. Good children could redeem some of this time for the little mermaid with their thoughts, but bad children's thoughts added on to the years of her misery. Any exciting sexual fantasies in childhood would have come into the category of "bad thoughts". We were able to consider why she may have found it necessary to "freeze": she was defending herself against overwhelming fears to do with shame and guilt. This consideration made it imperative for her not to allow me to be in a position to shame her. I found I was able to edge both towards the transference and towards sexual material in a way that she could tolerate.

## An increased sense of agency in the intrapsychic and external worlds

The third phase in the evolution of the patient's capacity to dream began after about three and a half years, accompanied by significant changes in her external situation, including advancement in her career consequent on her improved ability to relate to people. She began to feel some sense of agency over events in her own life, to be less helpless and angry, and hence to need less to control me. Around this time, the manifest content of her dreams became much more elaborate. My impression is that superego modification improved her capacity to sleep, to recall dreams and to become an active participant in the dream scene. As she improved, and secondary-process thinking began to achieve more autonomy, her dreams regained their wish-fulfilling function and showed signs of more normal structural conflict.

During the fifth year, my patient decided that she would like to cut down the number of sessions per week with a view to termination. Shortly after she talked about cutting down, saying that she felt the therapy had helped her considerably and that she wanted to try living without it (a major change for her), she reported the following dream, which had two scenes:

1. *N [a leader in her religious order]—or it could have been you—asked me to do a task—speak in front of a group. I had to read off a leaf-shaped page, and was told I must do it with the correct emotional expression. It was an impossible task. I waited my turn with trepidation. I eventually decided it would be easier to leave the room—not only for my sake, but for that of the whole group.*
2. *I was back at my childhood home, but my present age. The back part of the house could only be reached via a garage, around a side passage. I went through into the back room, and found my mother doing something in there, cleaning something. Mother seemed irritated to see me. She was in a bad mood. I realised mother's bad mood might be on account of something other than me. Mother said something about my brother having suffered a tragedy, something terrible had happened. I ran up to his room, but nothing seemed to be wrong.*

Work on the dream was very sticky. She was evasive and resistant to invitations to think about the content. Thinking about N, she said crossly that everything in religious life was backward, the reverse of normal. In ordinary life, people push each other aside to get into the underground; in religious life there is rivalry to be the most self-effacing. It was a ridiculous situation; it made her depressed and annoyed to think about it. She then remembered that I had said about her last dream (two sessions previously), "all the appropriate emotions are reversed". She remembered walking out of groups in the in-patient hospital when she felt overwhelmed. We could then understand that my insistence that she match up the correct emotions with her experiences (reiterated in the first part of the present dream) felt to her like another infuriating task from which she wished to escape, and further that she was becoming embattled with me about my wanting her to associate to her dream.

The second part of the dream, where her mother was angrily cleaning in the back room, to my mind fairly obviously related to the developmental stage of childhood where battles over cleanliness and control are paramount in the mother-child interaction, where the first "task" demanded of the child may have shame as the consequence of failure; and where, in her case, an enviously hated younger brother had been born. When asked if a tragedy had really ever befallen her brother, she said not, but she recalled a strong wish to bite off his toes when he was a baby; she also remembered her rage that he, being a boy, was allowed to be, and was admired for being, naughty, while she was forced to go on being good and was never admired. The two parts of the dream seem to have been temporally reversed, the first part illustrating the consequence of wishes fulfilled in the second.

I think this is a dream more typical of a neurotic, conflicted patient, than of a borderline, and I think it quite different from her earlier nightmares. In the form of the manifest dream, she no longer experiences herself as nothing but a speck of overwhelmed ego, frozen to the spot, nor as an ego desperately trying to shore itself up with some crude defences. This dream resonates between past and present, between the struggle with current demands and memories of past struggles. In it, there are disguised but recognizable wishes as well as fear of the consequences of the fulfilment of those wishes. Anxiety does not overwhelm the patient, and she is able to reassure herself within the dream that in fact her brother is unharmed, and that her mother's anger is manageable. She can say to me openly in the session that she is fed up with my demands and is not afraid to oppose me; also, however, she does not need to attack and demolish either herself or me. We can at last explore her conflicting feelings about the therapeutic "task" in a way that permits her to think about the topic in a way that would have been impossible if I had taken it up in the "here and now" when she was so flooded with hostility. Her wish to be admired and her mortification at any hint of failure, along with her tendency to walk out of groups and places where admiration is not sufficiently provided, are also much more available for exploration without arousing corrosive shame.

In the subsequent session, she said that she felt at last that she could exist at some basic level, a person among other people. She wondered whether she could continue to engage with people this well after ending with me, but felt that she would like to try for herself. Her model of self-other interaction had most certainly changed and developed. Her evaluation of the past had also changed, partly as it was better understood through the associative method of handling her dreams. I was convinced that our work together on dreams had helped her to develop a more realistic perspective on both internal and external reality.

## Concluding remarks

I have tried in this paper to illustrate how I was able to work with a borderline patient using a basically unmodified classical technique of dream interpretation. First, I was able to interest her in her own dream processes, and I was aided in this by her good intellectual endowment. It seems to me that patients with strong intellectual defences, the patients with insecure attachment representations and fear of emotion generally, are helped by the fact that affect can be reported at one remove in the dream. At the same time, though, the dream feels to them like an authentic experience. Through verbalizing the perceptual images and feelings in the dream in a non-threatening environment these patients can establish a more direct relation to their internal world, and ultimately to the world of objects. With the dream, there is always an escape clause – "after all, it was only a dream" – negation being the first function of the ego. As my patient's ego grew stronger, so the thoughts and affects expressed in the dream could be integrated. Childhood memories which were either unavailable to her (or which she consciously kept secret from me) made their way into the sessions via the dreams.

These memories also helped to create a bridge between thought and feeling. Perhaps most important, I believe it was therapeutically essential to convey to her that we were working on a joint enterprise, that I was by no means omniscient in regard to the contents of her mind. I think this helped assuage the cruel feelings of inferiority and envy that continually threatened her.

I am aware that my patient was relatively high functioning, and that her reality testing was not severely impaired. I have had a different experience with other borderline patients with whom the kind of dream interpretation I have described was not a useful road to analytic work because their dreams remained meaningless, "loose" associations of chaotic content; nevertheless, I continue to think that too many contemporary psychoanalysts define the patient in terms of his pathology and that we are in danger of losing sight of an individual's potential for change if we bring some over-arching theory of object relations to bear on his communications.

## Notes

1 This paper first appeared *J. Am. Psychoanal. Assoc.*, 51: 43–70.
2 I am grateful to Thomas Freeman for clarifying this point to me.

## References

Arlow, J. (1993). Transference as a compromise defence. Paper reported in Meeting of the American Psychoanalytic Association, New York. *Psychoanal. Q.*, 62: 702–704.

Baker, R. (1993). The patient's discovery of the psychoanalyst as a new object. *Int. J. Psycho-Anal.*, 74: 1223–1233.

Blum, H. (1976). The changing use of dreams in psychoanalytic practice – dreams and free association. *Int. J. Psycho-Anal.*, 57: 315–324

Couch, A. (1995). Anna Freud's adult psychoanalytic technique: a defence of classical analysis. *Int. J. Psycho-Anal.*, 57: 315–324.

Curtis, H. and Sachs, D. (1976). Dialogue on 'The changing use of dreams in psychoanalytic practice'. *Int. J. Psycho-Anal.*, 57: 343–354.

Federn, P. (1934). The awakening of the ego in dreams. *Int. J. Psycho-Anal.*, 15: 296–301.

Fonagy, P. (1991). Thinking about thinking: some clinical and theoretical considerations in the treatment of a borderline patient. *Int. J. Psycho-Anal.*, 72: 639–659.

Fonagy, P. (1999). Memory and therapeutic action. *Int. J. Psycho-Anal.*, 80: 215–221.

Fonagy, P. (2000). Dreams of borderline patients. In *Dreaming and Thinking*, ed. Rosine Perelberg. London: The Institute of Psycho-Analysis, pp. 91–108.
Freeman, T. (1998). *But Facts Exist*. London: Karnac Books.
Freud, A. (1965). *Normality and Pathology in Childhood: Assessments of Development*. London: Karnac, 1989.
Freud, A. (1976). Changes in psychoanalytic practice and experience. In *Writings of Anna Freud*, vol. 8. New York: International Universities Press, 1981.
Freud, S. (1900). The interpretation of dreams. *S.E.*, 4&5: 1–627.
Freud, S. (1911). The handling of dream interpretation in psychoanalysis. *S.E.*, 12: 89–96.
Freud, S. (1920). Beyond the pleasure principle. *S.E.*, 18: 3–64.
Freud, S. (1923). Remarks on the theory and practice of dream interpretation. *S.E.*, 19: 109–121.
Freud, S. (1940). An outline of psycho-analysis. *S.E.*, 23: 141–207.
Green, A. (2001). The passion of history confronted with the failure of psychoanalytic historical thinking. In *Within Time and Beyond Time: A Festschrift for Pearl King*, eds. R. Steiner and J. Johns, London: Karnac Books, pp. 25–38.
Greenson, R. (1970). The exceptional position of the dream in psychoanalytic practice. *Psychoanal. Q.*, 39: 519–549.
Grotstein, J. (1984). A proposed revision of the psychoanalytic concept of primitive mental states, part II – section 3, disorders of autistic safety and symbiotic relatedness. *Contemp. Psychoanal.*, 20: 266–343.
Joseph, B. (1985). Transference: the total situation. *Int. J. Psycho-Anal.*, 66: 447–454.
Kernberg, O., Selzer, M., Koenigsberg, H., Carr, A. and Appelbaum, A. (1989). *Psychodynamic Psychotherapy of Borderline Patients*. New York: Basic Books.
Khan, M. M. R. (1962). Dream psychology and the evolution of the psychoanalytic situation. *Int. J. Psycho-Anal.*, 43: 21–31.
Khan, M. M. R. (1972). The use and abuse of dream in psychic experience. In *The Privacy of the Self*. London: Hogarth Press, pp. 306–315.
Khan, M. M. R. (1976). The changing use of dreams in psychoanalytic practice – in search of dreaming experience. *Int. J. Psycho-Anal.*, 57: 325–330.
O'Shaughnessy, E. (1983). Words and working through. *Int. J. Psycho-Anal.*, 64: 281–289.
O'Shaughnessy, E. (1992). Enclaves and excursions. *Int. J. Psycho-Anal.*, 73: 603–611.
Reiser, M. (1997). The art and science of dream interpretation: Isakower revisited. *J. Am. Psychoanal. Assoc.*, 45: 891–905.

Sandler, J. (1976). Countertransference and role responsiveness. *Int. R.. Psycho-Anal.*, 3: 43–47.

Sandler, J. and Sandler, A.-M. (1994). The past unconscious and the present unconscious: a contribution to a technical frame of reference. *Psychoanal. St. Child*, 49: 278–292.

Segal, H. (1986). The function of dreams. In *The Work of Hannah Segal*, London: Free Association Books, pp. 89–97.

Sharpe, E. (1937). *Dream Analysis.* London: Hogarth Press.

Sterba, R. (1934). The fate of the ego in analytic therapy. *Int. J. Psycho-Anal.*, 15: 117–126.

Stewart, H. (1973). The experiencing of the dream and the transference. *Int. J. Psycho-Anal.*, 54: 345–357.

Stone, L. (1954). The widening scope of indications for psychoanalysis. *J. Am. Psychoanal. Assoc.*, 2: 567–594.

Tuckett, D. (2000). Dream interpretation in contemporary psychoanalytic technique. Unpublished paper given at the English-Speaking Conference, London, October 2000.

Waelder, R. (1987). Robert Waelder on psychoanalytic technique: five lectures. *Psychoanal. Q.*, 56: 1–67.

Yorke, C. (2001). The unconscious: past, present and future. In *Within Time and Beyond Time: A Festschrift for Pearl King*, eds. R. Steiner and J. Johns. 230-251 London: Karnac Books.

Yorke, C., Wiseberg, S. and Freeman, T. (1989). *Development and Psychopathology.* New Haven, CT and London: Yale University Press.

# 17

# HOW COME YOUR HOUSE DOES NOT FALL DOWN?[1]

Luis Rodríguez de la Sierra

João's mother telephoned me [in the autumn of 1998] as she was worried about her nine-year-old son and wanted to talk to me about him. I indicated that it would be a good idea if her husband could come along also. She told me that he was away on a business trip and she very much wanted to talk to me as soon as possible, so I gave her an appointment for two days later. She is an attractive woman in her late thirties, well dressed and slightly over made-up. There was something a bit anxious and irritating in her manner. I detected a subtle hostility in her, which provoked some negativism in me. I was bothered about my reaction to her, which I questioned. She spoke in slightly broken, heavily accented English and never spoke to me in her mother tongue in spite of the clear indication that I also spoke it. She is the youngest of a family of four girls and she described a rather typical, close Portuguese family background. She was quite concerned about her youngest son who, for the last few months, had been exhibiting a precocious and provocative sexual behaviour, that is talking about sex, making sexual gestures, easily stripping off his clothes, using four-letter words, etc. João was also very jealous of his older 13-year-old brother Xavier; he kept complaining that his parents favoured him, and he said he was unhappy at home. On the other hand, his mother said, he was very popular at school where both his peers and teachers thought highly of him. He admired his older brother enormously and got on well with him. The relationship with his father, though, was not so good. She seemed perplexed by the fact that, although he claimed not to like his father, his behaviour became worse when father was absent, like then, for instance. Xavier, on the other hand, gave them no reason to worry. I suggested we should meet again when her husband returned. She said she would try her best to persuade him to come; he travelled often and worked all the time so she did not know if he would find the time.

A week later they both came to see me: they immediately conveyed a certain tension between them. They had come to England 11 years ago, because of the father's occupation. They both came from upper class backgrounds. Mr. Y is a short, handsome and friendly man who dressed very smartly. He is the eldest of a family of three, with a sister two years younger and a younger brother in his early thirties. His father, to whom he had always been very close, had died two years previously, which had saddened him terribly. He was also concerned about João but, unlike mother, not so much about the so-called sexual precocity which, insightfully, he saw as connected to feelings of jealousy, envy and admiration towards his older brother. He thought that it was João's unconscious way of identifying with his pubertal sibling in an attempt to win the attention he thought his parents gave Xavier. However, Mr. Y's main concern was about João's apparent hostility towards him. The mother interrupted at this point and reproached him for not spending enough time with João and for being too disciplinarian when they were together. She told me he never played with João, he only tried to make him do his homework, etc. The father seemed embarrassed and tried, in vain, to reason with her. As the meeting continued it was clear that mother resented her husband's frequent business trips and that she felt abandoned and unsupported in the task of dealing with her sons, João in particular. I voiced these thoughts and although they appeared taken aback and said that they had not thought about it in this way, it made sense to them. I sympathized with mother, alone in a male household and deprived of the female support she would have enjoyed in her original family. I thought I could understand better now the hostility towards me (another man), which I sensed during my initial consultation with her.

The father then added that he had never seen the boy's sexually provocative behaviour and, with a smile, and in Portuguese, he said: "Typical, isn't it?" ("Típico, não é?"). I did not know if the comment referred to the boy's behaviour or if that was the father's way of seeking my support/complicity by making such a comment about "nagging" women to another man. I was aware of the danger of Mrs. Y feeling excluded. He also said that the boy alluded, occasionally, to dreams but never told him anything about them. He then told me that even if it was true that they (he and his wife) had their differences, they both loved their children and wanted to do whatever was necessary for their happiness. She agreed but said, with a certain pleasure, that they often argued in front of the children because her husband undermined her in front of them. He replied immediately that he would try not to do it again, but that it was not his fault completely because she provoked him by undermining him, in his absence, with her much more lenient attitude towards João. They both added, simultaneously, that the elder son never gave them any trouble. I ended the session by saying that the best thing would be for me to see João twice and have him tested by one of the psychologists at the Anna Freud Centre.

João came to see me the following Monday accompanied by his father who greeted me warmly. João initially appeared rather reserved, but he followed me willingly to my consulting room. He is a very good-looking, fair-haired boy, with huge blue eyes and long eyelashes. João was immaculately dressed in a rather continental-style adult suit that made him look like a little man, suggesting perhaps some pseudo-maturity. I noticed that the style resembled his father's. There was an intelligent and inquisitive expression on his face. He seemed to be covering his anxiety bravely, but I sensed his tension about meeting me. I felt sorry for him and liked him at once. I smiled at him and he appeared to relax and started talking to me in Portuguese. He said they thought they were going to be late because the traffic was heavy and his father had been late to collect him; he had just arrived from a business trip abroad. I said it must be difficult to come to see me, a complete stranger whom he had never met before. He nodded silently. I asked him if he knew what I was and if he knew why he was coming to see me. He replied that his father had told him that I was a nice man, a doctor who helped naughty children. I wondered what he meant by that and he told me that he was disobedient with his mother and, at times, was also rude to her. There was a brief pause and he added that his mother nagged him all the time and was always telling him off for not doing things the way she wanted. He then broke into English: "Do you see many children?"

I invited him to tell me what he thought and then, in Portuguese, he told me that he knew I saw children because his father had said so. I asked him which language he wished to use and he replied that although his written Portuguese was "not so good", he spoke both Portuguese and English perfectly. He then added that he preferred to speak Portuguese with me. At home, he said, he spoke it with his father all the time, because his father *always* used that language with him. With his mother, though, he alternated between English and Portuguese because his mother sometimes spoke to him in English. I found myself wondering about the mother's behaviour. I thought about her broken English and found myself thinking of the possible unconscious reasons why she would speak to João in a language other than her own. I have always been struck by the difficulties that must exist in the parent-child relationship when the parents choose to talk to their children in a language which is not their mother tongue and that very often they do not speak well. Relationships and communications are not solely and purely based on language, of course, but I have always wondered about the quality of the relationship when one of the parents is communicating with his children through an artificial, disguised, "as if" aspect of himself. I wondered if by not talking to João in Portuguese mother had denied her son access to a more intimate, close contact with her.

João then noticed a box on the table and looked at it with curiosity. I said there were toys and other things inside. Did he perhaps want to have a look? He smiled broadly and said: "Yes, let's see what's inside!" He selected a pack of cards and wondered what we could do with them. "We can play any game you like", I said. He paused for a moment and invited me to try and build a house with them. I would build one and he would build another one. I succeeded in building mine. He tried very carefully to build his, but it fell down on each attempt. I noticed he did not give up easily but persevered. I asked myself what was the nature of his communication to me, as expressed through the card game. What were his anxieties about himself, about his environment? He was disappointed when the session ended, asking: "May I come back another time to continue this game?" I said: "Of course, next week, same day and time".

When we returned to the waiting room, his father smiled at us and, looking at João, wondered if he had enjoyed it. João said he had. "Good!" The father had spoken in Portuguese and, in the same language, I said that his son wanted to come back next week. Mr.

Y replied that, unfortunately, he would not be able to bring him because he had to go abroad again and would not be back in time to collect João. His wife, though, would bring him to me. "Is that alright?" he asked João. The boy shrugged his shoulders and suddenly looked sad.

The following week, João's mother brought him to see me. They were ten minutes late and Mrs. Y apologized profusely: she had been delayed by a telephone call from her mother and therefore she had been late to collect João from school. He seemed quiet in contrast to his mother who came across as fussy and rather smothering. He withdrew physically from her when he saw me. I was struck again by the artificiality of his mother's unnecessary use of English with the two of us and noticed he spoke to me, or rather whispered, also in English. As soon as we entered the consulting room, he asked me, in Portuguese, if I had brought the cards, and he invited me to play the same game we had played the previous time. Again, his attempts to build a house of cards failed. He would not give up, though, and indeed persisted several times, but at one point he stopped and told me that he dreamt "every night" and that his dreams, at times, were bad ones. I asked him if he would like to tell me, for instance, his dream from the previous night. He seemed taken aback and said he could not remember. He added that he often forgot his dreams but that he knew in the morning that he had dreamt. He had tried to tell his mother sometimes, but she never seemed to have time because they had to rush to school in the mornings. I said that I thought he was trying to show me some of the difficulties he had with his mother and I wondered how he felt about discussing them with a stranger. He replied that he wanted to because Xavier was always on their mother's side and their father was very busy with his work, so he had no one to talk to. He paused for a moment and then said that he liked making things with his hands and colouring "something". I did not understand what that something might be and I said so. He replied that, if I wanted, he would show me next time. I agreed. I then realized I had not spoken to him about his seeing the psychologist who was going to test him as part of the assessment, but I knew that his parents had told him and had arranged for him to go to the Anna Freud Centre this week and the next one. I reminded him of all this and said that perhaps he could return to see me on Tuesday, rather than Monday when he would be seeing the lady psychologist. He did not reply.

When we returned to the waiting room, Mrs. Y. anxiously asked: "Did he do alright?" João looked rather diminished by this and moved to the other side of the room. I thought again that there was a fraught quality to their relationship and I wondered to what extent João's withdrawal was an expression of his being either annoyed with his intrusive mother (because he might have felt exposed by her anxious question) or of his feeling embarrassed by her attitude. I also wondered about his ambivalent communication about dreams and, initially, questioned myself for not having followed my temptation to make an interpretation about what I felt might be his unconscious motivation. Was he apprehensive about divulging too much about himself if he told me the dream? Was he thus recreating the sexual teasing of his mother or trying to convey his feelings about his father's absences? I then remembered a quotation from Anna Freud: "The analyst's task is not to create, i.e., to invent anything, but to observe, to explore and to understand and to explain" (1969 [1968], p. 270).

I was, nevertheless, left with an uneasy feeling about João and his mother. I sensed her hostility towards him and wondered how much of it was displaced from the hostility she expressed towards her husband. I was again puzzled by my reaction to her: I found her irritating and annoying and I was unable to know if the feelings came from me or from her. I decided to follow Anna Freud's advice and wait to see what happened.

A week later, João returned. He was his usual immaculate self, now on time and with a big box in his hands. The nanny had brought him: a pleasant young Portuguese girl with a warm and broad smile. While still in the waiting room, he said the nanny had come today because his mother had already accompanied him to see my "friend", the psychologist (a woman) thus implying that his mother did not have time to bring him twice the same week. The place was too far away, he said, as if trying to excuse his mother. João then followed me and, once inside the consulting room, told me that he had brought the box with the objects he had mentioned last time. It was a collection of beautiful little soldiers made of wood and painted in brilliant colours. He announced, full of pride: "I painted them. Do you like them?"

I asked him if he had any thoughts about whether I did or not, but he pretended to ignore me and instead told me that a teacher at his school liked them very much and had complimented him for his good taste. I said that I thought he was telling me that being liked was important to him and that perhaps he wanted to know if I liked him as well as the little soldiers. He nodded silently and looked at me expectantly. I asked him then if he liked coming to see me. He said he did because we talked and his parents had told him that he could tell me everything. It sounded more like a question than a statement and I voiced this. He nodded again. I said that perhaps he was not sure he could tell me everything because I had noticed, the previous week, a certain reluctance on his part to tell me his dream. He paused for a moment and said: "It was just a silly dream".

But he then told me:

> He had dreamt about a lady who had gone on a skiing holiday and she had got lost and was trying to see if she could find the others, but she could not. She then started skiing up and down the mountains and she had an accident. When the doctor arrived, he could not cure her.

He smiled and repeated that it was only a silly dream. Other dreams were frightening, but not this one. He then stood up and went to the window and tried to open it because he felt, suddenly, that the room was too hot. He could not open it and asked me to help him, which I did. He went back to his chair and looked inside the toy box. He got out some dolls: father, mother, grandfather and two children. Then he went to the soldiers and said they were going to fight because they were at war and, for a while, he played with them. He stopped and directed his attention towards the family dolls. He said grandfather had died because he was afraid of the war (I made a mental note about the reference to his own grandfather's death). The daddy doll was curious about the war that was going on outside and left. The mummy doll started crying because one of the children was ill and she did not know what to do.

I said I thought he was worried about himself and also about his family and was asking me if I could really help. I also thought, but did not say to him, that he resented my sending him to see the psychologist. I wondered if he had interpreted that as a rejection or as an indication that I needed the help of others to deal with him, like his parents. I also thought that the dream possibly contained hostile wishes against his parents, particularly against his mother. I wondered, as well, about his excitement *vis-à-vis* the possibility of having found someone for himself, me. (The Portuguese word he used for "mountains", *serra*, sounds very similar to part of my surname and actually means the same.)

He asked: "Well, can you help me?" I replied that the two of us might try to understand first what was wrong and then we both could possibly be in a better position to say if I could help. I wondered if he would like to come to see me more often and he said he could come after school if his mother had time to bring him in. I said I would talk to his parents and they would tell him when he could come to see me next. If he wanted, I said, he could come to see me every day from Monday to Friday, and then we could talk a bit more about his dreams, both the "silly" ones and the "bad" ones. He replied that he would very much like to do so.

After he left, I thought again about his dream and wondered how sensitive João was to his mother's feelings of sadness about being in a foreign country, feeling lost in a male household and without the support of the female members of her family. I then thought I could understand more about my initial reaction to her and wondered if her reluctance to speak to me in Portuguese was her way of showing me all that: was she conveying to me that using English was her way of trying to adapt to a new country as well as her way of avoiding missing her country and family, which she would do if she used her mother tongue? "*Olhos que não vêm, coraçao que não sente*". (What the eye sees not, the heart does not rue.) I thought João's dream also told me something about his possibly conflicted female identification.

I telephoned his parents and arranged for a meeting with them. I explained that João would benefit from intensive treatment. To my surprise, they seemed relieved and agreed without much fuss. I then said that although I would want to see them once a term to discuss how things were going, I would not be able to see or speak to them more often than that. The mother immediately wondered what they would do if they felt they needed to talk to me because João could be rather difficult at times. I said that I would like them to see a colleague whom they could see once a fortnight or monthly if they so wished. They accepted and we agreed that João would start his analysis the following week. While I have no doubts that the parental pathology influenced João, I was convinced that the boy had internalized conflicts that he dealt with through the defensive use of externalization, by making them appear as conflicts with his external world, with his objects.

The initial stages of the analysis were spent mostly with a variety of games and the occasional session where he would draw, showing a promising artistic talent. From time to time he chose to talk and when he did so, there was a pseudo mature quality to his conversation. His games, though, appeared appropriate for his age. Two or three times a week we would play the "build a house" game with the playing cards inside his box. His house would always collapse. I felt intrigued by this intelligent, charming little gentleman, inexplicably clumsy when it came to playing that game. Although he emerged as a very bright boy in the psychological testing, non-verbal skills appeared erratic. This was most noticeable while trying to build the house. Towards the end of the first term, it seemed that this was not due to any deficit but rather to conflictual interference. From time to time, he would also bring the wooden soldiers and one day I thought I was seeing some clinical indications of his aggressive impulses and wishes to retaliate. Two soldiers were fighting, one small and delicate, the other big and strong, with a moustache and a beard. The little soldier tried to start a fight with the bigger one several times, until the bigger one warned him. The little soldier persisted and then the big one kicked him. I said that perhaps he felt annoyed with me at times, for instance, when he tried to build the house and failed while mine stood up. He ignored me and continued playing. I said that perhaps he did not want me to notice these things because he was not sure yet he could talk to me freely, without being afraid that I might be annoyed with him and retaliate for his hostile feelings towards me. The following day he was brought by the nanny, who explained that Mrs. Y had guests from abroad and could not come. João reported a dream:

> He was coming back home from school, at night, when a big black man tried to steal his backpack. He tried to run but he could not move; he tried to cry for help but he could not utter a word.

I thought that his aggression, and his anxiety about punishment, was expressed in the dream. It conveyed a strong sense of guilt, as well as a sense of failing "to get away with the crime". I said it sounded like a rather frightening dream. He nodded, paused for a moment, and then laughed and said: "Don't be silly, it's just a dream".

I could see, more clearly than on other occasions, how he used denial as a means of defence. He was silent for a few minutes. He then said that he wanted to bring the little soldiers again because I had liked the way he had painted them, but he had forgotten to do so because he had got into trouble with his mother. He was playing with some friends and she was nearby and had got angry with him because he was telling some dirty jokes. She told him off and threatened to tell his father, who did not allow four letter words at home. I thought João's dream could be understood along the lines of castration anxiety. His dream followed a session where his play showed fantasies of mutual aggression. The black man who steals his backpack is a condensation of both his fears of being attacked and deprived of a highly valued possession, and of his own retaliatory wishes. The backpack is nothing but a disguise for his "front-pack", his genitals. He confirmed this in the session by "forgetting" to bring his precious little soldiers (which he assumes I like), a symbol of his genitals. I believe he "forgot" because he feared, unconsciously, I might steal them from him. Just before telling me the dream, he gave me an association to a situation where he behaved in a sexually provocative and excited way (telling "dirty" jokes), which he "exposed" to his mother. She reacted by threatening him with the image of a castrating father with whom, I believe, she gets confused in João's unconscious fantasies. I asked him if he had any ideas as to what this dream might be about. He moved his head silently from side to side. I said that I knew it was "only a dream", but that I also knew that dreams told us something about fears we had, and of which we were not necessarily aware. He listened attentively. I said that I thought that his dream might contain thoughts about us and asked him if it was possible that sometimes he might be afraid of me and of doing things that would make me angry. I added that he might fear what I would do to him if I got angry with him: that I might behave like the big black man in the dream or an angry rejecting mother/father who did not like the four-letter words. "No, you never get angry, anyway!" he replied. "My mother says you are very serious and that you have a very deep voice", he added, imitating my voice and trying to mock me.

I thought that he could accept my interpretation only by his defensive use of displacement (it is the mother who fears me and not him), as well as by trying to transform passive into active (plus possible intimations of identification with the aggressor), namely ceasing to be the one who fears me and transforming himself into the one who laughs at me. Afterwards, I thought that the dream might also contain anxieties about having to learn another language—i.e. which language to use with me or how to speak to me. Again, I thought of the identification with his mother and wondered if the dream revealed something related to it: similar anxieties about having to learn another language and, like her, a conflict regarding how and when to use it. The homosexual content of the dream and the confusion it engendered contributed to increase João's anxiety. I also wondered if the dream, in addition, might contain the memory of a developmentally earlier anxiety dream, experienced before language had partially or fully developed, a dream from pre-verbal times when he might have already experienced his mother as detached or perhaps unobtainable.

In his earliest statement about children's dreams, Freud said: "The dreams of young children are pure wish fulfilment and for that reason quite uninteresting compared with the dreams of adults" (1900, p. 127). Both in 1905 (p. 161)[2] and in 1916 (p. 126), he modified his views, especially in 1916: "Dream-distortion sets in very early in childhood, and dreams dreamt by children of between five and eight have been reported, which bear all the characteristics of later ones". In 1925, however, Freud stated for the first time: "Experience has shown that distorted dreams, *which stand in need of interpretation* [my italics], are already found in children of four or five" (1900 [1925 revised edition, footnote 1, p. 127]). In 1927 Anna Freud said:

> When it comes to dream interpretation...we can apply unchanged to children what we have learnt from our work with adults. During analysis the child dreams neither less or more than the adult; and the transparency or obscurity of the dream content is, as in the case of adults, a reflection of the strength of the resistance. Children's dreams are certainly easy to interpret though in analysis they are not always so simple as the examples given in *The Interpretation of Dreams*. We find in them all those distortions of wish fulfilment that correspond to the complicated neurotic organization of the child patient.
>
> (p. 24)

In a previous paper, I have commented that psychoanalytic authors with very few exceptions agree that the dreams of children contribute to the insight that we can gain into children's inner worlds (1996, p. 72). When Freud said of children's dreams that "they raise no problems for solution" (1900, p. 127), it is difficult to understand how he could put forward this view which seems, by definition, incompatible with his theories about infantile sexuality. Paradoxically, his attitude in attributing innocence and purity to children's dreams was curiously similar to what those before him thought about children's inner worlds. His initial formulations do not seem to take into account traumatic dreams, anxiety dreams and the many nightmares that we know occur. The dreams of children, as we can see in those of João, also possess, in addition to or "in lieu" of a wish fulfilment (which in João's dream seemed to be punishment by his father for his incestuous wishes towards his mother), a symptomatic value which should make us consider their developmental significance. They can show us the important concerns and tasks for children at different phases of development and in the course of their analyses, where they must be understood, also, in the context of the developing transference (1996, pp. 76–78). It was this latter aspect of João's dreams, as reported by him in the last two sessions which I chose to take up with him.

Like others, I often wonder if the interest in object relations, narcissism, attachment, transference phenomena, etc., has turned analysts away from the view, to which I subscribe, of the interpretation of dreams as "the royal road to our knowledge of the unconscious activities of the mind" (Freud 1900). At the same time, I no longer believe in the idea of dreams being only the fulfilment of a wish. There are dreams that refer to fears, to reflections, and which contain, as Freud stated several times, memories. They can reveal something about the developing ego of the child, particularly in relation to functions such as verbalization, language development, etc. The recognition of transference manifestations in child and adult analysis enables us to recognize the different and often complex aspects of the transference as they appear in the dreams of our patients. As we know, analytic dreams may be indicative of resistance, alliance, or both, in relation to the analyst and the analytic process. The fact remains, though, that in spite of the apparent revival of interest in dreams, children's dreams continue to be neglected and thus it is not surprising that in a book as fascinating as *The Dream Discourse Today*, edited by Sara Flanders (1993), there is hardly any mention of the subject of children's dreams (Rodríguez de la Sierra 1996, p. 76).

Towards the end of his first year of analysis, João emerged as a boy who was struggling with strong oedipal anxieties exacerbated by his father's absences and by his internal representation of father as a severe and potentially dangerous rival. Succeeding was therefore a frightening risk for him, as he showed me repeatedly by not being able to master the game of building [erecting] a house of cards. In addition, he was still engaged in a complex relationship with his mother. At times he related to her in a sado-masochistic way to which he often regressed whenever his oedipal attempts to seduce her failed. He felt rejected by her and would try to capture her attention through his provocative, apparently precocious pseudo-sexual behaviour. By adopting this behaviour, I thought (like his father) that he was trying to identify with his admired and envied pubertal brother, whose good relationship with his parents made João very jealous. The brother was a suitable object onto whom he could displace many of the feelings towards his father. Through the identification (with his brother), he could also keep up the homosexual attachment to both father and brother. When his attempts to deal with his oedipal anxieties failed, João would regress to a developmentally earlier phase with overtones of his oral and anal-sadistic struggles. His oedipal conflicts seemed to be further complicated by the fact that it appeared (both in his play and in the transference), as if the mother was at times experienced as the castrator. Then the father became the object by whom he felt protected as seen at the end of his first interview with me, when he looked sad and disappointed that his father was not bringing him to the following appointment.

After a year in treatment, an incident occurred which provided a turning point in the analysis: The previous summer, after many years of depending on my old manual portable Remington typewriter, I decided to buy a personal computer (a "laptop") in the hope that it would make my life easier. I soon discovered the opposite.

This coincided with the closure of the London Clinic of Psycho-Analysis (where I had always seen all my child patients) due to the Institute's move to new premises, which were not to be open for some time. I was compelled therefore to see this particular patient at my own consulting room, not far from the old Institute. I had installed both the computer and my Remington, side by side on the same desk, in my consulting room and one day, a Thursday afternoon, it was time for my session with João. For the first time, he noticed the computer and as soon as he saw it, he was fascinated by its presence. He was delighted with the idea of the many games we could play on it. He could not believe it when I said I did not know how to use the computer very well. I had sensed, immediately, his apprehension, his suspicion that I might be telling lies, that I was playing tricks. I had always been aware of his acute sensitivity to falsity in his objects.

"Really? I don't believe you; you are having me on", he said, "it's so easy that even a fool like me can do it". João is far from being a fool, quite the opposite, but I felt humiliated in my ignorance. He seemed disappointed. And then the Remington caught his attention: "What is *that*?" His voice was full of surprise, curiosity and astonishment. A typewriter, I announced victoriously. João wanted to know what the typewriter was for, and once I explained he came to the conclusion that he would never be able to learn how to use such a mysterious and complicated machine! He spent the rest of the session trying to decipher the secrets and intricacies of the intriguing contraption. Finally, with some hesitation, he proposed an exchange. Although he still believed that I was mocking him by pretending not to be able to use the computer, he would go along with me and we would play a new game in which he would teach me how to use the computer, while I would undertake the "awesome" task of trying to teach him to use the typewriter. This was a defining moment in the analysis. The next session he brought another dream:

> I dreamt that the Pope was getting bored in Rome because he had no friends and his housekeeper kept nagging him. Fidel Castro heard about it and because they had become good friends, he invited the Pope to go to Cuba to play football with him. The Pope accepted the invitation and wanted to stay in Cuba, but the Swiss Guard did not want him to and ordered the Pope to return to Rome because Fidel was a communist and a bad man.

(The words for "Pope" and "Dad" (papa—papá) are very similar in Portuguese, as they are in other Latin languages.) My association and countertransference reaction to João's dream were Calderón de la Barca's words when in "La vida es sueño" ("Life is a dream") (1982) Segismundo tells us:

> *Pues que la vida es tan corta,*
> *soñemos, alma, soñemos*
> *otra vez; pero ha de ser*
> *con atención y consejo*

*de que hemos de despertar*
*deste gusto al mejor tiempo*

(2358–2363)

(And since life is a dream,
Let's dream, my soul,
Let's dream, my soul,
Let's dream again but this time with attention
And bearing in mind that at some fine time
We're going to wake up from this pleasure.)[3]

A friend of the family had brought a video recording of the Pope's visit to Cuba. Before telling me his dream, João said that his mother had told him off for being naughty because he had eaten his brother's dessert. Afterwards, ignoring both computer and typewriter, he suggested that we should play, once again, his favourite game. We played at least five times and for the first time, he said: "How come your house never falls down?" "Because I am not afraid that mine will", I replied. He looked at me inquisitively. I said we had been playing that game for over a year so I assumed it meant something important to him that he could not express with words, so I had made it my task to try to understand his message. I said to him that I thought it must contain some anxiety about himself and about his family, something to do with his future. He replied immediately he often thought he would have to go to work and would not know how to do it properly and would be sacked. I asked what made him think so. He remained silent, looking sad. I said I thought his dream made me think he feared some kind of loss or split at home and I wondered if he had ever heard or thought anything that made him think that. He then said that, when his parents quarrelled, his father threatened to leave. I said I understood that part of him, at times, might want his father to leave so that he could be "the man of the family". He replied that if anything ever happened to his father, Xavier was the eldest and the one who really wanted to be the boss. I said that he felt guilty about his wishes, about wanting to be "the man of the family". I added he seemed to be afraid he would not be able to take his father's place properly (and would be sacked) because he was only a child and therefore it was easier for him to imagine that it was his brother who wanted to do those things. He replied: "Can you teach me to make sure my house doesn't fall down?"

I said that we could both try, in the same way that we were teaching each other with the computer and the typewriter. It also occurred to me that his dream contained wishes to leave, both home and the analysis when the two situations put him under stress, but we had come to the end of the session and I felt he had had enough with what I had said to him already. I wondered, after he had left, if the game was a way of conveying more primitive anxieties about himself. I have not found any evidence of this so far. I thought though that the dream about the Pope and Fidel Castro, in the transference, also referred to us and his ambivalence about the analysis, the Pope representing João (as well as his father) and Castro standing for me.

My meeting with João's parents was due and I made arrangements to see them. Much to my regret, Mr. and Mrs. Y never saw the colleague I had referred them to. There were all kinds of excuses for their avoidance. I thought they were afraid of facing some of their marital difficulties and, in addition, of confronting their feelings of inadequacy as parents. Mrs. Y frequently wondered if it was really necessary for João to come to see me so often and, occasionally, would mumble something about how "when we were children, nobody had to send their children to the psychiatrist". I was aware of her feelings of guilt, and of exclusion from her son's relationship with me and thought she could boycott the analysis if under threat. I now felt more certain of my initial understanding that the presence of the housekeeper and the Swiss Guard in the dream represented both his mother's and his own ambivalent feelings about me. The father, as if he could read my mind, came to my help by saying it was important that João should continue because he was much happier and gave them less trouble at home since he had started analysis. Our meeting took place the day after the session in which João told me his dream with the Pope. In the course of our meeting, I raised the question that João had put in my mind the day before: had they, during their difficult moments, ever considered separation? They appeared taken aback and denied it. There was a difficult silence, which Mrs. Y broke to tell me she had never thought about it; she had married for life, she said. Raising her voice a little, she turned towards her husband and told me he often said that when the children finished school and were ready to go to university, he would leave. "To do what, he has never explained", she added angrily. She said she did not know if their sons knew about his plans, but she would not be surprised if they did. Mr. Y looked very embarrassed and I felt sorry for him. He did not seem to know what to say and I said that was the sort of thing I would have preferred them to discuss with someone else. He said that perhaps he needed to talk to someone like me. He felt that he had married very young and, being the eldest, had always had responsibilities he had not asked for. He felt that once his children went to university, he would have his chance "to do my own thing". "And what about me then?" Mrs. Y said, with tears in her eyes. He said he had never meant to leave her, only to have the freedom to come and go as he pleased without feeling compelled "to perform". I silently wondered about possible sexual problems in their relationship. He said he wanted to reassure me that their troubles would never stand in their children's way, João would continue seeing me "for however long it was necessary". Time was up and, reluctantly, I ended the session. As they were leaving, he turned around and said that they would make an effort to arrange an appointment "to go to see the lady you recommended". Alas, they never did.

I am grateful to Abrahão Brafman for his comments on yet another way of understanding João's dream about the Pope and Fidel Castro. I should like to quote him: "I could not resist imagining that 'papá' (father) had been making many references about the 'Fidel', the Spanish you—a fact/wish he confirms by saying he needed to speak to someone like you".

The incident involving the computer and the typewriter marked a turning point in João's analysis. His discovery of a parent/analyst, with whom he could engage in learning and teaching, gave a new character to our relationship. João found it difficult to believe I knew nothing about computers. It took him some time to accept that it was true. He derived pleasure from being able to teach me something that he knew. This de-idealization of adults who are not omnipotent allowed for a reciprocity where we taught and helped each other. Those unfamiliar with the concept of "developmental help" (Edgcumbe 2000, pp. 160–195; Gavshon 1988; Hurry 1998, pp. 32–73) as part of psychoanalytic technique with children may, erroneously, see this as a mere countertransference enactment. Instead it provided João with a newly acquired confidence and the growth of a trusting and productive therapeutic alliance.

Like Segismundo (Calderón de la Barca's hero), João tries in vain to convince himself that life in his inner world is just a dream, attempting to avoid both disappointment and punishment in his life in the external world:

*Yo sueño que estoy aquí*
*destas prisiones cargado,*
*y soñé que en otro estado*
*más lisonjero me vi.*
*¿Qué es la vida? Un frenesí.*
*¿Qué es la vida? Una ilusión,*
*una sombra, una ficción,*
*y el mayor bien es pequeño,*
*que toda la vida es sueño,*
*y los sueños sueños son.*

(I dream that I am here
Bound down by these heavy chains
And I dreamed that once I lived differently
And was happy.
What is life? A frenzy.
Life's an illusion
Life's a shadow, a fiction,
And the greatest good is worth nothing at all,
For the whole of life is just a dream
And dreams…dreams are only dreams)

It is my hope that analysis will help João to come to terms with the difficulties his instinctual wishes, and the complex object-relations which they shape, and that analysis will enable him to go forward to the next and more difficult developmental stage he still has to master: adolescence. Perhaps then, like Basilio (Segismundo's father), his internalized father could say to him:

*Hijo - que tan noble acción*
*otra vez en mis entrañas*
*te engendra - príncipe eres*
*A ti el laurel y la palma*
*se te deben; tú venciste,*
*corónente tus hazañas.*

(My son, in your nobility you are reborn.
You are prince; the laurel and the palm of victory

Are yours. You overcame. Your achievements
Give you victory.)[4]

## Notes

1 *Acknowledgement*: Special thanks to Pauline Cohen who patiently and in vain waited for João's parents to contact her, and to Jenny Kaplan-Davids whose comments are integrated in the thinking behind this paper. I would also like to express my gratitude to Abrahão Brafman, Sheilagh Davies, Felicity Dirmeik, Audrey Gavshon, Anne-Marie Sandler and Sharon Stekelman for their useful suggestions and comments.
2 "Experience derived from the analyses – and not the theory of dreams- any wish left from waking life is sufficient to call up a dream, which always emerges as connected and ingenious but usually short, and which is usually recognized as a wish fulfilment" (Freud 1905, p. 161).
3 The author's translation.
4 The original says: "My son, in your nobility you are reborn from my entrails".

## References

Calderón de la Barca, P. (1982). *La vida es sueño*. Edición de Ciriaco Madrid: Ediciones Cátedra, S.A., pp. 173, 164–165, 205.
Edgcumbe, R. (2000). *Anna Freud: A View of Development, Disturbance and Therapeutic Techniques*. London: Routledge.
Flanders, S. (ed.) (1993). *The Dream Discourse Today*. New Library of Psychoanalysis. London: Routledge.
Freud, A. (1927). Four lectures on child analysis. In *The Writings of Anna Freud*, Vol.1. NewYork: International Universities Press, 1974, pp. 3–69.
Freud, A. (1969). Difficulties in the path of psychoanalysis: a confrontation of past with present viewpoints. In *The Writings of Anna Freud*, Vol. 7. New York: International Universities Press, 1981, pp. 124–156.
Freud, S. (1900). The interpretation of dreams. *S.E.*, 4 127 SE 5. 161
Freud, S. (1905). Jokes and their relation to the unconscious. *S.E.*, 8: 1–247.
Freud, S. (1916). Introductory lectures on psycho-analysis. *S.E.*, 22. 127
Gavshon, A. (1988). Playing: its role in child analysis. *Bull. Anna Freud Centre*, 11(2): 128–145.
Hurry, A. (1998). *Psychoanalysis and Developmental Therapy*. London: Karnac Books, pp. 32–73.
Rodríguez de la Sierra, L. (1996). Is it true that children seldom report their dreams? *Psychoanal. Europe Bull.*, 46: 66–81.

# 18

## MEASURE FOR MEASURE
## Unconscious communication in dreams

### Joan Schächter

**Introduction**

Cecily De Monchaux (1978; Flanders 1993) argues that the dream is "not only a source and container of phantasy content, but also a unit of phantasy employed by the patient in the enactment of the transference relationship" (p. 196). She suggests that certain unconscious messages can only be communicated through the action of reporting a dream. The dreamer can maintain the illusion of not being responsible for his/her dream and thus it is safe to put unwanted thoughts into it. "It [the dream] functions as a place of asylum, in which split-off elements can be kept alive until conditions are prestigious for their integration with consciously acceptable elements" (p. 203). In my paper I give a series of one patient's dreams after the first analytic break which revealed elements of his experience through the evocation and representation of his central unconscious conflicts. The dreams and the reporting of them had the function of containing some of the traumatic effects whilst offering a privileged space for unconscious communication. Whilst verbal interpretation was limited, I will illustrate the importance of the experience of the unconscious affective content of the dreams within the analytic relationship.

Freud noted the decline of psychoanalytic interest in dreams in his 1932 Introductory Lecture "Revision of Dream Theory" when he observed that the section headed "On Dream Interpretation" in *the*

*International Journal* had disappeared. The continuing debate about whether dreams still have a special place within psychoanalytic discourse has a long history. In the discussion of the dream in the "Wolf Man" (1918) Freud linked dreaming with remembering, drawing an implicit connection between the process of dreaming and the transformation of early experiences, introducing the important concept of nachträglichkeit. My own reading of Freud's differing emphases in the subsequent papers (1916, 1923, 1932)—for example " a dream is a thought like any other…"—is that he maintains the role of the dream within the field of the analytic process.

In my view a psychoanalytic discourse that privileges the transference and counter-transference relationship may lead to the dream becoming *only* a thought like any other. One of the consequences that can arise from this seems to be a "collapse" in levels of thinking, an example of which is the lack of differentiation between the manifest and the latent content of the dream. Loden (2003) also suggests that an exclusive focus on the transferential meaning of a dream in a session, that in itself expresses a listening *for* rather listening *to*, may counter the patient's own thought connections and capacity for self-enquiry.

The element of the dream which Freud evocatively termed a "child of night" (1932) is of relevance in this debate. Freud's recapitulation of dream theory in the New Introductory Lectures describes the one repudiated thought, "a child of night", that belongs to the dreamer's unconscious: "this unconscious impulse is the true creator of the dream". Ella Sharpe in her book *Dream Analysis* (1937) illustrates how "the material comprising the latent content is derived from *experience* of some kind" (p. 15). Experiences including not only actual past occurrences, but also emotional states and the body sensations, painful and pleasurable accompanying such experiences. Language and therefore the language of dreams, Sharpe suggests, is born of the body. It will be evident in my clinical illustration that the patient's anxieties and fears of intimate contact expressed in the series of dreams are rooted in bodily states and memories.

## Clinical illustration

I will focus on some unconscious elements in the dreams which refer to the central conflicts of the patient that, though not directly articulated in verbal interpretations, formed part of my preconscious and unconscious understanding that was conveyed to the patient. A few weeks after these dreams appeared in the sessions, aspects of the unconscious conflicts contained within them were brought more explicitly into the transference relationship. The dreams and the reporting of them in the sessions had the function of containing some of the traumatic effects whilst offering a privileged space for unconscious communication.

In a recent session David came upon the words "measured" and "measure" when he was reflecting on his partial identification with me—using a similar inflection in his voice to mine, which he had noticed when speaking to colleagues at work. He "played" for a while with the various meanings of the words: measured, a measure, rhythm, calm, Shakespeare's play "Measure for Measure". I felt affectively and silently involved for several minutes before the atmosphere changed and a distance emerged. His emotional engagement with himself and the analytic process had become a performance. Woven into this shared verbal and non-verbal experience in the session was the disturbing presence of his sexual excitement that drew him towards me and pulled him away; sexual excitation which needed some measure in order not to overflow and create chaos.

A week later in the last session before David left for a week's holiday, he said he was thinking about the word "deciduous" in his dream the previous day. He realised that it refers to "you and us", meaning doing things by himself or doing things together. Noticing the pattern of the cushion on the couch led him to recall being sick at school and reading his medical notes when he was left alone. He remembered staring at the pattern on the curtains. He was frightened and did not understand what he read. He recalled his mother's shame about taking an anti-nausea drug when she was pregnant with him, fearing it had caused him damage. He then spoke of a phone call in which his father had complained to him that mother did not like pasta which he wanted to eat. David felt angry and wondered why father could not just make it for himself. I commented: "the you and us issue again".

Just before the end of the session, thoughts of a baby emerged in David's mind. He recalled that walking home the previous day he had thought of an ill, feverish baby and realised he was feeling hot. Then, on leaving the room he averted his gaze which was quite unusual. This felt to me a significant moment in which his avoidance seemed to carry his sense of vulnerability and shame and his anticipation of not receiving the narcissistically enhancing look he wished for from his analyst. I was left thinking of the feverish baby in need of attention which had emerged just before he left to go away.

## Background

David came to treatment after a depressive episode which was precipitated by the ending of his first serious relationship with a girlfriend. He was worried by intrusive suicidal thoughts and felt disturbed by his difficulties in sexual relationships, both of which were connected to his conflicting feelings about needing to seek help. This was evident in his arriving late for the first consultation. He spoke of the difficult relationship with his girlfriend, who in some ways was like his mother. His father was not mentioned until near the end of the first meeting when he spoke of father leaving the "emotional stuff" to mother, being depressed and rather fragile, like David himself.

He had a dream on the morning of the third consultation when he had woken up feeling anxious.

> In the *dream* I was sitting cross-legged on a metal structure, he thought it was a fire escape.

He smiled about the double meaning of wanting therapy and seeing me as a calm figure, and wanting to flee (the fire escape). One of the aspects which struck me about this dream was the static quality of the figure of his analyst. I also wondered about being placed outside the room, did this signify a lack of a container or David's need to escape an object which threatened to become a prison? In considering beginning the analysis, David had expressed his fear of using the couch in bodily terms. He told me he sometimes suffered from oesophageal reflux and thus lying down could be difficult.

David was sent away to boarding school aged eight, where he was unhappy and homesick or "people sick" as he put it. He suffered frequent and heavy nosebleeds during childhood. This experience has assumed the shape of a defining trauma for him, enforcing an attitude of self-sufficiency which became a source of pride and sense of identity. He spoke of his feelings of anger and rage with his parents sitting alongside but not connected to his understanding of them. He had learnt later that they were distressed about sending him away, which left him with a sense of confusion as to why they did. In an early session he spoke of his love of red clothes and shoes, and of his difficulty in throwing some of these precious things away. He described keeping a tattered pair of red trainers under his bed for months before he could bear to throw them away; and not before he had taken a photo of them.

David brought many dreams to his sessions after the holiday, which was his first experience of an analytic break. He had brought dreams before with a palpable sense of pleasure and excitement associated with pleasing his analyst whilst gratifying his exhibitionistic impulses in an acceptable way. His early dreams expressed anxiety in various forms about not getting to his sessions, with more subtle references to an emerging erotic transference. He gave scattered references to sexual identity conflicts; his conscious fear of intimacy with women, his attachment to red objects, his awareness that some of his mannerisms are camp.

## A series of dreams

In the second week after the break he was eight minutes late to the first session of the week. Towards the end of the session he brought a dream:

> There was an unhappy baby in a front room of a house, a bit like the consulting room; he commented that at this point in the dream he was a kind of observer. His mother and her sister were there, both are nurses. Mother decided the baby had something in its ears and she was going to do a surgical intervention using the handle of a cheese grater, his aunt said are you sure that's the right thing to use? Mother insisted it was.

This reminded both of us of his having syringed his own ears using equipment sent by his mother some weeks before the break. When I explored this with him, he said he had done it to save money. He was going to buy some expensive headphones which needed fitting to his ears and he thought the suppliers would charge him extra because his ears were full of wax. Having syringed his ears he suffered from dizziness for a while and regretted doing it, recognising he was again trying to do everything by himself without asking for help. He could link this with his position of being an observer of the sick baby in his dream. He mentioned two further dreams from the weekend, one in which he was having sex with his sister who then disappeared, the second involving a ghost of a friend's father to whom he spoke reassuring words.

He arrived ten minutes early for the next session. He had recently been able to notice that his time of arrival for the sessions, whether early, exactly on time or late, had an important emotional meaning. When he had arrived early on other occasions, sometimes more than ten minutes early, I had the impression that he was unaware or wished to be unaware that there might be another patient before him. This elicited some irritation and a sense of intrusion in me, but also curiosity about his apparent lack of awareness of his behaviour. I speculated to myself that his action expressed an aspect of an early problem of bodily rhythms connected with disturbances in the relationship with his mother, underlying the more obvious meaning of his wish for attention. Initially when I had attempted to explore this with him, he felt criticised and intruded upon.

He remarked on his being early and having to ring the bell twice before I answered. He wondered whether his early arrival meant I had to stay in the room, which evidently on this day I had not done.

He had a dream:

> he was in his bedroom in his parents' house, there was a new baby and it would be in his room, so a cot had been put in his room. But it was more like a cage than a cot.
>
> In the dream he knew it was his parents' baby. He thought of his younger sister but he said this felt a bit theoretical, imagining what he might have felt about her arrival. I was reminded of his dream of being in bed having sex with his sister, and his earlier anxiously laden communication of having intrusive thoughts about his sister's genitals for many years. Having in mind his early arrival, I spoke of the baby representing his passionate feelings which he feels he has to cage, feeling fearful that I may not want him in my room.

The following day he began speaking of how he comes into the room saying hello or good morning, and then he turned his back on me whilst he took off his coat and put down his bag on the chair in which he first sat for the consultations. He related this to feelings of sibling rivalry aroused by meeting a female colleague the day before whom he knows is in analysis with me. He imagined she and I having a friendly chat before she lies down for her session. He went on to speak of how hard he works to gain approval and how furious he feels when he doesn't receive it. He later made a reference to masturbating the previous evening using internet pornography.

The next week he arrived 15 minutes late for the first session. He commented on the previous week's flowers being gone. I noticed that he was wearing a great deal of red. He reported that twice this week he had gone to something a day early. He accepted my interpretation that the Tuesday session seemed to be more of focus of his mixed feelings about his therapy because it is the first one of the week after the weekend break. He acknowledged that he had felt a wish not to come to the session but rather to stay at home and watch Obama's inauguration on T.V. Generally, he thought he was trying to squash too much into too little time. But he wanted to tell me that he was pleased to have spoken to his male flatmate Steven about how depressed he seemed and Steven had responded positively to him. David continued in a slightly complaining and perplexed tone that he wakes up early when Steven gets up for work even though Steven is very quiet. It is as if he has an internal alarm clock; that thought seemed mad to him. I noted to myself the appearance of his homosexual wishes and fears. He then spoke of the book he was reading entitled *Love's Executioner* written by a therapist, with tales of therapy. He thought of how he tries to control what happens here whilst he knows that to use it, he needs to be as open as possible.

Then he reported a dream which was in three parts, he described it as follows: "it went from love to anxiety to terror".

In the first part he was alone with a girl his age with long dark hair. They were in a beautiful winter landscape that was sort of blue, they were skating. She was in love with him and, they were in love with each other. She said she'd never felt this way before. Then she disappeared, she became like a hologram.

In the second part he was being offered erotic books for sale.

In the third part he was in his own bedroom; a woman came in who he recognised as male, someone from work, who is a female transgender person. She looked like a prostitute, a dodgy person; she was looking for something in his room, maybe drugs. Then suddenly she was on top of him, holding him down. He had already been offered a drink he thought might be tainted – drugged. He was terrified thinking he was going to be injected. He woke up.

He spoke of feeling ashamed talking about using pornography; he thought it must be unpleasant for me to hear. He recalled thinking the previous week whilst looking on the internet that he liked some of the images and he could pay for more, then he thought why stop there why not pay for a prostitute. He supposed it was about male desire implying both that I should be able to listen but also that I would not be willing to accept him. He thought the figure in the dream had given up his maleness to become a woman. He laughed, he quite liked this person; they were at a meeting the day before discussing a project. He is full of projects at the moment, this makes him worried about the possibility of becoming manic.

I noticed that David responded to most of my comments and interpretations with a "sure" which felt like a rapid dismissal as though he could not listen and had to defend himself against taking anything in from me. I thought of it as his way to "measure" the distance and emotional contact with me; an awareness that he came to in a later session as I have mentioned at the beginning of this clinical account. David thus conveyed his experience of an element of his dream, of a threatening intruding analyst, whom he transforms into a prostitute whose services he buys and for whom he may be ready to give up his maleness to form a homosexual couple and to avoid rejection. David's latent dream thoughts may be related to Shakespeare's play *Measure for Measure* in which Angelo's initially repudiated male desire for Isabella is later expressed in his determination that she should listen to him and prostitute herself to him in exchange for her brother's life.

David arrived five minutes early for the next session. When I collected him from the waiting room, he was self-consciously putting a book back on the bookshelf. Once on the couch he wondered whether he should ask permission to look at a book, but he thought he need not because they were there in the waiting room. He told me he was looking at a book titled *On not being able to paint*. I suggested this was connected with yesterday's session. "What about yesterday's session?" he mused out loud, "I was late, the dream, yes I was being offered books".

I commented on a kind of reversal, in the dream a woman/man came in to his room looking for something, today he is looking in my room.

He acknowledged feeling a sense of excitement in being caught out, and he linked this with the scene in his dream where he is being offered erotic books.

Later in the session he spoke of several women with whom he has been friends.

I commented: "a series of sisters".

After a brief silence David replied: "you've hit the nail on the head Joan".

The ambiguity in his expression struck me alongside his use of my first name, which seemed to emphasise the aggressive feelings aroused by my comment, which I had made rather spontaneously without thinking too much about it. He continued talking about the string of sisters. He commented that this was not the word I used, wondering about his use of the word "string". He thought of knots in string which mean problems to be untied, and tying the knot means marriage.

The following day he was on time but spent two minutes in the toilet thus keeping me waiting. He spoke about having thoughts of when he would finish his therapy. He had felt intensely competitive feelings towards the husband of the colleague who is in analysis with me, because he was doing a course which would improve his job chances. Then David recounted a very long *dream* which he announced as very symbolic, that occupied the rest of the session.

I will only give an outline of the dream:

> he escaped from a house where there was a fire in the bathroom started by a woman, then he got on a bus to go home but it went the wrong way, finally he was in a house where a man who was a kind of vampire gripped his wrist tightly, he resisted and pricked the man with a knife to see if he would bleed.

At the end of this account David commented that the dream was becoming a bit of a cliché, like a film where all the people have been taken over by vampires.

The following week he complained of feeling depressed again, he had intrusive suicidal thoughts seeing a window without a safety catch. He was late for the first session of the week, which unusually he did not mention. He felt tired and had fallen asleep on the bus on his way to the session. Later in the week he reported feeling very annoyed hearing a line from a song "danger in the eyes of a stranger". He wondered what he looked for in my eyes when he leaves. He had been looking at flats on the internet and saw one nearly next door to my house, but he thought he might play his music too loud and it would come through the walls. Subsequently he developed a mild inflammation in his eye, a symptom he had suffered before when he was depressed.

## Discussion

David has engaged with enthusiasm in his analysis; his intellectual interest is used not only defensively but is also allied with his wish for understanding and help. He conveyed a palpable sense of relief at having found a place and a person who can listen and think about him. Alongside this there is also an element of performance, needing to be noticed, to be the good patient and avoid criticism. In the initial weeks I became aware of his need to control the contact and control me, such that at times I felt myself in the role of an onlooker, a passive listener. David is clearly pleased and excited with the creative dream/gifts he can bring to his analyst, in telling the dream there is a sense of mastery (De Monchaux 1978 in Flanders 1993). The dreams are both a communication and a form of action in the sessions. As Pontalis points out, the dream is an object invested libidinally by the dreamer "the bearer of dread and enjoyment" and the telling of the dream to the analyst is "a sensorial exchange of the visual and hearing" (Pontalis 1974, 1993, p. 112).

The first dream David brought was on the morning of the third consultation, a dream in which I appeared undisguised sitting cross-legged on a fire escape. At this point neither he nor I were certain about whether we would begin an analytic journey together; in fact, I had intended to refer him to a colleague. David meanwhile made it clear that he wished to see me; the male senior colleague he had spoken to about getting help had recommended me. No doubt this dream was an expression both of his wish to escape and his fear of being cast out. Anna Ferruta (2009) discusses the obstacles to symbolisation encountered when the analyst appears undisguised in the first dream of an analysis. She suggests that this realistic representation indicates that the function of the other in the construction of the psychic world has been abolished. There is an aspect of this in David's analysis, an expression of his difficulties with otherness, with separateness that leads him to an imitative identification (Gaddini 1969), adopting the same inflection in his voice as mine. This is also apparent in his evident need to try to control his analyst, to come to his sessions with a certain level of prepared "script" enabling him to anticipate my responses and interpretations and to keep me in a safe place where I would not disturb or threaten him too much.

In the sequence of dreams following the first break, a reiteration in some ways of the earlier "break" between the consultations and starting therapy, central aspects of David's core complex (Glasser 1979) and oedipal conflicts are represented. The analytic process now shaped by the impact of the holiday break is full of his castration anxieties, the surgical operation to be performed by mother on the baby's ear, intensified by his fear of abandonment that evokes fantasies of cruelty and murderousness. To an extent his production of dreams in itself acts as a reassurance that he is not damaged by his analyst's comings and goings, an expression of his self-sufficiency. The other dreams of the first weekend—having sex with his sister who disappears and his encounter with a father ghost—suggest oedipal conflicts; his desire for his mother is rendered more acceptable to his super-ego when represented as his sister, and his death wish towards his father is disguised as a reassurance to the ghost father that he will find or recover what he has lost.

In the next dream there is a new baby produced by his parents, perhaps evidence that he has not killed his father after all. Following my interpretation of his fear of my rejection of his passionate feelings, he is drawn to internet pornography to satisfy his sexual desires in a way that avoids contact with a separate person. The internet functions as a container for his narcissistic rage that would otherwise threaten to break out into action in the transference. In the subsequent dream there is an image of an idealised relationship, they are in love with each other, but he is skating on ice in a state of narcissistic merger that threatens a loss of self. She disappears to be replaced with erotic books. This last vague scene is replaced by the entrance of a very threatening woman he recognises as a man, who wants to kill him in a barely disguised sexual encounter.

My verbal interpretation at this point of his fear of his passionate loving and aggressive feelings clearly lags behind the specific unconscious meanings in the dreams to which I have just referred. In the dream he brought the following week, the dream in three parts, is "framed" by his ambivalence expressed in his lateness and stated preference to watch the American president's inauguration. Behind his idealised wish for heterosexual love are his homosexual wishes and fears in the form of the transgender person who is both male and female. That he can bring such a dream suggests that he has experienced his analyst as able to hear without reacting as the feared prohibiting father or the intrusive seductive mother.

In David's dreams the representations of phantasies of the primal scene evoking his passive feminine wishes and anxieties, show that the traumatic impact of the first break and the excitement and rage provoked by my return, stirred up his most basic bisexual identifications and conflicts. These phantasies might be said to form the "child of night" of his dreams. The representation of the mother/analyst in the dream of the sick baby is of a phallic intrusive object who threatens castration (the operation in the ear); does he have to give up his masculinity or to simulate in order to survive? (Glasser 1992). The appearance of the baby in his dreams and subsequently in his waking thoughts suggested David was becoming more tolerant of accepting his dependency needs in relation to his analyst. After he left for his holiday, I thought of the baby representing the hated rival sister and the "sister patient" in the analysis. His memories in the last session before his departure for a week's holiday, of being sick alone at school and his mother's fears of taking a toxic drug in pregnancy, seemed to be condensed representations of early traumas which are beginning to emerge into the analytic space.

David's thoughts about the word "deciduous" in a session the week before an analytic break also carries the meaning of loss; green leaves that fall, as our emotional contact does not last. There is also the seasonal rhythm implied in the coming and going of leaves on a tree: they are not lost forever. I think this image reflects David's "deciduous" solution to his core complex anxieties, an oscillation between evergreen/fusional contact and a never-ending winter of isolation.

Apart from recurrent nosebleeds in childhood and adolescence, David suffers from a snake phobia and a needle phobia, both of which seem to be hysterical symptoms linked to unconscious sexual phantasies (Freud 1908). His history of prolonged and frequent nose bleeds which required cauterisation leading to damage of his nasal septum producing a hole, has perhaps the unconscious meaning of a circumcision further intensifying his castration fears and bisexual conflicts (Nunberg 1947). The nosebleeds and his attachment to red objects point to the presence of an unconscious identification with a woman who is menstruating and thus not pregnant, or a woman bleeding after childbirth. Anna Freud's (1967) view about the displacement of the reaction formation against death wishes from human beings to material objects and the identification with the lost object is relevant in understanding David's attachment to the red objects. At a more fundamental level there is a representation of his body with insecure boundaries in danger of losing its contents, opening the way to the dread of annihilation.

The flood of dream material had the aim of capturing my attention and offering an outlet for some of his aggression and pleasure in dreaming (Pontalis 1974, 1993). David thus transformed me into a more passive less threatening analyst as well as reversing through projection his own experience of being overwhelmed. However, at the same time the dreams have a genuinely communicative meaning and their content usefully alerted me to the active presence of transference currents that I needed to take into account when framing my interpretations. For example, the fragility of his masculine identifications which render him more vulnerable to fears of merger with the maternal object/analyst.

These elements of his psychic reality which have shown themselves in his dreams remain to be further elaborated and worked through in his analysis.

## Conclusion

De Monchaux (1978, 1993, p. 198) in her elegant argument for the special features of dream telling, suggests there is no final latent content "buried at the end of the rainbow". She refers to the temptation to yield to the simplistic idea that "the latent content is waiting like "sleeping beauty" for the prince's interpretative kiss to release her from the curse of resistance". This does not contradict the Freudian concept of "a child of night" but rather places it firmly within the context of the transference relationship and the whole field of the analytic session. De Monchaux's view that there is no final latent content can also be understood as corroborating Freud's concept of the dream's navel: "There is at least one spot in every dream at which it is unfathomable—a navel as it were, that is its point of contact with the unknown" (1900, p. 111 footnote). Freud returns to this theme in the theoretical chapter of *The Interpretation of Dreams*; he writes about the tangle of dream thoughts which cannot be unravelled:

> This is the dream's navel.... The dream thoughts to which we are led by interpretation cannot, from the nature of things, have any definite endings; they are bound to branch out into the intricate

network of our world of thought. It is at some point where this meshwork is particularly close that the dream wish grows up, like a mushroom out of mycelium.

(1900, p. 525)

In reporting a series of dreams from the beginning of an analysis I have suggested that the unconscious emotional experience generated is an important aspect of the developing analytic process. Birksted-Breen (2009) introduces the notion of "reverberation time", referring to a particular quality of the earliest "back and forth" internalised exchange with the mother, that is the basis of the capacity to dream. She posits that "reverberation time" is also the building block of the analytic process leading to "unfreezing" psychic time.

David's dreams in this early phase of the work had the function of evoking a level of unconscious communication which stimulated an emotional reverberation and resonance that allowed for the later elaboration of important transference phantasies, conflicts and affects.

## References

Birksted-Breen, D. (2009). Reverberation time: dreaming and the capacity to dream. *Int. J. Psycho-Anal.*, 90: 35–51.
Ferruta, A. (2009). The reality of the other: dreaming of the analyst. *Int. J. Psycho-Anal.*, 90: 93–108.
Flanders, S. (ed.) (1993). *The Dream Discourse Today*. New Library of Psychoanalysis. London: Routledge.
Freud, A. (1967). About losing and being lost. *Psychoanal. St. Child*, 22: 9–19.
Freud, S. (1900). The interpretation of dreams. *S.E.*, 4–5.
Freud, S. (1908). Hysterical phantasies and their relation to bisexuality. *S.E.*, 9: 159–166.
Freud, S. (1916). Introductory lectures on psycho-analysis: Symbolism in dreams. *S.E.*, 15: 149–169.
Freud, S. (1918). From the history of an infantile neurosis. *S.E.*, 17: 3–122.
Freud, S. (1923). Remarks on the theory and practice of dream interpretation. *S.E.*, 19: 109–138.
Freud, S. (1932). New introductory lectures, XXIX: revision of the theory of dreams. *S.E.*, 22: 7–30.
Gaddini, E. (1969). On imitation. *Int. J. Psycho-Anal.*, 50: 475–484.
Glasser, M. (1979). Some aspects of the role of aggression in the perversions. In *Sexual Deviation*, ed. I. Rosen, 2nd edition. Oxford: Oxford University Press, pp. 278–305.

Glasser, M. (1992). Problems in the psychoanalysis of certain narcissistic patients. *Int. J. Psycho-Anal.*, 73: 493–505.

Loden, S. (2003). The dream in contemporary psychoanalysis. *J. Amer. Psychoanal. Assn.*, 51: 43–70.

De Monchaux, C. (1978). Dreaming and the organising function of the ego. *Int. J. Psycho-Anal.*, 59: 443–453. In *The Dream Discourse Today*, ed. S. Flanders. New Library of Psychoanalysis. London: Routledge, 1993.

Nunberg, H. (1947). Circumcision and problems of bisexuality. *Int. J. Psycho-Anal.*, 28: 145–179.

Pontalis, J. B. (1974). Dream as object. *Int. Rev. Psycho-Anal.*, 1: 125–133. In *The Dream Discourse Today*, ed. S. Flanders. New Library of Psychoanalysis. London: Routledge, 1993.

Sharpe, E. (1937). *Dream Analysis*. London: Hogarth Press.

# 19

# REGRESSION, CURIOSITY AND THE DISCOVERY OF THE OBJECT[1]

Rosemary Davies

I started to consider therapeutic regression during a difficult period in the analysis of a patient who I intuited was regressed, and not in a state of what some call "psychic retreat". My researches reminded me of old battles. During the Controversial Discussions, for example Ernest Jones (King and Steiner 1991) recognised regression as a potentially explosive concept when he described it as "this quarrel-provoking word" (p. 323). Neither the adherents of the "nurture regression" school, nor the "psychic retreat" school, resolved the problem. However, Winnicott's linking regression with primary narcissism seemed to me to provide a sound theoretical underpinning for a technique that recognises the therapeutic value of regression, whilst avoiding the pitfall of failing to address the destructiveness inherent in the discovery of the object's otherness (1954b).

Psychoanalysts cannot embark on treatment without consideration of the possibility of the patient's regression. Faced with patients who regress over extended periods of time, rather than the moment-by-moment movements that characterise any analysis, it seems to me that clinicians are somewhat unschooled in contemporary psychoanalytic culture as to how to work creatively with the patient in this state. Earlier discussions of therapeutic regression got bogged down in issues that amounted to breaches of technique: physical contact with the patient during sessions for example, or in the analyst's self-disclosure (Balint 1968). It may have been in response to this that discussion of the centrality of regression in clinical practice diminished. This seems to be a characteristic of psychoanalytic debate in Britain. By contrast, in 1997 the American Psychoanalytic Association debated this topic under the heading: *Therapeutic regression, essential clinical condition or iatrogenic phenomenon? (Goldberg 1998).*

Therapeutic regression has a distinguished provenance. For Freud regression was a central concept of psychoanalysis: he outlined a threefold theory of regression: topographical, temporal and formal (1900) He argued, for example that transference, "the most delicate of instruments", was a clinical manifestation of regression (1912, p. 139). In the context of therapeutic regression, he counselled against "neglect of regression in analytic technique". He was concerned, in his dispute with Jung, that such neglect was tantamount to a dangerous "scientific regression" in itself (1914, p. 11). In 1935 Kris famously described "regression in the service of the ego". But it is Winnicott (1954a) whose work is quintessentially associated with the concept of regression. His work both theoretical and clinical privileged the role of "regression to dependence" as he called it.

Bion summarised the various views vividly in his controversial Cogitation of 1960 on why people might think he was not a Kleinian. He wrote "Winnicott says patients *need* to regress: Melanie Klein says they *must not*: I say they *are* regressed" (1992 p. 63). Bollas (1987) described the clinical phenomenology of regression to ordinary dependence and the "generative regressive process" (p. 258). In accord with Bion, he maintained that the analytic structure "invites regression" so *ipso facto* many patients are regressed. Stewart (1992) summarised this position as follows "regression acts as an ally of therapeutic progress" (p. 105).

Currently there seems to be less overt dispute, but there remains a subtle manifestation of the distaste for the clinical concept of regression. The debate devolves around a false dichotomy between those who argue that regression should be fostered and those who assert that it is tantamount to a psychic withdrawal: the "dialogue of the deaf" as Green (1986) describes it. Britton (1998), for example, considers that regression has appropriately fallen from our psychoanalytic vocabulary. Indeed, Spillius et al.'s *New Dictionary of Kleinian Thought* (2011) contains no entry on regression. Britton prefers that the term regression is reserved to describe a retreat into a pathological organisation that "reiterates the past and evades the future" (p. 72). However, I think the state of regression only provides an evasion of the future when there is a failure to recognise the therapeutic potential of a state of mind which might more readily than others, give up its unconscious secrets (Parsons 2014). Drawing on Freud's notion of "formal" regression, it can be seen how in the regressed state, primary process, the language of the Unconscious supersedes secondary process: more primitive modes of expression and representation take the place of the more structured thinking.

Let me set the scene by describing an episode in the analysis of a patient who regressed in analysis:

## Stephen

When Stephen started treatment, I conjectured that he might fall into a depression when analytic work touched some of his defensive structure. His history indicated the probability of some highly charged oedipal feelings towards a cold, demanding and humiliating father and a narcissistic mother who he described as "sweeter than the sweetest cup of tea." However, I did not predict the regression that characterised the first years of treatment.

In the second session of treatment Stephen reported a dream that became, as early dreams do, a sort of icon in treatment. He dreamt he saw a beached frigate and he knew he could not board it for on board there were diseased people. We saw this as a clear representation of his anxiety about embarking on treatment where he would have to encounter his own diseased and frightening internal objects. He feared that his characteristic defense of "going numb" would be breached: curiosity about his internal life was consciously experienced as a dangerous venture.

Stephen was often in tears and silent during the early months of treatment Indeed he commented, "Every time I think of talking to you I feel like crying." He spoke little and laboriously and in his own words described himself as "lost in a forest and don't know my way back." He described feeling utterly dropped during breaks and was difficult to pick up again. At the same time, whilst regressed in analysis he completed his professional studies and finalised a divorce.

Towards the end of the first year of treatment he told me he felt "intrigued by you". The intrigue was characterised by an erotic element and a very critical censorious element. Despite being analytically informed he was particularly critical of elements of the setting:

he disliked the lack of eye contact and was a stringent critic of any minor lapses in time keeping. He disliked seeing other patients and worked hard to persuade me that I should alter my schedule. When he told me of these complaints, he would then subside into a terror of the consequences of telling me: an anxiety about the father's cruel injunctions that did not allow for the young boy's curiosity and rivalry.

The silence and hesitancy continued. Then at the beginning of a session in the second year of his analysis he reported: "I felt very disturbed yesterday. For a split second when I left my session I thought of following you through the door when I heard you going into your house. I thought I would do something horrible or something horrible would happen to me." He pondered about this frightening image and told me that it reminded him of being a small child when his father would shout brief intense words at him and he would crumble: "a small child reduced to a grain of sand… but I know also (remembering a dream he reported the day before) that I can be harmful and damaging."

This was a turning point in his analysis, he was very frightened by the thought of following me. As he walked in his mind through the door into my mind would he come to grief as he broke through to my house or would I be damaged by his aggressive intrusion? In his associations to this image during the session he remembered "something fundamentally wrong with my parents' relationship." I think he was permitting himself curiosity about his parental objects who faced him with some very murderous feelings. His parents seemed at loggerheads all through his early childhood. But their cruel deception of him was revealed when they had another baby when Stephen was in his early teens.

Stephen gradually emerged from the regressed state and allowed himself to look at the aggression and the libidinal longings inherent in his curiosity about, and discovery of me as a separate object. He felt assailed by murderous oedipal feelings and reported a dream about the film Alien in which a terrifying monster emerges from the body of the heroine. He described his wish to make the danger safe by recruiting the aid of the Ghostbusters.

## Regression and the discovery of the object

Emerging from the regression Stephen was faced with the reality of me as a separate object. I think for many months I had been experienced as little more than a narcissistic extension of his own mind. But crucially that recognition revealed the danger of separateness to him. Would he or I be damaged? This clinical moment exemplifies what I regard as one of Freud's central tenets:

> The antithesis between subjective and objective does not exist from the first
>
> (1925, p. 237)

The conceptualisation of the nature of the discovery of our own subjectivity and the existence of another lies at the centre of the notion of "object usage" where the complexity of the subject placing the object outside the area of their omnipotent control defines a crucial developmental stage. This rich seam of clinical theory has recently been elaborated by Rousillon (2018) in his notion of the need for what he calls the 'pliability' of the maternal environment. This pliability will facilitate, in the emergence from the state of primary narcissism, the recognition of an object separate form the subject but, crucially the recognition that the object is a subject too:

> If the object "survives", then the infant has the experience that what he thought he had destroyed has in fact not been destroyed; he then discovers that the object eludes his omnipotence, that the object resists this, and the infant discovers that the object is another subject (another self), whose mode of presence, whose inner desires and impulses are not dependent on him, even if they are connected to him. …The problem is not one of "perception" but one of "conception"; it is one thing to perceive the object as being separate, but quite another to conceive of it as "another subject", that is, as possessing its own desires and impulses.
>
> (p. 13)

This elaboration makes a crucial link with the centrality of what Laplanche (1999) details as the "enigmatic signifiers": that which the mother brings into the equation as her desire, when the infant recognises her as a separate other. This conceptualisation enhances my understanding of my patient's concern as he recognised my separate existence.

In this context, Winnicott's writing on primary narcissism and its clinical manifestation in regression, proposes a theory of technique which addresses the recognition of human subjectivity: curiosity and the discovery of the object are central. In 1954, he wrote: "In primary narcissism the environment is holding the individual, and at the same time the individual knows of no environment and is at one with it..." (1954a, p. 283). So here the clinical state of regression is equated with primary narcissism. Linking regression with primary narcissism crucially differentiates some writers from others. Balint, a central exponent of therapeutic regression, disagreed with the idea of primary narcissism, preferring to think of primary love. Positing a notion of primary love presupposes the existence of a relationship that is substantially different from the individual who "recognises no environment".

This is a hotly contested topic theoretically. However, in my view the concept of primary narcissism provides a helpful clinical descriptive tool. It describes a primitive, undifferentiated, wordless state that can characterise the analytic encounter at certain moments. Contemporary evidence points to the recognition of an object from early life, that gives credence to the psychoanalytic view of object seeking behaviour over and above instinctual gratification, but it does not entirely account for the detailed phenomenology of the infant's internal state. As Green (2002) puts it:

> These observations are behavioral; we still do not know what is going on in the child's mind...The baby's reactions to the primary object...do not prove that the baby can experience the situation as a separate entity in relationship with another separate entity.
> (p. 647)

Indeed, from quite another psychoanalytic school the support for maintenance of the notion of primary narcissism is outlined in Pine's (2004) re-evaluation of Mahler's work on the "symbiotic stage". He argues for the notion of "symbiotic moments". Laplanche and Pontalis (1973) suggest the value of the notion of primary narcissism designating "formative moments" (p. 338). In Gibeault's (2004) discussion of cure in psychoanalysis he considered primary narcissism and narcissistic regression as the "mainspring of analytic material".

## Regression, curiosity, discovery of the object

A clinical theory which allows for the concept of primary narcissism demands then an explanation of what happens at the point of movement between hallucinated pleasure, and dependence on an external object. It is my view that Freud's metapsychology addresses this point. In 1915 Freud's preoccupation with the internal/ external axis leads him to postulate the presence of aggression inherent in the discovery of the object in the external world:

> When, during the state of primary narcissism, the object makes its appearance, the second opposite to loving, namely hating, also attains its development.
> (p. 136)

His well-known assertion that

> Hate, as a relation to objects, is older than love.

is often cited. However, the following elaboration is often not quoted

> It derives from the narcissistic ego's primordial repudiation of the external world with its outpouring of stimuli.
> (p. 139)

Here Freud's postulation of the hate that is meted out by the narcissistic ego on that which is not "I" is central. Following Freud, Winnicott (1969) asserted the inevitability of aggression in the discovery of the object:

> ...the subject is creating the object in the sense of finding externality itself, and it has to be added that this experience depends on the object's capacity to survive. ...If it is in an analysis that these matters are taking place, then the analyst, the analytic technique, and the analytic setting all come in as surviving or not surviving the patient's destructive attacks. Without the experience of maximum destructiveness ... the subject never places the analyst outside and therefore can never do more than experience a kind of self-analysis, using the analyst as a projection of a part of the self.
> (p. 714)

The analyst is required to survive the subject's attacks and nurture curiosity and discovery of an object rather than fostering projective repudiation of the object's otherness. Winnicott makes a crucial distinction between those who argue that projective mechanisms create external reality and his own view that:

> projective mechanisms assist in the act of noticing what is there but are not the reason why the object is there…orthodox psychoanalytic theory…tends to think of external reality only in terms of the individual's projective mechanisms.
>
> (p. 714)

He goes on to argue in the context of the reality principle that destructive feelings are present when the object is discerned. Such a conceptualisation indicates the risk of an eruption of destructive phantasies as the patient emerges from the regressed state, placing the analytic object outside of the self. When Stephen recognised a version of me with my own thoughts, my own life, the other side of the door, he or I were indeed in danger.

Primary narcissism is ruptured by the reality principle. The reality principle ushers in a caesura: the subject can no longer live on hallucinated pleasure alone. This is central to clinical sensitivity. This moment of rupture may reveal much about the nature of the patient's internal world. The technical challenge will surface when the subject momentarily notes there is something he is not at one with. The analyst is experienced as a representation of the world of "otherness", the "disrupter" so to speak. In the human infant's uniquely lengthy state of dependency, an inevitable loss and rupture occurs: the nursling is faced with a notion of a separate other who gives or withholds the breast. As Freud (1933), at his Platonic best, wrote:

> the child … never gets over the pain of losing its mother's breast.
>
> (p. 122)

Absence fuels exploration and here we see the centrality in psychoanalysis of what drives that curiosity. It is the interruption in relation to the fantasised, inexhaustible breast that initiates her researches: the disruption of the primary narcissistic state.

I conjecture that the regressed state is ruptured, just as the primary narcissistic moments are disrupted, by the recognition of dependence within the analysis: this can be a life or death moment. Rosenfeld (1987) considered:

> When he is faced with the reality of being dependent on the analyst... [the patient] would prefer to die, to be non-existent, to deny the fact of his birth...Some of these patients become very depressed and suicidal.
>
> (p. 107)

If the regressed state is assumed to be a pathological withdrawal, the default position is often a reliance on interpreting the regression as an attack on the analysis. Following Freud, I am arguing that hate finds expression when the patient emerges from the regression, rather than the regression being the consequence of hatred: the pathological retreat. Destructiveness is definitively present as the subject recognises the presence of a discrete other. However, this is more usefully assumed to be a representation of self-preservative aggression, not the deadly envious aggression that is assumed in the interpretation of the regressed state as an attack on analytic work, as a pathological withdrawal.

I focus on a particular moment in Stephen's analysis because when he imagined following me into my house, erasing the wall between the analytic space and my home, walking through the door of his mind into mine, I conjecture that this shattered the regression which had characterised the first years of his analysis and faced him with the object beyond his control: it evoked difficult destructive feelings. Stephen required resilience on my part to contend with this psychic movement. This can be achieved without recourse to a technique that ignores the destructiveness inherent in the discovery of the object's otherness. I think this acknowledgment helps the analyst to survive without retaliation: to be an object for another day so to speak. In the detail of the clinical moment the analyst becomes a regulator of the regression through the creative, receptive attitude, not through breaches of the setting. It seems to me that the rule of abstinence and the analytic stance can be maintained without forgoing a view that regression is a viable and interpretable state. The analytic stance is not only tested during the regression but, particularly as the patient discovers the hitherto "unknown environment" as Winnicott described it. Stephen confronted this "unknown environment", the "external world with its outpouring of stimuli"; the triadic world of oedipal danger, as he imagined crossing the threshold from my consulting room to my home: would he be murdered or murderous, or could a benign, boundary-setting third be summoned. This part of his analysis was indeed characterised by violent imagery.

I think that a more active interpretative technique, aimed at levering Stephen out of his regression in the first months of his analysis, might have precipitated a pathological psychic withdrawal or a premature termination of treatment: the regression would not have been mutative. I felt vindicated by the technical approach to Stephen's state since he managed gradually to recover and recount something of his own history that had been lost to him (he is a second-generation Holocaust survivor). Thus, he was enabled to embark on what Loewald (1960) described as one of the aims of psychoanalysis: to restore the patient's sense of historicity "turning ghosts into ancestors".

Allowing receptivity to the experience of the regression provides a context within which the destructiveness apparent in the discovery of the object can be analysed. Sandler (1993) suggested that there may also be a type of regression which takes place, "in a controlled way" for the analyst in identification with the patient (p. 1104). Just as the patient is required to give himself up to the associative path, so perhaps, in identification with the patient, the analyst surrenders to a sort of parallel regression. Similarly, Parsons (2005) in his discussion of formal regression writes: "analysts may need to accompany their patients into this domain, relinquishing their grasp on verbal representations and the logical connections between them". C. and S. Botella (2005) draw our attention to this "mutual regression… an inclusive movement like a double primary identification operating simultaneously in both partners in the session" (p. 105). Sandler likened this sort of mutual regression to certain uses of projective identification as counter-transferential markers.

I would like to consider two elements that are illustrated by this technical conceptualisation of the analytic attitude to the regressed patient: first, curiosity and second, what I call a deficit in the language of affect.

## Curiosity

In his initial presentation Stephen seemed curious about himself but his first dream of the beached frigate which could not be boarded for fear of what might be encountered therein, indicated an anxiety about investigating too far. However severe the pathology, patients who arrive in the analyst's consulting room retain something of their sense of curiosity. They may just be curious to see a "shrink" in real life, but more likely they are curious about themselves and their predicament. This may vary from conscious recognition of the curiosity about self, to unconscious communication of curiosity about the self in a projected form.

Spillius (1992) describes the centrality of curiosity and the fragility of its sustenance. In her discussion of Steiner's (1994) differentiation of *analyst* and *patient* centred interpretations she writes that the *analyst-centred* interpretation suggests a less blaming world

> ...which fosters curiosity, increased capacity to bear loss and awareness that other people are separate from oneself but have minds fundamentally similar to one's own even though they may have different thoughts.

Emerging from the primary narcissistic shell in the analytic context faces the subject with another who has "different thoughts", not just a projective entity, but also an entity in its own right. Spillius's point alerts us to the "blaming world" the patient often inhabits, which augurs against ordinary curiosity. Sometimes there is a dizzying reflection of this blaming world which envelops both patient and analyst. This can swamp clinical discussion and perhaps represents a defence against being accused of failing to see the aggression and destructiveness in the patient's material.

Curiosity is a part of a fundamental concept of psychoanalysis: the epistomophilic instinct, the search for knowledge. It is that curiosity which Freud demonstrated throughout his work: curious to hear the "reminiscences" of the hysterics in 1895 and still curious in 1939 in his last papers to discern the scope or limits of psychoanalysis. He assumed a curiosity in us all and intuited its absence as pathological. Little Hans' enthralling explorations of his body in relation to his mother, father and newborn sister come to mind as a fine example of the researches of the child. And, of course, it is that epistomophilia which fires psychoanalysts' continuing researches into how the self comes into being. The child's curiosity and explorations interweave with the essential existential plight: where did I come from? That question confronts the child with the parental couple, the primal scene: that union of difference that further alerts her to an environment beyond the not knowing state of primary narcissism. The primal scene in all its fantasised forms provides a screen on to which all sorts of projections and identifications are beamed. Crucially, the child's oedipal curiosity is tempered as desire meets prohibition: curiosity might stimulate dangerous discoveries., for example in Stephen's realisation of *"something fundamentally wrong with my parents' relationship"* when he reflected on his fear of his own curiosity about me.

In clinical practice, anxiety about our technique sometimes augurs against the pursuit of natural curiosity: an over weaning psychoanalytic superego can be a constraint on taking risks, pursuing unlikely threads. As Pontalis (1981) wrote, it is as if "in contemporary psychoanalysis the individual is captured in another's system" (p. 146). Green (1986) makes a similar point when he writes of:

> imprisonment within the interpretative matrices which translate the unknown into the already known and are revealed as inappropriate to a mode of relating in which the analyst, by his tolerance of the regressive needs of the patient, might facilitate evolution by declining to fix the experience in a mould which limits his freedom of movement in his psychic functioning.
>
> (p. 200)

So, far from the notion of the patient needing to discover the analyst, the as yet unknown environment, the patient can find him or herself trapped in a labyrinthine web of interpretations that can deflect curiosity rather than fostering the free associative process, and the mutative analytic endeavour. Perelberg (2015) makes a useful differentiation in this context between "open" and "closed" interpretations. This differentiation elaborates a clinical technique aimed at a responsiveness to curiosity, avoiding the trap of Green's depiction of the patient "imprisoned in the interpretative matrices".

Current controversy in clinical theory reflects Freud's contradictory remarks on, for example, the interpretation of the transference. In his famous papers on technique he writes, "every conflict has to be fought out in the transference" (1912, p. 104). Then, in the same series he writes and italicises, *"so long as the patient's communications and ideas run on without obstruction, the theme of the transference should be left untouched"* (1913, p. 139). Freud's postulation of this unobtrusive transference in my view underpins Winnicott's description of his technique:

> it is only in recent years that I have become able to wait and wait for the natural evolution of the transference arising out of the patient's growing trust in the psychoanalytic technique and setting, and to avoid breaking up this natural process by making interpretations... If only we can wait, the patient arrives at understanding creatively... I think I interpret mainly to let the patient know the limits of my understanding. The principle is that it is the patient and only the patient who has the answers.
>
> (1969, p. 711)

Sometimes it seems that less heed is paid to the excitement of discovery, of being the privileged listener, and more ascribed to preconceived notions of the patient as saboteur. And all this despite deference to Bion's recommendation that psychoanalysts should approach a session "without memory and desire": an injunction which has all but lost its meaning in its wearisome repetition (Sandler 1992, p. 196). I think, for example, without joining forces with the self-revelatory Intersubjectivists, that there can be recognition that the analysand's curiosity about his analyst can be interpreted as creative and generative, rather than malign and intrusive. For example, when the analysand makes enquiries of the analyst, the balance has to be held between maintaining a neutral, abstinent stance, whilst recognising that these enquiries reveal much about the patient's internal world via projection and identification. Fisher (2006) describes the inevitable tension between the questions that keep the curiosity alive, spawning more enquiry as compared with answers which foreclose further investigation. He elaborates Bion's thinking on curiosity and postulates a drive for curiosity linked with the establishment of the reality principle. He concludes that:

> This [curiosity] surely is the essence of psychoanalysis, the opening up of the analyst to the emotional experience of wanting to know the patient, thus making possible by the patient's internalization of this relationship, a wanting, and being able, to know oneself.
>
> (p. 1235)

Ogden (2004) specifically addresses the vexed question of the patient's curiosity about the analyst. He argues that in order for the analyst to participate in the process of getting to know the patient there is also an element of the analyst getting to be known by the patient. He is critical of the view that a patient cannot really "know" his analyst because he does not know what occurs outside the analysis. This idea is flawed according to Ogden because:

> it does not sufficiently take into account the fact that, to the extent that the analyst's life experience both within and outside of the analytic setting are significant, they genuinely change who the analyst is. The alteration in his being is an unspoken but felt presence in the analysis
>
> (p. 865)

Stephen's fear of his own curiosity was illustrated when he described being panic stricken in a bookshop when he caught sight of a woman behind a stack of books. He wanted to see her better but was fearful of being seen to be interested. He associated to a meeting earlier in the day when he described as he put it, "itching" to say something, but worried that if he did speak his "passion" and "aggression" would be revealed. He agreed that the fear of speaking and the intensity of his curiosity in the wish to see the "bookish" woman behind him, his analyst, exposed him and me to disturbing libidinal and aggressive feelings.

## The deficit in the language of affect

To conclude I would like to consider another problem in analytic technique which sometimes emerges in the treatment of the regressed patient. In the clinical vignette, Stephen was assailed by an intensity of affect as he contemplated the fear of what he might expose himself to if he followed me through the door. In the moment of affective contact, the regressed state was breached. He found himself assailed by powerful affect, and recovering his equilibrium required some hard analytic work. The regressed patient requires the analyst to recognise when to hold off and when to hold forth. When the patient begins to discover the object who has waited, words to describe these affects, return are a crucial vehicle of the analysis. Indeed, recognising the affective self faces the subject with the notion of the other: "The affect is the epiphany of the other for the subject" (Green 1999, p. 215). This can present something of a challenge. The wording of affect may leave the patient feeling deficient. The patient's psychic survival may depend on the disavowal of the existence of another who may evoke intolerable feelings. This is constantly under threat in treatment where the analyst is attempting to help the patient to be curious about his internal world and give voice to his affective state.

In my view this affective dimension is particularly problematic, for the patient is faced with a cruel disjuncture. The analyst's scrupulous attention to his or her affective state in the counter-transference, contrasts and conflicts with the patient's confused emergence into a world of "otherness" which evokes intense affects. Stephen rather poignantly described this to me when he progressed in treatment and started a relationship with a woman. He returned to a silent state and complained to me of a sense of deficiency, "both you and she have a language that I cannot use". This can leave him feeling that my emotional fluency as he sees it, usurps his sense of emotional agency, just as his mother usurped his early experience when she could not let him out of her sight.

Current psychoanalytic theory of technique rightly focuses on the need to pay careful heed to our affective echoes of the patients' material and our interpretive response. It is generally argued that recognising the affective content within the analytic setting is required before interpretation (e.g. Chused 1996; Fonagy and Target 1995; Rosenfeld 1987). In the treatment of the regressed patients where wording may be problematic Chused's (1996) conceptualisation is particularly apposite. She describes what she calls the *informative experience*: an affective, sometimes nonverbal communication which lays the foundations for an interpretation. *Informative experiences* are seen as arising out of interactions where the expected reaction is not forthcoming. The resulting emotional dissonance between expectation and experience "informs" and may provide an impetus for psychic change. Chused argues that in this way interpretive communication may be heard without being severely contaminated by superego projections:

> learning is always easier from experience than from explanation, which can feel critical to the one-who-didn't-know.
>
> (p. 1069)

So, whilst the analyst is schooled to be mindful of his or her affective state and its meaning counter-transferentially, the patient may be thoroughly compromised in terms of his affective world. Heimann (1960) in her famous restating of the notion of the counter-transference exhorts us to *sustain* our affective state

> what distinguishes this relationship from others is not the presence of feelings in one partner, the patient, and their absence in the other, the analyst, but the *degree* of feeling the analyst experiences and the use he makes of these feelings.... [and his ability]... to *sustain* his feelings as opposed to discharging them like the patient
>
> (p. 152)

But the patient may be ridding himself of difficult affect that may alert him to the terrifying possibility of the existence of a separate other. So, the analyst's capacity to reflect on and verbalise his or her own affective experience, whilst essential technically, may also intensify the patient's sense of isolation. The analyst who brings these feelings to the patient's attention, is underscoring the presence of a mind, the analyst's, which is not the patient's to colonise, but thinks and feels for itself. The patient's observation of the analyst's attempt to deal with these highly charged moments can be mutative, but the patient may also feel threatened by an assumption of a more sophisticated psychic range which he enviously observes in his analyst. McDougall (1989) asks,

> How can we give life to those who ask only that we help them keep their prison walls intact – and our emotional reactions to ourselves?
>
> (p. 117)

## Conclusion

Regression in the clinical setting is characterised, in my experience, by a highly charged affective encounter difficult to word, but crying out for accompaniment. I take the view that this state is, in some senses, a return to an earlier "frozen experience" (Winnicott 1954a). But in another way, it is an entirely new experience for the patient who has taken the risk of letting himself be known in this narcissistically vulnerable state. In this formulation, where there is a dominance of primary process thinking, the potential for change may be greater, for defences are breached and access to unconscious material may be enhanced. I think if we can maintain a structured analytic stance within our clinical practice, patients in a state of regression can be helped to psychically arrange and rearrange their internal objects in a way that allows them to bear the inevitable realisation of separateness. Thus, regression is not the immobilised, atrophied state that critics assume, but an inevitable and mutative aspect of many good enough analyses.

## Note

1 An earlier version of this paper appeared in *Time and Memory*, ed. R.R. Perelberg. London: Routledge, 2007.

## References

Balint, M. (1968). *The Basic Fault*. London: Tavistock.
Bion, W. (1992). *Cogitations*. London: Karnac. Books.
Bollas, C. (1987). *The Shadow of the Object*. London: Free Association Books.
Botella, C. and Botella, S. (2005). *The Work of Psychic Figurability*. London: Routledge.
Britton, R. (1998). *Belief and Imagination: Explorations in Psychoanalysis*. London: Routledge.
Chused, J. (1996). The therapeutic action of psychoanalysis: abstinence and informative experiences. *J. Am. Psychoanal. Assoc.*, 44: 1047–1071.
Fisher, J. V. (2006). The emotional experience of K. *Int. J. Psychoanal.*, 87: 1221–1237.
Fonagy, P. and Target, M. (1995). Understanding the violent patient: the use of the body and the role of the father. *Int. J. Psychoanal.*, 76: 487–501.
Freud, S. (1900). The interpretation of dreams. *S.E.*, 4&5: 1–627.
Freud, S. (1912). The dynamics of the transference. *S.E.*, 12: 97–108.
Freud, S. (1913). On beginning the treatment. *S.E.*, 12: 121–144.
Freud, S. (1914). On the history of the psycho-analytic movement. *S.E.*, 14: 1–66.
Freud, S. (1915). Instincts and their vicissitudes. *S.E.*, 14: 109–140.
Freud, S. (1925). On negation. *S.E.*, 19: 233–240.
Freud, S. (1933). New introductory lectures on psycho-analysis. *S.E.*, 22: 1–182.
Gibeault, A. (2004). Cure in psychoanalysis (unpublished discussion paper).
Goldberg, S. (1998). Regression: essential clinical condition or iatrogenic phenomenon. *J. Am. Psychoanal. Assoc.*, 47: 1169–1178.

Green, A. (1986). *On Private Madness*. London: Karnac.
Green, A. (1999). *The Fabric of Affect in the Psychoanalytic Discourse*. London: Routledge.
Green, A. (2002). A dual conception of narcissism. *Psychoanal. Q.*, 71(4): 631–649.
Heimann, P. (1960). Counter-transference. In *About Children and Children-No-Longer*, ed. Margret Tonnesmann. London: Routledge, 1989, pp. 151–160.
King, P. and Steiner, R. (1991). *The Freud-Klein Controversies*. London: Routledge.
Kris, E. (1935). The psychology of caricature. *Int. J. Psycho-Anal.*, 17: 285–303.
Laplanche, J. (1999). *Essays in Otherness*. London: Routledge. See also *Reading French Psychoanalysis*, eds. D. Birksted-Breen, S. Flanders and A. Gibeault. New Library of Psychoanalysis. London: Routledge, 2013.
Laplanche, J. and Pontalis, J.-B. (1973). *The Language of Psychoanalysis*. Hogarth Press: London.
Loewald, H. (1960). On the therapeutic action of psychoanalysis. In *Papers on Psychoanalysis*. New Haven and London: Yale University Press. 221-256
McDougall, J. (1989). *Theatres of the Body*. London: Free Association Books.
Ogden, T. (2004). This art of psychoanalysis. *Int. J. Psychoanal.* 85: 857–877.
Parsons, M. (2005). Psychoanalysis, art, listening, looking, outwards, inwards. (unpublished paper presented at the British Psychoanalytic society).
Parsons, M. (2014). *Living Psychoanalysis*. London: Routledge.
Perelberg, R. J. (2015). *Murdered Father, Dead Father*. London: Routledge.
Pine, F. (2004). Mahler's concepts of "symbiosis" and separation-individuation: revisited, reevaluated, refined. *J. Am. Psychoanal. Assoc.*, 52(2): 511–533.
Pontalis, J.-B. (1981). *Frontiers in Psycho-Analysis*. London: Hogarth Press.
Rosenfeld, H. (1987). *Impasse and Interpretation*. London: Tavistock.
Rousillon, R. (2018). Emergence and conception of the subject (self). In *Donald W. Winnicott and the History of the Present. Understanding the Man and his Work*, ed. A. Joyce. London: Karnac Books, pp. 1–16.
Sandler, J. (1992). Reflections on the developments in the theory of psychoanalytic technique. *Int. J. Psychoanal.* 73: 189–198.
Sandler, J. (1993). On communication from patient to analyst: not everything is projective identification. *Int. J. Psychoanal.* 74: 1097–1107.
Spillius, E. (1992). Discussion of Steiner's paper. Presented at UCL Conference. Unpublished.

Spillius, E. et al. (2011). *The New Dictionary of Kleinian Thought*. London: Routledge.
Steiner, J. (1994). *Psychic Retreats*. London: Routledge.
Stewart, H. (1992). *Psychic Experience and Problems of Technique*. London: Routledge.
Winnicott, D. W. (1954a). Metapsychological and clinical aspects of regression within the psycho-analytical set-up. In *Through Paediatrics to Psycho-Analysis*. London: Hogarth Press, 1975. 278-294
Winnicott, D. W. (1954b). Withdrawal and regression. In *Through Paediatrics to Psycho-Analysis*. London: Hogarth Press, 1975. 255-261
Winnicott, D. W. (1969). The use of an object. *Int. J. Psychoanal.*, 50: 711–716.

# Name index

**A**
Aisenstein, M. 1, 160, 161, 163, 166, 167
Akhtar, S. 208, 211, 231
Alexander, F. 251, 256, 257
Althusser, L. 49, 53, 65
Anna Freudians 2, 9, 31, 58
Anna Freud Centre 9, 11–12, 16, 21, 26, 71, 74, 77–82, 86, 236, 238, 311, 313
Anzieu, D. 275, 279
Arlow, J. 216, 290, 297

**B**
Baker, R. 120
Balint, M. 234, 236, 251, 252, 255, 348
Bion, W. 173, 210, 226, 270, 275, 344, 355
Birksted-Breen, D. 48, 64, 341
Blum, H. 119, 257, 261, 294
Bollas, C. 70, 85, 86, 217, 226, 260, 281, 344
and Sundelson, D. 227, 229, 230
Botella, C. and S. 31, 352
Brenman, E. 223

Brent Adolescent Centre 11, 95
Brierley, M. 54, 55, 57
Britten, B. 22, 188, 197, 200
Britton, R. 344

**C**
Chasseguet-Smirgel, J. 212
Chervet, B. 49
Chused, J. F. 27, 357
Contemporary Freudian group 1–11, 15–17, 19–21, 23–28, 31, 35–36
Controversial Discussions 2, 5–6, 35–36, 48, 53–59, 65, 343
Couch, A. 25, 293

**D**
Dejours, C. 169
De Masi, F. 224
De Monchaux, C. 29, 276, 328, 340
Deutsch, H. 196
Duncan, D. 25

**E**
Eagle, M. N. 262
Eissler, K. 256–57

*Name index*

**F**
Faimberg, H. 47, 67
Fairbairn, W.R.D. 255, 256
Feldman, M. 226
Ferenczi, S. 117, 169, 223
Ferruta, A. 337
Fisher, J.V. 355
Fonagy, P. 290, 292
  and Target, M. 9, 10, 112–13
Freeman, T. 298
Freud, A. 1, 2, 8, 11, 14, 17, 21, 26, 30, 43, 57, 77, 79, 96, 139, 141, 247, 314, 319, 339
Freud, S. 1–8, 10–11, 14, 15, 17, 19, 20, 24–26, 28, 30–31, 37, 39–40, 43–44, 47–54, 58–61, 65–67, 89, 97, 108–09, 119, 126–130, 138, 141, 149, 155, 157–160, 162, 171, 179, 189, 195, 199, 222, 225, 234, 251–52, 269, 279, 287–291, 293–95, 319–20, 328, 329, 340, 344, 345, 347, 349, 350, 351, 353, 354
Friedlander, K. 54–57

**G**
Gaddini, E. 234, 337
Gibeault, A. 348
Gill, M. 64, 256
Glasser, M. 10, 21–22, 24, 165, 217, 223–24, 235, 338–39
Glover, E. 54, 57, 223
Green, A. 31, 48, 52, 55, 63–64, 70, 158–59, 161–62, 171–72, 293, 344, 348, 354, 357
Greenacre, P. 252
Greenson, R. 252, 289, 302
Greenspan, S. I. 144, 235

**H**
Hampstead Clinic 1, 8, 12, 89, 139, 145
Hayman, A. 36, 53
Heimann, P. 6, 48, 60, 155, 211, 358
Hoffer, W. 9, 21, 54–55, 60–61, 127
Horton, R. 189–190

**I**
Independent (Middle) group 2, 36, 54, 58, 257
Isaacs, S. 6, 36, 48, 54, 56, 58–60
Isakower, O. 290, 293

**J**
Jones, E. 55–56, 343
Joseph, B. 291

**K**
Khan, M. 84, 269–70, 273, 276, 293–94
King, P. and Steiner, R. 35, 36, 48, 53–54, 56, 59, 60–61, 343
Klein, M. 4, 19, 43, 54–57, 59, 61, 210, 344
Kleinian (group) 2, 4, 36, 54, 59–61, 253–54, 257, 344
Kohon, G. 59, 67
Kohut, H. 235, 242, 255, 257, 263
Kris, E. 269, 280, 344
Krystal, H. 141

**L**
Laplanche, J. 1, 31, 67, 169, 347
  and Pontalis, J.-B. 19, 50, 90, 348
Laufer, E. and M. 11, 14, 238
Lebovici, S. 90, 92
Lemma, A. 226
Lewin, B. D. 269–70, 273, 275
Lichtenberg, J. 234–35

Lipowski, Z. J. 139
Loewald, H. 27, 91, 115, 119, 245, 253–55, 257, 260–61, 263–64, 352
Low, B. 60

## M
Mahler, M. 348
Malcom, R. R. 64
Marty, P. 1, 157, 161, 165, 167
Marx, K. 49, 65
McDougall, J. 140–41, 144, 358
Moran, G. 9, 253

## O
Ogden, T. 112, 201, 356
O'Shaughnessy, E. 226, 291, 293

## P
Payne, S. 54–55, 59–60
Pears, P. 22, 188, 200–02
Perelberg, R. J. 5–7, 10, 21, 166, 354
Pine, F. 348
Pontalis, J.-B. 1, 276, 337, 340, 354
Portman Clinic 10, 21–23, 206–07, 229

## R
Reiser, M. 290
Rolland, J. C. 51
Rosenfeld, H. 263–64, 272, 351
Rousillon, R. 347

## S
Sandler, J. 4, 9, 26, 64, 120, 167, 211, 245, 259, 264, 291, 352, 355
and A.-M. 1, 3, 4–6, 15, 64
and Joffe, W. G. 242
Schore, A. 201

Segal, H. 256–57, 264, 270, 280, 283, 296
Sharpe, E. F. 54, 59–60, 119–20, 236, 289, 329
Smadja, C. 1, 160
Sodré, I. 47, 64, 210
Sophocles (and *Oedipus Rex*) 96–97, 107–08, 111, 114, 124
Spillius, E. 35, 344, 353
Spitz, L. 280
Steiner, J. 353
Sterba, R. 289
Stern, D. 234, 255
Stewart, H. 263, 300, 344
Strachey, J. 52, 253–55, 263
Szwec, G. 161

## T
Tähkä, R. 121
Thomä, H. and Cheshire, N. 51
Tolpin, M. 235, 257
Treurniet, N. 252, 261

## V
van der Kolk, B. A. 208

## W
Waelder, R. 290
Williams, G. 279–80
Winnicott, D. W. 1, 5, 11, 13, 17, 31, 36, 71, 73, 82, 109, 112, 115, 117, 119–21, 123–24, 159, 169, 171, 196, 234, 237, 245, 251–52, 255, 257, 260, 262, 264, 270, 293, 343–44, 348–51, 355, 358
Wittgenstein, L. 2

## Y
Yorke, C. 3–4, 15, 20, 153, 293

# Subject index

**A**

abandonment, fear of 24, 98, 191–92, 248, 270, 272, 275, 284, 338
adolescence 18, 24, 63, 93–95, 97, 115–17, 126–37, 157, 166, 177, 183, 214, 235, 238, 253, 271–72, 276–77, 283, 285, 326, 339
aggression 3, 8, 10–11, 30, 103, 110, 112, 147, 152, 191, 198–99, 245, 297, 317–18, 340, 346, 349, 353, 356
  binding of 21, 236, 248
  concept of 6, 19–24, 234
  destructive 6, 14, 19–22, 31, 135–37, 146, 185, 242, 293, 349–51
  self-destructive 13, 21, 23, 94, 146, 164, 192, 235
  self-preservative 20–21, 191–92, 351
  sexualisation of destructive 21–22, 192, 201, 224–25
analyst as a new (developmental) object 12–14, 26–27, 79, 87, 96, 118, 121–22, 251–66, 301

analytic boundaries 29, 123, 217, 251, 269–70, 273–76
annihilation, fear of (anxiety) 21–22, 24, 191, 235, 284, 340

**B**

body 2–3, 11, 14–17, 25, 95, 99, 101–03, 126–37, 141, 150, 155–73, 176–86, 189, 197–98, 205, 219, 235–36, 241–42, 248, 277, 279, 282, 302, 329, 353
  attacking own body 14, 21, 23, 132–33, 137
  damaged, disgusting 99, 102, 133, 176, 242
  language 16, 142–43, 152
  libidinal 17, 21, 155–73
  and mind 17, 142, 144, 277
  representation 11, 15, 17, 101, 141–42, 145, 340
  and soma 16–17, 25, 155–73
  woman's unconscious use of 16, 18, 176–86
borderline patients and states 10, 25–26, 28, 45, 101, 263, 288, 293, 294–96, 300, 304–06

366

## Subject index

**C**

castration anxiety 8, 29, 47, 54, 61, 114, 136, 189, 318, 338–39
compulsion to repeat (repetition compulsion) 7, 19, 47, 53, 65, 70, 97, 261, 292, 296–98
core complex 10, 21–24, 165, 191–95, 199–201, 203, 235, 338–39
countertransference 42, 66, 71, 75, 155–73, 238, 258–61, 264, 287, 291–92, 322, 325

**D**

death instinct 19–20, 54
defences 15, 25–26, 43, 84, 217, 236, 239–40, 248, 272, 289–90, 292–93, 295, 298, 304–05, 359
denial 115, 129, 147, 150, 215, 224–25, 317
depression 20, 75, 95, 98–99, 100, 102, 145, 150, 176, 191, 196, 198, 200, 209, 238–42, 272, 304, 331, 334, 336–37, 345, 347, 351
developmental disturbance 26–27, 57, 153, 252–53, 266, 294–95
developmental help 12, 26, 30, 80
developmental lines 10–11, 16, 140, 142
developmental perspective (approach) 2, 7, 9, 3–15, 18–19, 31, 40, 50, 57, 71, 80, 83, 85, 90, 97, 105, 113, 127, 129, 137, 139, 141, 144–45, 159, 176–77, 191–92, 235, 248, 270, 280, 289, 294, 304, 319–21, 326, 347
developmental phases (stages) 13, 57, 91–92, 177–78, 288
dreams
  function of 4, 29, 280–91, 294, 298, 301, 303, 328, 330, 341

formation 291, 329
interpretation of 287–306
classic 288–90, 293–94
and transference 4, 28, 287, 290–92, 329, 340–41
growth of ego capacities 4, 28–30, 269, 275–76, 280, 284, 285, 288–89, 294, 300, 303–04, 337, 341
and play 5, 108–09, 270, 294
royal road to the unconscious, as 4, 24, 28, 288, 320
symbolic capacity 4, 169, 269, 275
unconscious communication 4, 29, 328, 337
with borderline patients 294–305

**E**

economic perspective 2, 8, 160–62, 168
ego, bodily 8–9, 23, 279
ego ideal 20, 60, 226
empathy 25–27, 239, 246, 251–53, 257–58, 264–65
enactment 14, 18, 26–27, 86–87, 99, 119–20, 149, 210–11, 246, 291–92, 325, 328
engulfment (fusion), fear of 10, 24, 185, 191, 199, 224, 248, 339–40

**F**

father, absent (lost) 10, 12–13, 18, 21, 76, 90–105, 183, 185, 201, 283, 310, 314, 321, 338
fixation 7, 10, 53, 57–58, 65
fragmentation 17, 167, 171, 207, 214, 240
  fear of 21, 235, 248
free association 24–26, 43
fusion, desire for 22, 24, 191

367

## G

guilt 82–83, 91, 117, 134, 141, 176, 178–80, 186, 214, 220–21, 224–26, 228, 231, 245, 246–47, 277, 285, 302, 317, 324
  unconscious 15, 182–83, 242

## H

helplessness (hilflösichkeit) 20, 150, 166, 225, 269

## I

id 24, 38, 44, 50, 254, 298
identification 7, 15, 19, 40, 62, 70, 85, 87, 94, 101, 105, 112, 128, 131, 135, 149, 167, 177, 194–97, 203, 226, 254, 277, 316, 319, 321, 330, 337, 339–40, 355
  analyst with patient 167, 352
  distinguished from simulation 22, 196, 199, 201–02
  pregnancy, in 177–78, 180, 185, 188
  projective 36, 40, 43–44, 210, 223, 263, 352
  with the aggressor 21, 43, 70, 222–24, 241, 318
identity 178, 182, 212, 280, 331
  gender 11, 15, 177
  insubstantial 22, 195–96, 222–23, 235
  sexual 10, 13–14, 94, 104, 110, 112, 177–78, 183–84, 332
incest 91, 93, 94, 115, 124, 213
  barrier (taboo) 13, 61, 90, 115, 224
infantile neurosis 7, 61
insight 20, 148, 244, 252–53, 256–57, 262, 282, 287, 289, 295, 319

interpretation 138, 141, 151, 198, 206, 214, 217, 252, 256–57, 264, 274–75, 280, 282
  extra-transference 25, 254
  here-and-now 259, 261–62
  mistakes in 252, 262–63, 265
  transference 120, 252–56, 262, 265, 270
  implicit 27, 120, 262–63, 266

## L

libidinal phases 7, 15, 57, 321
life and death drives 20–21, 160
  fusion and defusion of 17, 20–21

## M

masochism 197, 281
metapsychology 4, 6, 17, 47–48, 50, 54, 57–58, 65–66, 157, 171, 349
mother: woman's relation to in pregnancy 18–19, 176–86
motherhood 11, 172, 177–79, 183

## N

Nachträglichkeit (après-coup) 5–7, 11, 50–67, 73, 170–71, 222, 329
narcissism 7, 21, 41, 179, 203, 224, 234, 236, 320
  destructive 263, 272
  primary 31, 166, 171, 191, 343, 348–50, 354
negative therapeutic reaction 20, 298
neutrality 25, 27, 57, 120, 179, 227, 251–52, 254–56, 262, 264, 355

## O

obsessional neurosis, 20
oedipal phase 6, 10, 11–14, 29, 42 59–60, 89–105, 108–24, 127,

129, 130, 136, 176, 181, 183, 186, 199, 202, 213, 320–21, 338, 345–46, 351, 354

## P

Paris (French) School of Psychosomatics 1, 17, 20, 160
parricide (patricide) 13, 91, 93, 108, 115
perversion 116, 191–92, 194, 212, 223, 224–25, 235, 248
pregnancy 11, 18–19, 176–186
pre-oedipal development 10, 13–14, 18, 57, 89, 91–94, 97, 104, 127, 130, 133, 164
psychic change 25, 27, 245, 251, 253–55, 257, 261, 263–66, 283, 290, 301, 352, 354, 357–59
puberty 7–8, 18, 56, 113, 130–37, 284, 300, 310, 321

## R

reconstruction 7, 39, 42, 52, 102, 136, 256–57, 265, 288, 292
representation 15–17, 55, 141, 144, 149–50, 152–53, 158, 160, 165, 167, 172, 185, 199, 321, 328, 339–40, 345, 350–51
  self- 11, 40, 44, 83, 176, 180, 194–95, 245
regression 6–7, 17, 30–31, 48, 53–58, 61, 65, 103, 141, 152, 160–63, 166, 172, 178, 251, 262, 269, 280, 288, 291, 343–59
repression 3, 38, 50–51, 53, 59–60, 70, 127, 129–30, 140, 150, 224–25
  repression barrier 5–6, 39
return of the repressed 7, 53, 65
role responsiveness 26, 211, 213, 291

## S

Sadism 10, 18, 20–23, 95, 180, 192, 220, 224–25, 235, 248
sado-masochism 149, 196–97, 201, 239, 241, 248
safety (principle) 9, 43, 76, 114, 191, 237, 262, 268, 273, 298, 336
separation and indivuation 10–11, 17–18, 75, 79, 85–86, 92, 105, 128, 177, 184–85, 272–73
sexuality 10–11, 13, 21, 47–48, 51, 53, 56, 59, 61, 66, 112, 127–28, 157, 171–72, 177, 183, 188–90, 202, 225, 234–36, 240, 247–48, 283, 293, 302
  infantile 6, 8, 15, 61, 65, 111, 320
shame 15, 40, 214, 220–21, 224, 228, 263, 302, 304–05, 330
skin 16, 151–52, 156, 164, 169–70, 237, 275, 279
somatisation 142–43, 147, 150, 155–73, 282
structural model 24, 38, 44, 51, 289
superego 7–9, 24, 38, 44, 59–61, 93–94, 105, 141, 226, 249, 253–54, 303, 354, 357
  benign 20, 94, 245, 248, 253, 298
  punitive 13, 20, 23, 94, 102, 195, 220–21, 225–26, 230–31, 245, 253, 295–96, 298
symbolise, capacity to 4, 16, 20, 139, 141, 144, 163

## T

technique 3, 5, 15, 24–31, 36, 58, 64, 252, 262, 264–65, 288–306, 325, 343–44, 348–49, 351–57

## Subject index

therapeutic alliance 24, 148, 253, 258, 260, 289, 295, 298, 301, 320, 325
time/temporality 6–7, 24, 47–53, 58, 61, 63–66
topographical model 2, 4, 24, 37–39, 44, 47, 160
transference 3–4, 6, 24–29, 35, 38–43, 47, 64–66, 75, 96–97, 105, 118–22, 130–31, 170–71, 179, 222, 228–29, 251–56, 270, 287–97, 320, 329, 344, 354–55
transference neurosis 25, 26, 253
trauma 5–6, 17, 23, 47, 52–3, 65–6, 70–1, 117, 138, 171, 208, 222–23, 252

**U**

unconscious 2–7, 19, 24–29, 37–9, 44, 47, 50–51, 53, 57, 157, 169, 177–78, 186, 211, 291, 345
  dynamic 3, 6–7, 28, 47, 291
  phantasy 3, 5–6, 36–38, 40–42, 47–66
  present and past 3, 6, 39–40, 42, 44–45, 64
unconscious communciation 29, 162, 169, 172, 211, 328–41, 353

**V**

violent patients 10, 21, 98, 134, 215–16, 221, 271